W9-CLB-182

THE THIRD AGENDA IN
U.S. PRESIDENTIAL DEBATES

THE THIRD AGENDA IN U.S. PRESIDENTIAL DEBATES

DebateWatch and Viewer Reactions, 1996–2004

DIANA B. CARLIN, TAMMY VIGIL,
SUSAN BUEHLER, AND
KELLY MCDONALD

Praeger Series in Political Communication
Robert E. Denton, Jr., General Editor

Westport, Connecticut
London

Library of Congress Cataloging-in-Publication Data

Carlin, Diana B., 1950–
   The third agenda in U.S. presidential debates : debatewatch and viewer reactions,
1996–2004 / Diana B. Carlin, Tammy Vigil, Susan Buehler, and Kelly McDonald
        p. cm. — (Praeger series in political communication, ISSN 1062–5623)
   Includes bibliographical references and index.
   ISBN 978–0–275–96773–4 (alk. paper)
   1. Presidents—United States—Election—1996.   2. Presidents—United States—
Election—2000.   3. Presidents—United States—Election—2004.   4. Campaign
debates—United States.   5. Communication in politics—United States.   6. United
States—Politics and government—1993–2001.   7. United States—Politics and
government—2001.   I. McDonald, Kelly M.   II. Vigil, Tammy.   III. Title.
   JK5261996 .C37   2009
     324.973'0929—dc22   2008038702

British Library Cataloguing in Publication Data is available.

Library of Congress Catalog Card Number: 2008038702
ISBN: 978–0–275–96773–4
ISSN: 1062–5623

First published in 2009

Praeger Publishers, 88 Post Road West, Westport, CT 06881
An imprint of Greenwood Publishing Group, Inc.
www.praeger.com

Printed in the United States of America

The paper used in this book complies with the
Permanent Paper Standard issued by the National
Information Standards Organization (Z39.48–1984).

10   9   8   7   6   5   4   3   2   1

To the memory of Abraham Lincoln and Stephen A. Douglas in recognition of the 150th anniversary of their historic debates.

Contents

Preface

While DebateWatch is now a regular part of the Commission on Presidential Debates (CPD) voter education programs and has a prominent position on its Web site (http://www.debates.org/pages/dwoverview.html), all of its processes, questions, and procedures were initially developed by a research team that we coordinated. The grant proposal that supported creation of DebateWatch was written by Diana Carlin and submitted to the Ford Foundation through the University of Kansas. The DebateWatch research center in 1996 and 2000 was housed at the University of Kansas. It was important to have the CPD's support for the program in order to institutionalize it as a voter education tool. Without the CPD staff's knowledge of professional associations and nongovernmental organizations to contact as potential partners, as well as their media access to publicize the project, the scope and diversity of participants would not have been possible. The CPD provided staff and monetary resources to supplement the grant funding as well. The authors are fully aware that DebateWatch and this book would never have happened without a partnership with the CPD, and it is only through the CPD's adoption of the project that citizens had and will continue to have a voice in the presidential debates beyond the initial grant funding and our participation. The CPD ensured sustainability and expansion as is proven by the participation numbers in 2004, when the management of the program was solely theirs.

One of the authors, Diana B. Carlin, served on the Commission's advisory board from 1987 until 2000 and provided advice on formats, research, and voter education projects, including DebateWatch. She participated on several postelection panels from the perspective of a university researcher who has studied debates since 1980. The access the authors had to the Gallup group in San Diego in 1996 and to venues for DebateWatches involving audience members at several debate sites happened only through access to CPD staff.

Because of DebateWatch's relationship to the CPD, it is important to clarify that the contents of this book are solely the work of the authors. No one from the CPD read drafts or saw a prepublication version. Interpretations of the data and analysis of complex and controversial issues such as third party candidates do not in any way reflect the opinions or interpretations of decisions and events of anyone associated with the CPD. Diana Carlin's reflections on the third party selection process are hers alone and are based on her notes and documents used in making recommendations regarding candidate inclusion. This book represents independent research conducted within the open marketplace of ideas. The Ford Foundation grant was awarded to the University of Kansas with the expectation that the strengths and shortcomings of presidential debates and DebateWatch would be fully explored and exposed. Individuals involved with the CPD believed that academic researchers would develop a voter education program and conduct research with a level of integrity that would withstand the media's and public's scrutiny. The use of National Communication Association (NCA) members to conduct control groups for comparison to overall groups was supported by the CPD as a way to further validate the results. CPD Co-Chairman Frank Fahrenkopf stressed the importance of the research groups and recruitment of a wide variety of partners to ensure representative results when he and Co-Chairman Paul Kirk launched the program at a news conference on July 16, 1996.

Because the authors had an opportunity to observe the debates firsthand and to work with the CPD, they are aware of the high stakes involved in producing presidential debates as well as the legal issues and the public expectations surrounding their production. Thus, we want to acknowledge the association with the CPD but also want to emphasize the independent nature of the research.

It is also important to note that because this was a longitudinal study, other articles and book chapters using partial results were produced after each election cycle. Some of that research is included in the more expansive study this book represents. Previously published material is noted and in most cases is referenced for its conclusions rather than quoted directly. Direct quotations are noted and constitute relatively short excerpts. Chapter nine, which reports a nonvoter study conducted after the 1996 election, is the exception. That chapter was presented as an unpublished conference paper and it was indicated on the manuscript that it would serve as a chapter in this book.

Acknowledgments

The authors gratefully acknowledge the Ford Foundation for its $200,000 grant to the University of Kansas and principal investigator, Diana Carlin, which made the creation of DebateWatch possible. Marcia Smith, our program officer, provided support and advice throughout the project. The Commission on Presidential Debates (CPD) saw the value of DebateWatch as a way of enhancing the presidential debate viewing experience and adopted it as a voter education program. CPD Co-chairs Frank Fahrenkopf and Paul Kirk were highly supportive and eager to use the results to improve the presidential debates. CPD Executive Director Janet Brown provided staff support, advice, supplemental funds, publicity, and technical support for creating Web-based DebateWatch materials in the three election cycles reported on in this book. Heather Ballas, John Hofland, and Samantha Hojo were especially helpful in coordinating data collection and dissemination. The University of Kansas General Research Fund provided additional support for the 1996 and 2004 phases of the study.

Special thanks goes to those who were on the ground to make DebateWatch happen: hundreds of university faculty members and members of professional associations in every state who hosted DebateWatches, especially Mitchell McKinney, Mark Kuhn, Michael Mayer, Mari Tonn, Bob Smith, John Splaine, David Parkhurst, William Darby, Mary Kahl, Jack Kay, Teri Avis Wichman, Kristin Marshall, David Levasseur, Kevin Dean, Judy Edelhoff, Barbara Pickering, Peter Bicak, Mary Banwart, Val Endress, and William Dow for their extra efforts; the National Communication Association (formerly the Speech Communication Association), especially Jim Gaudino and Sherry Morreale, for encouraging members to host groups; the more than 125 partner organizations that signed on to promote and participate in DebateWatch and that made it possible for an idea to mushroom into what is becoming a common feature of debates at all levels of political activity; the individuals who answered the invitation to watch, listen, analyze, and talk; and the staff of the DebateWatch research centers—graduate and undergraduate students at the University of Kansas. Of the dozens of students who assisted with DebateWatch, a few deserve special recognition for putting in hours beyond what classes required: Brooke Ward Payne, Becky Halstead, Shawna Smith, Cydney Fowler, Karen Anderson, Jenifer Lewis, Jay Self, Eric Morris, Dan Schill, Carolyn McKnight, Khisu Beom, Mark Silver, McLean Thompson, Taleyna Morris, Mohammed Al Ghamdi, Justin LaBerge, Abby Pierron, and Anthony King. A special thanks goes to the other three members of the DebateWatch '96 team, Scott Sponholtz, Thomas Moore, and Jarius Jones, who spent hours answering phones and making the first DebateWatch a reality. Jim Schnoebelen and Ben Warner assisted with last-minute research and made some very helpful suggestions for improving the manuscript. Brian Frederick provided research assistance to update the manuscript. Many thanks go to our editor, Brian Foster, and everyone at Praeger for their patience through the numerous family hardships we all experienced that delayed the book's completion. Finally, a very special thanks to Joe Pierron who edited drafts and provided an informed but nonacademic reader's viewpoint, made food runs during intensive writing weekends, gave up part of a Sedona vacation so that Kelly and Diana could work in Arizona, put up with research materials on the kitchen and dining room tables for months, and provided much-needed moral support even when he wasn't sure the book would ever be completed.

Chapter One

Revealing the Third Agenda

In their study of the 1960 and 1976 presidential debates, Marilyn Jackson-Beeck and Robert Meadow[1] determined that of the three agendas or issues of importance in a political debate—candidate, media, and public—the public's was represented the least. This finding is not surprising given debate formats that feature journalists as interlocutors. David J. Lanoue, a political scientist, and Peter R. Schrott, a political communication scholar, examined the role of journalists in political debates and concluded that "journalists have their own goals, which may not be entirely consistent with the overall goal of informing the public about the issue positions of (and differences between) the nominees."[2] This conclusion was further confirmed by a content analysis of journalists' questions from 1960 through 2000 that matched question content with polling data of public agenda items. The study revealed that "In only one debate (1960) do journalists' questions have significant positive correlations with the public's interests."[3] Likewise, candidates have particular debate objectives that may not dovetail with the public's major concerns or their answers to questions are framed so generally that the public's concerns may be left largely unaddressed.

The problem, however, is not just with the debates. In general, there was a perceived lack of a clear public agenda in politics, which underscored much of the problem with the political climate in 1996, when the research for this book began. Despite polling and focus groups by candidates and the media that were intended to reveal the public agenda, many Americans were not hearing, reading, or seeing much in political messages or news that interested them or represented their concerns. Apathy was high and was reflected in 1990s books such as E. J. Dionne's *Why Americans Hate Politics*.[4] Harvard political science professor Robert Putnam argued that a sense of community and engagement with civic life was declining and that Americans were "bowling alone."[5] Political scientist Stephanie Greco Larson connected a lack of civic engagement to the way the media report on political opinion. According to Larson's analysis, the emphasis on "closed-ended questions" to measure public opinion restricts the issues to what the authors of polls think is important, and the result is that polls take control of public opinion "out of the hands of the public and put[s] it into the 'machinery of polling,' keeping political outsiders outside and restricting public debate. Consequently public opinion is constrained by having polls replace other kinds of expression."[6]

Public voices from the 1996 election cycle showed a great deal of cynicism and apathy as a result of being left on the outside, and discontent was evidenced in low voter turnout and high interest in alternative political voices. Between 1996 and 2004, cynicism and apathy did not disappear, but the disputed election of 2000 and events of 9/11 changed the way that viewers thought about voting, foreign policy, and the importance of politics in their lives. Voter turnout took an upswing in 2004. The growth of the Internet and expansion of political programming during the time period was dramatic. The convergence of print, broadcast, and digital communication, as well as citizen takeover of political talk via blogs and interactive Web sites, changed political participation among citizens as well. There were far more opportunities for a public agenda to be stated in unfiltered terms. This book provides insights into what remained constant and what changed about the way people consume political messages related to presidential debates.

STUDYING CITIZENS' VOICES

When many of us think of political communication, especially those of us who study or report on political messages, we often think of those messages that bombard the average citizen—speeches, advertisements, debates, Web sites, e-mails, blogs, text messages, and the many forms of news reporting. We seldom, however, think about the other messages involved in politics—those from the public. And when we do, they are often reduced to percentages reflecting horse race preferences or reactions to statements created by pollsters. Occasionally we might think about the words of C-SPAN or talk radio show callers who usually have a sound byte of time to comment. Finally, our thoughts may include the wide range of comments on political blogs that include informed and analytical comments as well as less than G-rated rants.

Beginning with the 1992 presidential election, a team of researchers throughout the United States created opportunities for citizens to participate in the public sphere and comment on their concerns. The concept of a public sphere relates not so much to a physical space but to "citizens deliberating about common affairs, as distinct from personal or private concerns."[7] German philosopher Jürgen Habermas gave prominence to the concept of an ideal public sphere, which he considered as outside the family, or private sphere, but not part of the state or marketplace. It involved "the public reason of private citizens."[8]

Within discussion groups held after the debates, average citizens talked about politics and expanded their part in the democratic process.[9] What was said in those discussions provided the impetus for this book. As the book's title suggests, the emphasis in the pages that follow is on the third agenda in the 1996, 2000, and 2004 presidential debates—the public's agenda. The third agenda is revealed through postdebate discussion groups, surveys completed by the participants, e-mails to the researchers, online discussions, and postelection surveys and focus groups. While the book includes analyses from scholars and political observers, the heart of the book was written by average citizens who decided to be talking heads rather than listen to them. Debate statements made by candidates and debate moderators are referenced, but only as they help explain or frame citizens' comments. Historical context is provided to remind us of the times in which these discussions occurred and to provide depth to the analysis. In other words, this is not so much a study of the presidential debates themselves but a study of the public reaction to the debates, the candidates, and the larger political climate in which the debates took place. The value of such an approach is that "Understanding how voters make their decision is tantamount, at some very basic level, to understanding how democracy works."[10]

The public sphere project upon which this book is based was called "Debate-Watch," a voter education program originally associated with the presidential debates and the Commission on Presidential Debates (CPD). As the book was completed in 2008, the term "debate watch" was used to describe any gathering of individuals to view a political debate. During the 2004 election and 2008 primaries, candidates' supporters were urged via e-mails to hold debate watches with other supporters. It is unlikely that the formal discussion structure our project promoted was followed by most of those watches, but the fact that they happened indicates the need for and importance of talk about politics and creation of shared political experiences. After most debates during the 2008 primary season, online focus groups sponsored by media outlets were found on media Web sites such as CNN. Anyone logging in could then watch and learn what others thought about the debates and the candidates.

The idea for creating the DebateWatch program was suggested by participants in the 1992 study that was sponsored by the CPD to determine the effectiveness of new debate formats introduced that year. The participants indicated that the discussions following the debates were as valuable, or even more valuable, than the debates themselves in gaining a better understanding about the candidates and the issues. Many of the 625 participants in 60 focus groups across 18 cities in 16 states indicated that they "never" or "rarely" discussed politics, especially not with individuals they did not know or who held differing political beliefs. Those early participants suggested that in 1996 and subsequent election years all citizens should be encouraged to watch and listen to the debates with groups and hold discussions of their own. Based on that suggestion, the idea for DebateWatch '96 was outlined in the concluding chapter of the report on the 1992 study.[11] DebateWatch was developed during the intervening years, and the project was initiated through a grant from the Ford Foundation.

The 1992 research project was conducted by university researchers at 18 sites who gathered a diverse group of voters to talk about what they had seen and heard. Several weeks after the 1992 election, the focus group facilitators met to discuss their experiences, and they were eager to see the study expanded into a full-fledged program because of several important "side effects" of the discussions:

- first-time voters learned from more experienced voters;
- individuals could disagree without becoming disagreeable;
- many participants were inspired to seek out new and varied sources of political messages to better understand topics introduced in the debates;
- group members indicated that if the candidate they supported did not win, they were at least willing to give the winner a chance because they realized that all of the candidates had good ideas;
- participants left with a sense of community because they found that individuals from different walks of life were concerned about the same basic issues that they were.

The enthusiasm among the 1992 study participants and facilitators to find a way for citizens to engage in political dialogue gave the researchers reason to believe that it was possible to generate greater enthusiasm for politics, create a better-informed electorate, and influence the political agenda to include the public's voice. The belief that a democracy must engage citizens in order to survive is shared by many, among them political scientist James Carey who wrote:

> Democracy originates among ordinary people in acts of conversation, among citizens who begin to question the disparities between their experience and what politicians are currently feeding them ... what is required is that citizens engage their environment and dissipate their anger constructively in political work.[12]

Thus, the motivation for developing DebateWatch was two-fold. First, the Commission on Presidential Debates wanted to continue to learn how to provide debates that better served the public interest. Second, and perhaps more importantly, DebateWatch appeared to be a way to address the lack of a citizen agenda in political discourse, the growing apathy among the electorate, the lack of civil discourse about the issues that separate us philosophically, and the fragmentation of our society.

The timing seemed right to give citizens more of a voice. Voter turnout in the 1994 mid-term elections was at an all-time low. Dissatisfaction with business as usual was high and resulted in a Republican takeover of both houses of Congress for the first time in 40 years. Veteran election observer Curtis Gans described the results as a "dealignment rather than realignment—a turning away from both major political parties ... without offering much hope for long term citizen re-engagement in the future."[13] The annual Gallup poll of ethics and honesty ratings of 25 professions showed Congress at an all-time low of 10 percent.[14] As a result of the growing discontent, many Americans were eager to have new candidates or new parties from which to choose a president in 1996. This was clear in the well-publicized push to "recruit" Colin Powell as a candidate and the conversion of Ross Perot's independent candidacy in 1992 into a third party.

The approach taken in this book to study the public's discourse is not unique, but it was seldom employed by political communication scholars and political scientists until the 1990s. The messages that most researchers or political observers seem interested in are those of the candidates and the media. In fact, even highly respected scholars such as Thomas E. Patterson in his book *Out of Order*, diminish the role that the audience plays in political discourse. Patterson's book, for example, includes a chapter entitled, "Reporters' Issues versus Candidates' Issues," in which he acknowledges that "society has urgent problems that need the government's attention."[15] However the chapter discusses the issues as a competing struggle between the candidates and the media to establish priorities with little suggestion that either set of issues is driven by or responsive to public needs.

Granted, prior to the Internet's development and growth, it was difficult for researchers to capture the public's comments about political messages. Members of the public typically do not give speeches, report on messages, or provide extensive documentation beyond letters to the editor or comments at local public hearings. However, researchers such as political scientists Marion Just and James Fishkin[16] found ways to create public spaces in which citizens could voice their opinions. Just and her colleagues used research methods similar to those in this study, and Fishkin brought a large group of Americans together in a single place to mingle with experts, talk about key issues, and give their opinions via a new type of polling. The focus group transcripts and feedback via the postdebate surveys, online chats, and e-mails generated by the DebateWatch project provided communication scholars with a source of political messages from the audience that was far more expansive than other projects. As the influence and presence of the Internet grew, we expanded our analysis of citizen talk to include more e-mail reactions and online discussions after the debates. Access to public talk means that researchers can analyze messages from candidates and public messages that reveal how the public reacts to them. Since communication scholars emphasize the importance of audience in the creation of politicians' messages, the audience data informs a study of political communication in a way that solitary analysis of political elites' texts alone cannot.

As indicated previously, much has changed since the 1992 election: the prevalence of talk radio and caller/Internet audience participation on news shows and blogs, extensive use of town hall meetings, the growing power of the Internet to create virtual communities, interactive candidate Web sites, and text messaging to remind potential voters to show up at the polls. These changes afford an opportunity to analyze citizen talk and to place the public's agenda front and center for the purposes of influencing the candidate and media agendas. In the process of privileging citizens' voices, the art of rhetorical criticism and political communication research is also broadened. By using the presidential debates to generate citizen talk about politics, the authors were able to learn far more than the typical

"Who won?" question asked by the media after a political debate. Nowhere in this book is a winner or loser asked for or declared.

As the précis of the chapters that follow suggest, DebateWatch viewers had a great deal on their minds besides winners or losers. This book provides a window into the American political experience at three distinct periods in our recent history. The similarities in what was important, valued, or learned across the cycles are clear, but the differences in attitudes over time are equally clear. There were tens of thousands of participants in various aspects of DebateWatch from 1996 through 2004. The authors sorted through thousands of pages of focus group and online chat transcripts, surveys, and e-mails that collectively represent citizens in all 50 states, the District of Columbia, and those living abroad. We analyzed the content for recurring themes and selected quotations that would represent as broad a slice of America, both geographically and demographically, as possible. However, our primary consideration in selecting a quotation to represent a theme or finding was that it best capsulated ideas expressed by many others—often in similar words. As a result, you may see some states or regions cited numerous times and others not at all. Quotations are presented "as is." There was no attempt to edit by correcting grammar or spelling in the case of e-mails or facilitator reports. However, disfluencies such as "uh" or "um" were removed, as were fillers such as "you know," which provided no substantive content or insight.

The book is organized thematically to incorporate the major issues related to political debates and to the DebateWatch project. All chapters are not organized chronologically as a longitudinal study might suggest. Some chapters lent themselves to a chronological presentation because it was important to show changes across cycles. For example, chapter three on methodology shows the progression of the project as technology became a larger factor and as the oversight changed from a funded research study to an institutionalized voter education project. Chapter eight on youth and chapter ten on third parties were also better served by isolating each election cycle for comparison and contrast. Other chapters required a topical or thematic approach because there was more consistency across the debates or comparison and contrast were better shown by discussing similarities side-by-side rather than through references to a previous debate cycle described in another section. Chapters four and five on format and candidate image are two good examples of this approach.

CHAPTER SUMMARIES

Chapter two establishes the importance of presidential debates in the electoral process. Over 40 years of research on political debates and their effects on voter education and vote choice are summarized to demonstrate why debates serve as focal points for public talk about presidential elections. The concept of the public sphere and the need to create dialogue on public issues is also presented as justification for a focus group methodology as one source of data. The research questions that guided the study are presented.

Chapter three explains the DebateWatch project and details the methodologies used to collect the political dialogue and opinions presented in the book. This chapter chronicles how the project was organized and publicized and it tracks the number of participants in each election cycle, the results of surveys used to collect demographic information, participants' use of media for political information, and the impact of the debates on candidate choice.

Chapter four examines the role of format on content and voter learning. While no new formats to rival the town hall were developed in the three election cycles, changes were made in staging—with candidates seated in some debates—and question and answer structures varied. Reactions to the changes—both positive and negative—are reported as well as research indicating the impact of formats on the way candidates debate and what viewers learn. Special attention is given to the town hall debate—a new format in 1992 that was considered to be the most useful for introducing the public's agenda into the debates when it first appeared. This chapter follows reactions to the changes in the town hall format over the next three election cycles. Of particular interest is a summary of the discussion with citizens who were on the stage as questioners in San Diego in 1996. A summary of the formats used in each election cycle is presented to provide context for comments.

Chapter five examines image and issues to help explain how voters make choices and how they interpret verbal and nonverbal messages sent by candidates in debates. The character issue was an important one, and the findings provide insights into how viewers assess a candidate's overall presidential fitness. Issue analysis includes reference to topics citizens indicated they wanted to hear when surveyed before the debates. Issues considered helpful or important, issues that were unimportant, and issues that weren't discussed are identified. Citizens' analysis of what is important and not important is potentially informative for anyone who reports on or participates in debates. The question of whether or not issues really matter to voters is answered and the overall impact of image and issues in terms of learning and vote choice is examined.

Chapter six looks at concerns expressed by participants that went beyond the candidates and the issues in the debates. This chapter presents views on the media, politics, visual elements of the debate, media coverage of DebateWatch, and the impact of participating in DebateWatch.

Chapter seven centers on running mates and their debates. It considers what the role of vice presidential debates should be and how well the vice presidential nominees fulfilled their roles. Participants' reactions to the debates illuminates the utility of the vice presidential match and the successes and failures of format and moderator to exploit the unique elements of the vice presidential match.

Chapter eight takes a detailed look at a group of voters that traditionally is missing in large numbers at election time—young voters. After a surge in youth voters in 1992, numbers dropped until 2004 when 9/11 and its aftermath brought politics closer to home. Special attention is given to why young people do not participate and how projects such as DebateWatch can motivate them. Reactions from this group are compared to those of other demographic groups.

Chapter nine explores the issue of nonparticipation at the polls and alienation from politics. It builds on postdebate comments from youthful participants and adds voices of a broader range of citizens. Surveys comparing voters' and nonvoters' views about politics and politicians are analyzed and comments from focus groups of nonvoters are presented to provide insight into the survey findings. This chapter grew out of comments from 1996 DebateWatch participants who felt alienated from the process and who didn't believe that their voices were represented by the candidates. The chapter taps into the political mood of the times as it was reflected in 1990s publications.

Chapter ten discusses one of the most controversial aspects of presidential debates: inclusion of minor party and independent candidates. A summary of policies for inclusion beginning with the 1976 debates is presented along with a review of the controversy surrounding noninclusion of minor party candidates in the three election cycles studied in the book. Citizen reaction as voiced in e-mails, letters, and DebateWatch groups is analyzed for consistent themes in arguments for inclusion.

Chapter eleven summarizes the lessons from the previous chapters to answer the research questions and to consider further improvements in political debates. This book was completed after the power shift in Congress that resulted from the 2006 mid-term elections and as the country was engaged in one of the more competitive, protracted, and historical primary seasons in recent years. The public spoke at the ballot box in 2006 and they were speaking there again, as well as through a number of media and online outlets, during the primaries. The desire for feedback into and engagement in the political dialogue was clear in 2008. Thus, this chapter summarizes citizens' insights to help shape future political debates to better realize their potential for voter education and an improved public sphere.

The appendices include all of the surveys and forms used for each Debate-Watch cycle. Surveys and procedural materials for the 1997 postelection study of nonvoters as well as tables with statistical test results are also included.

Chapter Two

Why Study, Watch, and Talk about Debates?

Participating in political debates has become as common for candidates as kissing babies, eating "rubber" chicken dinners, raising money, and launching attack ads. Every presidential election cycle since 1976 has included debates. The 2008 primary elections broke all records for the number of nationally televised debates for both parties. The Democrats participated in 21 debates from April 2007 to April 2008 and the Republicans were close behind with 18 when they settled on a nominee in February. Local, state, and Congressional election debates are ubiquitous as well, even if many are held in front of small audiences and have limited media coverage. Candidates, especially those running for Congress and governorships, might still try to avoid them or have as few as possible, but the reality is that debates are institutionalized in the American political system and are becoming more common in countries throughout the world. The media broadcasts, reports on, and analyzes debates. Candidates participate in them—either willingly or because it is expected. Potential voters watch, and then they talk about what they've observed and learned. Citizens' reactions may be voiced to a spouse, partner, family member or friends in the comfort of a living room or in the growing number of organized watch parties.[1]

Debates are essentially the focal point for a campaign.[2] A campaign is, in and of itself, an extended debate with a variety of candidate messages that state positions on issues, recall past accomplishments, emphasize credentials, make comparisons to the opponent(s), criticize opponents' positions or records, and defend against attacks on qualifications, positions, and records. Debates often include references to what was said in other campaign messages, and candidates extend and further refine their messages from the campaign trail during a debate. After a debate, they capitalize on their strongest arguments and try to explain away their gaffes. Over the course of a series of debates, a majority of the key issues the media, the candidates, and the public think are important are explored. One of the authors of this book has stated on numerous occasions that if someone fell asleep during a political campaign and woke up in time for the debates, he or she would know most of what had been said previously and would be prepared for the arguments waged during the remainder of the campaign.

Political scientist Thomas Holbrook examined the role of campaign information to close the knowledge gap between high and low interest political observers. He concluded that "as campaign events go, presidential debates are likely to generate more interest and to be more accessible than any other events in the fall campaign" and that "the information presented in debates is more likely to be new information to low information voters than to high information voters."[3] Political scientists Richard Lau and David Redlawsk, who studied how voters process political information, provided further validation of the importance of debates by noting that "when information flows in a relatively chaotic environment and is not easily managed by the decision maker, the task of comparing candidates to one another is not so simple. It is easy if you have the information in a handy to use, side-by-side format, and the amount of information is limited."[4] While their analysis did not specifically mention debates, the final sentence of the quotation describes the debate environment perfectly.

The 1992 focus group study of reactions to debates revealed that nearly one-quarter of the participants did not start following the campaign until after Labor Day.[5] The same was true in 1996. In 2004, a subset of participants revealed that 16 percent had not followed closely until a few weeks before the debates. Given how close the 2000 and 2004 election results were, a potentially significant number of voters can be influenced by a debate. A male focus group participant in Murray, Kentucky, after the first 1996 debate summarized the importance of debates for those who are latecomers to the political spectacle: "I thought for someone who really wasn't following the campaign that this debate would have given them a political overview of the positions of the two candidates. It didn't present any particular depth due to time and the variety of questions, but it sort of gave us an opener."

To set the stage for the voices that are presented throughout the book, this chapter provides an overview of debate research that establishes the ability of debates to reach large numbers of voters, promote learning, and influence votes. It then moves to a summary of salient research regarding the elements of debates, such as formats, that can affect their utility and outcomes. Next is a more general examination of the role of discussion in a democracy and how political talk among average citizens can enhance both the debate experience and democratic processes. Finally, the specific research questions addressed in the study are presented.

RESEARCH ON POLITICAL DEBATES

Several major summaries of over forty years of televised debate research were published in recent years.[6] They all concluded that debates have an impact on voters, and the way debates are staged influences the content of the debate and voters' perceptions. The 1992 focus group study that served as the catalyst for the creation of DebateWatch presented research showing the importance of debates as an education source and in making or reinforcing voting decisions. Additional research since 1992 further confirms those conclusions. In fact, the 1992 study clearly supported previous research suggesting that debates provide new information, enable viewers to compare candidates' positions, reinforce existing positions, assist undecided voters in making a vote choice, and demonstrate a clear relationship between image development and candidates' positions on issues or their past records. Since there is a sufficient body of research to support the importance of debates in campaigns, this chapter does not summarize all of the past research but emphasizes new research since 1992 while highlighting classic studies. Additional research is cited in chapters throughout the book to provide context for what was learned from focus group members.

The Reach and Influence of Debates

Candidates have countless ways to reach voters, including traditional speeches, direct mail, town hall meetings, advertising, broadcast e-mails, automated phone calls leaving recorded messages from the candidate or prominent supporters, and one-on-one encounters with voters. Internet options keep growing, and the pervasiveness of cell phones brought about the use of text messages to rally supporters or to get out the vote. Even with the explosion of Web sites, blogs, and free media through online news broadcasts and numerous network and cable channels, nothing compares to televised political debates for sheer reach. In addition to reach, debates provide a shared experience that largely happens in real time. This enhances viewers' ability to create both a face-to-face and a virtual community in an era of fragmentation. The Internet, cell phones, and text messaging have all contributed to the creation of virtual communities at the expense of face-to-face discussions. Additionally, news reporting about debates influences how viewers translate what they observed and shapes the opinions of those who did not watch. Media communication researcher Lynda Kaid and her colleagues examined the amount of coverage given to various key campaign issues and events on major networks between Labor Day and Election Day and found that "debate-related news segments are among the most frequent of all campaign stories."[7] Through what another media researcher, Diana Owen,[8] refers to as an "interwoven" communications environment, even nontraditional media parodying debates extend the influence. The Racine Group's summary of research on traditional and nontraditional media influences on perceptions of candidates cites Owen and others and concluded that "debates and 'new media,' such as political talk radio, TV entertainment shows, TV talk shows and TV news magazines, exerted the greatest influence on prospective voters' perceptions of candidates."[9] How the media shapes perceptions through debate coverage was illustrated in 2004 through research reported by Senja Post at Media Tenor, a media research institute (see www.mediatenor.com). In a content analysis of both print and broadcast coverage of the debates, the researchers found that "The TV debates were the single most important opportunity for John Kerry to change his image as a flip flopper. However, TV news after the first two debates continued to report on John Kerry as a politician who waffles on the issues."[10] Thus, the impact of anything Kerry said in the debate to change his image was potentially lessened by the reports. For those who did not view the debates, the media's framing of the issue was unlikely to change perceptions of Kerry.

Entertainment media's treatment of political debates, such as the long tradition of debate skits on *Saturday Night Live*, has likely done more than entertain. This is especially true since "9% of Americans got most of their news about the 2000 presidential campaign primarily from television entertainment talk shows and another 6% got most of their news from television prime-time comedy programs."[11] The 2008 primary debates illustrate the power of comedy to also be commentary. In a debate against Barack Obama in February 2008, Hillary Clinton referred to an SNL skit to make her point that she was getting the tough questions and the media was more concerned with making Obama comfortable: "If anybody saw 'Saturday Night Live,'" she said, "you know, maybe we should ask Barack if he's comfortable and needs another pillow."[12] James Downey wrote the skit and had written others on debates. The reporter who commented on Downey's ability to capture the political moment wrote, "When Downey has taken aim at the presidential debates, he has consistently defined the candidates before they could define themselves: His send-up of the 2000 debates between Al Gore and George W. Bush coined the Bushian malapropism 'strategery,' an invention that is sometimes attributed to Bush."[13] Similarly, as chapter eight demonstrates, a reference to a 2000 debate skit is made by one of the participants to the instant recognition of others in the group, thus proving the power of debates to capture attention of both the mainstream and alternative "news" sources.

Statistics clearly illustrate the reach of presidential debates in terms of viewership. In 1996, the two presidential debates averaged 41.2 million viewers, and 36.3 million watched the vice presidential debate. In 2000, an average of 40.6 million viewers tuned in and 28.5 million saw the vice presidential candidates. In 2004 when voter turnout increased, so did debate viewership. Nielsen reported that 62.4 million watched the first Bush-Kerry debate, 46.7 watched the second, and 51.1 watched the third. At 43.5 million, viewership for the vice presidential debate was higher than the average presidential numbers in 1996 and 2000.[14]

The only other candidate speech that has the potential to draw a large live audience from start to finish is the nominating convention acceptance speech; however, convention viewership is significantly lower. For example, viewership for the final night of the Republican convention in 2000 was 21.1 million[15] and the Democrats drew 23 million in 2004.[16] Video streaming on the Internet and reruns on C-SPAN make it possible for millions who weren't able to get to a television or see debates in real time to watch. The Internet makes it possible for those outside the United States to tune in. Of the approximately 6 million Americans in military and nonmilitary positions living abroad,[17] a significant number can now be part of the debate ritual and even DebateWatch. Starting in 1996, the Department of Defense's Federal Voting Assistance Program, which provides voting support to military and civilians abroad, circulated information about DebateWatch.[18] Groups reported from Austria, Brazil, Canada, Germany, and Japan.

Not only do potential voters watch in large numbers, but they consider debates to be a superior information source to most other ways of learning about candidates. A *USA Today* report in 1996 indicated that 36 percent of the respondents in exit polls listed debates as the "most valuable [television information source] in making their ballot choices" while only 6 percent listed paid television advertising.[19] Exit polls in 1988 and 1992 had similar results with 48 percent in 1988 and 70 percent in 1992 identifying debates as helpful in deciding for whom to vote.[20] A 2002 study conducted through the Debate Advisory Standards Project funded by The Pew Charitable Trusts found that 20 percent of the 1,000 respondents rated debates—in a general sense—as "the best, most useful information" about political candidates, compared to 3 percent for candidates' advertisements.[21] The same study also revealed that 76 percent of the registered voters across the country who were polled said that "debates are either very helpful or somewhat helpful in deciding how they will vote in elections for president."[22] A study by The Pew Research Center for the People and the Press prior to the start of the 2004 debates found that 29 percent said "the debates will matter in their decision of whom to support, which is about the same as in 2000 and 1996."[23] Pew's analysis of polling data from 1960 until 2000 taken before and after debates clearly revealed that debates do move polls, especially when the race is close or there are lingering questions about personal character.

Focus group participants were asked to evaluate the debates against other campaign messages. We heard consistent comments that provide insight into the statistics. An exchange within a group in Winston-Salem, North Carolina, after the second Clinton-Dole debate in 1996 is illustrative:

Female: I think I learn more from the debate.... I feel that it comes a little bit more unadulterated. I get to see what's really going on, and how they're going to address the issues.

Male: I agree with her. Compared to conventions, it's not just Democrats listening to Bill Clinton or Republicans listening to Bob Dole; you have a cross-section. Their message isn't catered to just one group of people.

A male who was in the live audience in Hartford, Connecticut, for the first Clinton-Dole debate provided another reason why debates were more valuable than other forms of information—a lack of selectivity in exposure to messages: "When we get campaign information [from other sources] it's from somewhere that we're interested in anyway. So we just reinforce what we believe anyway. But here we're forced to actually listen to what both opposing parties have to say about it." And a woman who was selected by the Gallup organization to be one of the questioners in the 1996 town hall debate summarized the thinking of many regarding the advantage of debates as an information source this way: "The debate format is far superior to anything that involves the media any more than it does. Because we don't get little chopped clips of the candidates."

A majority of participants in focus groups from 1992 to 2004 indicated that they learned something new from the debates. This confirmed what research on less extensive subject pools in previous elections had reported. The specifics of what was learned are provided in chapters five through eight. McKinney and Carlin's summary of voter learning research found that "debate effects are dependent largely on the contextual dynamics of a given campaign, including the particular candidates engaged in the debate and also highly dependent upon the different types of debate viewers."[24] Their analysis of the research further explained what factors influence the impact of debates on learning acquisition. Context is one factor and includes prior knowledge about the candidates (a factor that is more important in nonincumbent races), whether or not viewers are decided, if the race is close, and if there is weak party allegiance. In addition to context, the "disposition of viewers" has an influence. Level of interest, partisanship, commitment to a candidate, and level of viewing—part or all of a debate or more than one—contribute to the attitudes viewers bring to the experience. When all of these factors are taken into consideration, past research—including focus group research—does indicate that there is a reinforcement factor for those with a candidate choice[25] and that reinforcement can result in greater likelihood of voting. Viewers who are undecided or soft in their commitments can decide or change, and most viewers learn something new about the candidates whether it is related to issues or leadership/character traits. Salience of learning is largely dependent upon what was known coming into the debate.[26] The 2004 debates illustrate their power to move votes as well. Political communication scholar Robert Friedenberg analyzed polling data after the first debate and concluded that "before the debate Kerry had not led in any national poll, two of the thirteen polls taken in the week after the debate gave him a lead and three others found that the race was a tie. The 6-point lead that Bush had enjoyed in the RealClearPolitics poll average before the debate had diminished to 2 points in the week following the debate."[27]

It is clear that the research on reach and impact confirms what media scholar James Lemert and his colleagues concluded after conducting a survey of 1,000 voters in four states in 1990: "the public's overall sense is that it [the debates] may be the best game in town."[28]

Factors Affecting the Usefulness of Debates

Being the best game in town has not stopped political debates from being castigated for their shortcomings. In every election cycle since the Kennedy-Nixon debates, researchers and commentators uncovered limitations and flaws. It appears that no one has crafted the "perfect" debate. Rhetorical critic J. Jeffrey Auer called the Kennedy-Nixon debates "counterfeit" because they did not adhere to the traditions and structures of academic debate, especially the use of a clearly stated topic and sufficient time to develop arguments.[29] Lloyd Bitzer and Theodore Reuter picked up on the theme in 1976 with their book, *Carter vs. Ford: The Counterfeit Debates of 1976.*[30] Despite complaints about the short response times, lack of rebuttal opportunities, randomness of questions, topics not covered, candidate evasiveness, lack of follow-up questions, or redundant themes across debates, there is evidence that political debates are not counterfeit.

Political communication scholar Diana Carlin used argumentation and debate theory definitions of "debate" in an analysis of the 1988 debates to illustrate that the debates met the definitions. She argued that the structure, length of speeches, and lack of a single topic did not deny the encounters the right to be called debates because debate takes many forms outside academic structures, such as legislative debate. She further argued that there *is* a single topic in a debate—who would make the better president, governor, and so on—and the cumulative set of questions and answers addresses that topic.[31] Ultimately, debates compare issue positions, and political debates do that. Both the 1988 debates on which the Carlin essay was based and subsequent debates had clashes of positions and ideas. The following excerpt on the issue of tax cuts from a 2008 Republican primary debate features Senator John McCain and Governor Mitt Romney. It illustrates the ability of debates to force comparison and clash through carefully worded questions:

Janet Hook,
Los Angeles Times: Senator McCain, you're talking about making the tax cuts permanent. And as Governor Romney pointed out before, you opposed the Bush tax cuts the first time around. Now, more recently you've been saying that the reason why you opposed the tax cuts at first was because they weren't off-set by spending cuts. But back when you actually voted against the tax cuts in Congress, you said you opposed them because they favored the wealthy too much. So which is it? And if they were too skewed to the wealthy at first, are they still too skewed to the wealthy?

McCain: Actually, I think lower and middle income Americans need more help. Obviously, I think that's the case today. That's one reason why we're giving them rebates. I was part of the Reagan revolution. I was there with Jack Kemp and Phil Gramm and Warren Rudman and all these other fighters that wanted to change a terrible economic situation in America with 10 percent unemployment and 20 percent interest rates. I was proud to be a foot soldier, support those tax cuts, and they had spending restraints associated with it. I made it very clear when I ran in 2000 that I had a package of tax cuts which were very important and very impactful, but I also had restraints in spending. And I disagreed when spending got out of control. And I disagreed when we had tax cuts without spending restraint....

Anderson Cooper, CNN: Governor Romney, what do you think of Senator McCain's response?

Romney: I appreciate his response and appreciate the fact he was part of the Reagan revolution. I think that the Bush revolution and the downturn that we faced when he came in office suggested that we needed a tax cut. There's no question in my mind that Ronald Reagan would have said sign it and vote for it. And Senator McCain was one of two that did not. And again, the justification at the time was because it represents a tax cut for the rich. I believe in getting rates down. I think that builds our economy. When we talk about spending, however, I hope people in the country understand that most people in Washington, most politicians, generally want to talk about the $2 and $3 and $4 relative items. And they want to talk about the big one. Right now, federal spending is about 60 percent for entitlements—Social Security, Medicare and Medicaid. And that's growing like crazy. It will be 70 percent entitlements, plus interest, by the time of the next president's second term. And then the military is about 20 percent today. No one is talking about cutting the military, we ought to grow it. So people talk about the 20 percent and how we have to go after that 20 percent. There's not enough in the 20 percent to go after if we don't go after the entitlement problem. And you listen to all the folks running for president, no one wants to talk about it. But we have to talk about it. We have to put together a plan that says we're going to rein in the excessive growth in those areas, promising to meet the obligations we made to seniors. We're not going to change the deal on seniors, but we're going to have to change the deal for 20 and 30 and 40-year-olds, or we're going to bankrupt our country.[32]

Romney took advantage of the situation to criticize McCain's vote and also to separate himself as a former governor from someone who is in Congress and who he wanted to position as being part of the problem. Since their inception, political debates have countless examples such as this one that include questions asking for comparisons and candidates who delineate differences or create clash—a primary prerequisite of a debate.

Further evidence that debates provide a unique way of comparing candidates side-by-side is based on the extensive research led by political communication scholar William Benoit. His research shows that debates consist of acclaims, attacks, and defenses, which are all an integral part of what constitutes debate.[33] Benoit's research and earlier research by media researchers David Sears and Steven Chaffee demonstrated that the majority of debate content is on issues.[34] Media Tenor's content analysis of the 2004 debate transcripts found that "Debates are highly issue-oriented (almost 9 out of 10 statements dealt with issues like foreign policy, tax policy or health care."[35] If candidates are discussing issues, then comparisons are possible between or among candidates. Essentially, a debate is about making comparisons of policy options and determining which candidate presents the most benefits and the fewest risks.

If one accepts that the encounters deserve to be called debates as opposed to forums or joint news conferences, it is still important to take the criticisms seriously and find ways to improve the formats. Research can provide direction. The Commission on Presidential Debates' proposed use of a single moderator for the 1992 debates resulted from a symposium on formats that included a summary of academic research and opinions of individuals who had served as panelists.[36] The continued use of a single moderator and the town hall format after 1992 was a result of the 1992 focus group study. Additional changes since then reflect feedback from the DebateWatch groups and general public commentary about the debate formats.

Research does demonstrate that the way the debates are structured affects their utility for viewers. According to the Racine Group's White Paper on debates, "The format and the questions asked have an influence on the degree of interaction and the clash between or among candidates."[37] Clash is important for two reasons. First, it allows viewers to compare candidates' issue stances, and, secondly, it provides opportunities for attacks and defenses that further illuminate issues and reveal something about a candidate's mettle. Several content analyses of debates have shown that clash is affected by the format.[38] Among the findings is that multiple rebuttal periods within a single question cycle or topic and follow-up questions produce more clash. Participants in the 1992 focus group study were especially critical of the panelist format that allowed the first speaker two minutes to respond and the other candidates only one minute for rebuttal and no follow-up questions for any candidate.[39]

Research also indicates that individual candidates perform differently with different formats. The 1992 formats provided a perfect laboratory since each debate was different and "viewer reactions and polls taken after the debates indicated that Ross Perot performed best with the traditional format, Bill Clinton 'ruled' the town hall meeting format, and George Bush performed best with a free-flowing single moderator structure."[40] This finding argues for the use of multiple formats across a series of debates to provide both variety for viewers and a more level playing field for candidates with different debate skills. The various formats also mimic different types of communication settings in which a president functions—formal speeches given standing behind the presidential seal, conversational talks originating from the Oval Office, and town hall meetings or news conferences held in a variety of settings. If the purpose of debates is to demonstrate to the public how a candidate "enacts the presidency" as communication scholar Edward Hinck has suggested,[41] then the mix of settings provides a more realistic view and a clearer window into presidential qualities.

American presidential debates rely on a series of questions as the basis for debate, and how they are asked and who asks them also influence content, strategy, and clash. Research on questions reveals that "citizens ask different types of questions than professionals and that the questions influence the type of argument as well as the language choice used by the debaters."[42] If the same question or a variation on a theme is not asked of all candidates, the opportunity for clash and real comparison is reduced. Similarly if all candidates do not have an opportunity for rebuttal, comparison and clarification are reduced. This is especially problematic in primary debates with numerous candidates.

The structure of questions also influences the value of a response. For example, a question that directly asks candidates to compare a policy to that of other candidates is designed to elicit "debate," as the example from the 2008 Republican primary debate illustrated. Questions such as the ones that Jim Lehrer asked in the second 2000 Bush-Gore debate also forced the candidates to respond to one another and to stay on topic. For example, Lehrer asked the following question: "Vice President Gore, the governor mentioned the Middle East. Here we're talking at this stage in the game about diplomatic power that we have. What do you think the United States should do right now to resolve that conflict over there?" He then simply said, "Governor?" to solicit Bush's response. He followed Bush's analysis with the following to Gore: "So you don't believe, Vice President Gore, that we should take sides and resolve this right now? A lot of people pushing say the United States should declare itself and not be so neutral in this particular situation." After Gore's response, Lehrer then directed the nature of Bush's response with, "You agree with that, Governor?"[43] The format was conversational with the only time limit being that no response could exceed two minutes. There were no restrictions on the number of rebuttal speeches or follow-up questions; Lehrer could take a topic as far as he felt necessary to get the candidates to expound and clash. This approach is becoming more common and was a choice for many primary debates in 2004 and 2008 when the number of participants reached two or three. Questions, however, can also produce bad debate or at least discussion that viewers think is unimportant or irrelevant. This is discussed at length in chapters four and five.

Mass communication researcher William Eveland and his colleagues[44] analyzed the questions asked by journalists and citizens in the 1992 debates—the first time citizens had questioned general election candidates. They found clear differences in tone, with journalists being more aggressive and argumentative. Citizens were less concerned with foreign policy and wanted more specifics on policies. Focus group participants in 1992 detected the differences without a formal content analysis. They were highly critical of panelists' questions that they believed were irrelevant or too general, with one group member calling the panelists' questions in the second half of the Lansing, Michigan, debate "leading and aggressive and antagonistic."[45] Participants recognized that the town hall produced a different type of question—more what they would have asked. While they believed the questions fit their agenda, they also recognized the need for an expert moderator in the debates to direct the flow, enforce the rules, and provide a knowledge level of the issues that average citizens might not have. Chapter four provides a summary of viewers' reactions to the various aspects of debate format and how they relate to past research. The importance of promoting citizen talk about politics is examined in the next section as a means of providing a framework for the use of discussion groups in the study.

DISCUSSION AND DEMOCRACY

Because debates do matter in elections, it is only natural that viewers talk about them. DebateWatch was built on the premise, as mentioned in the introduction, that discussion and feedback to elected officials are integral parts of a democratic society. Political theorist Benjamin Barber argued that "at the heart of strong democracy is talk."[46] This belief is rooted in western philosophy going back to Plato, who believed that dialectic leads to knowledge or understanding. Rhetorical scholar James Benjamin explained, "The purpose of Plato's dialectic was to advance understanding. This was accomplished through discourse, since in Greek society pursuit of knowledge was conceived as a communal affair rather than an individual activity. Plato considered dialectic to be a way of searching for truth through question and answer discussions."[47]

Public policy researchers Fay Lomax Cook, Michael Delli Carpini, and Lawrence Jacobs noted a growing interest in "discursive participation" or public talk in the United States.[48] They identified "President Clinton's initiative on race in the early 1990s...Televised initiatives such as James Fishkin's 'deliberative polls,' town-hall meeting style presidential debates, *Nightline*'s or *Hardball*'s occasional public forums, even talk shows such as Oprah"[49] as promoting public deliberation. Their 2003 survey of 1,001 randomly selected adults in a national survey found that "fully 74 percent of Americans reported having engaged in at least one *type* of discursive act in the past year."[50] This included informal conversations about public issues, attendance at formal meetings, e-mailing or text messaging about policy issues, or participation in Internet chat rooms or online discussion groups.[51] A 2007 study of political talk in the workplace by Vault, a career information organization, found that 66 percent of respondents indicated that their "co-workers discuss politics at the office" and that 52 percent of those surveyed indicated that they were "open about [their] political views at work."[52]

The research findings on the prevalence of political talk in daily life and the response to DebateWatch through group discussions, online chats, and feedback reports suggest that the public desires to participate in politics as more than sideline observers. One of the audience members at the 1996 Clinton-Dole debate in Hartford participated in a DebateWatch afterwards and stated his belief that "Most Americans crave information, and I think most of us want to get together and talk about these issues." Finding out what public talk sounds like and how people learn through it, as the Greeks intended, is what DebateWatch is all about. Normative theory suggests how modern society should proceed to learn through talk. In summarizing the normative research on public talk or deliberative democracy, Carlin et al. wrote that "it should center on the 'common good' rather than on self-interest; involve equal, free, and informed participants; be governed by reasoned argument; and incorporate a diversity of perspectives."[53] The Carlin et al. study of 2004 DebateWatch groups and writers on newspaper-sponsored blogs, as well as an earlier study of the 1996 DebateWatch transcripts by Levasseur and Carlin,[54] revealed that much citizen talk was more egocentric than collective in its focus. In other words, citizens were more concerned about the impact of public policy on their personal lives than on the common good. Given that issues such as education, Social Security, taxes, and health care dominate much political discourse, that result is not surprising. These are policies that have highly personal consequences and the manner in which they are addressed by politicians personalizes them far more than focusing them on societal costs and benefits. As psychologist Drew Westen wrote when explaining "the political brain," "*Every* appeal is ultimately an emotional one to voter's interests—what's good for them and their families—or their values—what matters to them morally. The question that decides elections is whether the appeal is a weak or a strong one."[55] Studying political talk exposes the emotional reactions, but it also reveals how reactions can moderate through discussion.

Eveland examined the role of discussion in producing informed citizens and achieving normative standards of democratic knowledge and participation. He concluded "that the normative ideal of an informed citizenry is not an empirical reality, at least in the United States. A considerable body of research suggests that the American public is poorly informed about basic civics, political and current events information."[56] Through his research, Eveland concluded "that the act of engaging in discussion forces meaningful information processing—elaboration— and thus increases learning due to an influence on information processing during discussion."[57] The ideal public sphere in which "citizens deliberate about common affairs, as distinct from personal or private concerns"[58] may not be what dominates the DebateWatch texts or other public discussions of politics. However, the analysis of the three election cycles reported in this book does indicate that citizens learn from discussion and that events such as 9/11 had an impact on the issues that citizens found were important and on how they discussed them. The DebateWatch project comes closer to rhetorical theorist Gerald Hauser's belief that an "ideal form of discourse...seldom, if ever, has materialized," thus, we should study "discourse as it actually occurs in existing democracies."[59] In doing so, this study addresses several key questions:

1. What are viewers' expectations of political debates as an information source about candidates and issues and were they met?

2. How do debate format and questions affect learning acquisition?

3. How does information gleaned from debates help viewers decide who would be a better president?

4. What are the salient issues for voters and how are the issues related to formation of candidate images?

5. Do debates change or reinforce vote choice?

6. How do the debates compare to other campaign and news sources for learning acquisition?

7. Do news reports of debates and discussions after debates affect original views of the candidates or the debate outcomes?

8. Are the discussions a valuable source of information? Do they impact how the campaign is followed after the debates?

9. What motivates prospective voters to participate in the electoral process and what is the best way to engage young people?

10. Are vice presidential debates valuable?

11. Who should be included in the debates and why?

The scope of this project was large in that it covers three election cycles and includes tens of thousands of participant responses to surveys, nearly two thousand voices from focus groups, several thousand facilitator reports, and over a thousand e-mails and letters. The discussion provides insights into the numbers behind polling data and why viewers may not always vote for the person who "wins" the debate according to postdebate polls. The responses provide suggestions for how to improve debates and how candidates need to address an audience to maximize the impact of their words. One additional question the research sought to uncover was who chose to participate in DebateWatch. The next chapter addresses demographic information as well as the methods used to publicize the program and process the results.

Chapter Three

DebateWatch: Developing the Study

DebateWatch was a major research effort that produced a vast amount of quantitative and qualitative data. In addition to the information garnered about the influence and importance of the presidential and vice-presidential debates, this effort produced insights into vote choice, participation and nonparticipation at the polls, and public attitudes about politics, politicians, elections, and the media. While the other chapters in this book provide an outlet for DebateWatch participants' specific comments, this chapter focuses primarily on the study's quantifiable aspects. This chapter provides an overview of the DebateWatch program features that were consistent across the three election cycles and those that were unique. It then breaks down the data for each of the three years to provide a better understanding of who the participants were.

STUDY DESIGN AND IMPLEMENTATION

DebateWatch was created through a $200,000 Ford Foundation grant to the University of Kansas and principal investigator Diana Carlin in 1996, and it was operated in collaboration with the Commission on Presidential Debates (CPD) as one of their voter education projects. DebateWatch provided a grass roots structure to encourage individuals and organizations to host debate viewing parties in their homes, community centers, schools, places of worship, union halls, and other venues suitable for viewing and discussing the debates. It gave average citizens an opportunity to discuss the debates in a more formal manner than the next-day conversations in break rooms. It also provided an opportunity to give feedback to the debate sponsor and to have viewpoints reported to the media. The feedback helped improve debates and made citizens' voices—the third agenda—part of the debate process. Two important elements of DebateWatch were that the facilitators were not to ask who won or lost and discussion was to begin at the conclusion of the debate—no commentary or spin were to be viewed prior to the start of discussion. The idea was to have citizens give their thoughts without influence from the media or the campaigns. We know that these procedures were followed for the research groups since there are transcripts. Many facilitator forms and e-mail comments indicated that groups for which there were no transcripts followed the suggestion.

DebateWatch Packets and Surveys

Distribution of DebateWatch materials changed across the cycles. In all cases, the materials to conduct a DebateWatch and provide feedback were free of charge. In 1996, the packet included the following: an explanation of the program and its origin; suggestions for organizing a group; facilitator's instructions; explanation that a facilitator's report of the group's collective opinions was to be called in, faxed (to a toll-free number), or e-mailed within 24 hours of the debate; a form to assist in note taking; a viewer's guide to debates designed to enhance the debates' learning potential; an individual participant survey; and a resource list for information about voter registration guidelines and candidate information. Over fifteen thousand packets were mailed from the CPD's offices in Washington, D.C., and from the DebateWatch '96 research center at the University of Kansas. Researchers did not track downloads on the CPD Web site. In 2000, the packet was reduced to four pages with the individual participant survey, notes page, and other supplemental information eliminated. Internet distribution was encouraged and expanded and approximately three thousand packets were mailed. Participants had a dedicated e-mail address and toll-free fax number at the University of Kansas to send facilitator reports and additional comments. In 2004 everything was on the CPD Web site and paper distribution no longer took place. The National Communication Association (NCA), one of the CPD's voter education partners, engaged in additional research and had a separate facilitator report that was returned to the University of Kansas online. NCA data was also included in the CPD's totals. Copies of the DebateWatch materials from all three years are included in Appendices A, C, and D.

Marketing and Recruitment

DebateWatch was publicized through several channels. First, a group of approximately 125 partners was recruited from a variety of organizations, professional associations, and universities (see Appendix A). The rich variety of the partners added demographic and political diversity, and allowed each partner to develop its own DebateWatch groups using the adaptable packet information and to inform members through newspapers or other forms of communication about the program.

A second recruitment strategy was through numerous public notices. A public service announcement was prepared and distributed to broadcast outlets by the National Association of Broadcasters in 1996. *Parade Magazine* (1996) carried an article that generated over three thousand phone calls to the toll-free information number at the research center within 48 hours. Newspaper editors wrote editorials about the project and many others carried news stories. The Commission's Web site (http://www.debates.org) included the packet for downloading. On June 16, 1996, DebateWatch was launched in a news conference held in Washington, D.C., and included comments by voter education partners as well as the co-chairmen of the CPD.

Universities and organizations located in each of the cities that hosted a debate also organized a variety of DebateWatch activities each cycle. For example in 1996, after the vice presidential debate in St. Petersburg, Florida, the *St. Petersburg Times* hosted a large viewing party and then followed it with a discussion. Across town, Eckerd College and the League of Women Voters jointly hosted an intergenerational DebateWatch with students, community members, and Eckerd College Elderhostel participants who were from across the country. The day after the debate, the Elderhostel group continued the discussion with three of the Elderhostel faculty members and the event was carried on C-SPAN. In 2000, St. Louis University held a full day of activities on campus, including a panel featuring MTV personalities, as a way to generate participation in its DebateWatch activities. St. Louis also partnered with local news media to encourage DebateWatch groups throughout the city. In 2000 and 2004, DebateWatch groups were held at most sites and were of various sizes. Many were town/gown events. Internet discussion groups were sponsored by some of the partners and one of the SCA members hosted a discussion in the C-SPAN chat room in 1996.

A final recruitment strategy took place through the Speech Communication Association (SCA, but now the National Communication Association, or NCA). At least one communication faculty member was identified in each state in 1996 to serve as a coordinator to host a group for research purposes and to assist in organizing groups on campuses. Collectively, the SCA groups served as a control group against which grassroots results were compared. In 2000 and 2004, NCA members also organized research groups, collected individual participant surveys, and taped discussions. In addition to these recruitment strategies, individuals selected by Gallup for the San Diego town hall debate also agreed to hold a discussion after the debate that was aired by C-SPAN.

DebateWatch Procedures

Discussion groups were asked to describe their expectations for the debates and whether or not they were met, what they had learned, what they still needed to know, how well the formats served the purpose of providing debates that aided comparison of candidates, how debates compared to other information sources, and any other comments they had about the debates and the political process. The questions used in the three cycles are included in Appendices A, C, and D.

Research group organizers were encouraged to invite individuals representing as many age, racial, ethnic, and socioeconomic groups as possible. For the most part, an acceptable mix of participation was achieved by combining the research and voluntary groups in 1996 and 2004. Younger participants dominated in 2000 and racial diversity varied across cycles.

One of the most important features of DebateWatch was the voluntary group facilitator report. The facilitator report varied in content each cycle, but generally asked for basic demographic information about the group—number of participants, city and state, place of discussion (school, home, etc.), race and estimated ages of participants, participants' sex, partner organization affiliation if applicable, and how the group learned about DebateWatch. The report had three questions to serve as feedback to the sponsors in 1996: (1) which questions or topics did participants find most useful; (2) were any questions considered irrelevant or unimportant to participants; and (3) were any topics overlooked by Debate questioners or candidates which DebateWatch participants wanted to hear discussed. The answers to these questions were compiled from reports received within 24 hours of the debate and were disseminated to media outlets. The same strategy was used in 2000 and 2004. The 2004 CPD survey did not ask about irrelevant or nonuseful topics; the NCA survey did, however. The 2004 CPD survey asked for a comparison of the town hall format to the others used that year. A phone survey was conducted in 1996 prior to the debates to ask what topics citizens wanted to hear discussed in the debates. The CPD asked the same question in online surveys prior to the debates in 2000 and 2004. The results are discussed in chapter five.

The final stage of data collection involved nonvoters. Because of the low voter turnout in 1996 and common expressions of cynicism among group members, the original research design was altered to include a postelection study. Through surveys and intergenerational focus groups, voters' and nonvoters' attitudes about politics were compared. Although these individuals were nonvoters, many had watched or followed the debates and weighed in about them during the discussions. Research questions and details about the methodology along with the results are reported in chapter nine.

1996 RESULTS

Reports were returned from 824 groups over the three debates. The reports represented 8,376 individuals. Since completion of the forms was voluntary, there is no way of knowing how many people held groups or used the materials with family members. The DebateWatch research center also received anecdotal evidence via e-mail and telephone calls that suggested the number of focus groups actually conducted was much greater, but that many simply did not submit a report. The results, however, provide one of the largest databases of public opinion on presidential debates ever collected. One hundred twelve group discussions were taped and transcribed. Excerpts are included throughout the book.

The facilitator reports and participant surveys arrived via the DebateWatch fax, e-mail, and U.S. mail. Viewership was highest for the first debate and lowest for the vice-presidential debate. DebateWatch participation followed that pattern. Following the first debate in Hartford, Connecticut, 360 group facilitators submitted reports, representing 3,459 group members. The San Diego, California, debate resulted in 287 groups, representing 2,865 participants. The vice-presidential debate in St. Petersburg, Florida, produced 177 facilitator reports claiming a total participation of 2,052.

In addition to the facilitator reports, 6,178 individuals returned participant surveys. Overall, 3,103 Hartford participants, 2,727 San Diego participants, and 1,480 St. Petersburg participants submitted surveys. The participant information was not reported to the media.

Participant Demographics

The demographic breakdown of the information received indicates participation from a cross-section of Americans. Across the three debates, 52.6 percent of the participants were female and the remaining 47.4 percent were male. The first debate was represented by 51.2 percent females and 48.8 percent males. The participants for the vice-presidential debate in St. Petersburg had the largest margin of difference between male and female participants, with 54.3 percent female and 45.6 percent male. The presidential debate in San Diego had 52.2 percent female and 47.8 percent male participants.

The age of participants also varied only slightly across the debates. The 18- to 25-year-old age group made up the greatest percentage of the first debate's participants. This was not surprising for two reasons. First, it is easy to organize events on campuses and many campuses viewed this as a way of stimulating interest among young voters. Second, these groups were more likely to return their forms than groups organized by neighbors or friends because faculty were recruited specifically to provide data and their groups were dominated by students. In addition, the late starting time (9:00 P.M. ET) was a deterrent for older viewers, especially those on the east coast. To encourage participation from older adults, intergenerational groups were organized at several sites, which also provided transportation. In Wichita, Kansas, community participation was further encouraged by the mayor, and public and university facilities were available around the city. Because reports had to be faxed or e-mailed within 24 hours and it was quite late on the east coast by the time groups concluded, many did not report their results. Very few groups used the 800-number to call in reports. For the first debate, 37.5 percent of those who returned participant forms were 18 to 25 years old. This group was followed by those under 18 (25%).[1] Participants between 26 and 40 made up 14.2 percent, followed by 41- to 55-year-olds at 12.7 percent. Those over 55 made up the remaining 10.6 percent. This number is significantly disproportionate to voting patterns. The fact that the initial participant population represented almost the exact opposite of the actual voting population was not viewed as a problem, however. It was considered an opportunity to hear from and engage a cohort most frequently ignored and disengaged. As chapter eight reports, this cohort is most likely to learn from and be influenced by the debates. In terms of the findings, few differences, other than learning, were found across the various demographics in their reactions to the debates.

Participants for the vice-presidential debate in St. Petersburg were more evenly divided in the established age categories. While still the largest group, 18- to

25-year-olds made up 28.5 percent, while those over 55 surged to a high of 19.1 percent. This is likely the result of Elderhostels held in conjunction with the debate and with several venues encouraging intergenerational activities. The 41- to 55-year-olds also outnumbered the 26- to 40-year-olds with 16.9 percent and 14.6 percent respectively. For the third debate in San Diego, the numbers more closely followed the distribution of participants involved with the first debate.

The ethnic background of the participants from the first debate was also diverse, though not quite as diverse as the population as a whole. With 80.9 percent of participants indicating their ethnicity as "white," the remaining 19.1 percent was divided among other ethnic groups. The largest minority group represented in the research was that of "black-African American Descent" at 12.9 percent. Asians and Hispanics constituted 2.9 percent and 2.3 percent, respectively. People indicating "American Indian or Alaskan Native" as their heritage made up 1 percent of the participants from the first debate. In the 1990 census, approximately 75.6 percent of the population was white/nonhispanic. In the 2000 census, the total "white only" population was 69.1 percent. Thus, our participants overrepresented the white population by several percentage points. African Americans constituted 12.1 percent in the 1990 census and 12.3 percent of the population in the 2000 census; thus, the sample was representative of this demographic. Where the results were skewed was underrepresentation of Hispanics who were 9.0 percent of the population in 1990 and 12.5 percent in 2000. There was a slight underrepresentation of Asians, who constituted 2.9 percent of the population in 1990 and 3.6 percent in 2000.

The ethnic background pattern was consistent across all three debates, with two slight variations. In the San Diego debate, the percentage of Asian participants was twice as much as in any other debate (6.6%) and there was also a slight increase in the percentage of Hispanic participants (3.8%), which led to a decrease in the percentage of White participants (76.3%). This is likely because several large DebateWatch groups took place in and around San Diego since the debate was held there.

In both of the presidential debates, the majority of participants indicated their primary occupation as being a student with 54.4 percent listing that category for the first debate, 55.5 percent for the second, and 44.2 percent for the vice presidential. Many students also listed an occupation, either part-time or full-time, with the majority in the service sector. The second most frequent occupation was "professional/ specialty occupation," with 14.5 percent, 12.7 percent, and 13 percent of participants listing this category (all percentages are in the order of first presidential, second presidential, and vice presidential). This was the only occupation other than student to break into double-digit percentages for all three debates. Considering the large number of older participants for the vice-presidential debate, the only major change in occupation occurred with retirees. The percentage of respondents reporting their primary occupation as retired more than doubled in those groups, with 13.6 percent reporting "retired" in the vice presidential groups, compared with 6.4 percent who were retired in the Hartford watch groups and 5.0 percent in the San Diego groups. "Executive, administrative, managerial" was the third most frequently listed category with 7.1 percent, 6.7 percent, and 6.6 percent employed in that sector. Service occupations constituted 5.7 percent, 6.0 percent, and 5.2 percent of the participants. The only other categories that had more than 2 percent of the participants employed in that sector were "marketing and sales" (3.6%, 4.6%, and 5.7%) and "administrative support/clerical" (3%, 3.6%, and 4.8%). It is interesting to note that there was relative similarity in the proportions of individuals listing a category across the debates.

Other areas of consistency across the three debate participation groups include campaign information sources and level of exposure to campaign coverage. When participants in all three debate groups were asked to rank their sources for campaign information, the two most cited sources were nightly network news and local newspapers. The third choice varied across the three debates with first presidential debate participants listing national newspapers, vice-presidential debate participants listing C-SPAN, and second presidential debate participants listing National Public Radio. The C-SPAN choice for the vice presidential debates reflected the increased number of retirees participating. Given the large number of student participants, it was surprising that traditional news sources were more favored than Internet resources. However, in 1996 the prevalence of news on the Internet did not compare to what it is today.

When participants were asked about their exposure to campaign coverage in the six to eight months before the debates, the results were fairly consistent across the three debates. In each instance, over half of all participants (54.7%, 56.3%, and 58%) indicated that they were regular viewers, watching or reading information on a daily or weekly basis. Of the Hartford debate participants, 16.5 percent indicated they irregularly followed campaign coverage up until the debates, with the response "3–4 times per month" being the second most common (14.4% and 14.3%). "Irregularly until the debates," was the third highest response for the second presidential and vice presidential groups (13.4% for each). When the categories of "Regularly in past two months" and "Regularly in the past month" were combined with the responses for "Irregularly up until the debates," it became clear that an average of 23 percent of participants did not start following the campaign regularly until September. This was similar to the 1992 results and further supports the importance of the debates to summarize the campaigns for less informed viewers.

Less consistency was found in the participants' response to their party affiliation. The respondents for the first debate were primarily unaffiliated (35.9%), with Democrats following closely behind (35.6%) and Republicans coming in third (26.5%). For the vice-presidential debate, Democrats made a stronger showing as 45.2 percent of the respondents. Republicans took over the second place at 27.5 percent, followed by unaffiliated voters (26.3%). Of the third parties, only the Reform (average of .26%) and Libertarian parties were represented in all three of the debate participation groups, with the Libertarians representing the largest of the third party constituency groups among participants (average of .46%).[2] However, at no time did more than 0.6 percent of any participation group indicate themselves to be affiliated with a specific third party.

The diversity of the participants went beyond ethnic, age, and party differences. It also included geographic differences. DebateWatch groups reported from 44 states, the District of Columbia, and several international sites.[3] Of the states reporting, Kansas had the greatest number of participating groups with a total of 205 from across three debates. There was considerable statewide coverage of the national project headquartered at the University of Kansas. The media attention and resulting levels of participation indicate how important free media is to spread the word about DebateWatch and encourage participation. Ohio produced 53 reported groups, with Illinois and Maryland reporting 48 groups each. The other states in the top ten were California (43), Missouri (33), Virginia (30), Texas and the District of Columbia (25 each), and Connecticut (18). The remaining groups were evenly dispersed across the other states. The groups represent a combination of research groups, groups hosted by participating associations or organizations, and groups hosted by individuals or unaffiliated organizations who heard about DebateWatch via advertisements.

Survey Results

With a basic understanding of the 1996 participant demographics, it is possible to next look at the specific perspectives and opinions reported in the participant surveys. In addition to getting people to see that they could "disagree without being disagreeable," the project sought to understand the role both the debates and the discussions had on the participants' knowledge and vote choice. To gauge the effect of the debates and discussion on candidate preference, participants were asked before the debates whether or not they had a preference.[4] After the debate, but before the discussion, they filled out a portion of the survey that included questions about the effectiveness of the debate and if it affected their preference. Similar survey questions were completed about the influence of the discussion after its completion.

The majority of participants entered the debates and DebateWatch solidly supporting a candidate. Of the Hartford debate participants, 79 percent had a candidate preference. For both San Diego and St. Petersburg debates, over 82 percent of participants indicated a preference. There were no significant changes in candidate preference following either the debates or the discussions. However, this does not necessarily indicate there was no effect at all. These specific survey questions asked only about changes from one candidate to another, from a candidate to undecided, or from undecided to a candidate. What the questions failed to measure was if the debate or discussion strengthened or weakened the participants' support for their initially preferred candidate. This was addressed in other portions of the survey and those results are reported in chapter six.

2000 RESULTS

The results from DebateWatch '96, as well as the follow-up studies on voters and nonvoters, demonstrated a consistency among findings across the large number of participants. Although the groups crossed many geographic and demographic boundaries, the repeated data patterns show the DebateWatch results can be generalized to larger populations. For DebateWatch 2000, the research methodology was expanded to include participation through the World Wide Web. While thousands of DebateWatch packets were again sent through the mail, an electronic version of the packet was also available on the CPD Web site and from over 100 partner organizations. Groups were encouraged to register to receive updates on debate schedules, reminders about filing reports, and information about other groups in their areas. It was again impossible to know exactly how many groups and individuals participated. DebateWatch 2000 activities and groups were promoted and organized both nationally and locally through newspapers and other partner organizations in cities where the debates were held. DebateWatch had a prominent place on the CPD Web site and many inquiries for packets or explanations about the program came to the research office via an e-mail link on both the CPD and DebateWatch '96 sites. Unlike in 1996, there was no external funding to promote the program outside of its Web presence and the number of groups reporting to the research center declined. Nevertheless, there were still significant numbers.

A total of 363 groups participated across the four debates. The largest participant response was in the last presidential debate—the town hall style meeting. For this debate,148 groups returned reports. The second largest number was the first debate, with 115 reports. The second debate included reports from 74 groups, and the vice presidential debate included 26. The total number of participants was 5,949 and groups ranged in size from four to over five hundred, with the larger groups viewing the debate together before breaking into smaller discussion groups. The average size of discussion groups was 16 participants. The groups represented 31 different states and the District of Columbia, as well as Canada and Germany. As was the case in 1996, DebateWatch was only able to track the groups that returned a facilitator report. The groups were composed of 52.6 percent female and 47.4 percent male participants for the first debate, an even 50 percent each for the second, 52 percent women and 48 percent men for the third presidential and the vice presidential debates.

E-mails comprised a significant source of the feedback in 2000. E-mails did not always contain a person's place of residence, but a large number of correspondents did include at least a state of residence. Many e-mails were sent as addenda to facilitator reports because groups had something to say beyond what was asked for in the report. It was impossible to relate e-mails to specific facilitator reports since they were sent separately and most did not have any identifying information. Postdebate e-mail messages, however, were identified as coming from 24 states, the District of Columbia, and France. Predebate e-mails were sent from 28 states. Overall, 35 states were represented in the e-mail comments. While demographic data was not provided by e-mail senders, a wide range of political viewpoints was expressed and many writers indicated something about their professions, age, educational background, state of residence, political experience, or socioeconomic status that suggested nearly all of them were more experienced voters, that is, they were not in the 18–25 age range. In fact, only a few correspondents identified themselves as students. Nearly all e-mails came from the general public rather than NCA research groups. Over one thousand e-mails were received prior to and after the debates. Nearly half, as will be discussed in chapter ten, related to third party inclusion. A high percentage of e-mails—around two hundred—were received with comments specific to the moderators. A summary of the comments was sent to the CPD after the debates. In both 1992 and 1996 there were virtually no comments about moderators from either the focus groups or the facilitators' reports. Focus groups in 2000 also spent considerable time discussing the moderators as is reported in chapter four. The remaining emails discussed topics related to the format, the candidates, and the issues. Comments from the e-mails are interspersed with the focus group and facilitator report comments given in later chapters. E-mails did not always contain a person's place of residence, but a large number of correspondents did include at least a state of residence. It was also impossible to relate e-mails to specific facilitator reports because they were sent separately and most did not have any identifying information.

Since the 1996 postdebate transcripts and the follow-up study transcripts yielded the richest materials for analysis, the 2000 methodology also included taped discussion transcripts. The pairing with organizational partners and groups recruited by the National Communication Association continued and these organizations provided video and audiotapes that were transcribed and used for analysis. Because there was so much similarity across the transcripts in 1996 and fewer resources available in 2000 for transcription, a random sample of 30 groups was transcribed and used for the analysis.

Participant Demographics

A total of 798 individual participant surveys were collected, with the largest number coming after the third debate. Of these reports, 262 were submitted after the first debate, 89 after the second, 421 after the third, and 12 after the vice presidential debate. Fourteen surveys did not indicate which debate was viewed. Because several major efforts were made to involve students on campuses to try to reverse the low voter turnout from 1996, a higher percentage of participants were students in 2000 than in 1996. The 18–25 cohort represented 74 percent of the total individual participant surveys (592). Participants ranged from under 18 to over 70. A high percentage of facilitator reports did not include demographic data beyond male and female distinctions; thus, the only age data we report is from the individual participant surveys that were completed by the research groups led by NCA members. An analysis of the similarities and differences among the age cohorts in their responses to the questions regarding topic importance, news sources, and usefulness of debates is given in chapter eight on youth voters; thus, detailed results are not provided here.

Female participants represented 52 percent of the total in 2000. This is consistent with recent trends that show female voters outnumber male voters. According to Census Bureau statistics, women constituted 53.5 percent of the total votes cast in 2000. Age was the major discrepancy between voter turnout demographics and

DebateWatch participants. In 2000, the data collected from individual participants and from facilitator reports was heavily weighted by voters 18 to 25. Results reported in chapter eight indicate that there were no significant differences across age cohorts as to what issues were the most important; however, there were differences in what was learned.

2004 RESULTS

For the 2004 election cycle, DebateWatch continued to evolve and accommodate citizen participation using both face-to-face interaction and technology. The increased voter turnout for the election was also reflected in increased participation in DebateWatch. The CPD's DebateWatch Web site provided a summary of all groups reporting across the four debates.[5] Data from NCA research groups was fed into the overall data. According to the CPD, the cumulative number of DebateWatch 2004 participants across the four debates was 30,044, and the number of DebateWatch groups was 2,002. There were 511 groups for the first debate, 434 for the second, 771 for the third, and 286 for the vice presidential debate. The largest number of participants was for the first debate, with 13,522 reporting their reactions. The second highest was for the last presidential debate, which drew 8,231 participants. The second presidential debate yielded 4,692 participants, and the vice presidential results yielded 3,599.

Geographically, the online survey results represented each of the 50 states, the District of Columbia, Puerto Rico, and international locations.[6] One of the voter education partners, the National Communication Association (NCA), separated its results from the overall DebateWatch results in order to ask questions that the CPD online survey was not asking. There were two key questions. The first was whether or not the debates influenced predebate vote choice and the second asked which topics were considered irrelevant or unimportant (see Appendix D for the surveys used by the NCA research groups).

Participant Demographics

The most common location for DebateWatches continued to be colleges and schools, with 50 percent of the facilitator reports coming from those venues. Private homes provided the sites for 35 percent of the groups, and community locations such as libraries, civic clubs, or restaurants composed the remaining 15 percent. Demographic information from the CPD's data indicated that 43 percent of the participants were male and 57 percent female. Once again, younger viewers made up a high percentage of the participants with 5 percent fewer than 18 and 45 percent 18 to 25. The next highest level of participation was for those over 55, who comprised 21 percent of the total. The remaining 29 percent was split between the 26 to 40 cohort, at 18 percent, and the 41 to 55 cohort, at 11 percent. Ethnic diversity was greater for 2004 than it had been in the two previous cycles. White participation was 60 percent, African American was 27 percent, Hispanic was 7 percent, Asian American was 3 percent, Native American was 1 percent, and all others constituted 2 percent.

In addition to the CPD data, the NCA groups submitted more detailed surveys similar to those collected in 1996 and 2000. A total of 884 participant surveys were collected. These represented 20 states and the District of Columbia. The top three news sources demonstrated the growth of the Internet and also reflected that the majority of individual surveys came from younger voters. Nightly news continued to be the most common information source, listed by 67.6 percent of participants, but the Internet moved into second place, with 50 percent listing it among their top three. This change reflected the large cohort of younger participants. National newspapers were ranked third, with 43.4 percent, and local newspapers were fourth, with 32.6 percent. This group was more likely than those in other years to have followed the campaign prior to the post–Labor Day period. In 1996, the average across debates of those who followed the campaign regularly was 54 percent. In 2004 the average was 66.4 percent.

As was expected from the overall DebateWatch results, younger voters dominated in completing the individual participant forms. NCA members had primarily university groups from which to draw. A total of 80.4 percent of respondents were 18 to 25 years old. The remainder was distributed as follows: 1.9 percent of respondents were under 18, 8.3 percent were 26 to 40, 6.8 percent were 41 to 55, and 4.5 percent were over 55. Females comprised 53.8 percent of the total and males the remaining 46.2 percent.

Vote Choice Data

The NCA analysis of vote choice indicated that the greatest degree of shift from predebate vote choice occurred after the first debate. Going into the debate, 14.2 percent of the 666 participants indicated that they were undecided. After the debate, 9.5 percent remained undecided. Of the 85.8 percent with a predebate choice, 3.2 percent switched to a different candidate. Changes for the other debates were insignificant.

Other Questions

The CPD survey asked if DebateWatch would influence how closely participants followed the election. Twenty-four percent of respondents indicated that it would increase their level of information gathering. The CPD survey also asked if the town hall format was more valuable than the traditional format. Thirty-two percent indicated that it was. Other CPD questions relating to participants' opinions on the most useful debate topics and what they wanted to hear about during the remainder of the campaign, as well as the NCA questions regarding irrelevant questions, are discussed in chapter five.

QUALITATIVE DATA ANALYSIS PROCEDURES

All transcripts were coded in broad categories to correspond to book chapters: format (with subcategories for setting, time limits, questions, answers, moderator, and comparisons or preferences), vice presidential debate, town hall, expectations, issues (most useful, irrelevant or not useful, new information), character/presidential qualities, media critiques, comparison to other news sources, influence on vote choice, and third party. Facilitator report comments, e-mails, and letters were coded similarly. Once general coding was completed, each category was examined to look for trends. Themes emerged and these are reflected in the analysis that follows. Because facilitators used the same interview protocol, it was relatively easy to find each of the major categories of comments because they occurred at similar points in the discussion. This also allowed us to determine that the facilitators had followed the protocol and that all groups were asked nearly identical questions, though follow-up questions varied. Quotations were selected that best represented the themes, were the best articulated for a theme, or were the most interesting way of framing a theme. Often nearly verbatim language was used across focus groups to respond to a question. Nearly all themes are explicated with multiple responses across the three debate cycles.

CONCLUSION

By using a combination of focus group and survey data, along with open-ended comments on facilitator reports and e-mails, the DebateWatch research project yielded information about the value of the debates and the discussion, as well as information about political news consumption and vote choice. Unlike traditional questions regarding winners and losers, the DebateWatch survey and focus group questions provided insights into how debate viewing affects knowledge about candidates and issues. While research groups had a higher percentage of younger voters than both the overall DebateWatch groups and the electorate as a whole, the data obtained from these groups provides insight into how less experienced and less informed voters can benefit from debates and discussion by watching with members of their cohort or with intergenerational groups. The numbers of participants representing other age groups comprises the largest subject pool for debate research. With the exception of the increased use of the Internet as an information source in 2004, especially among younger viewers, there were few differences across any demographics in relation to news consumption, length of time following the campaign, topics considered important or unimportant, or usefulness of debates. As later chapters reveal, differences were found between younger and older voters in terms of learning and vote choice. Differences also existed based on previous knowledge of candidates and issues prior to the debates. These findings were consistent with past research on learning from debates. The remaining chapters include data primarily from the focus groups; however, quantitative data related to issues, attitudes about politics, usefulness of the debates and discussion as information sources, and vote choice are included to underscore findings from the focus groups.

Chapter Four

Why Format Matters

During each presidential debate season, political pundits and scholars complain about the formats and the lack of "real" debate. As noted in chapter two, critics have gone so far as to label the match-ups "counterfeit debates" because of their failure to meet academic debate standards. Lanoue and Schrott summarized the reaction to the panelist and news conference formats, standard until 1992, in their history of political debates through 1988: "the format of American presidential debates has not been especially popular with journalists and scholars. As early as the very first televised debates in 1960, critics were assailing the 'press conference' format" because "the debate agenda is set by the panelists—if the journalists want to talk about abortion, or civil rights, or taxation, the debaters have no choice but to address those issues."[1] Additional criticisms relate to the types of questions asked and the tendency of journalists to try to call attention to themselves through antagonistic or "gotcha" questions.

Of course, critics of formats always believe that their format ideas are better. An article in *Broadcasting* after the 1984 Reagan-Mondale debates indicated that Frank Stanton, who was president of CBS in 1960, and J. Leonard Reinsch, a retired president of Cox Communications, believed the 1960 formats and production were superior to what the League of Women Voters had done from 1976–1984:

> The purpose of the presidential debates would be better served if the League of Women Voters were not involved. To a degree, that feeling grows out of the conviction that they had done it better in 1960...without the League's participation. But Stanton recalled proposals he had made in 1963 for a series of presidential debates whose format would have marked a sharp departure from those of 1960—and would also require radical changes in the format currently in use.[2]

Although the traditional panelist format has not been used from 1996 through 2004 for the general election debates, criticisms persist. One of the most common format complaints is that contemporary debates don't live up to the quality of the Lincoln-Douglas debates, which were "real" debates. Discussion group and written comments referencing the Lincoln-Douglas debates were common across the three election cycles. Several comments from 1996 DebateWatch groups revealed the iconic power of the Lincoln-Douglas debates and how they impact expectations. A man in Kansas City, Missouri, reacted to a question about the format by proclaiming, "I was just going to say Stephen Douglas and Abraham Lincoln would not recognize this at all." Someone else in the group responded to the comment with "No!" Another went on to provide an inaccurate historical record of the debates, but made a valid point about the differences in the times:

> If you showed them this, first of all they'd be shocked to be alive! One person would talk for like three hours and everybody would go home and come back the next day to hear three to four hours of rebuttal on one issue. That was really a debate. In McDonald's fast food have it your way right now whatever, you're not going to get anything approaching that. I think it's more of a dialogue. It's not even a dialogue. It's a diatribe. It's an opportunity for me to give my little monologue. I would like a dialogue.

Additional "channeling" of the nineteenth-century debaters produced a similar analysis in Manhattan, Kansas, with this statement from one of the women in the group:

> It's made for TV. I grew up learning about the Douglas-Lincoln debates. Abraham Lincoln and Stephen Douglas would fall off their chairs and roll over in their graves at this point. They would have to go 90 seconds? No great orator would agree; in 90 seconds you don't have time to be orator. You have time to be a sound byte. That goes for either side.... If you have a complicated point to make, forget it.

In Detroit, a group was complaining about the lack of clash and someone noted: "We want to see them slug it out. That goes back to Lincoln-Douglas." In making arguments for direct clash, one woman who e-mailed her reactions to the 2000 debates told us: "I checked out the Lincoln-Douglas debates, but can't seem to find the name of the Moderator. It seems they were able to do just fine without one. I think the debates should be ONLY between the two candidates. The Moderator would ONLY keep time, maintain proper rotation, and dampen any incivility." Finally, this interchange from Murray, Kentucky, further illustrates the benchmark nature of the Lincoln-Douglas debates:

Moderator: Going back to what this gentleman said earlier, you said you didn't really see a debate here. Why not?

Male: Well a debate is when two people go after each other—give and take.... When Lincoln and Douglas debated, Lincoln and Douglas debated. There was no Jim Lehrer there to follow-up and cut off. They could have talked all day.

Lincoln and Douglas did come close to talking for an entire day—21 hours total— by the time the series concluded, and the events surrounding the debates certainly lasted much of a day.

While many people talk about the Lincoln-Douglas debates, few know much about their structure or content. Each debate was three hours long and was preceded and followed by parades and socializing. The first speaker spoke one hour and the second for 90 minutes. Afterward, the first was given time for a 30-minute rebuttal. There were seven debates—each in a different Congressional district and Lincoln and Douglas negotiated the details privately with an exchange of letters. While they did debate the greatest issue of the day—one that had tremendous potential to tear apart a young nation as it attempted to find a resolution to the slavery question—the Illinois Senator and his challenger from a fledgling political party did not use their entire 21 hours engaged in such high-minded argument. Indeed, over the course of the seven debates, there were few new arguments—a common complaint about contemporary debate series. It is also suggested that the Lincoln-Douglas debates contained only high-minded policy arguments that were superior to contemporary argumentation practices. Research, however, indicates that was not the necessarily the case even though the debates developed a single topic in depth. One of the foremost scholars on the Lincoln-Douglas debates, David Zarefsky, wrote, "The most vivid of the debate arguments was the allegation of conspiracy. The charge was that the opponent was engaged in a secret plot to bring about detestable ends."[3]

C-SPAN reproduced the debates in 1994, and in a companion book, historian and C-SPAN consultant John Splaine's comments sounded as if they could have been written today: "The debate strategies and techniques used were sometimes working at cross-purposes; for example, winning the election versus the battle of right against wrong."[4] Students who read the debate texts or watch the C-SPAN videos are usually shocked that Lincoln, the Great Emancipator, sounded less like an abolitionist as he moved from north to south in Illinois. In other words, these debates were not perfect. Zarefsky argued, however, that even with their flaws, clear lines of argument were drawn in the Lincoln-Douglas debates. The debaters had to adjust to the political climate and to the overall rhetorical situation, but the debates worked well in their time.[5]

In chapter two, we made a similar claim about contemporary debates. They are designed to work for our time, or at least adapt to our time, as focus group participants suggested. We live in a mediated age where the camera doesn't blink, news anchors tell us all of the news we need to know, and sound bytes get shorter each election cycle. We are a society that would have difficulty watching a three-hour debate in the comfort of our homes without a commercial break, let alone in the hot August sun, especially if we couldn't cast a vote for either candidate. In 1858, there was no direct election of U.S. senators; they were elected by state legislators. Today we do cast votes for presidential electors, and great numbers of us watch debates and anticipate them each election cycle. While we watch and then tell exit pollsters that they are useful in making vote choices, we also join the scholars and pundits in criticizing the formats. This chapter provides an opportunity for viewers to be critics. Before reviewing the public's comments and relating them to past research, the formats used in 1996, 2000, and 2004 are described to provide adequate context for the comments.

FORMATS 1996–2004

There was no format change between 1996 and 2004 as dramatic as the introduction of the 1992 town-hall debate format that would be used in the next three election cycles. The major innovation was one borrowed from many primary debates—candidates were seated as a moderator guided them through a less structured format that allowed for an extended period on an issue. All debates were 90 minutes. The minor changes across cycles dealt with time limits. They are described for each cycle separately.

1996

The 1996 race between President Bill Clinton and Kansas Senator Bob Dole featured two presidential debates and one vice presidential debate between Vice President Al Gore and former New York Congressman Jack Kemp. The first debate in Hartford, Connecticut, was held in The Bushnell Theatre on October 6 and had a single moderator. Candidates had two-minute opening statements and two-minute closing statements. Candidates were questioned in turn, with the first candidate responding for 90 seconds, the second providing a one-minute rebuttal, and the first giving an additional 30-second response. The second debate took place October 16 on the campus of the University of San Diego and featured the town hall format. In terms of time limits and opening and closing statements, the format was the same as in Hartford. There was no opportunity for follow-up questions, but the moderator could ask a question or make a comment to clarify the question. The vice presidential debate was held October 9 in St. Petersburg, Florida, at the Bayfront Center's Mahaffey Theater. There were no opening statements but there were three-minute closing statements. The questioning followed the same pattern as the presidential debates. Jim Lehrer of "The News Hour" on PBS moderated all three debates, which included both domestic and foreign policy topics.

2000

The first of three presidential debates featuring Vice President Al Gore and Texas Governor George W. Bush took place October 3 in Boston in the shadow of the Kennedy Library at the University of Massachusetts. Jim Lehrer was the single moderator overseeing a format with no opening statements and two-minute closing statements; a two-minute response to a question was followed by a one-minute rebuttal. Lehrer had the option to extend the debate by three and one-half minutes but no response could exceed two minutes. The second debate was at Wake Forest University in Winston-Salem, North Carolina, on October 11. The candidates were seated and the format was described as "a conversation" with no response exceeding two minutes. Lehrer could stay on a single topic as long as he wanted. The third debate took place at Washington University in St. Louis on October 17 and was the town hall format. Lehrer moderated and explained the procedures this way:

> Tonight's questions will be asked by St. Louis area voters who were identified as being uncommitted by the Gallup organization. Each of them wrote a question on a small card like this. Those cards were collected and then given to me this afternoon. My job, under the rules of the evening, was to decide the order the questions will be asked and to call on the questioners accordingly. I also have the option of asking follow-ups. In order to get to more of the panel's questions, for the record, I plan to do sparingly and mostly for clarifications. The audience participants are bound by the following rule. They shall not ask follow-up questions or otherwise participate in the extended discussion. And the questioner's microphone will be turned off after he or she completes asking the question. Those are the rules. As in Winston-Salem last week, no single answer or response from a candidate can exceed two minutes.[6]

The presidential candidates had two-minute closing statements. The vice presidential debate featuring former Secretary of Defense Dick Cheney and Connecticut Senator Joseph Lieberman was held in Danville, Kentucky, at Centre College on October 5. Bernard Shaw moderated. The candidates were seated and had two minutes for each response or rebuttal, with the moderator having the option to extend with two-minute time limits per response. Each candidate had a two-minute closing statement, and all debates featured both domestic and foreign policy topics.

2004

The 2004 debate cycle also featured three presidential debates and one vice presidential debate. President George W. Bush and Massachusetts Senator John Kerry first met on September 30 at the University of Miami in Coral Gables, Florida. Jim Lehrer moderated. The candidates gave two-minute responses and 90-second rebuttals, and debate could be extended one-minute with the time divided equally between candidates; each candidate had a two-minute closing statement. The candidates stood behind podiums. The debate was on foreign policy and homeland security. As a result of the negotiated agreement between the candidates' representatives, the microphones were equipped with a light system that signaled a green light when 30 seconds remained in any given answer, a yellow light came on at 15, a red light at five seconds, and then a flashing red indicated that time had expired. There was a backup buzzer system if a candidate persisted after the time expired. The second debate was the town hall style at Washington University in St. Louis on October 8 and it included both domestic and foreign policy topics. Charles Gibson of ABC News moderated. Each candidate had a closing statement, and Gibson explained the format that would involve 140 undecided voters selected by the Gallup organization:

> Now, earlier today, each audience member gave me two questions on cards like this, one they'd like to ask the president, the other they'd like to ask the senator. I have selected the questions to be asked and the order. No one has seen the final list of questions but me, certainly not the candidates. No audience member knows if he or she will be called upon. Audience microphones will be turned off after a question is

asked. Audience members will address their question to a specific candidate. He'll have two minutes to answer. The other candidate will have a minute and a half for rebuttal. And I have the option of extending discussion for one minute, to be divided equally between the two men.

The final presidential debate was held on October 13 at Arizona State University in Tempe and was moderated by Bob Schieffer of CBS News. It covered only domestic topics, and the candidates were in a formal setting standing behind podiums as they did in the first debate. The format was a two-minute response, 90-second rebuttal, and, at the moderator's discretion, an optional extension of one-minute, divided equally. The single vice presidential debate between Vice President Dick Cheney and North Carolina Senator John Edwards was held at Case Western Reserve University in Cleveland, Ohio, on October 5 with Gwen Ifill of PBS moderating. Both domestic and foreign policy topics were addressed in a format that had the candidates seated. The format was the same as for the presidential debates and included two-minute closing statements.

OVERVIEW OF FORMAT DISCUSSION

The remainder of the chapter summarizes the major themes related to format. Participants were asked specific questions about format with the goal of comparing the formats in a given year to one another and to other debates participants had viewed in the past. The format discussions related to their utility for viewers. Comments made about format are arranged thematically and the specific year to which they refer is indicated. Comments relate to preferred format or comparisons, questions, answers, time limits, pros and cons of the town hall, and the moderator's role and performance. Quotations are from postdebate discussion groups, facilitator reports, and e-mails.

The major recommendations made by the DebateWatch participants included having something closer to a Lincoln-Douglas debate with less intrusion from the moderator. This would include cross-examination by the candidates, opening and closing statements in all debates, a limited number of topics per debate, different topics in each debate, more flexible time limits that would allow for more depth of analysis and clearer comparisons and contrasts between or among positions while avoiding discussion of a topic from a previous question during a subsequent topic, rules that allow the moderator to keep the candidates on the topic, multiple formats including continuation of the town hall, and a town hall debate with random selection of questions and follow-up questions or at least confirmation that a questioner had received a satisfactory answer before going to the next question.

FORMAT ELEMENTS PRO AND CON

There are subtle differences in the formats across the three cycles—time limits, opening or no opening statements, sitting or standing, follow-up questions or no rebuttals. But formats alone do not influence the quality of the debates and their value to viewers. Content analyses of debates that demonstrate variations in clash (comparisons, direct attacks or challenges, and responses to attacks or challenges) across formats also conclude that incumbency, standing in the polls, previous performance, and debate skills also have an impact on content and debate performance. As would be expected, format studies show that the more opportunity there is for rebuttal, the more likely candidates are to clash and provide comparisons or clarify their positions.[7] Participants in groups, respondents to online surveys, and reports from facilitators all related aspects of format to the overall quality of candidates' responses, execution of candidates' agendas, and acknowledgment of a citizen agenda. Considerable attention was given to the role of questions, rules, moderators, and time limits on responses and information acquisition.

Cross-examination

Participants were asked to identify the features they liked and disliked about each of the formats and to compare them to one another in terms of their value as a voter education tool. Clash and comparison were the primary features that participants wanted in a debate. They identified questions—who was and wasn't asking them as well as what was asked—as a key to clash, clarification, and content. Many participants expressed a belief that cross-examination would improve the debates by making candidates more spontaneous and by providing viewers with better information and bases for comparison. One of the major criticisms of all of the formats was that they did not produce enough interaction between the candidates, and it was suggested that cross-examination would change that dynamic.

After the 1996 vice presidential debate, a male participant in Norman, Oklahoma, suggested it would be good to "Maybe allow the candidates to cross-examine each other." A female in Hartford, Connecticut, after the first 1996 debate said, "I almost wish they had been able to ask each other their own questions. It would have gotten more interesting." A male in Manhattan, Kansas, explained why the interest level would increase with cross-examination: "[The problem is] you can't question each other. They didn't have much conversation. So you're taking out the spontaneity and making it very scripted." A man in Tampa, Florida, gave additional reasons why cross-examination would provide better debate and more useful information:

> I have a sort of rhetorical question: why don't they directly debate each other like you do in a real debate? This is an artificial type of debate. It seems to me if Candidate X asks directly Candidate Y and Candidate Y had to respond to X's question, and then vice versa, you would get a truer picture of what's going on. This is too artificial. If they directly picked at each other, we'd have a much clearer picture as to where each of these guys stand.

Participants in 2000 also expressed a desire for cross-examination. Arguments for cross-examination by a man in Washington, D.C., resembled those of the Tampa participant four years earlier:

I would also like to see the rules allow and even encourage a certain amount of cross-questioning by the candidates. We want to see how they disagree and what each candidate has to say about and to the other. I and many of my friends thought the second presidential debate was boring. Whenever there was a hint of friction between the candidates' views, it seemed that the rules forced Mr. Lehrer to jump in and change the subject. Come on, there's nothing wrong with letting the candidates mix it up a bit....Next time loosen up a bit. It will make for better television and better information.

A brief exchange in Harrisonburg, Virginia, in 2004 illustrates the consistent desire of debate watchers to have more interaction:

Female: I wish they could talk to each other. Have an open session.

Male: I think that would have made it a little bit more interesting if they had been able to actually argue with each other like maybe take out the gloves and start boxing.

This analysis of cross-examination among a group of professionals in Providence, Rhode Island, after the final 2004 debate summarizes the major arguments heard from groups in 2004:

Male: I don't particularly care about that particular format [standing at podiums with the moderator alternating questions and an option for extension]. I would much prefer the two candidates ask one another questions. Have the moderator there to make sure everybody has a fair chance.

Male: I would prefer a format where each candidate could question the other directly in which the moderator would, to the exclusion of other issues, insist that the candidates answer the questions directly before their turn had passed. Even if it meant returning to the topic again and again.

Moderator: What about follow-ups?

Male: Less useful than a more direct form of a debate. I think of a debate as less structured than this was. Much more of an open forum in terms of positioning direct call and response and focus like a laser on the issues.

Moderator: Holly?

Female: I would agree with everything that has been said so far. I think the format was a little too formal and stiff. I would like to see them a bit more flexible. I think it would be interesting if candidates were allowed to rebut questions to each other.

Male: I would like to see a provision in this format where the candidates question each other. Not necessarily in a free give and take. I think that would degenerate into squabbling. But just as the moderator asks a question then there is a two-minute response, I would like the candidates to ask one another a question and answer in that same context. Given the circumstances of the entire campaign and the involvement of the media in it, I am not sure you can let it be that loose without somebody getting totally nailed to the wall.

It was clear that participants from 1996 to 2004 wanted candidates to question one another. However, most indicated, as did the 1992 groups, that the exchanges needed to be well moderated in contrast to the hands off rules the moderator in 1992 had to follow. Focus group members in 1992 indicated that the vice presidential debate "resulted in more one liners than voter education"[8] without a moderator to intervene. Although group members in the 2004 Providence, Rhode Island, group expressed an interest in cross-examination, one member did provide a caution that is worth considering if this format is advanced in future debate cycles when he explained that "I was a television producer for many years and I have actually produced live debates like this. And I found that getting candidates to question each other can be a very dangerous thing. Not because it necessarily deteriorates into a shouting match but they tend to ask one another questions that are very esoteric in nature and sort of leaves the audience wondering, 'What are these two guys talking about?'"

Question Types and Content

What the candidates were talking about and whether it was what the audience wanted to hear was a subject of considerable discussion and comment. Some of the discussion is covered in other chapters that specifically address issues. Analysis of format elements, however, does have to consider content on some level. Regardless of whether candidates have two-minute or 90-second responses, a major element impacting what is said in a debate and what is learned by an audience is the content of questions that start the candidate's statements. If the content is not part of the public agenda, less is learned. If questions are repeated across debates, there is redundancy and omission of information on other important issues. If questions don't ask for comparisons, comparisons might not be made. If follow-up questions are not part of the format, then rebuttal is limited and issue resolution or clarification does not occur.

Even with the elimination of the panelist format, the single moderator or citizens in the town hall continue to pose questions. An unmediated debate such as the Lincoln- Douglas encounters or a debate structured around a single topic such as occurred in the 1948 Thomas Dewey-Harold Stassen Republican primary is a rare occurrence in contemporary debates, especially at the presidential level.[9] Finding a single overriding topic is difficult. The best we have done is divide debates into general themes such as foreign or domestic policy, and even that didn't happen in 1996 and 2000. In 2004, the first debate was only on Iraq and homeland security, the second, town hall debate covered both issues with seven questions on foreign policy and 11 on domestic policy or presidential qualifications, and the third debate was on domestic issues. The questions, in essence, do create a series of mini-debates that may or may not relate to or build on one another, especially in the town hall format. Collectively, however, the questions should answer the overarching issue of who would make the better president.

Viewers participating in postdebate discussions since 1992 have been critical of the questions, especially when topics are repeated across debates. To demonstrate the impact questions have on restricting information acquisition, Friedenberg analyzed the questions in the 2004 debates and found that in the last debate, the moderator "asked a total of twenty questions, of which seven were repetitions of questions asked in prior debates."[10] Focus group members did not need Friedenberg's count to know that they were not hearing anything new. The notion of having fewer thematic questions per debate to avoid repetition was expressed in many of the groups and in e-mails. A man in a Spokane, Washington, group in 1996 expressed the recommendation this way: "They ought to concentrate if they're going to have three or four of them [debates] on the subject matter and really get into that. Tonight we're only talking about foreign policy and not continually going back to how to grow the economy; have one session on the economy. And let them go at it. That would probably be more beneficial than they way they're doing it now."

An e-mail in 2000 also addressed the cross-debate redundancy problem: "Some of the same topics were rehashed all 3 nights. It seemed to me that the debates one year were assigned separate categories, like the ones in your survey. Then in depth discussions might come about." In addition to wanting a variety of questions across debates, there was a desire to have "questions that take the candidates off guard and aren't the typical expected, trained, programmed questions" as a 2004 Providence, Rhode Island, woman stated. Similar comments were made each year. An e-mail suggestion in 2000 succinctly summarized the need for what might be called "process" questions that many expressed a desire for. These are questions that don't address the candidates' agendas specifically but ask the questions to explain how they would "enact" the presidency. Examples from viewers include: "How do the candidates feel about a certain piece of legislation before Congress? How would candidates deal with a Congress of the other party? Hypothetical problems could be presented to see how they would handle them."

Participants clearly had issues they wanted discussed, as chapter five reveals, but they also appreciated questions that focused their attention on issues they hadn't considered important or relevant prior to the debate. A woman in Kansas City, Missouri, in 1996 indicated: "There were a lot of questions asked, too, tonight that I wasn't thinking about, but once they said it, I was like 'Oh, I really want to know about that.' So it brought more things to my mind that I haven't thought of but were important." This comment underscores why debates need all three agendas. Given that citizens concentrate on issues that impact their lives most directly—education, health care, or jobs—they may not draw the link between those personal issues and foreign policy, for example. The educational value of debate is only enhanced when questions and answers help draw links between personal agendas and more universal issues.

Answers and Time Limits

Questions are important, as the analysis indicates, but voter learning is most directly affected by the answers—regardless of who asks the questions or how they are structured. Answers were heavily criticized, and participants were clear about the types of answers that are useful and those that are not. Participants wanted substantive responses—not so necessarily with a lot of facts and figures—but answers that responded to the questions and were more than stump speech generalities and repeated commonplaces. They wanted questions that forced the candidates to think on their feet. They wanted sufficient time to answer fewer questions, and they wanted the answers to be given within the time constraints. Most importantly, they wanted the candidates to actually answer the questions that were posed to them. For example, a woman in a Detroit, Michigan, group in 1996 indicated: "They went off on tangents tonight. They went back. They kept reiterating their opening statements because they have their agenda. When they couldn't answer a question, they'd go back to their agenda and bring it up again. A lot of questions were not answered."

After watching Cheney and Edwards eight years later, a participant in Lawrence, Kansas, observed a similar attachment to the candidates' agendas: "Both of them came out I think with their party line. They were going to talk about the party line no matter what the question was." This approach resulted in viewer frustration and a perception that the candidates were not paying attention to the public's need for additional information beyond scripted answers. This exchange in DeLand, Florida, in 2004 further illustrates the frustration:

Male 1:   Bush just kept asking the same questions of Kerry and Kerry just kept responding with the same answer. It just seemed so repetitive. They said it like eight times. That is just ridiculous. Eight times Bush had the same accusation and eight times Kerry came back with the same answer. Why do you need to keep saying the same thing time and again? I did not like that.

Female: I think they confused things a bit because it was a different question and they answered it the same way and went back and forth and confused things more rather than making more of a concrete argument.

Male 2:   I agree with you because even the moderator had to say two or three times "Now this is your position. Now can I clarify that this is your position?" Because they kept going back and saying the same argument time and time again and I just wanted to bang my head against the wall.... but they just kept going back to the same argument and not moving the debate along.

A 1996 group in Winston-Salem, North Carolina, had a similar reaction to the repetition and nonresponsiveness:

Female: I wrote down at 10:10 that they should have ended. I thought after that, it was just the same thing over and over.

Male 1:   This goes back to what you were saying earlier. The candidates talk about what they want to talk about, no matter what the question is.

Male 2:   At one point I put down that one of them had gone into the stump speech.

Male 3:   Clinton gave that speech about how many jobs and that whole litany of five things about seven times. There was more repetition than I remember in other debates.

Female: Well, they spent so much time memorizing the best responses.

The complaints about repetition were not just because the viewers were tired of hearing the same answer. A woman in Winston-Salem, North Carolina, in 1996 pointed out that by adding content unrelated to the question, the impact of the answer to the question can be diminished: "When Clinton said, 'I'm for it,' I thought that expressed completely how he felt about it. Then when he goes on and talks about some other thing, which should have been left behind with the last question, it takes away from the forcefulness of simply saying, 'I'm for it; enough said,' and then we forgot about the question, rather than emphasizing how he felt about it."

Clearly, participants didn't want just any answer or response, even if it expressed the candidates' platforms or contained data or anecdotes. A common desire expressed throughout the transcripts was for "real answers." Viewers found substance lacking in terms of detailed, jargon-free explanations and relevance to the questions. An e-mail received after the final debate in 2000 was very clear on the point: "I want REAL answers to REAL questions—not the phony garbage we saw tonight. What a waste of time! If I wanted to hear canned speeches, I could have just watched the commercials. Why not let the questioners follow up. Why not say, 'Hey, you didn't answer the question.'" A New York City facilitator's report in 2000 also complained about the lack of real answers and provided a solution to the lack of substance and clarity:

> They do not give the viewers real answers. None of the formats provide the means to information. All three left each candidate saying the other was not being truthful. Now, a format that allowed for charts (a la Perot) would have given the viewers facts and concrete evidence to analyze and make decisions.... we are a very visual society! And, you can be sure, when a candidate is asked to write it down for all to see, he'll be very careful to write what he really means to do—maybe even how!

The idea that the candidates were not being truthful or that there was no way to check on their truthfulness was a repeated theme, as this point from a participant in Portland, Maine, in 2000 indicates: "Each candidate got away with their version of the facts without an independent observer clarifying inaccuracies articulated by either candidate." After the first debate in 2000, a group member in Boston had a similar reaction: "I am worried about those numbers. Gore was good with the numbers, but I want to know who is really accurate with the numbers. We are Joe Public. We do not have, or we cannot get, reliable information.... Whoever is making these reports must have some interest and I feel that these reports are manipulated to obviously favor their candidate." A woman in Providence, Rhode Island, was also concerned about whether or not she could trust the statistics and who to believe when there was a disagreement on the record: "The thing that puts me in a quandary is when statistics are thrown out there and it is refuted by the opposition. I want a little screen to pop up and say 'actual voting record.'" Later in this chapter, discussion of a moderator's role returns to this theme of guaranteeing accuracy of data with a suggestion for how to better ensure that viewers are getting "the facts."

Incomplete answers, failure to answer, repetition, or answering a previous question rather than the question at hand were seen as the result of time limits and question sequence structures. Time limits were discussed in a broad sense by several groups and were commented on in facilitator reports and e-mails. The main complaint was that there was no time for detail and adequate comparison. The 2000 format added a three and one-half minute extension to improve rebuttal, but one man in 2000 didn't think that had solved the problem and suggested that "responses need to be four minutes. Two minutes is just short enough to get by using doubletalk and mantras." Others recommended a minimum of five minutes and still others wanted something closer to an academic debate with 8–10 minute statements on issues followed by rebuttals of several minutes.

This comment from a woman in a Bloomington, Indiana, group in 1996 summarizes what many said in all three cycles: "One thing I didn't like is that when they asked a question, he had to quickly finish up on the previous question, and then he went on to the next question. I think once that question is done with, it shouldn't be brought up again." This exchange in Detroit in 1996 was more emphatic about the need for rebuttal within a given question period, not in the following one:

Male 1: Maybe if they don't answer the question, they don't get as much time the next time.

Female 1: You know, if you're talking about changes, maybe they need to do that.

Male 2: Actually, you know how they always take the first 15 seconds to add an additional rebuttal, why don't they just give them the damn 15 seconds, let them rebut, and then go on to the next question. At this point, they're like, "Oh, I'd like to add . . ." Maybe they need that second rebuttal so that these people can come in and actually start the question fresh, rather than answering the last charge that somebody made.

Female 2: Sometimes they went on for such a long period in that rebuttal after a new question that we kind of lost track of the question by the time they started answering it. They'd already taken a minute to rebut.

A woman in Las Cruces, New Mexico, in 1996 was equally frustrated by the continuation of debate from a previous question:

They ask a question; they get one minute to talk about it, then you get a 30-second rebuttal, and then you get another 30-second rebuttal. Then that's it, and they ask another question. If you ask another question, that question should be answered. Each person gets to rebut like twice, on almost every question, and then another question that has nothing to do with what we were just talking about before is asked, and they say, "Well, let me talk about that other one for a minute." That's wrong. That's the whole point of a debate, is that you get your time to answer the question. If the time is up, then that's your own fault. You didn't answer it—too bad.

An e-mail in 2000 echoed the sentiment that if a candidate isn't responsive, the candidate should be held responsible to the people: "Here's an interesting concept I would like to see adopted for future debates. When the candidate strays off topic, or doesn't offer a direct answer to the question, the moderator stops the candidate's answer and the candidate forfeits the remaining time allocated to the question. I'm really tired of the candidates using the time allocated as an opportunity to raise some other issue they are more comfortable with, while essentially ignoring the actual question." Forfeiture of time or a turn was a common recommendation to rein in the candidates. A woman in Chapel Hill, North Carolina, in 2000 explained the obvious reason why content matters: "when the candidates actually answered questions, their differences became clear." And that is why the public watches debates—to draw distinctions that confirm their choices or help them make one.

The comments about candidates' failure to answer the questions or limit rebuttal to the sequence when a question was asked followed an assumption that the time limits are equal and allow sufficient time for rebuttal. That, however, is not necessarily the case with all of the formats used for the debates. Most had uneven time limits per question for each candidate. For example, in 1996 the first candidate had twice as much time on a question as the respondent and the first candidate didn't have a rebuttal. In 2000 the difference was also two to one, but there was an option to extend for three and one-half minutes. The time limits were closer in 2004—two minutes versus 90 seconds and a one-minute extension divided equally. All of these structures limit the second candidate's rebuttal opportunities in varying degrees; thus it is not surprising that the respondent will give a rebuttal when the next question comes before responding to the new question. One prerequisite of debate is that candidates should have equal time. Even if the time is divided equally across the total debate, if one candidate has twice as much time on one question as the other candidate, it is only natural to want to counter a charge rather than leave it hanging. Given that all moderators do not build on the previous answer or that in a town hall it is a random set of questions, the problem identified by the focus groups will continue unless each speaker has equal time per question, or follow-up questions are used to further clarify until a topic is exhausted. The option to extend time helps alleviate some of this problem as the focus group discussions indicate; however, it needs to be more along the lines of the 2000 format with three and one-half minutes to extend rather than one minute as was done in 2004. And the decision to extend is the moderator's, not the candidates'.

A Redmond, Washington, male participant in 2000 wanted to see time limits eliminated as a way to better judge the candidates' ability to think on their feet: "I would love to see a free-form debate where a strong moderator would throw out a question and then let the candidates go at it hammer and tongs for as long as the moderator felt appropriate.... It would give the voters a much better sense of how well the candidates think when they're forced off script." In addition to thinking on their feet, the free form suggestion would also address the issue of candidates sticking with their agendas.

As was indicated previously by the suggestion that failure to answer a question or providing incorrect information should have a consequence, accountability to the public was seen as important. One way they defined accountability was a candidate's willingness to follow debate rules. Vice President Gore's behavior was highly criticized for breaking many of the rules in 2000. It was clear that viewers wanted a moderator to enforce the rules and that there should be some consequence for not following them. A man in Provo, Utah, suggested that "There should be punitive measures (via time or some other mechanism) if a candidate blatantly disobeys the rules set forth at the beginning. What Gore did was absolutely out of control." A facilitator's report echoed the sentiment and provided a novel recommendation:

> The rules were clearly stated before the debate began. Vice President Gore continued to break them.... There was no action taken by the moderator to stop Gore much less to penalize him for trying to take unfair advantage, thus he just continued to force his own agenda for the debate. How about trying a penalty box like hockey uses? Each time a candidate breaks the rules in a debate, he must go to the penalty box for two minutes while his opponent has the floor.

The concern about not following rules had deeper implications than going over time, interrupting, or extending rebuttals into the next question. As we discuss in the next chapter, not following the rules was also seen as an indicator of character traits.

While viewers wanted rules to be followed if there were going to be rules, they also wanted rules that allowed enough flexibility or discretion on the moderator's part to ignore them in the pursuit of better debate. Viewers were well aware that the candidates set the rules and that they could become too restrictive "in the heat of the battle." The rules were seen as impeding good debate. Another facilitator's report in 2000 discussed the rules this way:

> The RULES are a problem!!! In tonight's debate there were times that COULD have spawned conversations or actual debates if Jim Lehrer had stepped back and not enforced the "rules." It should be recognized that even though the campaigns construct the rules ahead of time, in the heat of the moment it is clear when both candidates just want to ENGAGE. As viewers, we have waited MONTHS for an actual exchange of ideas (in my case, YEARS!).

The discussion group moderators and the facilitator's reports asked for suggested improvements, which prompted many critical responses. However, the groups also had positive reactions to the debates. Specifics are provided in the next two chapters, but general support for the debates and their ability to provide voter information were common each year.

Sit or Stand?

In 2000, the seated format was introduced and was used in both the presidential and vice presidential debates. In 2004, only the vice presidential debate used this staging. "This format responded to public sentiment that debates should not be viewed as horse races or a sporting event but should be considered as a job interview with the public watching."[11] This comment from an e-mail accompanying a facilitator's report from Pittsburgh in 2000 compares the less formal structure's ability to produce more clash and summarizes the majority of positive features identified:

> I felt the best debate format was the "discussion around the table format." The good aspect of this forum was the high level of interaction between the candidates and with the moderator. When candidates must respond to follow-up questions, it provides voters the opportunity to evaluate the accuracy and quality of candidate arguments. Future debates should increase this interaction. The podium format was just a chance for candidates to deliver stump speeches and provide little opportunity for the voter to evaluate the accuracy of candidate claims or quality of the candidate's arguments. Additional interaction between the candidates and from the moderator would have improved this.

One analysis in 2000 explained that the format provided more opportunity to observe "their body language as well as hearing their words. It does speak volumes as to sincerity and confidence." Many comments about the format stressed the civility that occurred from the staging and there was a positive response to it. A participant in Littleton, Colorado, in 2000 commented on the staging as a contributor to civility: "the participants' proximity to each other almost demanded that they treat each other with dignity and respect, even when they disagreed." In addition to the civility, the interaction was complimented and a facilitator's report from Turlock, California, in 2004 indicated that "The group thought the vice presidential debate was more in line with their conception of how a debate 'should' look." This comment was consistent with the findings reported in other sections calling for higher levels of interaction.

One of the elements that made this format work or not work, as many participants noted, was the moderator's ability to create a civil tone, ask probing questions, and keep the candidates on topic. In addition to commenting on candidates' performances, discussion groups, facilitator reports, and e-mails also made clear what the viewers' expectations were for moderators.

MODERATOR

In a lead to his story about the twenty-first televised Democrat primary debate in 2008, *Philadelphia Inquirer* reporter Michael D. Schaffer wrote: "It used to be that the important parties in a debate were the debaters. Lincoln and Douglas. Kennedy and Nixon. Carter and Ford. Reagan and Carter. But the morning after Wednesday night's presidential campaign debate in Philadelphia, the names on the nation's lips were...Charles Gibson and George Stephanopoulos."[12] Gibson and Stephanopoulos were the moderators, and their questions—which went for 45 minutes before raising the top issues in the campaign such as health care, the economy, or Iraq—drew criticism from newspapers around the country and 17,000 postings on ABC's Web site complaining about the questions before the evening was over.

A reality of American political debates, as noted previously, is that they give a stage to journalists as well as to candidates. These individuals are as much a part of the debate as the candidates, both in terms of their questions and their personalities. Many participants in our study would like to eliminate the moderator except as a timekeeper and referee in favor of a more open style. This is unlikely to happen since the risks of facing off are too great, and candidates will only participate in debates if they can minimize risks. Since the presence of a moderator who asks the questions or guides the questions in a town hall is the reality, then it is important to know how the moderators are judged and how their performance can be improved.

As noted in chapter three, nearly 200 e-mails were sent to the DebateWatch headquarters in 2000 complaining about the moderator for letting the debate get out of control. The reaction reconfirms 1996 comments and made it clear that participants viewed the moderator's primary role as keeping the candidates on the subject. An exchange in Winston-Salem, North Carolina, after the vice presidential debate in 1996, showed agreement among group members for having an interventionist moderator:

Male 1:   I think he ought to be allowed to interrupt their responses if they're not answering the questions and keep them on track.

Female 1: I thought they used to be allowed to interrupt people in a debate. They could, very nicely say, "Stop, you, right where you were..."

Female 2: And tell them that they did not answer the question that was asked.

Male 1:   But they wouldn't tell each other that they hadn't answered the question.

Female 2: No, but the moderator could.

A woman in a group in Staunton, Virginia, in 2004 gave a good example of why this should be done when she suggested that "I'd like to see the moderators have the opportunity to call on either one of them when they are off subject. Because, you ask George Bush about affirmative action, and he's talking about schools. What the hell has that got to do with affirmative action or judges and so forth?" Moderators most likely would agree with this woman that the rules need to provide an opportunity for clarification and to keep candidates on topic. In an interview with Jim Lehrer, conducted after the 1996 debates by Diana Carlin and Kelly McDonald, Lehrer expressed his frustration about the restrictiveness of the rules. Referring to the candidates' use of unfamiliar terms like "enterprise zones," which were not explained in the context of their answers, Lehrer commented that "there were a couple of times I just regretted that I didn't [interrupt], just say the hell with it. It wouldn't have violated the rules. I could have gotten away with it and just stopped and said, 'What the hell does he mean by this?'"[13]

There are dozens of potential issues that could be raised in a debate, and when an important issue is not explained clearly, viewers consider the opportunity to learn as having been squandered. They know that the candidates are more concerned with their own agendas than with the public's, but they have some expectation that the moderator will at least see that each candidate provides an on-point response. When the question also represents the public's agenda, then the loss is doubled. A male participant in Los Angeles in 2000 gave specific suggestions for how the moderator could improve the quality of responses: "I like the job Mr. Lehrer did, but I would make some suggestions. First, some more follow-ups that are more like interview questions would be helpful. Second, as long as the networks are able to instantly assemble 'fact checks,' 'reality checks,' and 'truth squad' material, and the candidates are just blathering rehashed boiler plate anyway, why not have the moderator take on the candidates for the accuracy of their claims right on the stage?"

A woman in Charlottesville, Virginia, in 2000 summarized what the majority of focus groups, facilitator reports, and e-mails suggested about moderators: "For the next presidential debates, I think it is time to get a new moderator, or perhaps different moderators for each debate.... Having a different moderator for each debate would have the advantage of bringing three different perspectives into the debate formats." The Commission on Presidential Debates and the Bush-Kerry negotiators obviously agreed with the public because there were four moderators rather than the one in 1996 and the two in 2000, and one of them was a woman.

Moderator's agendas are reflected in the topics they raise through their questions. The discussion of issues and questions related to character in the next chapter shed more light on what viewers expect from moderators and the tension between a media and a public agenda in presidential debates.

TOWN HALL

The town hall format was the first major breakthrough since 1956, when the panelist tradition was introduced in the Adlai Stevenson-Estes Kefauver Democratic primary debate. Having nonjournalist questioners was a feature of some primary debates, especially in the 1980s and early 1990s. Most of those debates had limited television coverage. The choice to have citizens ask questions in a general election debate was a risk for the sponsors, moderators, and candidates alike. Because it is a departure from the norm, it deserves separate analysis. It is also important to examine the town hall format separately because the 1996 debate was the second time it was used and it was modified from the original. There were no follow-up questions from the undecided voters, but the moderator could ask a follow-up to clarify the question's intent if it was poorly worded. The moderator randomly selected questioners and did not know what the questions were. Each subsequent year, changes were made to the 1992 rules, and reactions to the format's evolution are instructive. The town hall analysis also pulls together the comments from the previous sections on questions, answers, and time limits to view them through the lens of a single setting.

The town hall was the most popular format in 1992 when it was first introduced for a general election debate. Political communication scholar John Morello summarized the features that made it so appealing: "In sum, the history of town hall debates has produced a conventional wisdom that questions will be less accusatory and argumentative, will better reflect the interest of average viewers, will be harder for candidates to evade, and, by virtue of random selection of questions from 'uncommitted' voters or so called 'soft supporters' (the criterion introduced in 2004), will not inadvertently advantage one candidate or the other."[14]

Diana Carlin, Eric Morris, and Shawna Smith also indicated that "the public has responded positively to the format because citizens ask questions that citizens want answered, and citizens perceive that candidates are less evasive."[15] Mitchell McKinney wrote that "the advent of the town hall debate was regarded by some as a rejuvenation of the public sphere in presidential campaigns."[16] Participants in Normal, Illinois, in 1996 illustrated why researchers reached these conclusions:

Female: If someone like you is asking the question, you kind of know where they're coming from.

Female 2: I think it also lets you see what's really going on in their [candidates'] heads behind all the props they've built because they have to think on their feet. I think it would be much harder to come up with something that's not the truth and how you really feel in a situation. Maybe you would have somebody that's like, "Well, you know, I have a 16-year-old son who has been on crack, who has a gun, what are you going to do to help him?" See them really have to act it out.

A woman in Winston-Salem, North Carolina, believed the type of question posed by the woman in the Normal, Illinois, group did force a different type of response: "I felt they were a little less prepared to deal with the types of questions that citizens ask—'how are you going to deal with my problem?' They're better able to talk about general policy, the kind of questions that a journalist asks." A male in the group expanded on the difference: "It's more of a personal aspect, inside our borders; whereas, the journalists would have chosen a much broader scale. I think both formats show a different view, which I think people should be looking at."

One of the more unique perspectives that came out of DebateWatch '96 was from the actual Gallup group members who constituted the town hall questioners. Following the debate, they had an opportunity to discuss their participation during a focus group that was televised on C-SPAN. Two of the participants talked about their role as public representatives and they supported viewers' perception that the individuals were there to represent average Americans and that they would ask questions to connect public policy to daily life. A woman member of the Gallup group explained, "I felt that as a representative of the communities I'm a part of I might be able to make a difference." A man in the group had a similar response: "Basically the thing I learned and I was concerned about was whether or not the whole thing was a sham and the idea of being real and interacting with all the people in here gave me a real clear consciousness of what's going on, as far as being produced or presented to people. It is showing some very clear issues and the questions are coming from real people."

If the questioners were viewed by the audience and by themselves as "real people," the experience of being on stage with the candidates also created an environment that was less sterile for the candidates. The Gallup group saw "the candidates as three-dimensional figures instead of the two dimensions we see on television," and as "very, very sincere and very knowledgeable about their philosophical beliefs and ideas." Group members attributed this to the fact that we "see them react to the different questions where it's not as structured as the other debate" and the lack of structure was found by one woman in the Gallup group "to be superior because they give you more of an opportunity to see them be spontaneous." These comments are consistent with research cited previously, indicating that audience members also see this format as providing a more human and sincere view of the candidates.

The value of the format was supported by most members of the Gallup group, but they also had suggestions for change. Several individuals thought that there should have been more prescreening, and they were surprised that there wasn't. Because Lehrer didn't screen questions, one man noted that "some of the questions were very repetitive and that there were many other very important questions that weren't asked." Others in the group agreed with his assessment. A woman in the group recognized the potential downside of having "real people" who want their personal problems addressed when she admitted "I would have asked questions that pertained just to me and not to the general public, even though they may be important to somebody else." Another woman indicated that they weren't as tough on the candidates as journalists—something that did change in 2004—and she explained why: "I think perhaps we were a little soft on them. I know person-ally I had things on my mind that I would have liked to have asked, but I would have been embarrassed to; whereas, a reporter might go right out there and dig into those."

Comments from DebateWatch participants in 1996 mirrored the Gallup group's self-assessment of the format's weaknesses, but generally the response to the format was positive. A man in Kansas City, Missouri, commented on the impact of the proximity between the citizens and candidates. His comment also identified the weakness with time limits discussed previously in this chapter: "I really liked the few times they would interact with the person who asked the question.... there were a few times they [the candidates] asked for clarification or follow up or what do you do for a living or something like that.... I wish there'd been more opportunity for it. I think one of the reasons they didn't do more of that interaction was they only had 90 seconds." A woman in Bloomington, Indiana, also commented on the effect of proximity: "When the person asked the question, they moved toward that person so that they could look at that person and that gave them a little more life than standing behind the podium."

Speech Communication Association member Mark Kuhn moderated an online DebateWatch through the C-SPAN Chat Room. In response to his question asking for reactions to the format, comments included: "This one was better," "I think the questions were better," "Better questions, better format," "I got a lot more out of this debate than I did out of the first one," and "I feel that one of the advantages of this type of debate vs. the first is that the questions were more along the lines of what the American public would like to know."

A man in West Chester, Pennsylvania, believed that the type of questions forced the candidates at times to leave the safety of their stump speeches. He explained, "The questions that seemed to be pointed directly at the candidates seemed to cause them to falter a little bit and seemed to cause them to really have to struggle with the answers." The overall positive reaction was grounded in the notion that there is a third agenda in a debate and this is the best way to reach it. That sentiment is exemplified by this comment from a man in Highlands Ranch, Colorado: I found it [the format] very useful. I think it's good. It's a sampling of what we want to hear as opposed to an agenda-filtered set of questions. . . . the moderator has his own bias. If you're picking randomly out of a group of people you tried to sample representatively, you're more likely to get the kind of questions that are going to be more appreciated by the audience."

Positive responses to the town hall format continued in 2000 and 2004 and were along the same themes as in 1992 and 1996—the candidates were more communicative, the questions were more easily understood, and answers were often more direct. A woman attending an Elderhostel in St. Louis in conjunction with the debate compared the town hall favorably against the first debate in 2000 where the candidates, especially Vice President Gore, were described as disregarding the rules. She commented that "last night was the best because the first one I felt Lehrer could not even control the men. And last night I think he did his best. But you felt like the people were part of it, and that's what the United States is about." Another woman indicated that "it seemed that the men had the freedom to walk around a lot and that encouraged them to speak more and to speak more freely their minds. It's like it sort of started things flowing." A participant in Lawrence, Kansas, was pleased that a question on taxes had produced more clarity than he had heard in previous debates, and he stated that "I definitely understand better what they both stand for, and I'm a lot more motivated to go out and vote now and to get more involved—even, like life-long now after this. Definitely." As did many others who compared the value of the town hall to other formats, a woman in Arlington, Virginia, found the 2000 town hall debate to be "the best I have seen in all my years of watching televised debates."

The positive comments in 2004 were along the same lines as in previous years. The candidates, especially President Bush, were seen as "being more relaxed and more comfortable instead of being behind a podium with the very rigid rules" and it was attributed to "people asking questions" by participants in DeLand, Florida, whose views were shared by other group members around the country. And a comment in Providence, Rhode Island, reinforced what had been heard since 1992: "The interaction of the town hall environment works better for the average American because they can identify with people in the audience."

Even with the positive comments, it was obvious in 2004 that the town hall was losing some of its luster as the novelty wore off and format changes impacted content. The online DebateWatch facilitator's report hosted on the Commission on Presidential Debates' Web site asked if the town hall format was more valuable than the others. Only 32 percent of the 4,692 individuals represented in the reports said it was.[17] With fewer people favoring the town hall format in 2004 than did in previous cycles, it was only natural that there were criticisms. Many of them were similar to those from 1996 and 2000. The majority of criticisms across the cycles fell into three categories: questions and lack of follow-up questions, nonrepresentative samples and parochial interests, and lack of time to fully explore an issue. There was a consensus that the format has value as part of a mix of formats and should continue with changes. Changes suggested by the groups are reviewed at the conclusion of this section.

After 1992, there were no follow-up questions from the Gallup group. In fact, microphones were turned off as soon as the last word of the question was spoken. In 1996, the moderator could ask a follow-up only to clarify a questioner's intent if questions were poorly worded. In 2000 and 2004, the moderator could extend the questioning using the same time limits as the more traditional format (three and one-half minutes in 2000 with no candidate having more than two minutes and one minute evenly divided in 2004). However, it was the moderator's choice to do so. This exchange in Cape Girardeau, Missouri, in 1996 summarizes the major problem identified by individuals in dozens of groups about the lack of follow up:

Female: The only bad thing about it, I think, is the people that asked the questions weren't allowed to ask if that was clarified. They just went on.

Male 2: We know that a number of times questions were avoided. I think the very last question was avoided completely by both of them.

Male 3: It is supposed to be a town hall meeting. Not a town hall question session but a meeting which to me implies a back and forth.

Moderator: So they should have some follow-up?

Female 2: What's the use of all these questions if they're not even going to answer. I don't think they answered a fourth of them.

In 1996, the Gallup group was surprised that their questions weren't screened, but starting in 2000, questions were written on a card and submitted to the moderator who selected the questions but kept the selections to himself. While this method does have potential for the media agenda to serve as a filter, overall it has advantages. The moderator can look for recurring themes and keep from jumping back and forth between domestic and foreign policy or having redundant questions as happened in 1996. This procedure also makes sense in that the average person is in a high stress situation and is typically inexperienced at framing questions and being on television in such a high stakes environment. The writing process helps focus their questions. However, viewers did not respond well to the artificial nature of the written questions or the prescreening as a woman from Easton, Maryland, complained in 2000:

The format of the third debate was best but could have been better if the audience had actually been called upon to ask their questions and not have to submit them ahead of time for prescreening. Just have the audience raise their hands, the moderator calls on them randomly, then let the question fly. This would seem to cover the real questions people have. The ones used during the debate were mainly repeats of the first two [debates].

Since no one knows the overall quality of the questions received, it is difficult to know if there were better questions or a wider variety than what were asked. Regardless, there was a sense that the moderators could have chosen better questions as one e-mail in 2000 stated: "I also was disappointed in the questions he (Lehrer) chose from the audience in the town hall debate." A second e-mail was more specific: "I think that the questions and dialogue were the weakest of the 3 debates. Many of the questions were not phrased in a well thought out manner and some were even in the form of personal attacks." Questions with personal attacks increased in number in 2004 as this analysis from Morello reveals: "Citizen interrogators, who in the past asked the candidates to eschew attacks, clearly had a different agenda this time. It started with the first question.... And it did not stop there. Citizens initiated 11 of the 18 rounds of questions (61.1%) by challenging the candidates to respond to an explicit or implied accusation."[18] While the personal attacks might not have suited the focus group members, the fact that the questioners broke with tradition had a positive side according to Morello: "the 2004 experience demonstrates that the unexpected still can and does occur, no matter what rules are imposed."[19] Citizens, as discussed in the section on questions, clearly do want to catch candidates off-guard to test their spontaneity and ability to adapt; however, off guard does not translate into aggressive, adversarial, or "mean" questions. As Faucheux learned from his study of preferred formats, ambivalence about format results from the fact that "features citizens want also can be the same features that create problems."[20]

Because the citizen questioners are selected from the city and surrounding area where the debate is held, it is only natural that their interests are regional. Since they are likely voters—those who have voted in the past—the potential for having younger voters or infrequent voters is also reduced as this comment from a man in DeLand, Florida, in 2004 indicated: "You have an audience who is selected in a particular demographic, that is in a specific geographic area using issues they want to have addressed. And most of the people were middle-aged, so that restricts it somewhat.... so you have kind of a cultural interpretation and the moderator selecting what does get addressed." The comments on the demographics and nature of the questions were common and one additional example illustrates statements made in many groups all three years. A Cape Girardeau, Missouri, group member in 1996 noted that the composition "tainted the questions. You'd get different questions from different groups of people."

A final criticism dealt with time limits and much of what was said is reflected in the comments in a previous section. This was especially a problem in 1996 with the 90-second responses and in 2004 with only one-minute extensions. Two women in Grand Forks, North Dakota, in 1996 summarized the reactions of many others across the country:

Female 1:   I think in 90 or 60 seconds you can't really get to the heart of any issues anyway. Clinton gave an answer and there were two sentences and that was it.

Female 2:   You can't answer in 90 seconds to where you know what they're talking about. You generalize—"I'm against it. I'm for it." But why? To get into something that's going to impact you as a voter in 90 seconds?

Although there were criticisms of the town hall, there was also an understanding that some concessions have to be made to guarantee that questions do represent what people want to hear and that the answers and flow of discussion are controlled. Reactions to the 2000 town hall debate provide examples of the reasonable type of critique citizens gave. A man in San Francisco sent an e-mail and suggested that changes were eroding the original town hall format but he acknowledged some realities:

> Thank you for inviting feedback to your debate formats and procedures. I am pleased that you offered the candidates and the voters three separate formats. Although I am not pleased in the way the Town Hall format was operated. I understand the audience and to some extent the questions must be prescreened, but last night's debate did not allow for the beauty of the town hall format to come out. It lacked interaction between the candidates. You should allow the candidates to converse, ask questions of the other and have a verbal debate between the two, and not go through a middleman (the moderator). In this format, the moderator should be used as a referee, making sure only one candidate speaks, each gets a turn to speak, and to move the discussion on when it becomes redundant. The example of what was needed was hinted during the Affirmative Action discussion. The debate was cut off because of certain rules. It was a sterile town hall. I know audience members can be nervous; therefore, I see the need for cue cards for the questions, but it came off as staged and predetermined.

A man in Hillside, Illinois, in 2000 had a similar objection to screening the questions as well as a suggestion for selecting questions in future debates when he said, "This was not, in my opinion, a true town hall debate. The questions were the choice of the moderator by way of a filtering system. I agree that the questions should be screened for credibility and relevance. I think a true town hall would have the questions numbered and selected alternately by each candidate randomly from a lottery bowl. Perhaps a real hardball question might make an appearance." One suggestion for making the town hall format more useful and for avoiding questions that repeated themes from previous debates was to have the town hall first. The following reasoning was given in a facilitator's report in 2000: "This would give the moderator(s) the opportunity to ask questions that people neglected to ask. There was far too much repetition of topics and answers in the three debates and many important topics were left out or barely covered."

One of the major criticisms outlined previously was the lack of follow-up questions from the citizens. An Ann Arbor, Michigan, woman in 2000 suggested an alternative to a complete follow-up that was recommended by several groups in each cycle: "I think people in the town hall format should be allowed to comment on whether they felt their question had been answered to discourage off-point prepared answers by the candidates." A woman in Portland, Oregon, in 2000 provided a modification that is interesting but highly unlikely to be used when she suggested that "after each candidate had spoken, the moderator would return to the person asking the question and ask if each candidate had answered the question posed. The moderator would 'keep score' by giving a point to each candidate who answered the question adequately. The person who answered the most people's questions—and this has nothing to do with agreeing with the answers—would be the winner." DebateWatch did not ask that participants about winners and losers, but we did ask if one format served the viewers better than another in terms of learning about the candidates and the issues. The next section summarizes reactions to the question and shows that there was no clear "winner."

PREFERRED FORMAT

Although some formats may provide more "debate" in the form of clash and comparisons than others, there is little consensus as to what constitutes the best debate format. A Pew study of debate formats conducted by Faucheux also used focus groups, and Faucheux's analysis of the responses from the two focus groups is not unlike ours when it comes to identifying the ideal format: "The relatively high level of consensus regarding the desirable and undesirable characteristics of debates breaks down when participants are asked about specific debate formats.... the major reason consensus breaks down over formats is that certain formats tend to engender both positive and negative debate characteristics."[21]

Total agreement on the ideal format is impossible to reach, but the 1992 focus group participants were nearly unanimous in their desire to eliminate the panelist format. The CPD took their advice and 1992 was the last time a panel was used in a general election debate. The 1992 participants gave high marks to the single moderator and town hall formats, and they were clear that these formats worked well because of follow-up questions and guided discussion.[22] The participants between 1996 and 2004 generally agreed with those assessments. Two groups in Detroit in 1996 responded to a question about the panelist format with similar reactions. The two sets of reactions are combined:

Moderator: [After complaints about the format] Would you rather go back to a team of four reporters asking the questions?

Female 1: No!

Female 2: Which were terrible. They were the worst.

Male: Because they were trying to one-up each other.

Female 2: But it gets you ridiculous questions.

Female 3: It just went wild.

A group in Highlands Ranch, Colorado (also in 1996), had a similar exchange:

Female: Originally, they had a panel of questioners instead of just one. I wonder if that worked better. I don't remember.

Male 1:   I think this format is better.

Male 2:   I felt like the panel of questioners wanted to be on stage, and they were trying to out-do the debaters, really, to make their jobs more secure back at the network.

Male 1:   Trying to one-up each other.

However, a few participants in each subsequent debate cycle were wistful for the panelist format—proving Faucheux's claim that unanimity is impossible. For example, after the first debate in 1996, a female participant in Normal, Illinois, commented, "I expected them to do a panel. It just seems so wrong to do it this particular way." An email in 2000 gave a valid reason for including a panel: "I prefer the panels of journalists which were used in the several debates in the previous elections. A broader range of questions are asked if there is more than one questioner." A woman in Providence, Rhode Island, in 2004 gave a sound reason for having experts or journalists involved and having more than one: "I wonder if there were three media people there asking questions if there might be a better opportunity to have an objective fact checker of the facts and statistics because you have three minds working on the same stuff constantly." It is important to note that the desire for panelists was registered by very few, but recognizing that some feel it is a valuable format is equally important to mention.

Aside from the few voices with a desire to return to multiple panelists, the most consistent response to questions about preferred format was that there should not be a single one. This 2000 New York City facilitator's report explained: "The three different formats allowed the candidates at least one opportunity to experience their preference." A man in St. Louis, Missouri, in 2000 had a similar reaction: "I think it may be important to have a variety of formats to see how the two candidates react, respond, and interact based on different conditions so that you can get an added sense of the man or his perspectives." A woman in Valentine, Nebraska, in 2000 provided another perspective: "I prefer the use of differing formats and was very pleased with beginning with the traditional format followed by increasingly less formal debate formats." An e-mail had a nearly identical reaction to the progression and concluded with the idea that "each served a purpose and allowed us to see these candidates in different formats." Another said "it gave me 3 different looks at the candidates." And a final example of why varied formats are preferred was stated as follows: "I liked the varied formats. You should keep that as it provides different challenges and doesn't favor one type of candidate over another." Content analyses of debates discussed in chapter two indicate that different formats result in different argument structures and strategies from candidates. It was also clear in 1992 that Ross Perot was at his best in the traditional panelist format, Bill Clinton "owned" the town hall, and George H.W. Bush was most comfortable with a single moderator. Thus, the overwhelming preference for multiple formats has benefits for the candidates as well as for the public.

If no single format is "the best" or most preferred, there were definite preferences regarding how to make any format work better. As indicated in many of the comments in this chapter, suggestions were to extend the time and the number of rebuttal opportunities to reduce returning to a question instead of answering the one on the table. One person in Kansas City, Missouri, in 1996 had a novel approach to resolving the off-question problem: "Build in every 20 minutes two minutes to clarify any point that's been raised so far. You can't raise any new topics, but it is your opportunity to clarify what's been said or address a question." Maintaining a period of time such as three and one-half minutes for follow-up can also resolve the problem. A woman in Staunton, Virginia, in 2004 expressed an opinion that was shared by many others that the best approach was a flexible one: "I thought the structure and the process were well-designed. I like the keeping of the time carefully and the limiting people in how far they can go and it seems to me they give a fair amount of room for response and are even able to extend the time so the judge can kind of moderate what is appropriate."

There was positive response in 1996 to inclusion of opening statements. That was the only year they were used and many participants recommended that they should be a part of every debate. A man in Washington, D.C., in 2000 provided a very pragmatic reason for doing so: "Candidates should be given a two-minute opening statement in all debate formats. Jumping right into a question is awkward, forcing the candidates to split their initial response time between a reasonable greeting to the audience and responding to the first question." A woman in St. Louis, Missouri, in 2000 noted that an "opening statement by each one gets that general philosophy out and makes all the generalizations you can and keeps the rest of the debate for specifics and specific answers."

A final recommendation that surfaced multiple times in all three years, as well as in 1992, was narrowing the number of issues in each debate to increase the information value and to reduce redundancy across the debates. A man in the audience in Hartford in 1996 wanted "six debates" and wanted the sponsors to "break the debates into issues." A facilitator's report from Virginia suggested that there be more debates (4–6) "and have each debate focus on one topic . . . this will allow the candidate to fully explain his/her ideas, thoughts, and plans. Furthermore, it will help citizens to understand truly what the candidates stand for." A 1996 participant from Highlands Ranch, Colorado, described his idea of focused debates: "I would love to see a debate just on the economy. . . . I think they should then be called up on a handful of more tailored subjects. Foreign policy would be good. Probably the whole health plan would be good." In addition to a debate focused on a single issue, a range of suggestions was given for the maximum number of questions or topics in a debate to further focus the content. A Lawrence, Kansas, participant in 2004 thought the maximum number for a debate should be "about eight questions." There are currently about 20 in each debate.

Whether it was fewer questions per debate to allow more time per topic, assigned topics that varied across debates, or more and shorter debates on a single topic, it was clear that viewers wanted more depth of analysis, fewer sound byte responses, less redundancy, and a better set of answers from which to judge the candidates. All of these features should be wrapped in a variety of formats moderated by a different moderator for each debate.

CONCLUSION

On the surface, the issue of debate formats seems simple—who should ask the questions, how many turns should there be for each question and how long should each response be? As the analysis in this chapter indicates, the answers are far more complex than what the brief introductions the moderator gives at the beginning of each debate would suggest. Format does matter. The Racine Group's report referenced in chapter two indicated that format affects the content and clash in a debate, which, in turn, impacts learning. The fact that campaigns participate in prolonged negotiations over the most minute detail of the format and the production also suggests that how the debates take place has consequences. The public understands the impact of format on information acquisition without need for any type of scholarly research. They know what they want from a debate and whether they are getting it, and they can detect what helps and hinders their knowledge acquisition. The comments from participants in DebateWatch clearly indicate that it is a team effort to produce a debate with educational value that serves all parties' agendas. It is also clear that no single format will do it all. Format may matter, but human choice intervenes as well. The differing opinions about what constitutes a good format or useful information were clear from the array of comments. Comments that were selected for this chapter represented what a majority of groups reported as problematic or preferred, but there was certainly no unanimity on the specifics. As the next two chapters reveal, even with flaws, viewers learned from the debates. Just as the Lincoln-Douglas debates were not as ideal or pure as the mythology surrounding them suggests, contemporary debates are not as flawed as they are portrayed by their critics.

Chapter Five

Searching for a President:
What Matters to Voters?

In 1996, "character issues" were listed on facilitators' reports as one of the least useful topics in the debates. When this information was released to the media as part of a report on DebateWatch, there was considerable interest since character was high on the media's and Bob Dole's agendas. The *New York Times* sent reporter Francis X. Clines to Lawrence, Kansas, to listen to DebateWatch tapes and review the data that was pouring into the research center. The subsequent article included quotations that summarized the salient point made about character that year: the public has "come to draw a pronounced distinction between a politician's private life and public performance." And Clines illustrated with some of the pithier comments from discussion groups: "Character is a dead issue." "Our lives aren't really affected by Bill Clinton's personal life." "So what if Clinton smoked a little pot when he was in college? That has no impact on whether I'm going to have a job or my kid is going to get educated." "The character issue has been done to death. Bush tried it, and it didn't work." "When Dole says you can trust his word, what that says to me is that he hasn't had a chance to screw it up yet."[1] The comments and fuller discussion did not discount the importance of personal qualities, but they represented a view that "this is an area for *their* [the public's] criteria and standards, and *they*, not some biased politician, will make this judgment."[2]

And viewers do make judgments about many aspects of debates and their participants—formats, the moderator, the questions, the answers, and candidates' likelihood of being a good president. Many of the judgments result from expectations of the debate and whether or not they were fulfilled. What viewers seek from a debate might be a better understanding of the candidates' positions on the issues, it might be insights into candidates' personal characteristics, or it might be a combination of the two. DebateWatch participants in nearly every group made it clear that there was specific information they wanted to hear from the candidates, and nearly everyone learned something new. A woman in Nashville in 1996 explained that prior to the debate, she "expected from both candidates, and more from the Republican side, [to hear] ideas of what they would do as compared to what was happening now." A man in Winston-Salem, North Carolina, in 2000 wanted to "see a little more attention paid to the Supreme Court justices." In 2004 a participant in Kansas City, Missouri, wanted to "sort out the flip-flop issue [with Kerry]" and a man in Commerce, Texas, indicated that "at my age the one issue that interested me was health care and Medicare." By the end of the debates, some participants were pleased with what they heard, some were not, and some were still hopeful that by the end of the campaign some of their unanswered questions would be resolved.

Chapter two's research summary indicated that the majority of viewers gather information to reinforce a predebate vote choice, and undecided voters use debates to help make a choice. Some have a weak preference at the outset and leave themselves open to persuasion as a woman in Hartford, Connecticut, explained when asked if the debate influenced her choice in 1996: "It's not going to change my feelings from before.... I was open if something unusual came up, but it didn't." A man in College Station, Texas, in 2004 further exemplified the reinforcement function when he said, "I saw exactly what I expected to see. Kerry looks better; he presents well.... George Bush is not a great speaker or a great debater. Never has been. I think he is a strong-minded individual. I think he understands what's going to happen. I think he is a good manager and he's doing that very well." Farther north, an undecided voter in Madison, Wisconsin, explained that "Bush would point out that Kerry supported something, but then he didn't go to vote for it. That's what I learned and it helped make my decision."

The DebateWatch project yielded consistent findings that in spite of any shortcomings or criticisms, viewers do learn from the debates. Generally, participants were satisfied with what they saw and heard even if all of their expectations were not realized. Comments in this chapter provide insights into how viewers use the information they obtain—both verbal and nonverbal—to judge the candidates' personal qualities and their issue positions. Every transcript had some discussion of personal characteristics even though no specific questions were asked, and the reasoning behind the reactions reported in the *New York Times* article is illustrated throughout. The majority of this chapter is devoted to the larger issue of image—the image the viewers have of the candidates and how well the image matches with concepts of presidential leadership. The difference between the public's "character" agenda and the way character is addressed through the other two agendas in the debate is clearly articulated. The issue analysis that follows discussion of image relates directly to the third agenda—what was important to the viewers and how well the questions and answers addressed the public's agenda. DebateWatch transcripts, e-mails, pre- and postdebate surveys, and facilitators' reports form the basis for the analysis. The analysis is dependent upon some theoretical grounding; thus, before presenting viewers' reactions to the candidates and the issues, the underlying theories guiding the analysis are outlined.

THEORETICAL FRAMEWORK

Three theories contribute to explaining what takes place as viewers watch debates and process the information. These theories are fundamental to understanding comments in this chapter: uses and gratifications, agenda setting, and the image/issue dichotomy.

Uses and Gratifications

Political communication researchers Judith Trent and Robert Friedenberg described the uses and gratifications theory as being

> concerned with determining those uses people make of the mass media in the circumstances of their own lives as well as the gratifications they seek and receive from such consumption.... While some of these functions may be obvious (we read a newspaper account of a candidate's speech to gain more information about the candidate and the campaign), others may be latent (we watch a television commercial about a candidate so that we have enough information about the campaign to maintain our social status as an informed citizen). In other words, the functions served by the media during a campaign are not necessarily what they appear to be. Information or cognitive gains may serve many important purposes for the individual, and the uses/gratifications perspective provides a way to examine them.[3]

The concept that the functions of the media—in this case in televised debates—may not be what they appear to be is central to understanding how viewers use debates. The word "debate" suggests persuasion, but most viewers don't anticipate being persuaded—only reinforced. Debates are previewed and debriefed by the media as if they are academic contests or sporting events. However, most viewers don't watch to determine a winner or loser. Viewers tend to believe that their candidate won or at least wasn't damaged fatally as the comment from Commerce, Texas, suggested. What is apparent from the DebateWatch study is that viewers do watch for information. Ultimately, the research underlying this project was designed to determine if presidential debates produce gratification in terms of information acquisition. In fact, groups were asked specifically to identify questions or topics that were useful, not useful, or had not been discussed but needed to be.

Agenda Setting

The degree of gratification attained is partially impacted by the debate format, as chapter four indicated. However, it is also influenced by the candidates' and moderator's competing agendas, which can overpower any format. The second theory that guides the analysis in this chapter is agenda setting. It has a direct relationship to gratification. One of the most widely cited explanations of agenda setting comes from Bernard C. Cohen, who described the media as being "stunningly successful in telling its readers what to think about"[4] if not exactly what to think. Trent and Friedenberg further explained that "the media may not always dominate, but they do have a significant impact on what we think about (our focus of attention)."[5] If a topic is raised in a debate that is not on the public agenda, the public is forced to attend to that issue. Some viewers will decide that it is an issue that should be added to their agendas as a focus group member in chapter four noted about questions on topics with which she was unfamiliar. The media agenda contributes to gratification in this instance. The information alternatively may be perceived as irrelevant, unimportant, or out of place in the debate. If it is, it can be rejected, thus denying gratification or at least reducing its measure. If, for example, someone is willing to accept an imperfect candidate out of partisan loyalties or a determination that the other candidate is even less desirable, discussion about negative character traits will have limited or no impact.

Regardless of the response to either a "character" or a policy-based issue raised in the debate, the issue becomes part of the debate's agenda. An audience has no choice but to process it, but how it is processed into the larger schema of puzzle pieces defining presidential candidates is not necessarily determined by the media or the candidates. As the definition of agenda setting stated, the media can make someone attend to or become aware of an issue, but they can't make everyone think about it the way it is cast. The DebateWatch transcripts demonstrate how information that is presented through a media or candidate agenda is processed, and the results are often surprising in their depth of analysis and how interpretations are made. The agenda-setting aspect of the debates also provides a means for analyzing specific issues and how the three agendas—media, candidate, and public—come together. If something is on the public's agenda that is not discussed in the debate, the issue's salience is not reduced. The media or campaigns may add something to a public agenda, but they don't delete something on the public's agenda that isn't on theirs. Many individuals said they would continue to seek out information from other sources (see chapter six) or at least hope for closure on the issue before Election Day.

Image and Issues Dichotomy

As a result of the relationship between issue agendas and candidate evaluations, scholarly research on voter learning through debates has often attempted to sort out the interplay of image and issue knowledge acquisition. The dominant theme in early research was that they were two separate sets of information. There was an assumption that political messages are intended to project one or the other or that viewers concentrate on one to the exclusion or dominance of the other. Political communication scholar Susan Hellweg, however, argued that "candidates' debate messages incorporate a dual strategy of highlighting issue differences while also emphasizing a positive self-image and a negative opponent image."[6] Several studies suggest that image content dominates, while others conclude the opposite.[7] McKinney and Carlin's analysis of the literature on the dichotomy suggested that one answer to the lack of consensus is that "issue and image learning are two message variables that work in tandem."[8] Carlin addressed the tandem nature more directly in an analysis of the 1992 and 1996 DebateWatch groups, and she drew the following conclusion: "debate viewers make judgments about those [image] traits based on the strategies the debaters employ, their issue choices, their demeanor...their willingness to address the questions directly, and the manner in which they attack their opponents."[9]

Analysis of the viewers' comments over the three debate cycles represented in this book reinforces research concluding that issue choice and stance impact image. Additionally, the comments demonstrate that viewers bring different goals (uses and gratifications) and different backgrounds or goals (agendas) to the debates, which may result in privileging image or issues. For example, a highly informed group will learn less about issues but is likely to gain more image knowledge from how the candidates talk about the issues or attack an opponent's stances. Conversely, a less informed group may form or adjust an image through acquisition of new issue knowledge. Most viewers—regardless of prior knowledge or vote choice before the debates—are looking for a "fit" with their concept of what constitutes a presidential image and what issue positions better dovetail with their values. An inarticulate explanation of a shared position or value is often more important than an articulate explanation of an unacceptable position. As a result, winning a debate does not mean that a person wins an election or moves any voters from one candidate to another or toward a choice. Likewise, a presidential image is not necessarily tied to debate skills in an oratorical sense. Image formation is tied to a large number of factors, with issues being just one. Given the emphasis on issues in debates and the relatively minor differences between the candidates on some of them, viewers look for cues beyond arguments in sizing up the candidates as presidential material. As the focus group discussions that follow reveal, complex thinking goes into processing the information and reaching conclusions. The DebateWatch data suggests that issues and image are clearly interconnected.

Nonverbal Communication and Metamessages

Image is based on many factors. In addition to the three theories described previously, two communication principles provide additional framework for explaining how image develops and contributes to perceptions of character. The importance of nonverbal messages cannot be underestimated as research shows that the majority of a message's impact comes from nonverbal communication rather than from the spoken words. In fact, it is estimated that as little as 7 percent of a message's meaning comes from the words. Body language accounts for 55 percent and vocal cues—volume, tone, or inflection—communicate 38 percent.[10] People tend to trust nonverbal messages because they are perceived as mostly unintentional or more authentic. Metamessages—unspoken messages that are deduced from the context and manner in which the message is presented—also contribute to interpretation of a candidate's meaning. Metamessages are what we commonly refer to as "reading between the lines." DebateWatch participants did a considerable amount of reading between the lines. Participants expressed confidence in their ability to judge a person's character based on nonverbal cues and metamessages. A woman in Madison, Wisconsin, in 2004 commented on the value of watching the debates over hearing news reports of them and explained that "I'm a visual person; I want to see someone answer a question or ask a question. I want to see the look on their face. I want to decide for myself if I think their reaction is sincere or if they are full of it or trying to pass the buck." Another woman in Providence, Rhode Island, in 2004 responded when asked if the debates helped reveal leadership qualities that they did so "in a very visceral sense."

DOES "CHARACTER" MATTER?

The visual and visceral cues result from the televised nature of the debates. In a review of Alan Schroeder's *Presidential Debates: Forty Years of High Risk TV*, journalist Evan Cornog discussed the power of the camera to emphasize image over substance.[11] He concluded: "Yet the rise of the image was already being lamented in 1960, when Don Hewitt worried that the impact of TV debates would be to elect a 'matinee idol,' and historian Henry Steele Commager feared that televised debates would elevate 'the glib, the evasive, the dogmatic, the melo-dramatic' over more sober virtues."[12] If DebateWatch participants' comments are indicative of what other viewers think, and the consistent responses over several debate cycles suggests they are, then neither Hewitt nor Commager should have worried. While image is important to voters, it is not entirely based on "good looks" nor does the "glib" always win out. Viewers want substance, and they want the type of information that helps them assess fitness for the office. Potential vot-ers have an image of a president that is based on leadership qualities, and as was discussed in chapter four, the various formats give them some sense of how a can-didate will communicate as a president. The analysis of comments about character in this chapter go to the next step to examine what groups said about behaviors and policy positions that reveal "presidential" qualities.

Journalist Chris Wallace raised several provocative questions about the type of personal qualities a president must possess. In his book *Character: Profiles in Presidential Courage*, Wallace observed:

> In choosing a leader every four years, we have no idea what challenges will con-front the president. Who knew in the fall of 2000 that the central issue of the Bush presidency—the central test of Western values—would be the clash with Islamic extremism and the forces of terror? In that sense, every election is a bet on a person. Who has the character to stand tall in the face of unimaginable pressures and fiercely competing interests in order to make the hard choices? Who can we count on?[13]

Wallace's concept of presidential character is more in keeping with what focus group members said they were seeking in a president—those immutable but often nebulous qualities that stand the test of time and trial to help carry out the predict-able and the totally unexpected turns of the most challenging job in the world. It sounds like an impossible set of demands, and perhaps it is. Often the qualities Wallace's questions evoke and what group members desired in leaders are less likely to be uncovered with the types of questions and attacks that occur in the course of a presidential campaign or debate. "Character" attacks are common and include everything from the personal indiscretions that haunted Bill Clinton to the choice of one's pastor as Barack Obama found out in 2008 or the release of a spouse's financial records as Geraldine Ferraro in 1984 and John McCain in 2008 learned. Sorting out the attacks, determining what to believe, and weighing their importance in judging a person's ability to deal with issues such as terrorism is the challenge voters face and DebateWatch participants discussed.

If, in fact, viewers do care about character, then it logically is part of a shared agenda. The problem is that they object to the means by which the agenda is revealed as a review of questions Jim Lehrer asked each year and reactions to them illustrates. In 1996 Jim Lehrer asked the following questions:

> Senator Dole, we've talked mostly now about differences between the two of you that relate to policy issues and that sort of thing. Are there also significant differences in the more personal area that are relevant to this election?
>
> (Follow up) Senator Dole, if you could single out one thing that you would like for the voters to have in their mind [sic] about the President on a policy matter or a personal matter, what would it be? Something to know about him, understand it and appreciate it.
>
> Mr. President, what do you say to Senator Dole's point that this election is about keeping one's word?

A common reaction to the questions was that "the personal differences question surprised me," and people were pleased that "Mr. Dole step[ped] back, taking the high road" (from the Winston-Salem, NC, transcript). Group participants commonly referred to the questions as "prejudicial" or "irrelevant" and expressed the belief that they were brought up because the media concentrates on negative character issues; "they go for the scandal" and "you don't hear about the positive ones" (Hartford, CT, and Highlands Ranch, CO).

As if to prove the point that the media is more concerned with scandals and different issues than those on the public agenda, Lehrer continued his tact four years later when he asked, "For you, Governor. And this flows somewhat out of the Boston debate. You, your running mate, your campaign officials have charged that Vice President Gore exaggerates, embellishes and stretches the facts, et cetera. Are you—do you believe these are serious issues? This is a serious issue that the voters should use in deciding which one of you two men to vote for on November 7?" A woman in Boston, when asked if any of the questions were irrelevant or not useful, responded that "I just want to say, 'Shame on Jim Lehrer' for ending the debate on the character issue," and another woman in Lawrence, Kansas, responded negatively for a practical reason: "You're not going to get any real answers from a question like that. I want something more concrete instead of talking about abstract ideas like morality." After the vice presidential debate, there were comments about the lack of "character" questions and how refreshing it was. A man in Danville, Kentucky, did not discount the importance of character, but he made it clear that a specific question on it didn't belong in a debate. He explained what Americans really want to hear about—the bottom line for them: "I'm glad that there was no discussion on the character of the running mates because it matters to me but to a majority of Americans it doesn't. And the Republicans are finally starting to realize that America doesn't really care what happens as long as they are making money. That's what most people care about or that the environment's good or whatever. But what the President does is his personal business."

The trend of criticism was as consistent as the questions inviting the candidates to "go after" one another. In 2004, Lehrer asked two character-related questions—one to each candidate. The candidates' initial reactions are included:

Lehrer: Senator Kerry, you just—you've repeatedly accused President Bush—not here tonight, but elsewhere before—of not telling the truth about Iraq, essentially of lying to the American people about Iraq. Give us some examples of what you consider to be his not telling the truth.

Kerry: Well, I've never, ever used the harshest word, as you did just then. And I try not to.

Lehrer: President Bush, clearly, as we have heard, major policy differences between the two of you. Are there also underlying character issues that you believe, that you believe are serious enough to deny Senator Kerry the job as commander in chief of the United States?

Bush: That's a loaded question.

DebateWatch participants agreed with the President. A man in DeLand, Florida, gave a very reasoned explanation for why this type of question had little import for him and potentially for others when he said, "I am going to guess that outside of the media spotlight and outside of the few personal dealings, Bush and Kerry don't know one another very well. So I think it's odd for Jim Lehrer to ask Bush to describe Kerry's character flaws and vice versa.... It was a no-win question. No matter how you handled that question it would have backfired."

HOW IS CHARACTER REVEALED?

If the traditional character questions backfire, and they did for many in the groups, what, then, should be asked? How do we get to Wallace's notion of character? The DebateWatch transcripts suggest that it isn't necessary for moderators to ask character questions and it isn't necessary for candidates to attack their opponents on the issue. The public has a wide array of candidate messages it decodes to detect character including nonverbal communication, personal style, metamessages, issue positions, and how the candidates answer questions. The relationship between issue content and character as discussed in groups lends additional support to the idea that image and issues do interact and are not judged separately. The various avenues for revealing character are discussed within the context of each election cycle. Conversations in groups usually touched on more than one trigger in their discussions of character or presidential image.

The candidates' on-screen behaviors cumulatively result in perceptions of their personal style. The power of "style" in debates was explored by the Racine Group with the conclusion that "Exploratory research suggests that candidate presentational style is important to success in televised debates. Presidential debate scholars report that political candidates who in their personal styles are able to reveal to viewers their likeability, trust, and similarity are viewed as more persuasive."[14] A man in DeLand, Florida, in 2004 summarized the concept of style and related it to the ubiquitous issue of character with this observation: "Your character is tied to your personality and how you present yourself. When you are the leader of a country you need to present yourself in a certain way and your character follows along and your convictions and everything else."

As the DebateWatch groups were interpreting the candidates' metamessages, they were creating many of their own. Just as leadership qualities were revealed on a "visceral level" as one participant indicated, participants revealed a great deal about the high degree of emotional involvement and investment they have in the debates. This was especially true in 2000. The tone of the comments in the three election cycles is decidedly different even if the methods used to unravel character are consistent. The 1996 Clinton-Dole race analysis that follows is more extensive than the others for two reasons. Character attacks were a major component of the challenger's strategy, and the number of groups in 1996 was considerably larger than in the other two years. There are numerous examples of each type of analysis. Through use of more extensive examples from 1996, the relationship between the theories presented previously in the chapter and their observed application across the three debate cycles is firmly and clearly established.

1996 Clinton-Dole Debates

As discussed in other chapters, the 1996 race was not awash with drama or uncertainty as to its outcome. Clinton held a solid lead in the polls from primary season until the final poll on Election Day. The burgeoning budget deficit of the 1980s was under control, the economy was good, welfare reforms were being made, and the country was at peace. The only campaign strategies the Republicans had at their disposal were to propose more tax cuts, remind everyone of Clinton's failed health care plan, and attack his fitness for office. An article appearing in June 1996 with the headline "The Strategy: Dole Tries to Make an Issue of Clinton's Trustworthiness," reported that "Senator Bob Dole offered a broad attack on President Clinton's truthfulness and character today, mocking him as a President who broke his word and stole ideas from Republicans. 'Bill Clinton invites the American people to ask whether he can be trusted,' Mr. Dole said."[15]

Dole and his surrogates continued to make Clinton's integrity an issue during the summer and fall. The first debate provided an opportunity for Dole to capitalize on the issue, but he "took the high road" and a civil encounter ensued. Prior to the second debate, speculation ran high that Dole had to do something to cut Clinton's persistent double-digit lead and the character issue might be it, as reported on CNN's AllPolitics: "Still suffering from a double-digit lag behind

Clinton, Dole has heard many advisers urge him to drop the niceties and attack the president on the so-called 'character issue.' In stump speeches over the last few days, the former senator has been getting progressively tougher on his opponent, previewing the areas that his campaign has decided to open for questioning." The report went on to mention a fact that was also clearly revealed by DebateWatch participants, that in going negative, "The line they are walking is thin....Polls indicate that voters, particularly the key demographic plum of women, don't like candidates to attack each other personally, but want to hear about the issues."[16]

This conversation in Normal, Illinois, emphasizes what the polling data showed and reveals the existence of multiple agendas in a debate:

Female 1:   On the personal issue question, I felt that Lehrer was fishing. That was the only the only question that bothered me. It seemed he was baiting Bob Dole, "Come on, say 'character, say character.'" The media could jump on that. I think both candidates did a good job of steering clear of that whole issue that was brought up. It was so totally pounded on by the media that obviously the candidates don't want to stir it up tonight.

Moderator: He asked that question, do you think on behalf of the voting public or on behalf of the media?

Male 1:   I think for the media.

Female 2:   They could have a story out of that for a week if he'd said character or drugs or something like that.

Male 2:   Oh, yeah.

Moderator: Do you feel like that it's an issue that America as a whole is interested in? Or, in your eyes, is that simply a media issue?

Male 2:   I think it's a media issue. That's what everyone here said, "Thank you for getting beyond the character issue." They wanted to get the character issue involved because it was such a big part of the '92 election. I think that Senator Dole...realized that the attack on character simply wasn't effective in '92.... I think President Clinton had his own reasons for staying away from it. I think they kind of offset each other there in avoiding that question. They kind of tap-danced together around it.

The Gallup questioners from the town hall debate also engaged in a discussion of the type of questions they asked versus those asked by Lehrer in the previous debate. One woman summarized the discussion this way:

Well the thing that became clear to me after listening to the candidates tonight and the questions that we kept asking, even though Dole would really get off on the morality issue and try to really pin Clinton down to some of the things that were moral issues, we weren't interested in that. As our questions were clear, we had specific issues; we all came with concerns that we wanted to address and we stuck to that. We didn't care about those other things.

What they did care about was the candidates' fitness for the presidency. There were numerous comments contrasting Clinton's and Dole's styles that related to both presentational skills and age. A Detroit group had this exchange, which emphasized the power of nonverbal communication to create a presidential image:

Female 1:   I think you learned who has the better speaking style. Clinton is a little more dynamic than Dole. He just doesn't appear "presidential." That's what the debate should do.

Female 2:   Yes.... I hate to say it, but Dole appeared old. Although he was very funny. He was a very funny guy. But I don't think I want somebody like that running the country. Some people will be offended by what he is saying. He appeared to be shaking a little bit to me. His eyes were driving me nuts. He kept blinking, blinking, blinking. I thought, fix the contact. Clinton always generally appears more relaxed on camera. Some people are always relaxed on camera no matter what they're doing. But Dole is probably a brilliant guy, but Clinton appeared more relaxed. When you put them side by side, you can really see a difference.

A man in West Chester, Pennsylvania, however, used a criterion other than appearance to settle the age issue. He relied on the answer to a question asked in the town hall debate about Dole's age and his ability to relate to younger voters: "I also felt that for Dole the most difficult question perhaps was about his age. And I felt he gave a very brief answer to it but it was a strength and then he redirected it to his economic plan."

The individuals selected by Gallup to ask questions in the town hall had a much better view of the two candidates and reached some different conclusions than the group in Detroit, thus proving that meaning is in the eye of the beholder. While the camera may not blink, it doesn't give the same picture as the one viewed up close and personal:

Female 1:   One of the things that I thought was very interesting is that the age issue had been a big issue for me, with Senator Dole. He seemed much more dynamic than I had expected in doing this, so it's not an issue for me anymore.

Female 2:   I thought while they both did very well, I was impressed with the difference that I saw in Senator Dole from what I normally see portrayed in television newscasts. I found him to be a much more personable individual than I ever would have thought. Very approachable and very much unlike coverage I have seen of him.

Discussions of the town hall debate revealed the importance of nonverbal communication to provide insights into how the candidates respond to their constituents. Two women in Las Cruces, New Mexico, discussed how the candidates' eye contact with the Gallup group told them about the candidates' responsiveness to the public. One noted that "I thought that Clinton was connecting more with the audience than Dole was," and the other responded that "any time Clinton got asked a question, Clinton directed himself to that person. If I'm asking somebody a question, I want you to direct your answer directly at me." And in what could have been a continuation of the discussion, a woman in San Francisco emphasized how direct eye contact is interpreted:

> Along the lines of Clinton, when people asked questions, he directly talked to them. He looked them in the eye and directly gave them their answer, while Dole went around the stage, and he kind of looked down. But he tried sometimes to directly address the person, but Clinton looked stronger. He was focused on that person, like "I'm going to answer your question." Plus, when you look at someone, that means that you're supposed to be telling the truth, looking directly and making eye contact.

Since the Dole campaign made an issue of Clinton's veracity, the ability to detect truthful answers was important to the group members. When a group in Mills Valley, California, was comparing and contrasting their perceptions of the two candidates, the moderator asked specifically "What do you think just visually? What strikes you?" A woman responded about Clinton, "To begin with, he's a vigorous man of 50, and charming." A man added, "There's hope in his voice; that's another thing." The conversation quickly shifted to Senator Dole and observations about personality. Comments brought past perceptions into play as an important component in how the candidates are judged in a debate. The conversation evolved into an analysis of truthfulness, and it ended with a cynical observation that further supports why the character issue, as it often plays out, fails to resonate the way the media or candidates expect it to. This is especially true, as it was in 1996, if someone has a proven record on issues that matter to the public such as the economy:

Female 1: Dole, on the other hand...I've listened to him in the Senate over and over again, and he's so negative. He never has anything positive to say about anybody or anything. Negativity all the way down the line. That's what made me feel that he didn't win. He came off well tonight because he wasn't all negative. He had some good things to say; he even joked a little bit. You saw a sort of human charm to him.

Male 1: People want to see people up there, not statistics and knowledge. They really want to see the human side of them.

Female 1: Yeah, they do.

Male 2: And if you look at the two candidates as humans, just as who would you like to break bread with, you're not going to want to break bread with Dole. Dole is the old-style paradigm. The thing is, there are still a lot of voters who feel that politicians need to be staunch and stern, but that is all a stereotype, and that has been broken, due to all the technology. People would rather see somebody be human than somebody who just says, "Trust my word; I keep my word."

Female 2: But how do you know whether they are coming clean with the truth or not?

Male 2: People have learned over the many decades of presidential candidates that none of them really tell the entire truth in any case. So what difference does it make if you vote for somebody who you think is lying as opposed to somebody who may or may not be lying? They're both lying in some way anyway, so vote for the guy who's been there already, who's done at least some things that have been positive for the country, who seems presidential. The economy is doing well. To say, "Vote for me, because I keep my word," doesn't mean anything anyway, because they don't keep their word.

Keeping their word was usually associated with issues—whether or not they followed through on campaign promises or what they did to promote issues of importance to the public. The major issues that groups wanted discussed in the campaigns are presented in a later section, but it is important to also relate issues to image as the image/issue dichotomy theory suggests. In 1996, it was clear that the two have a synergistic relationship. A woman in Nashville equated record with truthfulness when she analyzed Dole's record and brought in past knowledge to what was said in the debate: "Dole's past records show he has been inconsistent on a lot of issues like education. It's mainly education that I feel like he didn't tell the truth about, yet he still keeps saying he's a man that keeps his promises or whatever. But according to the newspapers, every one that I've read, it's always been the same thing, that he's trying to cut education, and he kept saying he was trying to make it better." As the issue discussion continued, another woman in the group took the analysis another step to interpret how issue positions reveal attitudes about the public:

> I'd like it brought out more as to why the Republicans don't seem more humanitarian as far as trying to extend a little bit more to help people less fortunate than themselves and from what I heard in the past, that's not really their agenda. They're more about economics. I think when you deal with economics you have to deal with people. I think that's why Bob Dole does not come across that well with people; he doesn't have a natural love for all people.

A man in Cape Girardeau, Missouri, gave a lengthy analysis of the issues and how they related to his perception of the candidates that got to the heart of the issue/image dichotomy:

> There is certainly concern about the trustworthiness of the people who are in the highest political position. No question about that. There are also questions, however, about the policies each would bring with him. A debate like this not only helps make clear the feelings that you may have about a candidate, about his intelligence and his character...but as well the baggage—either positive or negative—that comes with him as a consequence of the positions of the political party he represents.... The issues have been well hashed in this country for some time. Nothing new there, but [there was] a new impression about the principal figures as a consequence of these exchanges.

Examination of a record was further discussed as it relates to the scrutiny that one undergoes as a candidate. A group in Winston-Salem, North Carolina, noted that a sitting president is going to have far more to scrutinize than will a senator and that the apples and oranges comparisons create problems for viewers in their analyses:

There's a very big difference though in comparing a role as senator to a role as president. When you are president, you are in the spotlight 24–7, and somebody is going to pick up on a 5-word sentence that contradicts everything you've been trying to say, and will bring that out. A senator is not under that kind of scrutiny. The scope of the spotlight is very different, so it's very hard to compare track records of a senator and a president.

The differences between individuals who have held an executive office and senators also cropped up in a discussion about the candidates' ability to relate to people—a character trait that viewers were seeking from the men who were running for president. Two men in Kansas City, Missouri, were discussing Dole's attempts to related to the average American and one cited the advantage that governors have over senators in that arena with this exchange:

Male 1:   He's trying to convince Americans that he can relate, but he's been inside closed doors for the last thirty years.... His life is not like the average American's life.

Male 2:   That's an advantage a governor has. Governors have more contact with the people.

Relating, however, is not the same as "walking a mile" in someone's shoes. Groups discussed the need to have someone in the White House who understands the lives of average Americans. Individuals whose background was not that of a middle class white American male wondered aloud if a candidate could relate to America's diversity. A woman in College Park, Maryland, spoke to the issue in this way:

I know I'm never going to get a President who is like me, who understands me. I know I'm never going to get an Asian woman to become President of the United States. I know this. I know Clinton doesn't—he may say he knows the American people—[but] he doesn't know me. He doesn't know my culture, doesn't know my family; he doesn't know any of us. He knows what he is. He grew up middle class, lower middle class. He knows what they want. He knows what he wants. He knows what the people like him want. So for me to say I want someone who knows me in the Presidency, I would be so naive to say that.... So I'm not going to say anything like that. I want someone who's smart enough to win, who can get himself in the Presidency and succeed.

In the end, that is what most of the viewers wanted—someone who could succeed in the office and make a difference in their lives. As the analysis of 1996 demonstrates, a great deal of thought went into determining what does make a successful president and what constitutes presidential character. The same was true for the participants in 2000 and 2004.

2000 Bush-Gore Debates

The 2000 Bush-Gore debates produced some of the best examples of the visceral nature of "leadership" qualities and the highly charged reactions viewers can have to the candidates. The majority of comments related to character, image, and style applied to Vice President Gore. For example, Al Gore's behavior in the first debate that included aggressive verbal behaviors such as interruptions and nonverbal reactions to Governor Bush, such as sighing, provoked considerable negative response like this comment from a woman in St. Clair Shores, Michigan: "I would like to say that Mr. Gore's behavior was atrocious. I know that the First Amendment allows everyone freedom of speech and of expression, but his child-like behavior diminished the stature of the debates and the election process." An e-mail analyzing all three presidential debates provided a similar reaction: "Perhaps, Lehrer did us a favor by letting Al Gore steamroll over him in the first debate. It enabled Al Gore to show us what an ass he really is." Another e-mail writer was equally irritated with Gore's disregard for the rules but went further than simply venting to explain what the behavior indicated to him about trustworthiness: "If a candidate is going to break the rules (that he helped set up) that tells me that he will probably break the rules if he gets into office. What we need is an honest president who will follow proper procedures." Underlying that comment was an implication that Bill Clinton's trustworthiness problems were shadowing Gore, and a man in Boston came out and said what others were undoubtedly thinking: "I don't know how people can look at Al Gore without thinking about the Bill Clinton incident." A woman in the same Boston group after the first debate was more concerned with what debate behaviors might reveal about presidential style, especially diplomacy skills:

> One thing I think concerning Gore is that it seems he was belligerent at times. I thought it was plain. He was belligerent and petty. That sort of worries me a little in terms of diplomacy. If this is how he acts against an adversary, it sort of concerns me that he tends to zero in on some type of tiny detail and lose the big picture....he went for petty fighting, you know, about minutiae. So that really concerns me. I do not know what sort of impact that will have on his foreign relations, to be honest.

Gore notably changed his behavior for the second debate and there were comments about the change. A group in Winston-Salem, North Carolina, was discussing the importance of issues in judging a candidate's character when one man provided insight into the image/issue relationship with this analysis of Gore's transformation:

> After the first debate I think Gore lost a lot of credibility, and apparently he's better than everyone and having this snotty attitude. But from this debate, I don't know how much of it was his own adjusting or his campaign's coaching him on it, but he seemed a lot more relaxed. He wasn't interrupting. He didn't appear standoffish or anything like that, and I think that made his issues be looked upon a lot better. In the first debate, I think his attitude took away from a lot of what he was saying, and since he was acting a lot more mature in this debate, more was actually focused on what he was actually saying.

Gore's transformation was noticed by others, but some did not change their initial views. A participant in a St. Louis Elderhostel commented after the last debate of 2000 that:

I saw three different Gores in the debates. The first one, combative, a more aggressive type individual. The second, apparently, his handlers and all these people that are really expert in body language and all of that who are their advisors told him, "Hey, let's not do that anymore. People don't seem to like that. Let's calm it down." So the second one, here he's a very passive man that was sitting there and very passive. He dropped in the polls. So Bush comes ahead. The third debate, here he comes out very aggressive, and sometimes I thought that aggressiveness was not really assertiveness. I thought it was almost being pompous.

Two individuals in Boston also discussed Gore's personality and its shortcomings, but one of them reached a different conclusion about what is important in judging character:

Female: I would like to see Gore sort of personalize himself towards the American people and he did not really do that. He was very stoic, and there was just a wall there that you could not really penetrate.

Male: We need somebody in there who can get the job done. I really, I think it would be nice to have a likeable person, but can you come through on your word? When Gore said, "I will not let you down," I liked that part in his speech. I mean that is character.

As happened in 1996, the town hall debate provided a means for viewers to judge character based on how the candidates reacted to average citizens as opposed to one another. Gore's behavior was criticized on that front as well with a good example coming from a man who identified himself in an e-mail as a pastor from Ansonia, Pennsylvania. He looked at the overlap of Gore's agenda and the public's in making his assessment:

Gore was more interested in presenting his agenda on the issues and attacking Bush than in answering the people's questions. Bush always addressed each person personally by name before he answered the question. However, Gore did not address any of the questioners by name.... Bush appeared to be more personable, honest, and forthright; while Gore was in-your-face and deliberately putting his agenda before the questions as evidenced in the end when Gore had to answer the person's question in his closing remark!

While most of the comments about Gore's behavior were negative, there were some who compared the two candidates and reached a different conclusion based on a variety of nonverbal messages as this e-mail sender did:

I envisioned both Vice-Pres. Gore and Mr. Bush in President Clinton's place. Mr. Bush just did not come into focus. And after watching and listening to Bush during tonight's debate, I am even more certain. Bush just does not project a Presidential image. He is smug and appears to be the pseudo-school yard bully. The type that needs the urging of the other kids on the playground in order to summon the courage to bully another classmate. His shoulders are rounded and he walks as if he has a six shooter on his hip that he might draw at any minute. He doesn't have the stature, honed by years of experience, to be the President.... I don't want someone who is a good ole boy that could sit in a bar and have a beer with the other good ole boys.

Two women in the St. Louis Elderhostel had similar and more succinct comparisons based on the town hall debate, and they used a different standard of judgment than the pastor from Pennsylvania when one expressed the belief that "Gore looked a lot more comfortable last night, and I thought Bush looked a lot more scared. You know, he wasn't sure whether he was going to be prepared for the questions from the people. But that's who he's going to have to answer to." The other noted that "When I saw Bush's reaction to the question that they asked about the death penalty in his state that was the first time that I really felt that I saw Bush react without being coached. I thought that he felt really shaken by that question. And it was a real question. I appreciated having that visual response."

The visual cues were important in 2000 just as they were in 1996 because "what you get from this is this sort of 'grace under fire'—who under tremendous pressure performs the best and the analogy is that they will perform under pressure as president" as a man in Lawrence, Kansas, put it. Equally important were policy discussions and what they revealed about character. The Boston group had one of the best examples of a discussion that connected issues and metamessages to perceptions of candidates. It includes the complaint heard in 1996 about the candidate's abilities to understand what the public experiences as well as more specific issue examples and what they reflected about the candidates' character:

Female 1: I was keeping track of things like how many times Gore said positive things about Bush, which was six times. Bush said only one positive thing about Gore and at least eight character attacks. There were three phrases that I wrote down from both of them that I found sort of chilling. One thing that Bush said at one point was "cultural pollution." Something that Gore said was "inappropriate entertainment," which sounded in line with Tipper Gore's calling for censorship in music. A third thing was "K through 12 diagnostic tools" which Bush mentioned. This sounded like the kind of tracking thing they do in schools where they take very young people and decide who are going to be the smartest ones and who are not, which smacks of racism and classism in this country.... They just slipped out with the candidates not noticing, which I think are important things to look out for because that is who the candidates actually are, when they are not paying attention.

Female 2: I find it very difficult to look at people who come from a very high class and upper class education, family background, all the kind of baggage that comes with that, and really, actually believe that one, they understand what it is to be middle class and all the kind of stuff that comes with that, and two that they can actually do something about it. I do not know. Maybe that is just me. But that is one thing I find difficult with these two candidates.

Male 1: Well, they can do something about it, I mean, if they pass their laws through Congress and it is not that easy if you have a Democratic president and a Republican Congress. You can have a lot of problems. Bush is talking a lot about working with the Democrats and the Republicans.

Male 2: Well, Bush mentioned that he has two children that go to public school. That shows that he actually cares about his constituents.

Male 3: I was surprised to see Bush get sort of blind-sided in terms of foreign policy, suggesting that he could very easily have simply gone into an alliance with Russia....I think that is someplace where he has been very short-sighted....So I don't think Bush was really mindful when he said, "here's an idea" of what exactly that would entail. That is something that a president would need to think about.

Bush definitely had to think about foreign policy more than anyone would have imagined in 2000 and in very different ways than other presidents had, as Chris Wallace acknowledged. The fact that it was Bush making decisions about 9/11 rather than Gore was attributed by some to Gore's debate performance. As the Racine Group concluded in its analysis of the 2000 debates and Gore's relational style, "The media zeroed in on these relational gaffes, and Gore's substantive edge [in the polls] slipped away."[17] Comments from DebateWatch groups provide insights as to why just as they explained why the character issue did not work against Clinton in 1996. In 2004, less attention was given to character discussion than in the other years as discussion of the war and the failing economy dominated. However, the discussion that did take place continued to emphasize the relationship between issues and judgments of character, and nonverbal behaviors were once again topics of discussion.

2004 Bush-Kerry Debates

Ostensibly, the 2004 debates had more parallels with those of 1996 than those of 2000. There was an incumbent president. The challenger was a long-serving senator with a military service record. There were questions of character raised against the Democrat. But there were also significant differences. The race was not a foregone conclusion as in 1996. The incumbent president was not popular. Foreign policy was on the top of everyone's list of important issues unlike it had been since the fall of the Soviet Union. The economy was faltering. The country's prestige in the world was damaged as a result of the invasion of Iraq. Finally, unlike 1996, the debates had the potential to make a difference as they had in 2000.

In a predebate discussion of the debates on PBS, syndicated columnist Mark Shields provided the context for the debates when asked by news anchor Margaret Warner how much was riding on the match-ups: "Oh, I think an awful lot is riding on it, especially for John Kerry. I mean, over the last six to eight weeks the dynamic of the race has been changed by—effectively by the Bush campaign, they've made it a referendum on John Kerry rather than a referendum on the incumbent."[18] Character had become a major issue for John Kerry, and at the heart of it was a series of advertisements from a group called Swift Boat Veterans for Truth that claimed on its Web site and in its advertising that "John Kerry misrepresented his record and ours in Vietnam and therefore exhibits serious flaws in character and lacks the potential to lead."[19] Kerry was also accused of "flip-flopping" on several key issues and his famous statement, "I actually did vote for the $87 billion [supplemental appropriations for Afghanistan and Iraq] before I voted against it." The flip-flop issue was one that was listed in the introduction to this chapter as something that a DebateWatch participant expected to sort out—he was not alone.

In general, there was a different tone to the comments about character and leadership. Whereas participants in 1996 and 2000 had definite reactions to each candidate, there was considerable ambivalence expressed in 2004. Comments showed more balance and even internal struggles to sort out both men's strengths and weaknesses, as this excerpt from DeLand, Florida, illustrates:

Female: It really bothered me that when Kerry would respond, Bush would be looking off somewhere else or he would be smirking a little bit to himself. And Kerry did it a little bit too, but I noticed it much more with President Bush. That bothered me because it just seemed like a lack of respect. It is like even if you don't agree with the guy or don't agree with his policies, and yeah, he is trying to take your job, but he went to Vietnam and he was a Senator for twenty years, and that is pretty impressive to keep getting elected for that long. You should show at least respect and that touched me a little bit. But I wouldn't vote because of what President Bush looked like in the debate.

Male: The way that Bush really just leapt out of his chair is definitely going to pose a lot of questions depending on which side you look at it. From the left side they say "you know, he is just trying to attack Kerry and trying to get back to this issue quickly." The right side might say, "He is very passionate about this whole issue and he wanted to present his case; he wanted to defend himself from what Kerry had said."

A woman in Providence, Rhode Island, was obviously looking for something from John Kerry to counter her concerns about President Bush's leadership style and her comments reflect her attempts at self-persuasion: "I think the style I saw from Bush is the same old same old. Shooting from the hip, that jerkiness. That worries me when you have to make important decisions, and I kept writing 'Kerry's responses seem to be reflective.' Maybe they weren't; maybe they were studied. But he seemed to be in control of his responses. So from the standpoint of that, it reinforced my feeling that he would be a more reasoned leader." Another woman in the group was trying to reconcile her acknowledgement of President Bush's successes with what she was seeing nonverbally in the debate as she worked through reaching a vote choice:

I think that Kerry handles the question with more polish and command of the language and also with self-control. My concern is Mr. Bush is a smart man, and he has proven himself as an effective leader. But he does not strike me as someone who can manage a crisis unless he has the kind of people around him telling him what to do. That whole demeanor of being terrified of losing, it is about confidence and all situations of crisis threatening worries me about how he carries himself. The fact Kerry would handle with calm and reserve I think is the right direction. I think if it gets hot, he can handle it. He can marshal the forces.

The comment about "polish and command of the language" reflected the impact of four years of countless jokes about President Bush's inarticulateness. The metamessage for many was that Bush's consistent mangling of the English language reflected something about his intelligence. A man in Staunton, Virginia, was using the debate to confirm or deny that perception, as he explained that "One of the reasons I watched the debate was because I had such a negative view of George Bush that I wanted to see if that view was borne out by seeing the actual performance.... My general view of his abilities has been improved by having watched the debate, and I thought—not to be condescending—but I thought he was a brighter person than I anticipated him to be."

While the debates produced more positive feelings about candidates for some viewers, they had the opposite effect for others. Issue positions and metamessages contributed to some of the reactions as a woman in Madison, Wisconsin, explained:

> I found that I disliked Senator Kerry more after the debate than before. When people would ask him things about abortion or he was talking about that he said how deeply he respected the person and, you'll forgive me, but I had this irrelevant thought from the movies about how this is what men say before or after sex in the morning. I didn't like the word "stronger" being used in connection with the United States. I think to have a stronger America is what led us into this quagmire. I guess I had forgotten that he is in favor of welfare reform.

President Bush also received scrutiny for the way he answered questions from the group in Madison as one man's comments indicate: "Bush was defensive about things like he was guilty or feeling guilty about some of the decisions that he made and he couldn't admit any wrongdoing or any mistakes that he made except for maybe some appointment. So I don't think that he really had that sense of integrity because he didn't answer some of the questions that it would be okay to admit mistakes about and he's not willing to do that."

Most participants were far more guarded than the two individuals in Madison in revealing who they preferred, but they made it clear that they were making judgments based on nonverbal behaviors and the way that questions were answered. A man in Providence, Rhode Island, had clear criteria for gauging character and it was "to look and see who's actually answering the questions and who's not. That helps me form an opinion on what type of character this person has.... What their answer is does not matter to me as much as did they answer at all. That tells me more about their character than what their answer was." A man in Madison was also less concerned about the answers and was more interested in "the way that their personalities worked and the way that they dealt with problems." The relationship between personality and problem solving was also explored in DeLand, Florida, as represented by this analysis:

> Personality does influence some of how they execute policy and I think it is very clear from just watching the debates that the two have their different personalities. And I think that usually is going to influence how they relate to people, how they relate to foreign leaders, how they relate to their cabinet and all the other things related to foreign policy. So direct cause and effect...and less emphasis on character because character has a kind of virtue attachment to it or like a value attachment to it that I don't think is as relevant.

The final comment is similar to those heard in other years that expressed a desire to separate "moral" issues or "virtues" from less obviously judgmental qualities such as personality and style. Although five of the six presidential candidates were different, the comments about them and explanations of how evaluations were made were consistent. Many of the conclusions reached about the candidates were based on nonverbal messages, and interpretations were made with confidence as a woman in College Station, Texas, explained: "The nonverbals said a lot to me, the way they were reacting to each other. I'm not going to point out anyone in particular that I thought was any worse or any better than the other but I could tell by just looking."

Because the debates are televised and most people watch them, there is a great deal of "just looking" that contributes to what someone learns from debates. Chapter six goes into more depth on visual elements in the debates. This chapter's title suggests that people are not just looking, but they are searching for something. When all of the comments about character, image, personality, style, or leadership are put together, what they are searching for is someone who represents most closely the qualities associated with the presidency. Chapter two cited research by communication scholar Edward Hinck whose analysis of presidential debates concluded that they provide an opportunity for candidates to "enact" the presidency or show the presidential qualities they would exhibit if elected. An online participant from Denver in the 1996 DebateWatch hosted by the Interactive Distance Training Network provided one of the most succinct explanations of how debaters "enact" the presidency when he wrote that "just from the body language and the response, the whole factor of charisma is very, very important. You have to realize, these are individuals who are going to be speaking out on foreign affairs and very, very important issues, where confidence is a factor. If you're sitting in a debate, and you tremble, and you stammer, and you can't finish your thoughts, I think that's a good indicator of how well you're going to do." The examples from the three sets of debates were simply that—examples—of the numerous discussions groups had about the qualities they were seeking in a president. The word "character" was commonly used even if the groups didn't want moderators or candidates using it, and, thus, a public agenda was clear from these discussions. Most participants achieved gratification in terms of identifying the presence or absence of characteristics they were seeking, and the relationship between image and issues was evident from the analysis the participants applied.

Since issue discussions dominated the discussions and were the major emphasis of the facilitator's reports and many e-mails, the next section addresses the importance of issues in the debates and tracks the changing landscape in what was deemed important.

DO ISSUES MATTER?

Media Tenor research cited in chapter two indicated that 9 out of 10 statements in the 2004 presidential debates were issue oriented. Other research cited from previous debates found similar proportions. Transcripts from DebateWatch are also heavily issue-oriented. Questions about expectations yielded issue responses and specific questions about the usefulness of questions elicited considerable issue discussion. As indicated in the previous section on character, there is also a close relationship between issues and the images that candidates project. Further, comments such as "The American people want to know issues. They don't want to know about things that aren't relevant to them" (Clarksville, Arkansas); "Nothing is irrelevant. I think there is no way that a question can be deemed irrelevant or unimportant because there is someone out there who has not heard anything about either of these candidates and so whatever questions comes up, it is informative for somebody" (Providence, Rhode Island); and "I think the people [in the town hall audience] did a good job of focusing on the concerns that everyday Americans have" (Kansas City, Missouri) clearly indicate that issue content is important to viewers.

Participants were very clear that the debates should emphasize items on the public agenda. In addition to the comments that character questions were less important than policy questions, there were also comments about topics raised in the debates by either the moderators or the candidates that were not at the top of the public's agenda. In 1996 for example, foreign policy did not appear on the top five list of most useful topics discussed in the debates, and a man in Nashville reacted to Bob Dole's complaint about a lack of foreign policy topics this way: "Dole's comment near the end, he wished there'd been more foreign policy questions, this is consistent with what we saw tonight, it is consistent with all the polls. When people are asked, 'what do you care about?,' foreign policy is way down on the list." There were also objections to what were considered "soft ball" questions such as the one Bob Schieffer asked in the final debate in 2004 about what they had learned from the women in their lives, their mothers, wives, and daughters. A woman in Providence, Rhode Island, summarized the thinking of others who listed it as an irrelevant question: "I think asking them both about the women in their lives was irrelevant frankly. I would much rather have had him say, 'In the first three months of your presidency what is your action plan? In the next six months what are you going to do?' It was too soft. Too soft." The reason behind the objection to this type of question is obvious in light of the previous discussion in the chapter on how insight into personality or character is achieved. When people believe that they are capable of detecting character or personality traits without specific questions, they don't want to "waste" a question that could be used for a substantive topic. Results from facilitator reports demonstrate that there were always topics that needed more depth of discussion or topics that needed to be discussed even after a series of three or four debates.

Because there are expectations for what is going to be learned—and issue knowledge is usually at the top of the list—the DebateWatch project tracked the issues the public wanted to hear about, what issues they thought were important, what issues they thought were irrelevant, and what they still wanted to learn about after each of the debates. The results for each year are given in the next section along with an analysis of the similarities and differences across the three years.

SUGGESTED TOPICS

As indicated in chapter three, a phone survey was conducted prior to the 1996 debates to learn what issues voters thought should be discussed in the debates. Using randomly generated numbers, researchers contacted 244 individuals. The survey group was composed of 56.1 percent females and 43.5 percent males. The ages of the group were as follows: 6.7 percent were 18 to 24 years old, 23.1 percent were 25 to 34, 21.8 percent were 35 to 44, 18.1 percent were 45 to 54, and the remaining 30.2 percent were over 55. All but 10.5 percent were registered voters and of those who weren't, 52 percent planned to register before the election. Party affiliation was nearly equal, with 32.6 percent registered as Republicans, 35.6 percent registered as Democrats, and the remaining 31.8 percent unaffiliated. Nearly 32 percent had a high school education or less. Thirty-four percent had some college or an associate's degree, 18.4 percent had college degrees, and 13.9 percent had some postbaccalaureate work or a degree. The remaining 2.5 percent did not provide educational background. Forty-nine percent were employed full time and 18.3 percent were retired. The remaining respondents were employed part-time or were full-time homemakers. Of those providing information on ethnicity, 80.7 percent were white, 8.8 percent were African American, 1.3 percent were Asian, 5 percent were mixed race, and 4.2 percent listed themselves as other. Seventeen respondents indicated Hispanic ethnicity either exclusively or in combination with another race. A final demographic question addressed income, and 55.5 percent of the respondents earned under $40,000 with the greatest number earning $25,000–$39,999 (28.4% of the total group). This group was also highly engaged in the political process and 91.3 percent indicated that they planned to watch the debates.

Participants were asked to identify issues they wanted discussed and to also provide a question they would like to have asked in the debates. The major issues were the economy, including taxes, the budget, and jobs; education—both K–12 and higher education; crime, including drugs and gun control; health care and Social Security; foreign policy and military; social issues such as abortion and welfare; morality/character and religion and how they relate to the candidates; elections and cynicism; and general questions about legislative priorities or administrative style. Survey respondents were also given an opportunity to suggest a question they wanted asked in the debates. Some examples of the questions citizens would have asked included: What do you feel would be the most important think you could do to affect our children's education? Why is your economic plan better than your opponent's? In layman's terms, what would you do to get a balanced budget and lower taxes? What is the most important thing you could do in your administration that you could look back on and say "Only I could have done it"? What qualifies you to relate to the average American?

What is interesting about the proposed questions is that they are largely "process" questions. In other words, they ask how the president will go about doing something more than asking for the details of a proposal. The metamessage is "How would you lead?" Comments in chapter four indicated that facts and figures are viewed with skepticism—several people suggested instant "fact checks." A man in Grand Forks, North Dakota, addressed the relationship between facts and figures and character when he opined that "All the numbers that were thrown out make me wonder, where is the truth? Bob Dole said that people are watching the debates to find the truth, but I don't think that there's any truth in that.... if you really want to find the truth, then you'll have to do some research to see what the numbers are and what the facts are. They'll both manipulate them, but that's the game." Thus, asking questions that keep statistics and details to a minimum and concentrating on underlying ideology for a policy or a strategy to get it through Congress would more likely be viewed as helpful. A man in Clarksville, Arkansas, expressed his frustration with a lack of "how" in candidates' responses when he evaluated the Clinton and Dole tax plans: "I guess there is so much that they are promising—tax cuts and balanced budget and all that—and yet nobody can sit there and tell you what they're going to do." Finally, the logic behind the difference in the types of questions the public might ask and a moderator asks was explained by a woman in St. Louis, Missouri, in 2000, who believed that the public is looking for a philosophy of government: "How people react to them is going to depend upon how they feel about the approach to the federal government. Do they want someone who paints with a broad brush or somebody who wanted to be very interested in more of the details?"

The 2004 CPD online predebate survey also collected specific data related to suggested debate topic areas. The top six were economic issues, health and health care, education, Iraq and national security, environment and energy, and civil rights and liberties. The survey did not ask for specific questions. There are two interesting observations that can be made about the 2004 list. The first is that Iraq and national security came in fourth even though national security was a major issue on the candidates' and public's agendas and the focus of the Bush campaign was on who was better able to lead in war time. The second is that many of the issues that people wanted addressed were similar to those in 1996, such as economic issues, education, and health care, and foreign policy, suggesting that no matter how much things change, they truly do stay the same. Further analysis of the 2004 results follows in the next section.

MOST USEFUL, LEAST USEFUL, AND UNTAPPED TOPICS

In 1996, participants identified the five most useful topics as tax reform, education, the economy, social issues (e.g., race relations, affirmative action), and health care. In 2000, education, health care, crime (including gun control), taxes, social issues (abortion, civil rights, and gay rights) topped the list. In 2004, Iraq and national security topped the list for three of the four debates. Given that it was fourth on the list in the predebate survey of suggested topics, the shift represents an example of an issue gaining great salience as a result of the debate. The research by Levasseur and Carlin and Carlin et al. cited in chapter two provides some insight into the shift in priorities. Most people tend to concentrate on issues that affect their daily lives. While national security is something that affects everyone, the pocket book issues have greater salience. Questions and answers about Iraq and national security emphasized strategy and time lines for withdrawal and the region's stability. While the underlying current was whether or not we were safe from other attacks on our shores, the majority of the technical issues didn't hit home. Questions and responses that relate foreign policy to domestic conditions will have more salience because people do concentrate on what is in front of them. Even if some viewers didn't originally see Iraq and national security as a top three issue, debates can bring the agendas closer when connections are made and the ramification of policies are clear. With respect to Iraq and national security, the topic was on the predebate list but with 13 percent listing it as a top issue as opposed to the 23 percent who found it the most important topic in the third presidential debate. By the conclusion of the debates, national security was back to having 14 percent of the participants wanting to hear more.

Groups were asked which topics were least useful or irrelevant. It is important to note here that some of the topics that were listed were not necessarily unimportant in and of themselves, but participants indicated that the lack of depth in the analysis contributed to their selection of a given topic. The respondents in 1996 most frequently indicated character, military issues (e.g., gays in the military, Star Wars), and lifestyle choices. In 2000, questions specifically about character again were listed most frequently, followed by agriculture, campaign finance reform, abortion, and taxes. It is significant to note that some of the topics that appeared on the list of least useful or irrelevant did come from the town hall meeting. In 2004, the facilitator's report on the CPD Web site did not include the question about least useful topics. The National Communication Association survey did, however. The results from that sample of the total DebateWatch population listed the questions about wives and daughters of the candidates, the candidates' faith, homosexuality, and the flu shot shortage as the least useful or irrelevant.

Facilitator reports also asked for a listing of topics that participants wanted to hear discussed in future debates (the question was asked after each debate thus providing an opportunity for publication of the results prior to the end of the debate series) or what issues they still believed needed to be discussed throughout the remainder of the campaign (asked after the last debate). In 1996, abortion, education, foreign policy, social issues, and ideological differences (role or size of government and views of the presidency) were listed most frequently. The questions on ideology and views of the presidency were especially noteworthy because they were consistent with the types of questions the predebate survey group wanted asked. In 2000, foreign policy, education, crime (including gun control and capital punishment), abortion, and environment were listed. In 2004, the economy was listed most frequently, followed by health care, national security, education, environment and energy, and Social Security. As was the case with the most and least relevant or important topics, what remained to be explored in more depth was also consistent across debates.

A discussion from College Station, Texas, in 2004 after the final debate illustrates how seriously groups took the discussion of issues and how they used issues to form judgments about the candidates that would affect their votes. In response to the question regarding the topics that were most helpful to them, this discussion ensued:

Female 1:   Abortion, it's always a hard to win subject, but its one of those particulars that stood out to me as a specific to see their viewpoint on it and where they stand and what morals and ethics they have which is going to help me to chose which president or which candidate to pick.

Male 1:   Her thing right there, I thought one man up there had a viewpoint and the other one, really, you don't know where he stood on it.

Male 2:   I think the war on terror and the war in Iraq is definitely the focus of the total election. Those issues are very very important. But this election is hinging on our foreign policy right now.... I think that's really going to determine who in the end do you like better about the war?...your interpretation of that is going to ultimately affect your vote.

Female 2:   I think national security is number one...and how the candidate or president is keeping his faith, I think is number one.

When the discussion then moved to issues that still remained to be explored before Election Day, this dialogue indicated that it might not be so important to have the topics discussed because the group members could extrapolate the answers based on what they had seen and heard:

Male 1:   I had one they didn't discuss—gay marriage and also polygamy. That is something that definitely needs to be brought up on the domestic agenda.

Male 2:   Well I think those two things are probably covered under the fact of which one you want to vote for. One of them is going to be for social programs and socialist things and one of them is going to be for states rights and less government

In the end, then, what remains for the candidates to say after the debates may be less important because of the debates themselves and what is read between the lines.

CONCLUSION

The reactions to questions of character that were quoted in the *New York Times* were not an anomaly that could be attributed to Bill Clinton's charisma or a solid economy. Even when character was an issue, as it was in 2000 with Vice President

Gore, and in 2004 with both candidates, each in his own way, the public didn't want the moderator to raise the issue. It is clear that viewers do have their ways of discerning a person's suitability for the highest office in the land. In addition to the transcripts and e-mails, the facilitators' reports consistently listed character questions among the least useful, even when a significant part of discussions was devoted to the topic.

At the same time that viewers knew what they didn't want asked, they knew what they did want to hear. Debate viewers are issue-oriented and they have a clear agenda. However, they are willing to adjust their agendas based on what they learn from the debates. In response to the question the chapter's title asks—what matters to voters?—the answer has to include an element of peace of mind, in addition to discerning fitness for office or policy positions. It was clear that viewers want insight into the candidates' human qualities, but what they saw may have convinced them that the person didn't have what it took to meet the demands of the office. They also wanted some assurance that the candidates understand the people they want to lead. Most importantly, they wanted to know in their own minds that they have made a choice that is reasoned and comfortable. Regardless of whether it is partisan loyalties or a single issue or simply a desire for someone or something different that motivates a voter to select one candidate over another, voters use debates to reduce any dissonance they have or to make them feel even better about a choice with which they are already comfortable. Questions, issues, and answers help them find what they are seeking, but in the end, what they discern from interactions and demeanor within the high stress context of a debate is what provides the most insight.

Chapter Six

Citizen Talk beyond the Candidates and Issues

While the DebateWatch research project focused primarily on the debates and how to improve them as a voter education tool, questions addressed to the groups went beyond the formats, the candidates, and the issues. In keeping with the notion of a third agenda—the public's agenda—in the debate process, participants were free to raise whatever issues they wanted about the debates, campaigns, the media, and politics. This chapter includes comments on a variety of subjects, many of which developed organically from the discussions. The chapter begins with comments about the visual presentation of the candidates via shot selection and then moves to a larger discussion of the comparative educational value of debates versus other information sources and concludes with the benefits of DebateWatch participation.

VISUALIZING THE CANDIDATES

After the Lincoln-Douglas debates, one of the most commonly cited pieces of political debate history is the visual impact of the Kennedy-Nixon debates. Much has been written about Richard Nixon's makeup, the sweat on his brow, the color of his suit against the stage background, his facial expressions of discomfort with some of the questions, and his gaunt look after hospitalization for a staph infection. His appearance was contrasted with that of a confident, tan, and robust-looking John Kennedy. An oft repeated "fact" is that those who watched the first debate thought Kennedy won and those who listened thought Nixon won. Scholarly researchers have investigated this finding to determine if it is factual or is a myth that endures primarily through repetition rather than substantive evidence. There was, in fact, only one study conducted to compare radio listeners with television viewers and it had a relatively small number of subjects.[1] Two communication scholars, David Vancil and Sue Pendell, disputed the sufficiency of the sample size and the overall evidence to make the claim of a difference.[2] However, political debate scholar Sidney Kraus concluded that the available research supported the claim.[3] The reality may be somewhere in between the two positions in that some radio listeners beyond the group surveyed undoubtedly "heard" a different debate performance than those who heard but also saw the nonverbal messages that accompanied the televised version.

Regardless of how widespread the difference in perceptions between television viewers and radio listeners was in 1960, debate viewers do notice the candidates' nonverbal behaviors and they rely on them for insights into the candidates' character, as the previous chapter indicated. Communication researchers Susan Hellweg, Michael Pfau, and Steven Brydon concluded in their study of presidential debates that "the visual component of television communication dwarfs the verbal dimension."[4] As a result of the medium's power, several political communication scholars analyzed the visual elements of political debates, not in terms of candidates' nonverbal behaviors, but from the perspective of camera angles and shot selection. Content analyses of camera angles, reaction shots, split screens, or who is in a shot have suggested that some candidates are possibly advantaged over others. Robert Tiemens, for example, analyzed the 1976 Carter-Ford debates and concluded that Carter was shown smiling more than Ford was, and the overall composition of Carter's shots showed more direct eye contact and presented him more positively.[5] John Morello conducted a similar analysis on the 1976, 1984, and 1988 debates to determine if the shot selection suggested more clash between the candidates through the use of reaction shots, close ups, or two shots (using a wide angle shot of both candidates rather than a split screen) than what was actually contained in the verbal transcript. He concluded that across the three debate cycles he studied, shot selection to create a sense of conflict or clash did not always correspond with the actual degree of clash found in the transcript.[6] Other researchers have reached different conclusions about the evenness of coverage in their analyses,[7] but the fact remains that visuals attract attention and people form opinions of candidates based on them.

Proof of the recognition of the camera's power to influence is found in the Memoranda of Understanding (MOU) that came out of the quadrennial debate over the debates. The agreements typically have references to the way that the candidates are to be shown on camera. The 2004 MOU was similar to those of previous years in its instruction to the networks that "TV coverage will be limited to the candidate speaking. There will be no TV cutaways to any candidate who is not responding to a question.... The camera located at the rear of the stage shall be used only to take shots of the moderator."[8] However, since the networks are not a party to the agreement, they tend to ignore the candidates' dictates and show what they want to show to create more visual interest. CPD Co-Chairman Frank Fahrenkopf gave a realistic assessment of the agreement's ability to influence the networks when he told *The New York Times* that "the restrictions on what the networks can show are unenforceable."[9]

Split Screens and Shot Selection

The MOU also outlines various production logistics. For example, there is a different network in charge of the cameras for each debate and every network uses the feed from that network's cameras. This is called a pooled feed. There are multiple cameras throughout the auditorium focusing on each candidate and the moderator from different angles with some cameras showing both candidates and others only one. The official producer selects which camera to show at any one time, but in recent years the networks don't use the pool director's choices. As a result, each network varies to some degree from the others in how the debate is broadcast. For example, in 2004, C-SPAN chose a split screen for the entire debate. Others showed a split screen—some vertical and some horizontal—for part of the debate and supplemented with reaction shots and two shots. Still others only used reaction shots and two shots. Some concentrated almost exclusively on the candidate who was speaking unless there was a reaction of major interest; others used shots with both candidates for a large part of a response. The end result was that variations in shot selection and use of the split screen did not produce an identical viewing experience for everyone who watched.

Group members picked up on the camera work and illustrated the point that communication scholars made regarding the impact of the camera on perceptions. Many found the split screen distracting and also noticed that its use was not even for each candidate. This comment from an Eckerd College Florida, Elderhostel participant in 1996 summarizes what was said by many others across the groups: "I was distressed at the amount of time they had the split screen on while Kemp was talking. Whereas, when Gore was talking it was very seldom on. Maybe it's not right, but it seems to me that the split screen is very disconcerting. You're watching how Gore reacts to these things and you're not listening too much to what Kemp was saying. I thought that was a fault of the production." A participant in Madison, Wisconsin, in 2004 had a similar reaction to the continuous use of a split screen:

> We watched the vice presidential debate where they had the split screen rather than have the cameraman decide to look for reaction shots. I mean they had the camera just on both individuals all the time with the same angle. I think that affects things too because of some of the cheap shots they took of Bush with the camera. Granted he made the expressions and everything, but it really calls attention to it to have the camera swoop over there and catch him at it.

C-SPAN's approach that lets the audience see what someone sitting in the debate hall would see—both candidates simultaneously—has a certain logic. However, it fails to consider that even if a person in the hall has the ability to view both candidates, that doesn't mean the person will actually focus on both for the entire debate. Television also magnifies behaviors and enlarges the candidate compared to what is seen from an audience member's seat. The reality is that these are mediated events. Just as the newspapers in Lincoln and Douglas's day provided transcripts that were influenced by the newspaper's political leanings or the stenographer's abilities, the camera mediates what takes place. It cannot replace the experience of "being there." The split screen is more balanced than randomly selected reaction shots or shots of the person not speaking while he or she is engaged in something such as looking at a watch or sighing. However it has downsides as the viewers indicated in the previous quotations and as a second theme reveals.

Media Bias

A second problem with production decisions according to DebateWatch participants was that they created a perception of media bias. The following e-mail was received after the 2000 town hall debate and is an example of comments about media bias that specifically relate to the production decisions:

> In regard to the manner in which the debate was photographed by video camera, it appeared that either the camera operator was biased against Gov. Bush, or did not know what he or she was doing. The divided screen was smaller for Gov Bush, often the view of him was blocked out completely or Gore was viewed behind Bush as Bush spoke. The background color for Bush was dark and poorly lit, while Gore had a wider screen, lighter background and more lighting, and he was never blocked from sight as was the Governor.

The expressions of bias are due in part to the fact that most viewers have a candidate choice prior to the debates and they bring their own biases to the event as well. They will see and hear what helps them confirm their prior leanings—including convictions about unfair media treatment of "their" candidate.

Positive Visual Attributes and Media Reports

While there were numerous complaints about the video production choices, there were some positive comments indicating that the visuals contributed to a better understanding of the candidate's character. The comments in chapter five about facial expressions, body language, and movement and what they suggested about character are a case in point. The more an audience can see, the more they can potentially learn. This reaction from a man at the Florida Elderhostel in 1996 who had some experience in the media further expressed the positive aspects of having the camera as a roving rather than a stationary eye:

> I think there's another way of looking at this [split screen]. The reaction of the other candidate to what is being said is often quite revealing and I was very interested as a former professional in television, to see how Kemp handled this, the two of them. You noticed that Gore was always attentive, always listening, always apparently paying attention to what Kemp was saying; whereas, Kemp, when Gore was speaking, was fiddling, looking to one side, his eyes going all over the place, which is a definite no-no. I can tell you, he allowed himself to look flustered.

Not only did the group members talk about the role the camera played in giving nuance the debate, but they also commented on the way the media reports about the visuals and the candidates' nonverbal behaviors that they capture. Two examples from 2004 illustrate. The first is from a discussion in DeLand, Florida, about the casual, seated format for the vice presidential debate. The group watched a telecast with the split screen and they detected far more body language than in past debates; they also made references to media coverage of visual aspects of the debates. One person commented that "I think body language was a huge part." This set off the following:

Male: Their writing got distracting, but all of them do that on purpose. This could be a new strategy this year. I don't remember that there was as much obvious note taking in the past.

Male 2:   It makes sure they look like they are better committed, but they are ripping and flipping papers.

Male 3:   It's part of the strategy because it's a cut-away shot. It's very important. It doomed Bush four years ago and he didn't do it in that election. But he was kind of ridiculed for it. He has been ridiculed since last week. And they were saying it because every time they show Kerry, he was writing notes.

It was not uncommon for discussions to include references to the past debates and reporting on them. A comment about camera work and the impact of visuals in 2004 demonstrates the power of the Internet as a media source. By way of context, there was a widely circulated photograph taken of President Bush's back from the camera that was only supposed to show the moderator. The photo fueled Internet speculation that he had a "box" with a receiver on his back and a listening device in his ear so that he could be coached on his answers. This rumor was mentioned in several groups. During a discussion of the formats and production qualities of each type of format after the town hall debate, this conversation ensued in Providence, Rhode Island:

Female 1:   Obviously they would have to agree to all of the formats so that is probably why you have what you have. It's a smorgasbord.

Male: That's why you have a producer and why you have a moderator.

Female 2:   Or you have George Bush with a box on his back. Who knows?

With all of the talk of reaction shots, note taking, and boxes on backs, one person in DeLand, Florida, found a solution to the production issues, but based on what we heard from most groups, it was definitely a minority viewpoint:

In the next election in the next debates in 2008 I'm going to try and just listen to it on the radio. I think that would bring a new perspective to it not to be able to see facial expressions, to not see body language, to actually listen....and so next time I'm going to try to hear it on the radio.

Perhaps 2008 is the time for researchers to replicate the study that was done in 1960 and select a set of DebateWatch groups that will only listen to the debates. Comparing the reactions and interpretations of listeners to viewers would certainly be instructive and perhaps would add to the lore about viewing and listening. While this would be an interesting academic exercise, its utility is likely to be limited because presidential debates are televised events, and nearly everyone who follows the debates will listen *and* watch.

The fact that groups were so observant about the camera work and reacted to how it affected their viewing of the debates should give broadcasters some reason to review their past shot selections. Given the camera's power to influence perceptions and the many opportunities—planned or unplanned—to catch a candidate in an unflattering pose, finding neutral ways to show the candidates is not easy. The media should at least review research conducted by individuals such as Tiemens and Morello and DebateWatch viewers' reactions to past productions. A constant theme among DebateWatch participants has been a desire for debates that are as free from bias, external control, and shallow content as possible. Criticisms and suggestions for improvement clearly suggest that the public doesn't think this goal has been achieved to date. Any attempts to create debates that are viewed as more balanced or better publicity about the broadcaster's production plans and goals are likely to be well received by audiences and contribute to a reduction in negative attitudes about the media. Without some clear signals in the next round of debates that the public's desires are being heard, the type of outrage over the questions and direction of the ABC debate that was discussed in chapter four is only likely to grow with the expanded use of the Internet.

One definite conclusion from DebateWatch findings is that comments made about the visuals added validity to the conclusion reached by Susan Hellweg and her colleagues that visuals are more important than verbal cues in debates. The DebateWatch groups made it clear that the important visual cues came from the candidates during unguarded moments when candidates believed the MOU would protect them because they were not speaking. Campaign staffs need to take note that the camera truly does not blink in a presidential debate and there is no such thing as even a second in which no one is watching or interpreting more than what the candidate thinks is being communicated.

NEWS AND ADVERTISING VERSUS DEBATES FOR INFORMATION

The discussions about the media were not confined to camera angles, facial expressions, note taking, or the media's reports on any or all of the above. DebateWatch specifically asked how the debates compared to other news sources for information about the candidates and their positions and how participants would use the media to continue to learn after the debates. In addition to responding to these questions, participants raised issues related to DebateWatch coverage.

Except for individuals who devote considerable time to following campaigns from a variety of sources, most DebateWatch participants found the information received from debates superior to that of other news sources or to the candidates' own advertising. As a report from Turlock, California, in 2004 indicated, "The majority of participants said that the debate was THE key source of information that would impact their understanding of each candidate with the nightly news a distant second." Comments from groups confirmed the polling data cited in chapter two about the importance of debates in reinforcement or decision making. Since many participants were first-time voters, findings discussed in chapter five created an expectation for the authors that the debates would be perceived as a superior news source. The expectation was also based on the stage of the campaign when debates occur. Timing is critical, and debates come when attention is highest. A significant number of participants each election cycle (see chapter three) were latecomers to campaign coverage. A DebateWatch 2000 participant in Winston-Salem, North Carolina, illustrated the typical timeline for following a campaign:

> I think for a lot of people they don't even start paying attention to the debate until Labor Day....people's interest just doesn't peak until the debates really come around, and once the debates come and you have the opportunity to see the candidates clash in their own personal views and how they discuss things openly, that's when people start making it a major focus, I mean it's not like the information isn't there, it's just that the interest isn't there, you know, in June or July.

Thus, what is repetitive for the well-informed and is definitely old news for the media who have followed the campaigns for nearly two years by debate season, is new information for many viewers. The idea described in chapter two—that the debates focus attention on the key issues for both well informed and those who are casual observers—is supported by the North Carolina participant and by comments that follow in this chapter. The unevenness of viewer knowledge indicates the difficulty moderators and candidates have in providing baseline information along with detail on new or complex issues that require prior knowledge. As was discussed in chapter four, formats that allow for extensive discussion of an issue can get past the familiar for those with greater knowledge, while simultaneously enabling less informed viewers to understand past positions and how they relate to answers in the debate.

Less Filtered Content

Chapter five confirmed that nearly everyone learns something new from a debate or receives confirmation of a previous impression or candidate's position on an issue. In an online national DebateWatch, a participant from Nashville in 1996 summarized the thinking of many across the election cycles that even with flaws and camera shots that reduce the broadcast's perceived neutrality, the debates are still considered the closest thing to an unfiltered view of the candidates that the public is likely to get. The desire for an unfiltered view was expressed succinctly by a woman in Boone, North Carolina, in 1996: "What we know as news is determined by what the press puts on or not. Tonight, you turned off the spin doctors before they came on." The lack of a filter was often discussed in tandem with further comments about media bias as happened in Nashville in 1996 as expressed by this comment: "Well, the main thing is we just see what the news media wants. We see bits and pieces, and we don't have any coherent view of them and tonight we had a true coherent view of the fact that like this gentleman said, they're both good men and they're both human beings who just have somewhat different ideas." The final statement is one that was explored in depth in chapter five in the discussion of viewer learning. Because the debates are civil for the most part, the candidates are side-by-side, and comparisons can be made, viewers do come to realize that there are ideological differences. This is important in light of research presented in chapter nine that shows many who opt out of the electoral process do so because they don't believe the candidates differ on the issues. For those who watch debates, talk about them, and perceive clear differences, one factor contributing to cynicism has potential to be reduced.

The detection of media bias discussed in the visual section was not limited to the camera's selective presentations as the comment from Boone, North Carolina, indicated. A 1996 group in Towson, Maryland, also took a critical view of the media in discussing the "unfiltered" qualities of debates compared to other media. While there was not total agreement across all groups in the study that the debates were superior to other information sources, the overwhelming consensus was that they had advantages:

Male 1:   The media, as far as that's concerned, has already picked one candidate, and they keep telling you how good the guy is.

Female 1:   They're all opinionated, so I don't read editorials. And I read things that I think are factual, but when I do the research, I find out they're not factual.

Male 2:   Time out here. I'll tell you, I like seeing it live, and I'm going to use the word "unfiltered." But the fact is that television changes what we see and hear....All that colors what we see, so we lose a lot. But to me, comparatively, it's better hearing it "unfiltered," less filtered I should say, than reading it a week later in a magazine that's dated a week in advance, like *Time* or *Newsweek*, or something like that.

Viewing the candidates side-by-side in an unfiltered or less filtered setting with some degree of spontaneity was seen as the single most important value of the debates. A discussion in Winston-Salem, North Carolina, in 2000 after the second Bush-Gore debate echoes what was heard in many others:

Female 1:   I think it's different just to hear it coming from the candidate himself. When you hear it on the news, sometimes you get a minute clip of them actually saying it, but usually there's some kind of spin put on it. The candidates put a spin on it too, but I think it's different to hear it coming directly from them.

Male 1:   I agree. I think it's better to have the two candidates there. They don't have one candidate make some comment to the media and then the other candidate has a week or so to get together with his campaign people and come up with a response that they think will be good. They have to play off of each other right then and there. And like, when she said, the media tells you what they want you to know, the media with little sound bytes, they can put a really big twist on what a candidate says but when you have them both sitting right there, they're answering the questions right then and there not with time to prepare their words.

Male 2:   I enjoy watching the debates more because I kind of have a preconceived notion of what the two candidates stand for because of their policies, and then, and I've gotten that knowledge based on media and then you can watch and see how either they hide in a position on something controversial like for Bush, abortion; or for Gore, gun control or education. How they'll try to catch the other and in each position by saying things like, I supported that or how each candidate will try to draw out distinctions.

To demonstrate the consistency of groups' preferences for debates over other news sources, this dialogue from College Station, Texas, in 2004 is illustrative. The participants explain how debates are superior to asynchronous news reporting since the time lag limits reporters' ability to create a form of debate throughout the campaign that compares to the real thing:

Male 1:   I think it's important to see the two sides interacting as opposed to reading two columns in a newspaper or magazine. You can actually see how they differ and how they work off each other.

Male 2:   It also doesn't give as much time in between when one gives a speech and then the other one gives a speech they both spin it so much in between the two speeches. Whereas a debate, they just do it immediately.

Male 3:   From a publication standpoint, it's hard for people to catch both sides expressing their opinions. Maybe they might catch Bush or they might catch Kerry like at a time when they happen to be home or happen to catch a news broadcast. This just gives them a chance, I guess in all fairness, for both sides to catch opinions.

Once again, the information was not surprising as it confirmed what was learned in the 1992 study and what exit polling and other research found about the relative usefulness of debates compared to media sources. What is instructive, however, is the prevalent criticism of the media as biased. It is common to hear complaints that the media is liberal leaning or that a particular network or talk show host is conservative; however, the comments from DebateWatch groups did not emphasize a left versus right frame but considered a much broader context of the media as not fulfilling its duties to inform the public as completely and honestly as possible or as one person put it, the media has "a moral obligation to the voters to [help them] be as informed as possible when giving your vote." A group in Cape Girardeau, Missouri, in 1996 discussed the role of the media at length, and the discussion concluded with this comment: "The media's job, though, isn't to decide what is true. It's to report the facts that were stated in a particular event." Much of the discussion in DebateWatch groups about political reporting and reporting on the debates suggested that this view was shared widely. Comments were made that too much "news" is "expert commentary but that's not hard news reporting on what was stated at the debate." Participants distinguished between editorial pages or television programs that serve as the broadcast equivalent and "factual" reports of what happens in a debate or on the campaign trail. They found far more of the former as comments in this chapter indicate. The evaluations of politicians, as reported in chapter nine, are not flattering, and comments in chapter four suggested negativity and cynicism about the debate moderators. Scattered throughout the many pages of transcripts are comments that indicate widespread cynicism about the media as well. The results of responses to a neutral question asking for comparisons as information sources yielded far more than what was asked and did allow the public's agenda to be voiced.

Postdebate Coverage and Impact

Communication scholar Yariv Tsfati examined the impact of exposure to news coverage of debates to determine its effect on perceptions of winners and losers. He found that "exposure to news coverage of the debate significantly interacted with exposure to the actual debate, so that the impact of news coverage was stronger for those watching little of the actual debate."[10] While DebateWatch participants did not declare winners or losers or view campaign spin or media commentary before beginning their discussions, they had definite opinions about typical debate news coverage from previous experience. The discussion of news filters in the previous section provides some insights into Tsfati's findings. A comment from a participant in DeLand, Florida, in 2004 further explains why those who watch a debate in its entirety are less likely to be influenced by media descriptions of the debate than those who don't watch or watch only part: "As I was watching the debates, it was a completely different image from the sound bytes on the media where they drop all of the errors on both sides and it's just the quarreling." Another person in the group was critical of the media's emphasis on the visual elements: "The way the news coverage is and the way you see things sometimes changes your perspective. They talked about this during the news. There was this thing about Bush's facial expressions during the first debate and about Kerry being taller and the split screens. And to me, none of that made a daggone bit of difference. I wanted to hear the issues and I wanted to hear what the candidates had to say." And it is not just the images from the debates themselves that don't present the complete picture. This comment from a 2004 participant survey addressed the bias in reporting this way: "Fox news bringing up issues they said were discussed that actually weren't. They really focused on changing what the candidates said. The media adds stuff." A man in DeLand, Florida, in 2004 saw the bias as much broader than a single news outlet: "Depending on which newspaper you get, well, he [Bush] was either really compassionate or really defensive about what Kerry had said." A Detroit participant in 1996 made a similar comment: "I think that the thing you notice in reading the media the day after you watch the debates is the divergence in what you saw and what the media saw, which is very apparent."

One specific aspect of news reporting that many group members found unhelpful or uninformative was the concentration on winning and losing. Many found the DebateWatch opportunity an attractive alternative to postdebate commentary as a woman in St. Louis, Missouri, in 2000 explained: "it seems that all the newscasts after the debates focus on who won the debate, which to me is irrelevant and subjective. I more appreciate hearing different views on what the issues are rather than the winner or loser of the debate." A woman in St. Clair Shores, Michigan, had a similar reaction indicating that she didn't "think it is very important at all as to who specifically 'wins' the debate. What is important, is that the average voter becomes informed on the issues." Complaints about the media's infatuation with winning and losing were expressed in several groups in 1996 as well, and in keeping with the baseball playoff season, a Detroit group had this exchange:

Male 1:   I don't think these debates are meant to be won or lost. I think they're for the public to come out with more information about each candidate and what they stand for.

Male 2:   I think the win or lose part comes in the election.

Female 3:   Right.

Male 4:   That's the first question the media asks every time: "Who won?"

Male 3:   It's not a baseball game. It's a presidential debate.

Comments in 2004 were especially critical and equally insightful as to why the media's determination to declare a winner may not be all that important to viewers. For example, it is not uncommon for debate "winners" to lose elections. Comments in groups indicated that viewers often separate debate skills from presidential qualities or at least discount tallies of winners and losers. A Staunton, Virginia, woman commented after discussing the vice presidential debate that "After the first debate I watched just to see what the spin meisters came up with: Oh, Kerry won. Big whoop!" An open ended comment on a participant's report in 2004 was equally unimpressed with the emphasis on winning: "The media just talks about who won. They shouldn't be trying to claim a winner. These aren't real debates." A man in Providence, Rhode Island, also complained about the emphasis on winning and confirmed what was discussed in chapter five about qualities unrelated to debate skills that translate into winning elections and make declaration of winners and losers an academic matter: "There are some people who are just not good debaters. Debate as a format should not be the test by which a voter determines who they are going to vote for." In addition to believing that voters shouldn't base a vote on debate skills, a man in Commerce, Texas, believed that emphasis on winners and losers was tainted by bias when he said that "The liberals always take the party line no matter what. The conservatives seem a little bit more genuine in saying, 'Hey, we think George Bush lost the first debate.' But I don't see that in the media. The media keeps pushing all the time for the liberal person to have dominated in some way."

One important point that is worth repeating in regards to comments about media bias is that viewers watch through their own selective lenses. The person who saw Fox News as biased also made comments in the group to indicate that she was a Kerry supporter. The man in Commerce, Texas, had comments that suggested he supported Bush. The fact that there are numerous news outlets and people can pick those that more closely fit their philosophical leanings, is one of the positive elements of American media. This does not suggest, however, that the media should not change its emphasis on winners and losers of debates, emphasis on gaffes and conflict, and emphasis of nonissue content when reporting on debates. Research does suggest that for those who don't watch the debates, the media influences their judgments of the candidates. As DebateWatch participants noted, what nonviewers see or read is not the complete picture. Issues dominate debates and if the issues aren't reported as the most important information out of the debates, then the media has done a disservice to the public.

Candidates' Advertisements and Web Sites

In addition to the debates and news reports, political advertising and Web sites help complete what resembles a "paint by numbers" picture of candidates and issues. Participants weighed in on their relative merits as well. If the news media was the subject of negative reviews as an information source for viewers, the candidates' own advertising was held in even lower esteem. Candidates' Web sites have far more information about the candidates and the issues than 30-second advertisements, news reports, or short answers in debates. The information is also unfiltered by the media. Even with these strengths, Web sites were also found to be lacking in some respects.

After a discussion of the various information sources available to voters, the moderator in Auburn, Alabama, in 1996 posed this question: "If we're going to put the debates up here as a source of information, what do we put at the bottom?" Several members responded with "Commercials" or "The advertisements." The opinion was shared by many others each year including a 1996 group in Lawrence, Kansas, that concluded, "the ads are completely slanted." A group in Spokane, Washington, in 1996 also found spots to be less useful than debates and discussed the difference this way:

Male: Actually it's going to be interesting to contrast watching these folks in these debates with the hit ads and all that stuff coming up....These at least make these people a little bit more human than the hit ads that show the opponent in black and white.

Female: Another thing that struck me when you were talking about hit ads that there was this conversation from Kemp quite a few times about "your scare tactics." Yet I thought that's kind of interesting because that's what campaigns have become—scare tactics.

The issue of negativity or scare tactics was a common explanation for preferring debates to advertising. One man in Winston-Salem, North Carolina, in 1996 expressed the belief that the candidates were aware of the public's attitudes about negative advertising and used the debates as a counter to the ill will created by attack ads. He expressed the superiority of debates this way: "I think they were trying to be nice. They didn't want to come across as being negative because I think we as citizens are so tired of negative advertising that if they came off that way, it would have been a loss of votes for whoever did it."

A participant in a Madison, Wisconsin, group in 2004 labeled Web sites and advertisements as not being "honest" sources of information because "the ads aren't right; you know they are completely misleading. . . . these commercials on TV are completely false. Each of their Web sites are misleading." Kansas City, Missouri, participants in 2004 also had complaints about Web sites, but for a different reason. They didn't want the candidates to use the Web sites as an excuse for not giving a complete answer in the debates. The discussion went like this:

Female: John Kerry said he had a four step plan or whatever for Iraq and then he gave out his Web site to go find it there. He didn't actually tell you what it was. So I guess you can go find it written down by somebody else.

Male: I think the debate is a chance for him to get up on national television and explain what it says on his Web site. If someone has a question or something is unclear, he is supposed to get up there and explicitly say what he wants to do not say "go look it up."

This discussion made it clear that each form of information comes with expectations from the end users and that connecting dots or sorting out the truth is not what voters want to be doing. While not directly responding to the issue of using a candidate's Web site for clarification, a woman in a C-SPAN online DebateWatch in 1996 explained that she preferred debates over advertising and Web sites for accessible and complete information because "People hardly have time to do what they have to do to survive much less do all this research."

The discussion of the comparative value of information sources such as debates, various forms of news reporting, and advertising makes it clear that no single source of information is adequate to produce an informed voter. Debates have definite advantages over most news sources for depth, focus on issues, comparison of positions, and insights into a candidates' personal and leadership qualities. However, the news media, with its shortcomings, is still seen as needed to fill in gaps and to reveal how a candidate learns from a "losing" performance. The candidates bear the major responsibility for educating the public through their various forms of communication. What happens after the debates as reported in the media may tell as much about a candidate's ability to adjust to the ever-changing demands of the presidency as the debates themselves. Viewers do follow the postdebate candidate messages, and they look for candidates' adjustments. The public can be forgiving of debate gaffes or poor performances if candidates demonstrate recognition of the problem and take corrective measures after the debates. When damage control is not done after the debate, "winning" can be reversed. This happened in 1976 when President Ford misspoke in a debate about Soviet domination of Eastern Europe and did not change his position in spite of a follow-up question that suggested his analysis was inaccurate. As the week went on and Ford stuck to his position, media criticism increased and opinions of Ford's performance changed. Pollster Frederick T. Steeper found that Ford had a "54–36 percent lead" in vote choice immediately after the debate. Within 25 hours after news reports about the gaffe, Carter had a 17 point lead.[11] Since viewers and non-viewers follow the news after the debates, debates are not seen as singular events. Adjustments in perspectives on debate performance further emphasize the relative lack of importance of declaring winners. An example from 2004 also illustrates that the debate is really not over even when it is over. A man in DeLand, Florida, observed "changes after the first debate, starting the next day, in Bush's stump speeches. Bush was responding to questions he had responded to the previous night much more articulately and with much more preparation." He and others found this to be a compelling example of how Bush and his staff learned and adapted. By combining knowledge and insights gained through the debates with additional postdebate information obtained from the media and other sources, DebateWatch participants demonstrated that they became better media consumers and they underscored the synergistic nature of debates, campaign messages, and news reports. The benefit of greater media consumption after the debates and other "side effects" of DebateWatch participation are discussed in the next section.

BENEFITS OF DEBATEWATCH

DebateWatch was created largely because the 1992 research project (see chapter one) revealed a desire among participants to engage with others in discussion. The 1992 study revealed that there were several "side effects" of discussing politics with relative strangers. The research related to DebateWatch was designed to determine if the 1992 findings reported in chapter one were an anomaly or if benefits such as increased media usage, greater tolerance for differing opinions, and increased likelihood of voting were a natural outcome. The majority of DebateWatch participants in 1996, 2000, and 2004 did report similar effects. Even those who were seasoned political observers indicated that while they may not have learned anything knew or changed their opinions, the opportunity to talk about the issues with others was interesting and provided insights into how others viewed the issues. For those who were less experienced voters or who were not fully engaged politically, the benefits were greater.

Specific answers to the questions on the impact of debate viewing and discussion came in two forms. The 1996 and 2000, participant surveys asked several questions about the benefits of watching the debates and engaging in discussion (see Appendix A for a list of questions). In addition to the questions on surveys, group members were asked each of the three years to comment on the impact of the debates and discussion on learning and media consumption, attitudes about the candidates, vote choice, and increased interest in the election. It was clear that reinforcement was the major benefit of both viewing debates and discussing them. In 1996, the statement, "The debates reinforced my attitudes about one or more candidates," resulted in 72.7 percent of the respondents agreeing or strongly agreeing with the statement. The companion statement for the discussion had 58 percent agreeing or strongly agreeing. Twenty percent disagreed and the remainder were in between. When these results are combined with comments made in the discussions, it is clear that for those who are less informed, the discussion provides information, but has less utility for those who are better informed. In 2000, the same two statements produced 82.3 percent agreement for debates and 60.4 percent agreement for discussion. The statement, "The debates made me more likely to vote," received a positive response from 45.6 percent in 1996 and a nearly identical 45.1 percent of the participants in 2000. The same statement substituting the word "discussion" had a significantly lower affirmative response, with 35.6 percent in 1996 and 36.5 percent in 2000. While both sets of numbers are below 50 percent, they do emphasize that reinforcement has two dimensions. The first is to confirm a choice, but the second is to increase the likelihood that a supporter will actually vote. In a close election year, as 2000 was, any type of reinforcement for a vote choice or confidence builder that actually gets someone to the polls can make a difference. Two other statements were of interest. One only applied to the discussion, while the other concerned both the debates and the discussion. The first, "The discussion helped me understand why others view the candidates or issues differently than I do" produced agreement from 62 percent of the participants in 1996 and from 54.8 percent in 2000. While not significant majorities, the results do indicate that discussion can contribute to greater tolerance for opposing viewpoints. The statement, "The debates increased my interest in following the remainder of the campaign more closely" had a positive response from 60.5 percent in 1996 and from 75.9 percent of the respondents in 2000. Given the overall low interest in the 1996 campaign, the significantly lower result for 1996 is not surprising. For the statement on developing an increased interest in following the campaigns as a result of the discussion, 59.6 percent in 1996 agreed or strongly agreed and 63.8 percent did so in 2000.

The positive reaction to the statement about greater understanding of opposing viewpoints is especially important because it highlights the possibility for open, reasonable discussion between people who disagree. It demonstrates that politics does not need to be a taboo subject in "polite society" and that opposing viewpoints can be expressed without the heat and volume displayed in many cable television programs contrasting views from the left and the right. Transcripts from DebateWatch groups clearly demonstrated that people with opposing viewpoints expressed their opinions and engaged in civil discussion of differences. There are virtually no examples in any of the transcripts indicating heated discussions, put-downs, or critical reactions. People were respectful and felt comfortable expressing disagreement without concern for setting off a melee.

The degree of agreement with the statement related to postdebate campaign news consumption reinforces the educational value of DebateWatch. The fact that people learned from the total experience and wanted to continue to learn after the debates and the discussion indicates that creation of a public sphere that resembles the normative ideal is not impossible. The reactions of younger voters and those who admitted that they were not highly political suggest one way to increase political participation among traditionally disengaged groups. By simply inviting people to participate, their sense of efficacy increases.

One additional statement appeared on the survey in 2000 but was not included in 1996: "The information discussed in the debates differed from that presented by news media." Fifty percent of the participants agreed with the statement, thus demonstrating that there is informational value in the debates that distinguish them from other news sources as the previous section comparing information sources also revealed.

Comments from focus group participants provide far richer data than numbers alone. Specific comments from discussions emphasize how watching the debates and participating in DebateWatch affected media use after the debates, how participation increased tolerance for opposing ideas, and how confidence in the participants' ability to engage in the process increased.

Use of Media after the Debates

In addition to the question on the participants' report, DebateWatch groups and facilitators were asked if and how watching the debates and participating in DebateWatch would affect consumption of news. As expected, most well-informed viewers indicated that there would be little change. For a high percentage of participants who were casual observers or who didn't start paying attention until the fall, the debates increased interest in learning more about the candidates and the issues. A man in a postelection group in Detroit in 1996 indicated that "After being at DebateWatch, I'd go home at night and watch CNBC and watch any kind of media late at night. I got interested in what the issues were—a lot of the issues. I have a little boy; so education is a big thing." Many expressed a need to sort out confusion from incomplete ideas or confusing statistics as did a man in the Detroit group who indicated that he "looked at the media differently to try to find out: What are they saying? What sort of corroborating evidence do they have to support claims?" An online discussion participant from Portland, Oregon, in 1996 also wanted to use the media to follow up on what he had heard in the debate. As he explained:

> From here on out to the election, participating in DebateWatch 96 has really let me focus on the responses of the candidates. In the future when I see Bob Dole or Bill Clinton, I'll try to compare the answers that they give in the future to the answers that they gave during the debate tonight, and see if they actually stick to the same

answers that they provided this evening, or if from here on out they'll change their answers. I think that will really affect the way I vote come November.

Two women participants in a postelection discussion in Clarion, Pennsylvania, in 1996 had a similar experience:

Female: One thing I noticed that was probably a little different because of Debate-Watch was that I listened to more strictly political stuff on WPSU than I might have had the patience for previously

Female 2: I pretty much consulted *Newsweek* and television and I'd check different channels on television to compare what they're doing.

Numerous other participants in 1996 and the other two years made similar claims of increased news consumption as a result of DebateWatch participation. In 2000, several facilitator reports summarized the group's intention regarding postdebate follow up. The facilitator for a group of Americans living in Bonn, Germany, wrote that "They all said that because of participating and because of the discussion, their curiosity was sparked and they are more interested in following the remainder of the campaign." A group in Fullerton, California, indicated that "At least two thirds (out of 28) thought they would pay increased attention to the election now that they have heard the debate and gone through the discussion." College Park, Maryland, reported that "They said they were much more informed on the election issues than they were before they came and that being involved would motivate them to (1) read more about the election, (2) watch reruns of the earlier debates (which many of them had not seen) on C-SPAN, (3) register to vote, and (4) actually vote in the election." The report from Norman, Oklahoma, said that "All of the group members indicated that they enjoyed the experience and appreciated the opportunity to talk about the debate ... a majority of the group expressed an interest in following up on campaign information through newspapers, television and the Internet." An Elderhostel participant in St. Louis in 2000 expressed a belief that citizens had a responsibility to go beyond the debates because "we have to do our homework. We have to educate ourselves. That's what a campaign is for. The debate is just another vehicle of doing that."

A set of comments from 2004 provides one of the best summaries of the responses to the question asked each cycle about following the news after the debates. There were large DebateWatch groups in both West Long Branch, New Jersey, and Providence, Rhode Island, that provided a cross-section of participants. A facilitator's report summarizing the sentiments in West Long Branch indicated that "Most said this will influence how they pay attention to the election. This energized them."

One of the larger DebateWatch projects in 2004 was in Providence where organizers recruited community members, students, and individuals who had experience in politics or the media. The large group watched together and then was broken into smaller units with trained facilitators to guide the discussion. Some of the groups were taped and others only reported general reactions via the facilitators' report or participant surveys. The groups met for all of the debates. Comments from focus groups and from the facilitators' reports indicated that for those who "are extremely involved and well-informed in the process, Debate-Watch served no influence but they all enjoyed the discussion." Reports from groups that were primarily "experts" or long-term voters indicated that few, if any, would change viewing or reading habits. However, reports from groups with less exposure prior to the debates reported the following conclusions: "All of them said it would influence the way they watch the election"; "watching the debate and then following with discussion has moved [them] to watch more news and seek out Internet sites that offered unbiased information"; "some indicated they would attempt to get a better understanding of the foreign policy issues and global issues aside from the war on terror and many mentioned the Internet as a prominent tool for getting information on the candidates"; "participating in DebateWatch would influence the way they read about, watch, or discuss the election. However, it will most likely not change their preference for a candidate."

Increased Political Talk, Tolerance, and Confidence as Voters

No one associated with the DebateWatch project anticipated that the debates would change many minds. Reinforcement was the expected and actual outcome, except for the relatively few undecided voters. There were expectations, however, that by becoming a part of a community that shared the debate experience, viewers would become more politically involved or would be more likely to discuss the debates with others. Actual participation in DebateWatch was seen as an advantage for some who had not talked about politics in the past. A report from Americans in Montreal, Quebec, Canada, in 2000 explained that "There was overwhelming support for this forum that allowed them to speak their minds on several issues surrounding the debate. The sense of participation (and lack of apathy!) was a very positive thing for the attendees." Another 2000 group in Denver reported on the influence of the group viewing and discussion on how they saw the debate: "All agreed that it [the discussion] would influence their interpretation of the debate—lack of media commentary was valuable . . . viewing of the debate was quite different than watching it at home with distractions; watching the debate among peers made it a more enjoyable experience." A man in Detroit in 1996 also commented on the difference of watching and talking with others: "I just love this experience simply because when I watch these things by myself, I'm really far more biased than when I watch it with a group like this."

Along with the experience of talking in the groups, participants also talked more after the debates with friends and coworkers. Findings from the postelection study in 1996 provided some specifics. A woman in Detroit explained that her "personal level of interest didn't really go up because I was really interested before the debates and really interested afterwards, but my level of trying to get other people interested increased." A man in the same group believed that he "might have changed a few people's votes" through sharing what he learned with others. A second man added that he provided "information for someone else who didn't participate in the [DebateWatch] process or who wasn't going to vote" and that he "might have influenced them to vote." A third person in the Detroit group had a similar experience of finding himself "having opportunities maybe to persuade or be an advocate for a particular thing. If you're undecided about a particular candidate or you're not pro my candidate I would take it upon myself with the information after having watched the debate to inform you, or at least to try to put my two cents in toward your attitude change toward my candidate."

Similar discussions took place in Clarion, Ohio, in 1996 where one woman "noticed when I was talking to people who hadn't watched the debates but had heard about them or had read about them, it was amazing how much more I was able to discuss what they actually said rather than my feelings." Another man in the group corroborated her experience and said that he "found that those people, who, like you said, hadn't seen it were interested in it and I became sort of a vehicle for informing them." And a third person enthused that "I know I did talk to more people about it than I usually do. I couldn't stop myself. Probably more than I would have otherwise." A teacher in Staunton, Virginia, in 2004 who participated in several of the sessions did more than talk to others, he indicated that it impacted his lesson plans and that "I'm having students examine get-out-the-vote posters and analyze them and I'm encouraging them to think about it."

A comment from a woman in Clarion touched on one of the more important side effects of the discussion besides the willingness to talk: "I'm willing to talk to other people and I'm willing to see how they feel and why they feel the way they do." The openness created within the groups was appreciated because people felt comfortable expressing opinions, as the group in Montreal noted. The atmosphere resulted in increased tolerance for opposing viewpoints both during the Debate-Watch and afterwards.

A man in Detroit in 1996 demonstrated how debates can open a person's mind: "It gave me a greater respect for the candidate I'm not voting for.... There still isn't any doubt as to whom I'm going to vote for, but you gain more respect, and you understand that neither candidate is perfect, and that both candidates are trying." That sentiment was an important reason why participants thought that the debates and the discussions could help combat apathy. One woman in Lawrence, Kansas, in 2000 summarized the effect of the discussion, saying, "I think sitting down and talking in a group like this allows you to see the good points on both sides. Maybe, if you do believe the Republicans, you see a lot of the good points of the Democratic platform, and the other way around." Understanding more about the candidate a person wasn't supporting was a common theme as reactions in 1996 and 2004 illustrate. A woman in Clarion, Pennsylvania, had this to say about gaining appreciation for the candidate she wasn't supporting:

After DebateWatches I noticed that talking to people who were staunch Dole supporters, I could actually appreciate what they were saying; whereas, before I was just like, oh, I disagree with you, go away. But, I disagreed with them so much that I couldn't find any common ground. Whereas, watching the debates, watching Dole,

I can see where they were coming from and talking about it with people who were more positive towards Dole. It was really good for that.

And a man in College Station, Texas, eight years later in 2004 had a similar experience: "My understanding and maybe even, I'm not sure what the right word is, my ability to see the opponent, Mr. Kerry, in a more credible light, I think has gone up a few clicks. I still don't embrace where he's coming from. I don't see that ever changing for myself. You come up with a greater understanding to the alternate position."

A man in Detroit commented on the diversity within the group: "It's a group of so many different people. You get all of these different views from different people of different walks of life and you come out with a lot more knowledge of what different groups of people stand for."

A seasoned politico in Clarion, Pennsylvania, was very effusive about the impact of the experience on her understanding of people who aren't as active as she was:

The thing I found most valuable was I heard some opinions expressed in the Debate-Watch discussion which frankly blew my mind. It was really helpful to me to try to get inside other people's point of view. I have very passionate feelings about a lot of these issues and about politics and about voting and I've worked on many many many campaigns. But I was nothing short of astonished by some of the positions that people who were in the group I was with took about voting, about their role in a democracy. It shocked me into understanding more about voter apathy....I think I underestimated how complicated people's approaches to democracy are and that's part of why it's not an easy process. It kind of made me feel more understanding of what was happening. Not that I liked it, I didn't feel better. I didn't feel relief. In fact, I felt more worried than when I started, but at least I felt like I had a glimpse of something which I just never would have had any encounter with otherwise.

While this woman gained insights into how others think about politics, the experience for those who were apathetic or less informed was equally insightful and rewarding. The final DebateWatch benefit to participants was a greater sense of their own ability to participate in the electoral process. This was especially true for younger voters, but even those who were more experienced found themselves thinking differently. A facilitator's report from Pekin, Illinois, in 2000 summarized what was said in many groups and on many reports: "All participants welcomed the chance to view the debates (two did not have television in their homes). Although the debates did not change their minds, they all volunteered that their opinions were now more informed." A man in Detroit in 1996 explained a "personal benefit" as feeling "more confident and self-assured about the selection in the presidential candidate and being informed." A woman in Clarion, Pennsylvania, after the 1996 election admitted that "This may be a terrible thing to say, but this was the first time that I've gone to the polls with opinions about all of the candidates. Watching the debate got me started on a track of what to watch for, what to look for, how to form an opinion, and what I wanted in a candidate so when

I went to the polls, I felt like an informed voter for the first time." A woman in St. Louis in 2000 also felt better informed because of the diversity of opinions she heard and "the opportunity I had to discuss complicated issues that cross different economic, social, racial, religious boundaries. I never really got that input before. I usually watch with my family and that was a homogenized situation." Younger voters in Lawrence, Kansas, in a 1996 postelection group felt better informed and also indicated that participating and learning made them "feel important and we need more of that." One member stated that "If they're going to be asking me the questions, maybe I should get into it a little more."

CONCLUSION

"Getting into it a little more" is what DebateWatch does for citizens. They go from being passive observers to active listeners, analysts, and better informed voters. Eveland's analysis of political discussion and its impact on learning concluded that "individuals glean information from their discussion partner in much the same way that they would gain information from the news media directly. That is, during political conversations or conversations about the news, information that one discussion partner obtained from a news media source is recounted as part of the conversation."[12] The comments from DebateWatch groups further confirm Eveland's conclusion. This chapter covered a variety of topics that DebateWatch groups discussed, including their own knowledge acquisition through the watching and talking processes. They revealed a critical eye when talking about the way the media presents a debate, and they analyzed the shortcomings of political news while also acknowledging that the news media can help sort out confusion created by the candidates or previous media reports. The participants' discussions of their DebateWatch experiences provide important information for those producing, participating in, or studying political debates. First, debates do matter even if it is to serve a reinforcement purpose. Individuals expressed more confidence in their vote choice as a result of the debates or they recognized that they needed to dig a little further to reach the comfort level necessary to vote. Second, they expressed a genuine desire for substantive information, but they also indicated how complex that process is for several reasons. People are busy and don't have as much time to dig for information as they would like. While many recognized that it is a citizen's responsibility to be informed, they also expressed frustration with doing so in an efficient way that makes it easy to find "the truth." Politicians often shorthand their responses or get so caught up in strategy or their own agendas that they forget that the public doesn't have sufficient background on complex issues or that unlike the media, the public hasn't heard a politician's speech dozens of times. The media is concerned with competition and wants to create interest through the debate production itself, the declaration of winners and losers, and an infatuation with strategy and gaffes rather than substantive issues. The public wants the debates and news coverage to be interesting, but they also want to feel that they are presented in a manner that is fair and informative. This chapter raised many issues, and provided many simple solutions: don't declare winners, but help us understand who did the better job and why; concentrate on issues, but don't make them so vague or so complex that nothing is learned; and don't use the camera in unfair ways, but let us see the candidates under pressure so we can judge their fitness for office. The debates may not change many minds about the candidates or the issues, but the debates and the opportunity to discuss them can have important side effects that ultimately impact voting and democratic processes.

Chapter Seven

Who's on Deck? Talk about Vice Presidents and Future Presidents

Though public and media attention is primarily drawn to contests featuring candidates for the nation's top office, the introduction of vice presidential debates in 1976 was pivotal in political debate history. When President Ford challenged Governor Carter to debate in 1976, attention naturally turned to the candidates' running mates.[1] The official invitation from the sponsor, the League of Women Voters, included a vice presidential debate. The Kennedy assassination, Nixon's resignation, and attempts on President Ford's life all reminded the public of the fact that the vice president is a heartbeat away from the most powerful position in the world. The importance of the vice presidential choice was further emphasized by Spiro Agnew's resignation. The 25th amendment was applied for the first time with Ford's selection and ratification. When Ford became president, he had to select a new vice president. In 1976, neither the president nor the vice president had been elected. Additionally, the enthusiasm for a vice presidential debate resulted in part because it featured two veteran senators, Bob Dole from Kansas and Walter Mondale from Minnesota, who had engaged in many floor debates in the Senate and who were not reluctant to make history.

After their first appearance, vice presidential debates were held in every election cycle except 1980. That year there was only one debate between the two major party candidates, and scheduling a vice presidential debate seemed less important than getting the two major party candidates on the same stage. The vice presidential debates in the 1996, 2000, and 2004 election cycles saw five different men face off in innovative formats. With viewership reaching upwards of 43 million in 2004, the debates engaged large audiences. It is now difficult to imagine an election cycle without debates and without a vice presidential encounter. This chapter explores the unique elements of vice presidential debates and DebateWatch participants' reactions to them. Participants' comments are reviewed in light of vice presidential debate theories and research findings. Groups that viewed the vice presidential debates were asked specific questions about the utility of the contests and what, if anything, could be done to make them more useful.

DO VICE PRESIDENTIAL DEBATES MATTER?

Debates are, as we have argued elsewhere, "focal points" for the national campaign and are events with significant national audiences. Though a large and growing body of literature on presidential debates has developed in the last 20 years, research into vice presidential debates is relatively sparse. Given the reasons that the first vice presidential debate occurred, research on them is important. The research that does exist supports the need to examine these encounters and their impact. Romero[2] argued that the impact of vice presidential debates, as measured in terms of voting behavior, is negligible and its effects are transient on voter attention, but he admitted that partisan advantage may still be accrued from them. Moreover, Holbrook[3] asserted that "vice-presidential debates can influence both vote choice and candidate evaluations," and that they "have their own unique effect on public opinion during presidential campaigns" and "deserve more scholarly attention," even if they are but one of many factors influencing voters' decision making in a campaign. Tonn's analysis of changing voter attitudes about Ross Perot as a result of his running mate James Stockdale's performance in the 1992 presidential debates underscores the importance of running mates in impression formation about the standard bearer. In reviewing focus group comments, Tonn observed that "nearly all voters had been shaken by Stockdale's humiliating performance during the vice presidential debate. The Stockdale debacle not only had called into question Perot's personal judgment and his seriousness about the campaign but also had revealed some stark limitations of tapping persons without political experience for such important political positions."[4]

In 1976, Bob Dole had the requisite political experience to qualify for either the vice presidency or the presidency, but that didn't mean that his success in a debate was guaranteed that year or in 1996 as a presidential candidate. Dole's debate history and reactions to his performances indicate how much a vice presidential debate can matter. In what was an aggressive debate on both sides, Dole came out as the "hatchet man" in his encounter with Mondale. He was tough on his opponents, tough on Democrats, and even tough on the sponsor when he commented that the League of Women Voters 50 percent rating of his record was the result of their being "wrong half the time." His most caustic remark, however, came when he attributed casualties in World Wars I and II to "Democratic wars in this century." Dole's 1976 performance not only had an impact when it occurred, but it continued to haunt him 20 years later when he ran at the top of the Dole-Kemp ticket. In a *New York Times* postdebate analysis with the headline "Searing Images from Debates Past Are Continuing to Haunt Dole," Katharine Q. Seelye wrote about Dole's reluctance to go negative: "If Bob Dole was skittish about going negative in Wednesday's debate against President Clinton, he had good reason to be. When he began attacking Walter Mondale in their 1976 Vice-Presidential debate, Mr. Dole sealed a reputation as a partisan hatchet man, which he has been trying to live down since. And his ticket lost the race, too."[5] Both pre- and postdebate analyses of Dole's debate history and his demeanor in 1996 influenced some focus group members. There were several comments about Dole's reputation and a perception that he was negative in 1996, as this entry from an online participant in the Interactive Distance Training Network DebateWatch illustrates: "I learned that Bob Dole is a really mean-spirited person. I'm sort of young, so I don't remember the debates of 1988 [Dole also made some caustic comments in 1988 Republican primary debates] or the earlier debates when Bob Dole criticized people in the past, but tonight he was just downright mean to President Clinton."

As with presidential debates, negatives in vice presidential debates are remembered more than positives. Some may combine with other issues and contribute to electoral defeats; others are overcome. The latter was the case in 1988 when part of the Democrats' strategy was questioning George H.W. Bush's presidential timbre by casting dispersions on his choice of running mate, Dan Quayle. Quayle's lack of preparation to assume the presidency, especially in contrast to Senate veteran Lloyd Bentsen's credentials, was a major theme of attacks on Bush.[6] One of the most famous quips in debate history was Lloyd Bentsen's response to Quayle's comparison of his qualifications to John F. Kennedy: "Senator, I served with Jack Kennedy, I knew Jack Kennedy, Jack Kennedy was a friend of mine. Senator, you are no Jack Kennedy." Anything Bentsen gained from that line was lost a few nights later in another memorable and oft-repeated moment of debate history. Michael Dukakis's dispassionate response to Bernard Shaw's question about whether or not he would continue to oppose the death penalty if his wife, Kitty, were raped and murdered, confirmed perceptions that Dukakis was an unfeeling policy wonk.[7] And as chapter five discussed, image is developed from a variety of verbal and nonverbal cues within a debate. For most viewers, the most telling moments are the unguarded ones that reveal a great deal about the presence or absence of "presidential" qualities. However, the "presidential" test that is administered when candidates least expect it is not limited to the top of the ticket, as comments later in this chapter reveal.

VICE PRESIDENTIAL DEBATE GOALS AND STRATEGIES

While research on vice presidential debates is limited, it does go beyond the issue of whether or not the debates impact perceptions of the top of the ticket or contribute to a win or loss. Researchers have investigated vice presidential debates to determine if they serve a function that is unique from that of presidential debates or if debaters' strategies differ from those of the standard bearers. In their functional analysis of vice presidential debates, Benoit and Airne[8] noted that candidates for the number two spot emphasize leadership, employ more frequent attacks of their opponents, and highlight past deeds and character within their debates more than their presidential counterparts. Carlin and Bicak reached similar conclusions in an earlier study of vice presidential debates when they wrote that:

A vice presidential debate is a unique form of political debate in which a candidate must demonstrate fitness to assume the presidency—an office he or she is not actually seeking; define his or her role as a vice president and demonstrate fitness for that office as well; contribute to a better understanding of the presidential running mate's virtues; respond to attacks on policies and character in a manner that the presidential nominee could not; and lodge more direct attacks on the opponents, especially the presidential running mate, than could be made in a direct match up between presidential nominees.[9]

They further concluded that achievement of these purposes was enhanced by the format and the types of questions asked, especially questions specific to qualifications, role of the vice presidency, and how differences between the running mates would be resolved.[10]

The analysis of DebateWatch comments about the vice presidential debates takes the two studies on functions of vice presidential debates into account. Both the expectations for the debates and comments on the actual performance indicate that viewers perceived the purposes to be similar to those the scholars uncovered, and they judged the candidates based on how well they performed those functions. Before presenting analysis of the comments, context for the three vice presidential debates is provided.

CONTEXTUALIZING THE VICE PRESIDENTIAL DEBATES

The 1992 debates were known for their historical significance of having three participants, Admiral James Stockdale's lack of preparation for the debates, the unstructured format, the high levels of acrimony between Senator Al Gore and Vice President Dan Quayle, and the considerable material the debaters provided for *Saturday Night Live* writers. The formats in the next three cycles were far more structured and the debates were considerably more civil than in 1992, but they provided ample material for discussion in DebateWatch groups.

1996 Debate

With Election Day less than one month away, the exchange between Vice President Al Gore and former Housing Secretary and Congressman Jack Kemp should have produced considerable interest. Both men had sought the top office—Gore in 1988 and Kemp in 1996—and they were considered potential presidential candidates in 2000. Television audiences, however, were decidedly turned off—or at the very least tuned into another channel—on the evening of October 9 when the two men squared off in St. Petersburg, Florida. Audience numbers were down almost 50 percent from the 1992 vice presidential debate with only 26.6 million watching compared to 51.2 million in 1992. Doubtless some of the lack of interest can be attributed to the 20-plus point lead the Clinton-Gore ticket held over Dole-Kemp. Polling after the vice presidential debate showed the incumbent ticket's margin widening or holding ground. The format, as described in detail in chapter four, returned from the unstructured 1992 format to the traditional time-bound question-answer structure with a closing statement. The debate was marked by a high degree of civility—most likely this was Gore's attempt to avoid Dole's fate and undo whatever negative image he created for himself in 1992.

2000 Debate

Squaring off at Centre College in Danville, Kentucky, with a television audience of 28.5 million, former Secretary of Defense Dick Cheney and Connecticut Senator Joseph Lieberman defied conventional wisdom, the media, and pundits alike by producing a debate characterized by civility and even a bit of humor, rather than the political slash and burn techniques of their running mates in the presidential debates that year. Described as a "debate thick with policy, devoid of personal attacks and only occasionally leavened by spirited exchanges"[11] the Cheney-Lieberman match revealed each man's patient and tempered nature. Drawing a somewhat flattering critique in comparison to their running mates, reporters for New York's *Daily News* remarked about the duo that, "One of the most striking things about the 90-minute encounter was how much more in command of the facts Cheney seemed compared with his running mate, and how much more likable Lieberman came across compared to his."[12] Cheney and Lieberman were relatively specific in detail, comparative in their evidence and support for their positions, and acknowledged one another and the moderator by name. The civility did not go unnoticed in postdebate discussions.

2004 Debate

The 2004 vice presidential debate in Cleveland, Ohio, at Case Western Reserve University featured incumbent Vice President Dick Cheney and North Carolina Senator John Edwards. Though noting the historically minor significance of debates between vice presidential candidates, Barbara Kellerman, a professor at Harvard University's John F. Kennedy School of Government predicted that "this particular debate is likely to have greater interest for two reasons. This is a pretty lively horse race, so anything, even at the margin, could potentially have a greater influence than it otherwise might have, and, second, these are two such very different men."[13] It was the personal differences, perhaps, that brought more people to their televisions to view the 2004 vice presidential. Drawing 43.5 million viewers, the Cheney-Edwards exchange had nearly half again as many audience members as 1996 or 2000 vice presidential debates garnered.

The format was familiar to Vice President Cheney as it duplicated 2000. The two men were seated at a table and questions were posed by a single moderator. Based on Cheney's 2000 performance and his quiet demeanor, the staging was thought to benefit him more than Edwards, the trial lawyer. The expectations for the debate, however, were something altogether different from what occurred. Pundits and strategists projected that Cheney's strident attacks on Edwards's running mate during the campaign, and Edwards's ability to make powerful emotional appeals to crowds were sure to make for a tense exchange. The debate, at least partially, lived up to those expectations. As one writer noted, "the table lost."[14] In what the writer went on to describe as the "ruckus at the roundtable," the debate featured such occasionally sharp exchanges between Cheney and Edwards that at one point the vice president remarked, "Your facts are just wrong, Senator," and the Senator's later retort, "What the Vice President has just said is just a complete distortion."

EXPECTATIONS

Exchanges that were either respectful or heated characterized the three rounds of vice presidential debates. Discussions revealed that participants had definite expectations for the debates and those expectations operated on several levels. Within each cycle, there were expectations about the tone the debate would take, how well the candidates would perform compared to the presidential candidates, treatment of the issues, and how well the running mates met the qualifications as team players.

Tone

Theories regarding vice presidential debates cited previously suggest that these debates are more aggressive in nature than presidential debates. The thinking is that the vice presidential candidates have to demonstrate that they are suited for the presidency, but they don't have to act presidential—at least not until called to serve. Expectations related to the tone indicated that the public shares in the theory, and that comments were grounded in two sources. The first were media reports anticipating the strategies and level of heat. The descriptions of the context in the previous section make it clear that the media was on target some years and missed it in others. The second source for developing expectations was the viewer's own experience from watching previous vice presidential debates. The 1984, 1988, and 1992 vice presidential debates were spirited, and 1996 audiences were especially braced for another testy exchange as were those in 2004. Al Gore's aggressive behavior in 1992 and the expectation that Jack Kemp would be the attack dog that Bob Dole couldn't be resulted in DebateWatch exchanges of surprise and near disappointment that Gore and Kemp behaved more like respectful adversaries than fierce combatants. Some attributed the unanticipated civility to the candidates' previous relationship as House colleagues or to a strategic choice on Gore's part to reshape his image from 1992 as this group in Oxford, Ohio, speculated:

Male 1:   In my opinion, from the cordiality they displayed before and after, my best guess is that they're probably friends.

Female 1:   They are social friends. They are a couple of social friends. Did you like that or not like that?

Male 1:   My guess is that they're still friends.

Female 1:   I liked that because it was nothing personal. They were friends. They discussed the issues.

Male 2:   I saw it as a strategy. Vice President Gore started it to shut off Kemp. There had been so much talk that Kemp was going to have to go negative. I think he [started] right at the beginning by going so positive and saying it was so good to have someone so positive and who liked to stay on the issues.

Male 1: I think you're right about that.

Male 3: Really boxed him in so he couldn't go negative. The talk today is that Kemp was going to go on the offensive and become very aggressive.

Male 4: I thought the debate was too civil. Not to be mean-spirited, but they could have said, "No, that's not true." You can have a heated debate and not be mean-spirited.

Disappointment was also expressed in Towson, Maryland, and was summarized by one man who said, "All they did was act like each other's fan club and stroke each other for the whole hour and a half."

While expectations for fireworks weren't met, the complaint about too much civility wasn't shared universally. In addition to predebate speculation about the debate's tenor, expectations were also influenced by past viewing experience. A man in Bloomington, Indiana, shared the Oxford, Ohio, group's surprise at the debate's tone but appreciated the high road: "I had watched vice presidential debates in the past and usually they were just big mud slingin' fests where they say pretty much what the presidential candidates don't want to say. This one was nice in that they didn't do that; they kind of stuck to the issues and their visions for the country."

By 2000, expectations of aggression took a back seat to a desire for civility. The contentious first presidential debate in 2000 had viewers wanting something calmer and more substantive, and they got it. A Danville, Kentucky, group compared the vice presidential debate to the first presidential and concluded that there was a "different nature of this debate versus the presidential debate. There was a lot more language along the lines of, 'okay that is a prime difference and even though your policy has a little bit of merit, mine holds more merit.' It's recognizing your policy isn't evil versus good; it's 'I think mine is better and this is why.'"

After civil debates in 1996 and 2000, expectations about tone were mixed in 2004. The thinking for some was that civility would be the norm because of Cheney's demeanor in 2000, but for others, predebate media analyses suggested otherwise. Drawing comparisons to the debates in 2000, one woman in Kansas City, Missouri, observed, "Watching the vice presidential debate the last time, it was a much friendlier, chummier feeling. This did not have that feel whatsoever." In counterpoint, a male in the same group had anticipated more conflict and noted, "I honestly expected to see more of that. I thought it was very tame—boring really." Another group in Harrisonburg, Virginia, also expected a lively debate and there were clear differences in opinion regarding the level of conflict:

Male 1: I thought it was going to be more heated than it seemed from the beginning, but both of them seemed to get after each other pretty heavily during the debate. That was what I expected.

Female: I expected it to be more heated. They only interrupted one another once that I could recall.

Taken together, the comments thus far reflect the ambivalence that accompanies debates when the level of conflict is considered. There is a desire for clash and some level of aggression from the vice presidential candidates that is not typical of presidential debaters, but no one wants all-out warfare. People don't want to be bored—a term used several times to describe reactions to the calm 1996 debate—but they also don't want to end the evening cowering in a corner to escape the vitriol.

Comparing the Two Halves of the Ticket

In addition to developing expectations related to the debate's tone, the groups indicated that they expected to see greater differences in the performances than what they saw. Typically they expected the presidential candidates to have the stronger, more substantive debate and come off as more "presidential." The 2000 election, however, was a perfect example of expectations gone awry. Two comments represent the thinking of many who were disappointed in the first presidential debate but found solace in the vice presidential. A man in Leavenworth, Washington, judged the vice presidential candidates to be superior to the heads of their tickets and had high praise for the debate when he wrote in an e-mail: "The BEST debate I've ever seen. The VP candidates came off far more articulate, competent, professional, respectable than their counterparts—an excellent forum." A second e-mail from Michigan expressed a disappointment shared by others in 2000 that the ticket couldn't be switched: "Of all the debates, the only one that I found insightful was the vice-presidential debate. It was handled well. The candidates both answered the questions better and the flow of the debate was the best. After all is said and done, I would vote for Dick Cheney given the opportunity." A desire for a switch in the ticket wasn't limited to 2000, however. There were individuals who also thought the Republican ticket would have been stronger in 1996 with Kemp at the top as this participant in the online DebateWatch opined: "I have worked for Dole. But would rather have a Kemp-Dole ticket." Similar comments were made in Tampa, Florida, with one person going even further in suggesting reversals:

Male: After having watched the debate last night and also the one Sunday and having listened to the various speeches by the various candidates, I frankly, am much more impressed with Jack Kemp than I am with Bob Dole and I think Kemp should be at the top of the ticket.

Male 2: Yes, I must confess the same thought occurred to me last night—should we reverse the ticket? On both sides? It would be interesting.

An Oxford, Ohio, group agreed with that assessment:

Male: My opinion is I would be more comfortable with either one of these people winning than the two that are running for president.

Female: I agree.

Male: I wish they were running.

Perhaps it was the lackluster race in 1996 and the bad start Gore and Bush had in 2000 that had participants imagining other tickets, but comparisons also occurred in 2004 discussions. A woman in Kansas City, Missouri, said that "It seemed like Edwards and Cheney were a lot more gung ho about what they were talking about," and a man in the group expanded on the idea by saying that "in seeing Cheney's performance compared to President Bush's performance, it's an interesting comparison with how Cheney can make the case."

The ability to make the case was an important factor in how participants judged the vice presidential candidates. There were clear performance expectations as indicated by a woman in Tempe, Arizona, in 1996 who did not find her candidate's performance to be on par with her expectations when she stated: "I'm Republican. I'm for him, but I didn't think he answered the questions very well." In 2004 a woman in Kansas City, Missouri, also found that the candidates performed differently than she had anticipated, but she was pleased with the result: "I thought Edwards was really going to stumble on foreign policy ... but I was pleasantly surprised."

For the most part, vice presidential debates resemble presidential debates in that they are issue oriented. An analysis of the questions in the three debates revealed that 41 out of the total 52 questions posed to the candidates were about specific issues. The remainder covered strategy or issues related specifically to the vice presidency. There were clear expectations that the vice presidential candidates would handle the issues as well as their running mates. The comments about Kemp's and Edwards's performance were definitely tied to issues. Some particularly refreshing moments in the discussions were revealed when participants admitted they were surprised to have learned something new from the running mates. A participant in the 1996 C-SPAN online DebateWatch indicated that "the VP debate was clearer on the issues than the presidential debate" and a man in Highlands Ranch, Colorado, identified a specific issue when he observed that "one of the new things that was introduced tonight was Kemp mentioning revamping of the IRS. Dole didn't mention that at all." Another man in Tempe, Arizona, indicated that "Jack Kemp kind of explained really what the hole in the deficit really meant. Compared to the last debate, it was much clearer." A woman in Bloomington, Indiana, reported similar sentiments about Gore's performance: "I learned a little bit about what Clinton's tax policy is. It helped that Gore came out with what they're going to do. It was helpful to hear specifics."

In 2000, as discussed previously, the overall attitude was that the vice presidential debates were superior. While not agreeing with most of the praise for the vice presidential candidates, a man in Milwaukee, Wisconsin, at least found something positive from the vice presidential debate that he found lacking in the presidential when he expressed the opinion that he "was disappointed how by and large, Dick Cheney was the only exception, the candidates failed to answer the questions." The 2004 groups also made new discoveries via the vice presidential debate. A good summary of what was discussed in groups about new information was found in a facilitator's report from Providence, Rhode Island: "The fact that Cheney had never met Edwards until tonight. Edwards and Kerry's Senate voting record of missed votes. Bush/Cheney 'flip-flop' record regarding the 9/11 Commission, Homeland Security, etc."

Overall, the vice presidential candidates stacked up well when it came to issues, and transcripts all had lively issue discussions. The 1996 debates also had an additional expectation. As a man in Norman, Oklahoma, put it, "this debate would probably be the first presidential debate of 2000."

Gore and Kemp were definitely making a trial run for 2000, and analysis of the debate dealt with more than the two men's qualifications as "on deck" players. As indicated previously, some wanted the match to replace the top of the 1996 tickets, and there were clear comparisons of the two men's worthiness to replace their running mates in four years. The expectation of a 2000 Gore-Kemp race was half realized and perhaps it was only half because many found Kemp's performance lacking even though he did fill voids left by Dole. Comments made with an eye toward a future election are exemplified by this excerpt from Tampa, Florida:

Male: It has been stated many times that these might be the two candidates we'll be seeing in 2000. Well, I made up my mind last night. If Kemp is the candidate, I was very disappointed with the way he presented himself. He just seemed to be at such loose ends. He didn't seem to be focused at all and the contrast with Mr. Gore who was so well prepared and frankly, came over a lot more intelligently than I had ever seen him before. If this is 2000, I think Mr. Gore is going to win.

The Winston-Salem, North Carolina, group was less interested in who might win in 2000 but considered the prospective race as a tempering influence on their behaviors. One person commented that "as I heard the debate, they were very careful. They didn't want to say anything that would meet them again in 2000 if they decided to run," and another responded that "When you say something, it comes back to haunt you."

Just as comments about Bob Dole's 1976 debate performance followed him in 1996, the futuristic statements about Gore and Kemp further suggest that debates do not occur in a vacuum. Whether it is developing a vision of a debate based on past experience, taking the measure of a future presidential candidate, or comparing the two parts of the ticket, the vice presidential debates generated discussions that were unique from those about the heads of the tickets yet were grounded in references to them. There was yet another expectation about the vice presidential debates, and it related to the relationship between the running mates.

Teammates

The candidates for president and vice president do run as a team, but their history may also include having been primary election opponents as was the case with Dole and Kemp in 1996 and Kerry and Edwards in 2004. Thus, running mates may not always agree on every issue. One of George H.W. Bush's statements in a 1980 primary debate against Ronald Reagan in which he labeled

Reagan's economic proposals as "voodoo economics" came back to haunt him in his 1984 vice presidential match-up with Geraldine Ferraro. Panelist John Mashek asked, "Vice President Bush, four years ago, you ran against Mr. Reagan for the Republican nomination. You disagreed with him on such issues as the Equal Rights Amendment, abortion, and you labeled his economic policies as voodoo. Now you apparently agree with him on every issue. If you should be called upon to assume the presidency, would you follow Mr. Reagan's policies down the line or would you revert to some of your own ideas?" Ferraro picked up on the theme and attacked the Reagan-Bush economic policies this way: "I, too, recall when Vice President Bush was running in the primary against President Reagan and he called the program voodoo economics, and it was and it is. We are facing absolutely massive deficits; this administration has chosen to ignore it."

This exchange exemplifies one function of vice presidential debates identified by scholars which is to sort out the differences between the running mates and to determine how the candidates will work as a team in spite of them. Bernard Shaw in 2000 was the only moderator in the three debates to address the differences directly with his question to Dick Cheney, "Have you noticed a contradiction or hypocritical shift by your opponent on positions and issues since he was nominated?" Even without such a prompt, each series had references to shifts. Al Gore commented on Jack Kemp's shifts on Affirmative Action, and Dick Cheney pointed out numerous positional shifts in both Edwards's and Kerry's positions to bring themselves in line with one another and the most popular position on the war in Iraq.

As a result of the direct questions and the points made by the candidates, it was not uncommon for groups to discuss the philosophical differences between the candidates and use the differences to explain strategies or weaknesses. The philosophical differences and their impact on performance were especially noteworthy in 1996 as this exchange in Boone, North Carolina, indicates:

Male 1:   I think Al Gore helped his party out; whereas, I don't think Kemp was as helpful to Dole.

Male 2:   Kemp appeared to be holding something back, being more himself than he usually is.

Female 1:   I think the reason is because he and Dole are so different on a lot of their issues. That's the reason he held back.

Female 2:   He's had to change his point of view on a lot of things.

Male 3:   Kemp doesn't believe what he's saying.

Female 2:   Now he's had to go against everything he believes and what's gonna hurt him is people who would have voted for him are now gonna say, "Well, if he can change his mind like that, then why should I vote for him?"

The last statement from that exchange demonstrates how viewers bring past knowledge to their analyses and how important it is for candidates to be "honest" about the issues. This is an example similar to those discussed in chapter five, where "character" is judged by issue positions. Further proof that past debates inform the current one was found in a comment from a 2000 group in Danville, Kentucky, discussing the vice presidential debate and the way that candidates have to change to adapt to running mates. One of the men observed that "Vice president Gore was much more of a liberal candidate back in '92 than he is per say even now. When Clinton asked him to run he became much more conservative because Clinton for all intents and purposes as a Democrat is quite moderate. Gore has kinda had to cater to that, becoming more moderate. But he used to be much more liberal. I think that happens to an extent. I don't believe Cheney is changing much of anything. I think he and Bush are in pretty good agreement on all the issues but I think most candidates do change." This type of pragmatism was evident in several groups and was used as the basis for explaining candidates' weak responses. A discussion in Oxford, Ohio, in 1996 sounds very much like the one from Danville:

Male 1:   There were five times it seemed to me that Kemp absolutely ignored the question. I thought Gore constantly brought it back to the question.

Female 2:   But don't you think that's partially because Gore has not had an opinion for the past four years? It's been Clinton's opinion. . . . But Kemp has been his own person. He has come in under someone who he doesn't always agree with.

Female 2:   It's a problem.

Male 2:   If you saw the article a couple of weeks ago, it listed all the disagreements. I can't believe that Dole chose Kemp. After I read the article, I can't believe he chose him.

Kemp might not have answered the questions, but other vice presidential candidates did and viewers considered their answers to be a show of solidarity with their running mates. When someone complained in Tempe, Arizona, in 1996 that there was nothing new in the vice presidential debate, someone else responded that he thought "it shows how much they support their running mate." Another group in Bloomington, Indiana, had a similar discussion but also acknowledged the need for compromise to accept a position on the team:

Male: I believe that all of them, both of them, were saying exactly what their lead guys told them to say. They never expressed an idea, not one.

Female: Except, in a heartbeat they could take over the presidency. So I'm just assuming that they are their ideas as well.

Female 2:   Maybe they collaborated with their ideas and platforms to believe one thing. I think if you're going to be on a team of any kind, you have to compromise and meet down the middle so that you both have the same goals.

Eight years later in DeLand, Florida, a nearly identical discussion took place. When a woman saw Cheney's responses as "really associat[ing] ideas with being vice president, being part of the administration," a man in the group expressed a similar belief about Edwards' responses with a slightly more cynical tone: "They were going to talk about the party line no matter what the question was. Edwards especially was given Kerry's best lines from last Thursday and he was to talk about everything including Kerry's hidden [less well known] points."

Part of being a team member is to defend the running mate in ways that he can't do himself and that was the idea behind the comment regarding Kerry's "hidden points." Being a staunch defender of one's running mate is another idea coming from the theories about vice presidential debates. A discussion in Norman, Oklahoma, in 1996 touched on the character issue that was supposed to be a part of the first Clinton-Dole debate but never materialized and was instead dealt with in the vice presidential debate. One man noted that Gore did what a good running mate should do: "In the first presidential debate we saw Clinton and Dole being very civil to each other. I heard some commentary that maybe in the vice presidential debates they would attack each other's character. I felt like Gore really defined the issue." In 2000, Cheney was seen as helping out his running mate on one of the most contentious issues in American politics—abortion. A question was asked about Cheney's support of House Republican efforts to restrict distribution of the abortion drug RU-486. In commenting on Cheney's response, a man in Danville, Kentucky, sensed that there might be some disagreement between Cheney and Bush but that Cheney "covered up for Bush a little bit, who's basically said the whole time, 'look the president can't do this, the president can't get rid of this drug.' He could if he wanted to, if he tried. He diverted, he completely side-stepped the whole issue. Cheney helped him out a little bit. That's what I saw the most in that whole subject."

There was no doubt that discussion groups grappled with the realities of creating teams from two individuals with different political experiences and somewhat different philosophies—even if they are in the same party. Some were more critical in their views of compromise than others, but most expected that the running mates would have a unified approach, that the vice presidential candidates would make their running mates look good—perhaps even better than the tops of the ticket had done for themselves—and that seeing the complete team was important because the vice president is a heartbeat away from the presidency. That topic was a common one and is analyzed in the next section.

THE VALUE OF VICE PRESIDENTIAL DEBATES

The many voices from across the nation who came together in 1996, 2000, and 2004 to participate in DebateWatch expressed a range of complex and contradictory feelings about the meaning and importance of the vice presidential debates. Importantly, these expressions—taken collectively—give voice to the ambivalence, cynicism, optimism and trials that voters see in the political system. When asked specifically if "vice presidential debates are useful," one woman in Norman, Oklahoma, in 1996 offered an insightful observation of their potential dual use for voters when she noted that "the candidate or the President has chosen this person to be the Vice President. It kind of is a character trait of the President to see what kind of person the President is going to pick to be the person who would take his position if something happened to him. It gives us an idea of what kind of person he is by choosing his successor." The importance of knowing who a successor would be was expressed in several groups with comments such as, "It gave me a little more insight into the person who would be second in command," "but it is helpful to see the seconds-in-command," "you're dealing with the team and it's important to come to know both of them," and "these are candidates for a position that is a heartbeat away." The group in Spokane, Washington, felt that the issue was important enough that a generic question addressing presidential qualities and assuming the presidency should be asked. After talking about the lack of a vice presidential question in the debate, someone suggested that the candidates should all be asked, "What would you do if something happened to the President? What kind of president would you be?" Of course, the underlying reality that a president could die in office or resign was never far from the surface as the suggested question in these discussions in Highlands Ranch, Colorado, and Detroit in 1996 illustrates:

Female 1:   Oh, yeah. It's important because, for example, Dole's age.

Female 2:   You never what's going to happen. You never think much about the vice president. He's kind of just there.

Male: Just in case.

Male 1:   It gives us an idea of what's going on.

Male 2:   Or what might happen. Remember, like with Teddy Roosevelt. They made him vice president to keep him out of trouble and he's President. You have to remember this person is first in line for President.

Female: That's the other very important thing. We need to know, as the American people, in case something happens to the president, who is going to be the leader of our country.

And if a vice presidential candidate might happen to assume the role of president, many group members wanted that person subjected to the same types of tests that the presidential candidates underwent. There was a clear desire to see how they withstood pressure, and a woman in Tempe, Arizona, in 1996 believed that the debate gives "a pretty good idea of what type of men they are by standing up and having those questions fired at them and how they answer and how they deport themselves." A Kansas City, Missouri, participant in 2004 ruled out the value of the issue discussions and emphasized the performance under pressure value when he argued that the debates help us "to see where they stand and to see how they are going to respond under pressure—situation where they don't know the answer, when someone is attacking them. It is not, by any means, to find out the truth." A very specific example of how the "stress test" was applied came from a comment about the Gore-Kemp debate from a man in Towson, Maryland, who noted that:

I thought I learned something last time and in this debate. I think I was influenced by listening to the two candidates and taking notes. I learned a lot more about Jack Kemp. I thought I had known, but I really changed my opinion of that candidate and what I thought his abilities were under stress. I thought, under stress he didn't impress me with his ability to handle things under stress. I was surprised to see how Gore comparatively speaking handled things better under stress. I did not expect that to happen. I clearly did not.

In addition to seeing how the candidates comported themselves throughout the debate, others wanted to see questions specific to the vice presidency. This occurred only in the 2004 debate even though it is theoretically one of the functions of the debate and was common in years prior to 1996. The omission of such a question was duly noted in 1996 when someone in Norman, Oklahoma, commented that "In past debates they always got into some discussion about whether they're qualified to assume the office of the presidency. They didn't this year." Someone in Tempe asked a similar question that resulted in this discussion:

    Male: Why don't they talk about what they'll do as vice president?
 Female 1:   Their role as vice president.
 Female 2:   Because they're pretty helpless.
    Male: They don't have to talk the whole debate, but maybe they should include a part of it in there rather than repeating the same issues over and over again.
 Female 1:   If they're just going to discuss the same questions as they did before, then it's [the vice presidential debate] not necessary. But if they discuss what their roles are in the vice presidency then it's important.

Analysts of the vice presidency consider Gore to be one of the more powerful vice presidents with responsibilities for leading efforts to reduce the size of government and being an active presidential advisor. They also saw Cheney's central role in the Bush administration starting with handling the transition to being a key player in the war on terror as moving the office far beyond John Nance Gardner's claim that the office "wasn't worth a pitcher of warm spit."[15] Given that the vice presidency grew in importance under both Clinton and Bush, the desire for specific discussion of the running mate's role is a reasonable expectation bordering on being a convention for the debate.

Regardless of how qualified a person is for the office, presidents do use vice presidents differently. Just as the group members learned something about presidential character through the choice of a running mate, much can be gleaned from decisions regarding that person's role. And when all of the reasons given for having vice presidential debates are added together, they culminate in the possibility that the person who is selected as a running mate might just tip the balance in favor of the top of the ticket for those who are wavering or are undecided. Political scientist David W. Romero posited that theory when he explained that "it is possible they [vice presidential nominees] have an indirect influence through presidential candidate evaluations. For example, suppose a voter is pleased with the vice presidential selection and increases his or her presidential evaluation as a result. When considered independently of presidential evaluations, vice presidential evaluations would be minuscule to nonexistent. However, the original presidential evaluation update, if this scenario is correct, could be very real."[16] Several individuals did indicate that the choice of a vice presidential nominee influenced their views of the top of the ticket, as exemplified by a woman in Bloomington, Indiana, who "hypothetically" suggested that "If I were looking towards maybe voting for Dole, then Kemp would have been the person to put me over the edge. So I think it was important to have the vice presidents." Thus, the question posed previously in this chapter as to whether or not vice presidential debates matter, would have to be answered in the affirmative—at least for some viewers.

CONCLUSION

The comments from DebateWatch participants leave little doubt that it is important to have the vice presidential candidates both in the wings and on the stage. The three vice presidential debates discussed in this chapter had distinctive characteristics because of the individuals involved, the context of the election, the campaigns' strategies, and the types of questions that the moderators chose to ask. While fewer people watch the players who are on deck and fewer participated in DebateWatch activities for those debates, as the results in chapter three indicate, the individuals who did participate took very serious looks at the candidates and the issues they debated. The discussions demonstrated once again that viewers of debates are savvy in their analyses of what is taking place. They recognized the conflicts that are created for individuals who have to sacrifice something of themselves to take the number two spot. They were aware that the debates often do have a different tenor because the running mates can say and do some things that the presidential candidates are wise to avoid doing themselves. They offered effective suggestions as to the types of questions are needed to make the debates for the two offices more distinctive. Finally, they were not shy in stating their disappointment in either the candidates' performances or their desire to have the tickets reversed. Throughout this book, we have emphasized the many values of the DebateWatch project. One that should be mentioned again here is that Debate-Watch creates an environment for candor and an atmosphere of friendly disagreement. Nowhere was that better shown than in a reading of the comments about the vice presidential debates.

Chapter Eight

Generation Next: Youth as Political Actors

In 1942, with 18- to 20-year-olds defending their country in World War II, Congress began debating the wisdom of lowering the voting age to 18. The debate took on new urgency in the 1960s after many more disenfranchised youth had fought and died in Korea and were fighting and dying in Vietnam. Students were engaging in civil rights, pro-ERA, and antiwar protests, and it was obvious the youth of America were eager and willing to participate in the political process. In 1971, after 29 years of consideration, Congress passed the 26th Amendment and the states ratified it in only four months. The presidential election of 1972 was the first chance for 18- to 20-year-olds to exercise their newly granted right to vote. Their turnout that year would serve as a foreshadowing of their participation to come.

In 1972, only 48.3 percent of eligible 18- to 20-year-old voters cast a vote. While this number was a high rate in comparison to successive generations, it was a disappointing result. When the "youth vote" is expanded to include 21- to 24-year-olds, turnout for the 1972 election was 49.6 percent.[1] Although the turnout was a full 13 percentage points lower than any other age group, it is the pinnacle of youth turnout and a rate of participation that has remained unmatched a full three and a half decades later. While some might attribute the low turnout to a lack of understanding of the democratic process, the historical context of that race should have been a large draw for young voters. Not only was it the first chance for younger citizens to participate, a historical event of its own, but the country was embroiled in an undeclared and unpopular war in Vietnam and there were serious concerns of economic decline that would affect their employment in the immediate future. The controversy, concerns, and new capacity to have an input should have mobilized a larger segment of that population.

In 1976, the youth vote dropped. Only 42.2 percent of 18- to 24-year-olds, and just 38 percent of 18- to 20-year-olds, showed up at the polls. This 10 percent decline among the newest of voters drew concerns. While there was an overall drop in total voter participation, the 7 percent change from 1972 doubled the drop in any other age group. One presidential cycle into their enfranchisement and the group was already seemingly disinterested in exercising this right. Reports of "apathy" began to percolate. The elections of the 1980s did nothing to quell those reports.

During the first two elections of the 1980s, youth voter turnout hovered around the 40 percent mark.[2] However, in 1988, there was a precipitous decline in overall voter turnout. Only about half of all eligible voters made it to the polls that year. The Bush-Dukakis race seemed to inspire lower all-around participation in spite of unique factors such as the first female vice presidential candidate on a major party ticket. For youth voters, the decreased turnout was again amplified. Only 36.2 percent of eligible 18- to 24-year-olds voted.[3] The lowest turnout up to that point, the 1988 election was cause for concern among pundits.

YOUTH AND THE 1992 CAMPAIGN

In 1992, youth participation rebounded. The young voter turnout was a full 8 percent higher than in 1988, reaching a turnout second only to the 1972 results. Many factors contributed to the upsurge. For the first time in many election cycles, young voters were seen as a potential "swing vote" group.[4] Traditional campaign strategies necessitate appealing to issues important to the groups who historically vote in high numbers, such as seniors and the swing voters of the year, for example, "soccer moms," "angry white males," or "the religious right." Appealing to the interests of a particular group is often referred to as playing a particular type of "card." Most frequently, candidates are noted for playing the "race card" when discussing issues of particular interest to minorities and playing the "gender card" when discussing issues related to women's concerns.[5] Oddly, when candidates play the "youth card" they are almost never addressing issues of interest to young voters. The "youth card" most often relates to the candidate's demonstration of youth and vitality. Playing up a candidate's youthfulness is rarely primarily intended to appeal to young voters; rather, it is usually intended to reassure groups that already vote *en masse* that a candidate is fit for the job.[6]

The 1992 campaign was one notable exception. Candidates from both major parties specifically courted young voters. They appeared on television shows popular with the "under 30 crowd." One iconic image from the 1992 campaign was then-candidate Bill Clinton playing the saxophone on the *Arsenio Hall Show*. In addition, both Clinton and Bush appeared on MTV on more than one occasion. While many traditionalists deemed the appearances "unpresidential," younger voters seemed to be drawn into the campaign. Coupling the "boxers or briefs" questions with discussions of issues thought to be of interest to younger segments of the population, candidates did manage to mobilize these young voters. In fact, voters under 30 gave Bill Clinton a nine-point boost in the election.[7]

In addition to the major parties' concerted efforts, the emergence of a seemingly viable third-party candidate also enhanced youth voter participation. Ross Perot, with his folksy humor and lack of Washington experience, managed to seize the attention of many voters in 1992, including many young voters. The inclusion of popular third-party candidates, or viable candidates with unique characteristics, has traditionally sparked more participation from younger voters, not only in the United States, but also abroad.[8] The motivation is two-fold. First, the rebelliousness of a change from the norm appeals to the often-rebellious nature of young people. Second, the potential for a substantive change signified by even the appearance of viability for an "outsider" to the system appeals to the hope and vitality of the young. This effect was evidenced during the 2008 primaries when a record number of young people attended caucuses and voted in primaries.[9] According to a cover story on youth political involvement, *Time* reported that in their poll of the under-30 cohort, "Nearly three-quarters of the respondents said they feel the country is headed down the wrong track.... Their interest in the election exceeds their interest in celebrity news or sports—7 of 10 said they are paying attention to the race."[10]

A third factor influencing youth voter turnout in 1992 was an expanded and diversified "get out the vote" campaign targeting young citizens. Prior to the 1992 campaign, there were a few loosely organized efforts to mobilize young citizens. General get out the vote (GOTV) efforts were viewed as sufficient for mobilizing 18- to 24-year-olds although all evidence was to the contrary. In fact, as late as 1996, the League of Women Voters, a dominant voter advocacy group, dedicated only one line of their "Get Out and Vote: Encouraging Participation in Your Community" booklet to mobilizing young citizens. Their advice: members "may want to emphasize the importance of the election as it relates to their education and job prospects."[11]

In the early 1990s, two youth voter advocacy campaigns began encouraging young people to register, become informed, and vote. MTV sponsored a campaign titled "Choose or Lose." The campaign encouraged voter registration, included information on political candidates and issues of particular relevance to younger citizens. In 1992, it was a wildly popular effort, in part because it allowed young people to relate politics to their daily lives and because it gave a different view of the candidates. For the first time in a long time, many young people felt as though they were being heard and that their voices and votes mattered.

A second dominant youth vote advocacy group that was developed in the 1990s and impacted the 1992 turnout was Rock the Vote. Founded in 1990 as a nonpartisan political advocacy organization, Rock the Vote is often confused with the MTV campaign. They both used similar tactics for mobilizing young citizens—celebrity endorsements, music-based events, and nonpartisan issue-oriented discussions emphasizing young people's concerns. These GOTV campaigns and others gave young people a chance to become connected and engaged. They were also fairly novel and attention-getting, which resulted in higher turnouts.

In addition to specific youth vote mobilization campaigns, research projects in 1992 focused more specifically on young people. The 1992 focus group study included an analysis of the specific needs of youth voters.[12] The findings indicated that young people want to be a part of the system. The young participants also found political debates helpful sources of information, particularly innovative and interactive formats such as the "town hall" debate. They explained that questions posed by "common" people mirrored their interests and concerns more than those posed by journalists or other moderators. The usefulness of the debates as information sources for young voters reinforces the importance of holding presidential debates.

THE (LACK OF) YOUTH PARTICIPATION IN 1996

The factors contributing to the spike in youth voting during the 1992 campaign were not nearly so effective beyond that campaign. The Clinton-Dole race only drew 32.4 percent of 18- to 24-year-olds to the polls. The turnout for 18- to 20-year-olds was a paltry 31.2 percent, an all-time low for a presidential election. The youth, however, reflected the rest of the country. For the first time in modern campaign history, fewer than half of all eligible citizens voted.[13] The question, then, becomes, what changed in the 1996 election that dampened young citizens' enthusiasm from the previous election?

The attention paid to young voters decreased considerably during the 1996 campaign. The candidate who courted young voters so enthusiastically in 1992 was the incumbent and needed the group less than before. The race was not hotly contested; thus, candidate appearances in youth-oriented forums seemed perfunctory rather than sincere. Voter mobilization campaigns also lacked the unique flair of the 1992 effort. Many of the same appeals and tactics were used, giving young people a sense of having seen it all before. Even the unique third-party factor faded. Although many people again considered Perot a viable candidate, he'd lost his broad appeal and the attention of the younger voting demographic. He, like the mobilization efforts, was no longer novel enough to warrant their attention or support.

Although the actual majority of citizens failed to participate in the 1996 election, youth seemed to be singled out by pundits and scholars. Deemed "apathetic" and "lazy" by most, young people were labeled "slacker citizens" before the polls even opened.[14] Based primarily upon conjecture rather than research, media labels attributing the lack of participation to character flaws in young citizens encourages a sense of disempowerment and disconnect from the political process. In a 1997 focus group of nonvoters, young participants complained of the "bum wrap" they get by the media. A young man in Lawrence, Kansas commented, "If they are going to assume we don't care, why should I bother to prove them wrong?" Another in Detroit commented on his view of whose interests were met in campaigns: "I really don't see my best interests being represented....they think that we only exist just to vote, and it's just a means, but it's not a way to OUR means; it's a way to THEIR means."

The assumption of politician's ill motives or lack of interest among young citizens was widespread in 1995 and 1996.[15] The impact spread beyond simple editorializing. Even among nonvoters the attitude about nonvoters' motives was negative. As part of the larger project summarized throughout this book, nonvoters were asked to explain nonvoting behaviors. When asked about their own behavior, nonvoters seemed to have rational, socially acceptable explanations for not voting, including missing registration deadlines, busy schedules, paperwork mishaps, and so on. However, when asked to explain the behaviors of others, responses mirrored media reports—apathy and laziness were the top two responses. In other words, many participants in our study saw themselves as having good reasons for not voting but didn't apply that thinking to others.

For those who planned to vote, however, the DebateWatch project provided a means to understand their attitudes, motivations, and expectations for debates as a voter education tool. The focus groups and surveys conducted immediately after the debates provided a wealth of information about the impact the debates had on young citizens' attitudes about candidates and their perceptions of political processes, some of which were positive, but most of which were negative. In that respect, younger viewers were no different from other age cohorts. Some had positive comments about the debates and what they had learned, but others differed in their responses. Expectations played a major role, especially for first-time voters. For instance, one participant expressed frustration with the "unnatural" nature of the debates, stating, "it reinforced how I viewed the process. Not either candidate specifically, but the process in general, and that debates are really preplanned. Obviously they studied well, they had canned answers for when certain questions came up." A student in Murray, Kentucky, had a similar reaction: "This was a television show. It was a media event. You could never have, as these gentlemen said so nicely, a debate and have 90 seconds and 30 seconds. That is not a debate. It's time television devotes to this and that's all." Another student in Las Cruces, New Mexico, had hoped to hear something to help her prepare for her first time to vote but came away disappointed:

> This will be my first time voting, and I just figured you shouldn't vote unless you know what you're voting for. I wanted to get a taste for what the candidates stood for. Actually what I got was pretty much nothing. It's just a lot of lame rhetoric that didn't really mean much. I don't really see that much reason to vote right now just after watching this. It didn't move me either direction.

While similar frustrations were echoed in focus groups across the country, others discussed disappointment with the general issues covered. Even when "common" people asked the questions in the town hall format, young participants felt the questions did not adequately reflect their concerns. As one focus group participant said, "This whole town hall thing is just a masquerade because if you look at the questions they were either open questions or questions that were very, very, very predictable. The best issues did not emerge." A female in West Chester, Pennsylvania, agreed, saying, "I didn't like it at all. Who selected these people to ask these questions? Who picked them?" Participants also noted how few young voters were on stage at the "town hall" exchange. Interestingly, the young non-voters seem to be a fickle group. The favored "town hall" format of 1992 was questioned in 1996 for authenticity and lack of representation. The novelty of the format gave way to a critical view four years later.

An additional complaint from voters who were relatively new to complex issues such as taxes was that candidates' programs were not explained completely—even when citizens in the town hall asked for a direct explanation. As a result, there was room for skepticism. A young professional in Kansas City, Missouri noted:

> He's [Dole] saying he's going to give everybody a 15% tax break. Well, wouldn't I want a 15% tax break? I'm right out of college, and I'm not rolling in the dough. Of course, I want more money in my pocket. But, for some reason, I'm skeptical because he never explained to me...and that's all I ever wanted....and they asked him point blank. I was just, "God, thank God, somebody that's asking the questions I wanted to ask." And he completely avoided it; didn't give any explanation.

Despite these criticisms, the majority of comments demonstrated that the debates and participating in DebateWatch helped undecided voters select a candidate, provided a key to reversing apathy, and motivated others to learn more. For example, a woman in Detroit indicated that the invitation to participate in a DebateWatch altered her behavior: "I thought it would be interesting. I wasn't even going to watch the debate. I just, this year, am kind of apathetic to this particular election. I thought, 'Well, this is a good thing. This will make me listen to people.'" A student at Wake Forest University indicated that she learned new information: "I didn't know some of the things, or I wasn't aware. None of the information was earth-shattering, but it does help to draw a little bit of a finer line." A male in the group indicated that "I was an undecided voter into the tail end of the vice-presidential debate, and I watched this one in its entirety, and I think I have a candidate. So it has swayed me to one side."

Not all younger DebateWatch participants were less cynical after the debates and the DebateWatch experience, but even some of the more critical participants did find value in both. For example, one San Francisco student expressed a belief that the debates were a superior way to get information and responded to some of the more skeptical members of her group:

> I really liked this debate. If you go find stuff on your own, you're finding out through your boundaries....They're answering what they want to say. If you take it for a gimmick or not, that's them. You can read it on the Internet, but how do you know he really said that? You can read it in a newspaper, but the only way I'm going to know is if I watch him say it.

Another female in the San Francisco group expressed her belief that the candidates were not giving her complete responses but rather than check out of the process, she was motivated to learn more: "I think that the debates maybe could be a stepping stone to doing your own research. The whole time I was watching this, I was thinking, 'I can't wait to get the literature on this and read both sides of it,' because I know both sides are lying." A third woman agreed, "It made me think that I wanted to do research for myself and look for the real issues. What do Democrats really stand for? What do Republicans really stand for?"

In addition to reacting to the debates, the focus groups discussed the political process and the campaigns more generally. While there were additional expressions of frustration that topics in the debates did not always appeal to them, the younger participants in DebateWatch had advice for how to get them involved. In each group across the country, there seemed to be an acute awareness of the lack of attention paid to young people. As one young man explained, "the majority of us are younger and that seems like the group that should be targeted more. You always see [the candidates] visiting senior centers and the donut shops where you've got the majority of older people. If a politician would go to a high school or a university, the impression would stick with young people longer." A young woman also warned, "[The youth] is just a huge group of people and politicians just need to start targeting them or else its just going to increase everyone's apathy."

In general, the young people involved in the postdebate focus groups in 1996 found the discussion to be more enlightening and empowering than the debates themselves. Many were thankful for the opportunity to be a part of the process; they were grateful for a forum in which their collective voices could be heard. As one young woman in the Lawrence, Kansas, group said, "It makes me feel really special, even though I know I'm one of so many thousands of people. It feels like I mean something, just knowing that we are somehow going to get results back from this." Another woman in the group echoed the sentiment and took it one step further, suggesting that participation breeds participation:

> I think just asking people how they feel. "Why are you going to vote?" That makes people feel important, and if we had more of that, "Well, how you feel? What are the issues that are important to you?" I think that that would be helpful, just to ask people because I think that it makes you feel more important and it makes you feel like, "Hey, if they're going to be asking me the questions, maybe I should get into it a little more."

It is important to emphasize in analyzing any DebateWatch group that these were individuals who had sufficient interest or incentive via a class project to actually watch the debate and participate in a postdebate discussion. However, responses demonstrate that voter education programs are beneficial in combating apathy. Even if cynicism weren't erased, the young people in these groups were at least watching and talking—something that many of them said they would not have done absent the DebateWatch project. Universities across the country were able to generate large crowds during a year when most voters, and especially younger voters, stayed home in droves. The University of Maryland had nearly five hundred attend a DebateWatch the night of the town hall debate. It was broadcast live on C-SPAN. The University of San Diego, the host of the town hall, had approximately the same number in an arena. George Washington University hosted hundreds for each debate in the student center, and other campuses in our research group attracted anywhere from dozens to hundreds of students, faculty, and community members.

VOTING TRENDS AT THE TURN OF THE MILLENNIUM

Whether or not the young participants of DebateWatch in 1996 remained active in 2000 is unknown, but the new millennium did not see an upsurge in interest among young people, in general. During the Bush-Gore battle, 18- to 24-year-olds managed to reach a new low in turnout. Only 32.3 percent of 18- to 24-year-olds showed up at the polls—just under the low established in 1996. While Federal Election Commission data showed a 2.2 percent increase in overall voter participation from 1996 to 2000, the youth vote slipped another 10th of a percent. It was the first time in 20 years that the youth vote fell while the participation of other age groups rose.

The 2000 race was one of well-known names, faces, and strategies. The sitting vice president faced the son of a former president in a close race. The issues facing the nation were the same as usual—economics, education, and health care. While some candidates did make attempts to appear "personable" on talk shows and youth-oriented media, many of their strategies seemed "old hat" by 2000. MTV's once-progressive "Choose or Lose" effort seemed tame and overused. Young people no longer found the "boxers or briefs" question entertaining or evocative. In an effort to raise interest, the youth-oriented organization Choose or Lose paired with musician P. Diddy in a campaign dubbed "Vote or Die." While the title seemed edgy, the strategies were much the same as 1992 and 1996.

Interestingly, the low level of youth voting in 2000 was not an accurate representation of youth political involvement.[16] Many young people reported volunteering for political campaigns or issue-oriented organizations as their means of participating in the political process. For some, the experience seemed much more gratifying than the single act of voting. Young people often believe they have more of an impact and more of a voice if they are a part of a campaign or movement. The idea that young people are politically active outside of the voting booth is not new. In 1972, Sidney Hyman defended this tendency in his book *Youth in Politics*. Addressing the question of whether or not youth are apathetic, Hyman argued an emphatic "yes and no," explaining:

> It is yes when judgment is based on the superficial observation that student electoral participation fell far short of the springtime predictions.... The answer is no when it is recognized that the springtime predictions were pitched to such unreasonably high expectations that the failure ... to realize them resulted in an exaggerated impression of apathy on the part of the young. The answer is also no if the ... level of student electoral participation is compared ... with the extent to which the electorate as a whole participates in electoral politics beyond the act of voting.[17]

In fact, others have asserted that the true measure of youth political involvement should include rates of volunteerism. As volunteers, young people often outnumber older age groups. Many campaigns rely heavily on the free labor and high energy that young volunteers provide.[18]

DebateWatch 2000 once again targeted young populations as a way to increase their motivation to participate in the electoral process. When asked about the usefulness of the debates as sources of information in 2000, young people in upstate New York commented more on the "entertainment" factor of the debates rather than the factual information provided. In fact, one week after the debates, when asked what they remembered about what they had seen, many of the focus group participants cited comical satires of the debates more than the debates themselves. One young male explained, "I remember Gore's lockbox. I'm not sure what he wanted to put in it, but it sure was funny how he kept saying 'lockbox' over and over." A 20-year-old female in the group questioned, "Did he really say it that much or was that just SNL exaggerating? The skit was pretty funny, though." Such comments lend credence to the conclusions of research cited in chapter two that nontraditional media influence perceptions of debate performances and that younger citizens are attracted more to *Saturday Night Live* and *The Daily Show* for their political knowledge than they are to *The News Hour*.

A discussion among participants in an intergenerational group in St. Louis demonstrated the importance of peer pressure relevant to political participation. One male indicated that the DebateWatch project was useful for first-time voters because it encouraged them to participate when they might not have otherwise. He commented that "I didn't vote last time because my group of friends weren't interested in voting, so it never interested me." When asked what got the student interested, he indicated a government class he was taking. Participants for the intergenerational DebateWatch group in St. Louis were recruited out of such classes at Washington University where the town hall debate occurred. Someone summarized the impact of viewing and discussing the debate by noting that "primarily we've got a lot of preconceived ideas about what we're going to do; they are either reinforced or they're changed. Somebody must have really had an effect."

After the second debate at Wake Forest, a student group was asked specifically how the issues related to them. One male student mentioned a topic also discussed in St. Louis—gun control—and its relationship to the Columbine shootings and why it resonated more than the more traditional topics of Social Security and taxes. His insight into the way that issues are discussed and their broader appeal is instructive for candidates who have to talk about core issues but also need to appeal to a wide constituency:

> I think an issue that I was really looking forward to that hadn't been dealt with until today was the issue of gun control. For young people the whole Columbine thing, that was committed by young people, against young people. And anybody our age should be able to say to politicians, there needs to be a way that we get guns out of young people's hands and control all that type of thing, you know, the way that they can get the guns and things like that. With social security, with Medicare, with those things like that, it's not so much that they don't necessarily relate to us because they will soon enough, it's the way that they say the things that we really can't relate to. I can't really understand their whole, such and such tax cut, rather than if they said it affects certain demographics in different types of ways. It's just not as easy for me to comprehend. I don't see that as an immediately relevant issue to me in the way that they say it—in their wording.

Another male in the group addressed the question of issue relevance by saying, "I thought with Lehrer's questions and the way he did it, he raised some real important issues that are issues for all kinds of different people including, you know, the 18–25 age group. Like civil rights, the foreign policy issues, environment, those type of issues." Another participant indicated that Gore's discussion of college tax credits was the issue that resonated most directly. Another cited Bush as adapting well to young voters' concerns: "I think that specifically, Bush tried to reach our demographic by talking about how he wants to give people more control over how they invest their money."

Overall, the group after the second debate at Wake Forest felt that the major benefit of the debate was that it raised issues that hadn't been discussed in the first debate or in the campaign. One male participant summarized what others were also saying: "And I thought it was really interesting and cool in this debate that, you know, those issues that really hadn't been a focus of the campaign were discussed, and not just discussed but they were clearly delineated policy positions, and kind of approached these issues on these two sides."

Carlin and Anderson compared the differences across demographic groups participating in DebateWatch 2000 in terms of the usefulness of the debates, voter learning, and topic importance.[19] Using data representing nearly 5,000 Americans in 31 states, the District of Columbia, and abroad, a significant difference in the percentages of young voters compared to those over 25 was found in terms of predebate candidate choice. While over 90 percent of more experienced voters had a predebate choice, 72.8 percent of the 18 to 25 cohort did. The degree of change after the debates was not significant across the age cohorts; however, there was a significant difference after the DebateWatch discussions since more young viewers clarified their choices. Young viewers found the debates significantly more informative than did older viewers, especially when compared to those over 55; thus, the educational value was high in 2000, as it had also been in previous years. Similarly, younger viewers found the postdebate discussions more valuable than did the other age groups. When it came to issues, the top five (taxes, education, health care, international relations, and gun control) were on all groups' lists. However, young voters more often listed environment, energy policy, race relations, and abortion among their top 10 than did other cohorts.

Members of the National Communication Association DebateWatch groups also examined the reactions of younger viewers. Spiker, Lin, and Wells analyzed DebateWatch transcripts and reached conclusions consistent with our summaries.[20] They found that the discussions they analyzed from three groups in Missouri, Texas, and Ohio (one for each presidential debate) included three major themes: "(1) debates allow for critical evaluation of candidates; (2) participants feel they have low personal power but express a strong sense of civic duty; and (3) a generation gap exists since politics is perceived as not relating to young citizens."[21]

Perhaps the most disappointing aspect of the debates as they related to younger viewers was that the St. Louis debate offered an opportunity for the candidates to address issues relevant to that cohort; however, while both candidates talked philosophically about needing to bring younger voters around, neither seized the chance to dispel the view that candidates can't break out of their set campaign speeches. A member of the Gallup group asked, "It seems that when we hear about issues of this campaign, it's usually Medicare, Social Security or prescription drugs. As a college professor, I hear a lot of apathy amongst young people who feel that there are no issues directed to them. And they don't plan to vote. How do you address that?" Gore responded:

> We've got to change it. . . . Sometimes people who are very idealistic and have great dreams, as young people do, are apt to stay at arm's length from the political process because they think their good hearts might be brittle, and if they invest their hopes and allow themselves to believe, then they're gonna be let down and disappointed. But thank goodness we've always had enough people who have been willing in every generation to push past the fear of a broken heart and become deeply involved in forming a more perfect union. We're America, and we believe in our future and we know we have the ability to shape our future. Now, we've got to address one of the biggest threats to our democracy. And that is the current campaign financing system.

Unfortunately, campaign finance reform was not on the top-10 list of issues for this cohort. Bush came closer to addressing the heart of the problem, but his response also drifted back into his agenda:

> A lot of people are sick and tired of the bitterness in Washington, D.C. and therefore they don't want any part of politics. . . . There's a lot of young folks saying, you know, why do I want to be involved with this mess? And what I think needs to happen in order to encourage the young to become involved is to shoot straight, is to set aside the partisan differences, and set an agenda that will make sense. Medicare . . . is relevant for all of us, young and old alike. We better get it right now. Tax reform is relevant for old and young alike. I don't think it's the issues that turn kids off. I think it's the tone. I think it's the attitude. I think it's a cynicism in Washington and it doesn't have to be that way. . . . could an administration change the tone in Washington, D.C.? And I believe the answer is "yes," otherwise I wouldn't be asking for your vote. That's what happened in Texas. We worked together. There is a man here in this audience named Hugo Berlanga. He is the chairman of the health committee. He came here for a reason, to tout our record on health in Texas. He's a Democrat. I didn't care whether he was a Republican or Democrat. What I cared about is could we work together. That's what Washington, D.C. needs. And finally, sir, to answer your question, you need somebody in office who will tell the truth. That's the best way to get people back in the system.

To illustrate the inadequacy of the response, we can turn to the postdebate surveys that were submitted to the DebateWatch research center after the St. Louis debate. Among the list of topics that appeared for the first time in large enough numbers to be listed among the top 10 was "youth issues." Other issues mentioned as important to younger voters that appeared consistently across the lists of topics not covered adequately were the environment, education—beyond K–12 issues—and civil rights.

Ironically, while the campaign, including the debates, was rather nondescript, the conclusion to the 2000 election was incredibly unique and historic. For the first time in modern memory, one candidate won the popular vote while the other won the Electoral College vote. While Gore earned 48.3 percent of the popular vote, he fell short of the required number of Electoral College votes to win the White House. Bush's 47.8 percent earned him 271 Electoral College votes and the White House. Of course, the results were not that simple. The campaign dragged on for almost six weeks after the votes were tallied. Due to technical difficulties, votes in Florida were counted and recounted. The results were ultimately determined by the U.S. Supreme Court and announced on December 13, 2000. While the events were too late to affect the 2000 turnout, the controversial ending to the 2000 election cycle had profound effects on the electorate in 2004, particularly young voters.

YOUNG VOTERS IN 2004

The 2004 elections had a stunningly similar sociohistorical context to those in 1972. The country was engaged in an increasingly unpopular military action, and an incumbent president was running against a military veteran who opposed the action.[22] In the wake of the 2000 election controversy, the September 11 terrorist attacks in 2001, and the war in Iraq started in 2003, the world watched the 2004 campaign with great interest. So did young citizens.

In November 2004, the youth vote exhibited a resurgence in numbers not seen in decades. While fewer than half of the eligible youth population voted, the 47 percent turnout among 18- to 24-year-olds was the second highest showing since the ratification of the 26th Amendment. While still below the 55.3 percent turnout of all eligible voters, as reported by the FEC, the 15 percent increase among this cohort restored hope in the possibility of reviving the "slacker citizens" lamented in 1996.

The increased turnout among this population was again attributable to many factors. One factor influencing the increase was the 2000 election result. In 1996, focus group and survey results indicated that a significant number of nonvoters believed or strongly believed that "a single vote doesn't matter."[23] After 2000, the power of the individual vote was emphasized. Candidates, pundits, voter mobilization organizations, and others had fresh evidence with which to argue for the importance of a single vote. All citizens, young and old, were reminded many times of the importance of participation during the months leading up to Election Day. This emphasis also encouraged candidates to court new groups of voters.

Candidates' interest in courting new voters was aided by a second factor influencing voter turnout: the popularity of emerging communication technologies, particularly the Internet. Internet use by politicians in 1996 and 2000 was limited but grew between 1996 and 2000. The 2004 campaign was the first in which candidates actively used the new technology to reach out to individuals. The proliferation of new technologies encouraged higher involvement among young people. With candidates developing Web-based campaigns that appealed directly to younger citizens, the accessibility and interactive nature of online campaign messages encouraged engagement on a new level. Beginning with Howard Dean's use of Web-postings early in the Democratic primary season, the potential uses of the online medium were realized and effectively utilized. For example, "Deaniacs," young Dean supporters, were caught up in the spirited Democrat primary election largely because of the Web and MoveOn.org's emphasis on the war. By the time of the general election, the major candidates each had a well-established Web presence to supplement more traditional campaign strategies. Much like the alterations in strategy found in the 1992 election, the inclusion of online campaigning signaled an interest in reaching out to young people via the media they use most. It also afforded an unprecedented level of interaction between candidates and citizens.

When asked what they learned from the debates, younger voters often acknowledged learning about traditional topics such as health care that appeal more often to older voters. One woman admitted that she had not been following the campaign until the debates: "Obviously I knew nothing so everything they said was new." Hinting that he had not been following the news very carefully either, a male participant indicated that he "didn't know Kerry and Edwards changed their minds that many times [on the war]." A participant in DeLand, Florida, found a question about Supreme Court appointees interesting: "I hadn't really thought about the kind of justice that would be appointed by either candidate, so I thought that was an interesting question—something that hasn't come up at all in the campaign."

In addition to what they found interesting and what they learned, young voters also expressed disappointment in topics not covered. The draft was one topic that was mentioned in several Lawrence, Kansas, groups and was also discussed in the Harrisonburg, Virginia, group:

Female 1:   One thing I would kinda like to hear more about is how they are talking about implementing the draft. That would definitely affect us and there was no mention of that.…

Female 2:   I think that I have heard in the past couple of days that voter registration is up all over the country and a lot more teens, eighteen plus voting so you would think that they would have addressed issues more relevant to us, but I don't think they did. The draft—that is something that has personally affected a lot of my friends.

Facilitator reports from other locations held on campuses also listed the draft as one of the topics not covered sufficiently. A group of 21 young voters in Wooster, Ohio, listed the draft as a top issue along with the Patriot Act. A group at John Carroll University in Cleveland listed only the draft as the topic the 20 participants thought needed more discussion. The failure to address the issue was especially significant since a survey of 18- to 29-year-olds conducted by the Annenberg Public Policy Center found that only approximately 25 percent knew that "neither President Bush nor Senator Kerry favors the draft compared to 42% overall."[24]

The facilitator's report from Turlock, California, which identified 14 of the 18 participants as being between 18 and 25 years of age, indicated that the majority wanted to hear more on the environment. Another group from Orange, California, in which there were 56 participants between the ages of 18 and 25 listed hearing more about an exit strategy from Iraq and Afghanistan as a key topic, as well as discussion of international topics other than Iraq and the Middle East.

While all of their questions may not have been answered, the 2004 debates and the previous two cycles did serve two key purposes for young viewers. They strengthened young citizens' connection to the political process, particularly emphasizing the importance of democratic ideals.[25] Additionally, young people who watched the 2004 presidential debates experienced a confidence boost. Watching the debates gave young viewers high levels of what McKinney and Chattopadhyay deem "political information efficacy," or confidence in their political knowledge.[26] The combination of increased confidence in political knowledge and an increased conviction of the importance of democratic ideals can be an influence in mobilizing young people to vote. The same result was found in 1996 and 2000 as this quotation from a male participant in Normal, Illinois, in 1996 demonstrates: "The next debate I watch, I'll know what they're talking about and I'll be able to watch it and look for certain things. I'll focus how I watch it; I'll be able to watch it more critically."

Overall, the 2004 presidential race was interesting for many reasons. Concerns over the controversy four years earlier, fears of more terrorist attacks, continuing military action in Iraq and Afghanistan, economic worries, and health care were on the minds of voters. Additionally, the spread of new communication technologies and more ready access to political information brought about change in the campaign process. For young voters, access to information, a concrete example of the importance of every vote, and having candidates pay attention to them surely contributed to the increase in voter turnout in 2004 and in continued interest in the 2008 primaries.

CONCLUSION

Politicians frequently talk about the future and the kind of country they and voters will leave to their children and grandchildren. Young voters are those children and grandchildren, and they have the potential to shape their own future—but only if they participate. The results of DebateWatch demonstrate the importance of inviting, involving, and informing young voters in order to motivate them to participate in the electoral process. Campus DebateWatch organizers invited young people and told them their voices were important. By being involved in DebateWatch, they became more informed, and as a result, gained the confidence to participate in the process. While they may not have been completely happy with the candidates, their answers, or the issues that were emphasized, most admitted that they learned from the debates. This cohort's vote was more likely to be influenced by debate viewing and DebateWatch discussions than that of other groups. Since this group was historically underrepresented in the electoral process, the disproportionate level of participation in DebateWatch can be viewed as positive for two reasons. First, it engaged underrepresented voters in the process. Second, and perhaps more importantly, it provided insights into what it will take to continue to motivate young people. They want to hear messages that address their issues, they want to be made to feel like an important part of the process, they want to believe that a vote will matter both in terms of who is elected and what policies those elected implement, and they want explanations that are clear, understandable, and acknowledge the complexities of the issues. In reality, what young voters want is also what all voters want, as the study of nonvoters in chapter nine reveals. None of this is especially surprising information, but it does emphasize that democratic ideals can be attained only when individuals who are part of a democratic society are given an opportunity to voice opinions and believe that in doing so they can influence outcomes and ultimately their lives. The nonvoter study discussed in the next chapter was largely the result of the expressions of dissatisfaction with the political system from younger viewers that were reinforced by viewers of all ages. Chapter nine provides insights into the reasons behind some of the attitudes expressed in this chapter on youth.

Chapter Nine

Nonvoters Speak Out

The postdebate and postelection focus groups in 1996 provided the impetus for a study of nonvoters 10 months after the 1996 election.[1] Cynicism was expressed by many DebateWatch group members, and some made it clear that the debates had not convinced them to vote. For example, in response to a question about the impact the debates would have on vote choice, two participants in San Francisco had the following to say:

Male: It influenced me in the sense that it reassured me that there's no way that I would vote for any of these guys.

Female: My opinion has changed during this discussion. I would probably change my vote. I would not vote for any of them.

Across the country in Nashville, Tennessee, expressions of frustration with the choices and politics provided some insight into the reasons why people don't vote:

Male: People who have power are not going to do what's right. If we say that, then we're lost anyway. It doesn't matter who we vote for.

Female: Right. That's why you have so few people voting.

And there *were* far fewer people voting in 1996 than in the previous election as the statistics in chapter eight indicated. The second phase of the initial DebateWatch '96 research was developed to determine if issues raised in the postdebate focus groups could be explored in a way to provide more information about the roots of cynicism and decisions to opt out of the electoral process. While the research was done in only one of the three election cycles covered in this book, the information received does have applicability beyond the cycle in which it was collected. Focus group comments reported in previous chapters from all three cycles indicated some degree of frustration with the candidates, their policies, and the overall political process.

To tap into the sources of voter apathy, discontent, and cynicism expressed by DebateWatch participants and to further explore the political climate described in numerous books published in the 1990s,[2] a combination of survey and focus group research was used. The study was designed to determine if voters and nonvoters differ on the following: (1) attitudes about the importance of voting, (2) opinions about the relevance of politics and political issues in their lives, (3) reasons for nonparticipation in the electoral process, (4) level of exposure to and selection of political information, (5) language used to discuss politics and voting, (6) solutions to commonly identified political problems, and (7) evaluations of the value of campaign messages and news about politics. The methodology is explained in detail and the findings are informed through the survey data and focus group discussions.

METHODOLOGY

Data was collected over a three-week period in September and October 1997. Individuals who led DebateWatch '96 groups volunteered to participate in the study and were asked to either collect data from students or conduct a focus group of randomly selected nonvoters with the exception of one focus group that was composed only of students. Appendix B includes all of the recruitment procedures, instructions for collecting data, surveys, focus group questions, and tables with results including levels of significance for differences between and among groups. Focus group participants received a $25 honorarium. They were the only participants in any phase of DebateWatch to receive an honorarium.

Subjects

Survey data was collected from students at eight universities across the country.[3] A student sample was selected because the youth cohort had the lowest turnout of any age group in the 1996 election. This cohort represents a generation of voters that has the potential to influence politics for the next 60 years. If the voting trends discussed in chapter eight indicate that lifelong voting patterns are developed early, then it is important to know how to capture this group when they are first eligible to vote.

In all, the survey phase produced a sample of 587 self-reported voters and nonvoters. The second phase of the study consisted of nine focus groups representing a cross-section of randomly selected self-reported nonvoters and one group composed of students. Participants were in eight locations across the country.[4] A total of 75 nonvoters of varying ages, backgrounds, and occupations participated in the focus groups and filled out an abbreviated version of the survey administered to the student group. Focus groups' surveys were used for comparison with the student survey data to determine if those results could be generalized beyond a student population. As expected from the consistency of comments across cohorts in the DebateWatch groups, there was little variation between student and nonstudent responses.

Of the 587 student participants, 84.2 percent were 18 to 25 years of age; 11.9 percent were aged 26 to 40; 3.6 percent were between 40 and 55; and 0.2 percent were over 55. Just over 60 percent of participants were women. Following U.S. Census categories, survey respondents listed their ethnicity as follows: White, 64.9 percent; African American, 16.9 percent; Hispanic, 11.6 percent; Asian/ Pacific Islander, 2.6 percent; and American Indian/Alaskan Native, 1.9 percent.

While all participants were full- or part-time students, 22 percent listed an occupation as well. Most of those listing employment were in service-related jobs. The political affiliation given by the respondents was 33.2 percent Democrats; 22.7 percent Republicans; 31 percent unaffiliated, and 2.7 percent split among the various third parties. The majority of respondents were registered voters (80.4%), and 61.7 percent had voted in at least one previous election. In fact, 55.5 percent of respondents reported that they had voted in the 1996 presidential election.

Demographically, the focus group participants varied from the survey respondents. Of the 75 participants, 40 percent were 18 to 25, 42.6 percent were 26 to 40, 13.3 percent were 41 to 55, and 4 percent were over 55.[5] As with DebateWatch groups, it was difficult to get older participants because of evening meeting times for the groups. Twenty-six percent of the total group members were students, and they were all in a single group. One-third of the 18 to 25 cohort were nonstudents. Well over half (69.3%) were male and 30.7 percent female. Of the 73 who indicated their ethnic background, 60.3 percent were White, 37 percent were African American, 1.4 percent were Asian/Pacific Islander, and 1.4 percent were American Indian/Alaskan Native. Over half (55.4%) of the participants were registered voters, although 52.8 percent of the total group reported never having voted. Of those with past voting records, some had not voted since 1964 or 1976. Party affiliation included 17.3 percent Republican, 25 percent Democrat, 53.8 percent unaffiliated, and 3.8 percent other.

News Sources

Like the DebateWatch '96 participants, subjects were asked to indicate their top sources of news about politics and political issues. For student survey participants, nightly network news was the most common source with 86.6 percent of all respondents ranking it as one of their top three. Local newspapers were the second most cited source with 65.5 percent of participants listing it. Unlike the DebateWatch '96 groups, these participants cited news magazines as their third major source for political news (28.6%). DebateWatch participants had NPR, C-SPAN, and national newspapers in their top three. Talk shows and National Public Radio rounded out the top five for the nonvoter study. This information was important in painting a broader picture of political interest. Over half of the student respondents indicated that they were regular or frequent (almost daily) consumers of the news with 44.7 percent following regularly/weekly and 22.6 percent following three to four times per month. Thus, this was not a group that ignored political news, which is expected since there were voters in the group. The percentage following the news at least weekly was greater than the percentage of the total group that voted in 1996.

Focus group participants were less regular followers of political news, however. Only 32.2 percent reported following on a regular/weekly basis, 23.1 percent followed two to three times per month, and 21.5 percent accessed the news once or less per month. Even though regular attention to news media was lower than for the student group, over half followed the news on a regular basis. When they did tune in, 77.3 percent listed nightly network news as one of their top three sources, 65.3 percent indicated the local paper as a primary source, and 26.6 percent cited news magazines.[6]

Instruments

A 36-item questionnaire was designed that included 11 demographic questions, 15 opinion questions using a five-point scale (1-strongly disagree to 5-strongly agree), and 10 open-ended questions (see Appendix B for the complete survey). Questions were modeled after the University of Michigan National Election Study survey.[7] Focus group participants answered the first 26 questions of the survey administered to the student group to obtain demographic information and to compare baseline attitudes. Most of the demographic questions were similar to those used for DebateWatch. The 17 questions that covered the topics addressed in the open-ended section of the student survey were used to stimulate discussion in each focus group (see Appendix B). As a result, the focus group survey was an abbreviated version of the student survey.

Open-ended responses were content analyzed by two independent coders with a reliability of .9. Answers to the question, "Write the first thing that comes to mind when you see or hear the following words (your answer can be a word or phrase) and follow the word or phrase with a brief explanation as to why you answered as you did: politics, politician, elections/campaigns, news media, and political advertising," were coded as positive, neutral, and negative (see Appendix B for examples of each category). Nonvoters were asked to explain why they did not vote in 1996 and in the case of those who voted previously to also explain what was different in 1996. All respondents were asked to speculate as to why citizens, in general, do not vote. Responses were coded in one of the following eight categories: apathy, lack of empowerment, ineligibility, registration and voting processes, personal inconvenience, disillusioned with the system, candidate choices, and lack of information to make an informed decision. Respondents were asked to describe the major problems with American politics today. Answers were coded as public apathy, failure to address citizens' and the country's needs, campaign process is too costly and negative, media, candidates are flawed, and issues. They were also asked what they thought can be done to resolve the problems they identified. Responses were coded as accountability, broaden the candidate base, campaign reform, voter education, reform the media, nothing can be done, and not certain. The next question asked what could be done to get the respondent more engaged in politics. Results were coded as already interested, nothing, better access to information, candidates, increase empowerment, more relevant issues, and media reforms. The final question asked if the news media and candidates provide enough and the right kind of information to make an informed choice and what additional information is needed. Answers were coded in one of six categories: more focus on issues, more positive news, less analysis and more fact, more about candidate's stance and history, access to information, and accountability of information. Statistical tests were applied to determine if there were significant differences in responses between voters and nonvoters.[8]

Transcripts from focus groups were analyzed using the same categories used for open-ended questions. Because discussion topics often overlapped, making it difficult to get an accurate frequency count, repeated terms were counted only once and comparisons to survey responses were based on existence or nonexistence of terms rather than on frequencies.

ATTITUDES ABOUT VOTING AND POLITICAL RELEVANCE

To assess attitudes about the importance of voting and the relevance of politics to a person's daily life, subjects reacted to a series of statements. Both subject pools reacted to the statement, "A single vote doesn't matter." A significant difference was found between voters and nonvoters on this question (see Table 1 in Appendix B) with 80 percent of voters, 65.7 percent of the student nonvoters, and 58.8 percent of the focus group members disagreeing with the statement. While the majority of all three groups disagreed, the difference in the percentages across groups was significant (see Appendix B, Table 1).

While a majority of nonvoters believed in the efficacy of a vote, they didn't vote. The focus group transcripts provide insight as to why nonvoters do not exercise their right to vote. The major reasons had nothing to do with whether or not a vote influences the outcome of the election. In fact, no one in any of the groups gave that as a direct reason. Dissatisfaction with the Electoral College was the reason that came the closest to "lack of influence." It was mentioned in several focus groups. The most common reason for not voting was related to outcomes—nonvoters believe nothing will change regardless of who is elected. The change to which they refer is one of two types: change in the way government operates or change in their everyday lives. One woman in Detroit addressed the former this way:

> I voted in '92, and the only reason I voted then was because there had been Republicans in the office for so long and even though I was pretty skeptical and I didn't think it would make a real big difference. It was kinda like, well, there was suddenly this large chance that there would be somebody from a different party than was already in office, and I thought that might make some difference. But then, after it happened, it really made no difference at all.

A male in one of the two Wilmington, Delaware, groups noted that "there's no big drastic change from different president to different president since I was young." Another male in the same group got at the relationship between officeholders and daily life:

it really don't matter who wins, you're still going to be getting up in the morning doing your same job, raising your kids, getting food for your kids, caring about your wife, and your dog, and just the normal stuff. And I don't care who's in there unless it's Stalin or Hitler, you're still going to be doing the same things. The politicians change minute details way up there where we can't see what changes they make really affect our personal lives.

An additional, but less frequently mentioned reason for opting out was a loss of faith in the very tenets of democracy. A male participant in Bellingham, Washington, expressed the belief that "the politicians and the issues seem to be manufactured so that you're not really making a choice." Two participants in Detroit echoed this opinion, but in more cynical terms:

Female: It's really obvious to me that the system in which our politics and our elections and our elected officials exist is one that has as its only purpose to
uphold the power of the people that are there. And any sort of sham or whatever you want to call it that we actually have some say in it is not real. It's
fabricated to try and convince us that we have some kind of democracy.

Male: I think I said things like CONTROLLING AND MANIPULATIVE [in
response to word associations], and I tend to agree with Kate despite the
fact—one word popped out was DEMOCRACY. But I think that's just a
word we call it that lacks any real meaning. When some people heard that
I was gonna be participating in this focus group, they, of course, got tagged
on the fact that the focus group was those who didn't vote in the last election. And I got these evil looks as if I was not a patriot or as if I was evil
or something. I think that's the kind of reaction that a lot of people have
been convinced or persuaded to believe that they are part of something that
doesn't really exist. Their vote really doesn't matter much, and they just
keep contributing to something that doesn't work.

These comments directly relate to opinions about the relevance of politics and political issues in subjects' lives. It seems logical that if someone does not think a vote matters or doesn't vote, that person might also see the issues related to the vote as unimportant. Subjects responded to four statements that addressed this issue: "I do not have time for politics," "What goes on in Washington does not affect my life," "What goes on in the state capital does not affect my life," and "What goes on in the city/county government does not affect my life." Sig-nificant differences were found between student voters and student nonvoters for only one of the four statements: "I do not have time for politics." Sixty-five percent of voters disagreed with the statement compared to 43.1 percent of the nonvoters. When results from the general population of nonvoters were included, those comparisons also yielded a significant difference, with a larger percent-age disagreeing (51.4 percent) when compared to student nonvoters. However, the percentage was still significantly smaller than for voters. (See Appendix B, Table 1 for results of statistical tests.) Thus, time more than negative attitudes about politics or a lack of belief in political efficacy produced the most distinction between the two groups.

The agreement on three of the questions was consistent with results for the open-ended question, "Do the decisions politicians make at local, state, and national levels affect you personally? If yes, on what particular issues and how?" Of the individuals who responded, 443 (75.5%) said "yes," 77 (13.1%) said "no." In giving specific ways in which politicians affected them personally, respondents listed taxes, freedoms, salaries/minimum wage, college tuition, public education, gun control, cigarettes, health care, and drinking. Some of those who answered "yes" responded that they didn't know how they were affected or couldn't think of any personal examples, but knew that there was an impact. Some of those answering "no" indicated that they weren't affected "yet," suggesting that they weren't taxpayers or homeowners.

The following dialogue from the Detroit group demonstrates the thinking behind the numbers on this set of questions:

Male: I do feel that what politicians do affect us. It affects us every day in every way that we can imagine.

Female: Yes, I do. As far as Governor Engler, he's eliminated a lot of programs focused on lower classes, and it's really affecting them. . . .

Male: There was a time when I didn't think so, but I have yet to recover from the Nixon administration, so . . . (laughter).

Female: I'm affected. I am not buying groceries for the next two weeks. I work at a bakery, and I'm going to be living on toast because out of my $529 paycheck, a lot of guys running offices halfway across the country decided that they need $159 of that to spend on things that they think are important, and they never asked me about it. So I'm not eating anything but toast because some guy decided that he's gotta, ya know, have $257 nuts on his $2,000 toilet seat or some airplane that costs $8 million to fly 20 feet. Yeah, it affects me a lot. Every day.

Male: I just have an observation that's kind of interesting. Ya know, this is quite an arrangement of people here, and even though nobody here votes, we sure have a lot on our minds!

Female: I was gonna say that. Something I often think about when I hear things on the news about people who don't vote is there's a big vote of apathy. And I think a lot of people don't vote not because they're apathetic, but because of the opposite.

This discussion demonstrates that nonvoters do pay attention to political issues. The comments about military procurements clearly suggest that the woman knew about the Pentagon spending scandals and believed that those expenditures impacted the public in negative ways. The Detroit group's discussion and the previous one regarding the "sham" of elections reveal another reason for not voting: citizens do not believe that elected officials represent their interests.

As a result, politicians are seen as failing to meet the goals of representative democracy. Seven statements dealt with the perceived shortcomings of representative democracy: "Politicians do not listen to the public," "Politicians do not care about the public," "Politicians only care about people with money," "Politicians forget campaign promises," "Politicians should not be trusted," "Elected officials try to do the right thing," and "Politicians will say anything to get elected." There was a significant difference between the student voters and nonvoters for the statement that "politicians don't listen to the public," and that "politicians will say whatever it takes to get elected." On the statement that "politicians don't listen to the public," 56.4 percent of the voters disagreed; whereas, 43.8 percent of the nonvoters did. While a majority of both groups agreed that "politicians will say anything to get elected," nearly 30 percent of the nonvoters strongly agreed as compared to 16.7 percent of the voters. Conversely, only 7.5 percent of the nonvoters disagreed or strongly disagreed compared to 12.8 percent of the voters.

Students were willing to give politicians the benefit of the doubt, with over half of both voters and nonvoters disagreeing with the statement that politicians don't care and a similar percentage agreeing that they try to do the right thing. However, they were less charitable in their assessment of politicians' concern for money and their penchant for breaking campaign promises. Approximately 40 percent of both groups agreed with the former statement, and over 50 percent agreed with the latter. The open-ended word association statement, "politicians," yielded no significant differences in the types of words listed. Of the words listed by 538 participants, 53.7 percent of the voters included negative words as did 58.5 percent of the nonvoters; 42.6 percent of the voters had neutral descriptors compared to 35.2 percent of the nonvoters; and only 4 percent of the voters and 3 percent of the nonvoters had positive words.

On the seven statements that addressed the shortcomings of representative democracy, the percentages of focus group respondents agreeing with the statements were higher than were those for the nonvoting 18- to 25-year-olds. This resulted in significant differences for all but the statements that "politicians don't care about voters" and that "politicians only care about people with money" (see Appendix B, Table 1). Over half of the focus group members (57.4%) disagreed or strongly disagreed, but many of the participants who considered themselves middle class expressed the belief that politicians care about only those at the extremes. As a woman in Las Vegas noted, the middle class feels ignored: "I'm not rich enough, and I'm not poor enough. The campaigns, to me, seem that they're not talking to me." Others believed that politicians were generally too out of touch to understand or care about average citizens' needs. The representative anecdote of being out of touch from the 1990s was cited by the group in Martin, Tennessee, during their general discussion of politicians' attributes:

Female: I think that the politicians are so far out there that they don't even know what the real world's like anymore. They're up there in their big positions, and, ya know, they don't know what it's like to be, quote, common, or whatever...

Male: Like George Bush not recognizing the scanner at the grocery store when they scanned the UPC codes. When was that? Like 1990? Yeah, in 1990 he didn't know what it was. He thought it was some new-fangled machine in the super-market. He had no idea, not a clue. Besides that, George Bush hasn't been to the grocery store probably since '75. (Laughter) The computerized cash register was probably a surprise to him!

Male: So you're saying they're insulated? A lot of times politicians are, and I mean whether you like it or not, most of them are wealthy or very, very upper middle class and beyond.

Male: (acknowledging female member): I agree with her. They associate with each other all the time. They don't get to the local level, and see how...

Male: I would go so far as to say there's been many an honest politician who was probably corrupted by the system after getting in office who would never dream of doing the things that he or she did while in office, and yet, with the lobbyists and the temptations that's around them, it's almost just too much to say no.

This group expressed many sentiments suggestive of alienation from the system, but the discussion suggests that politicians have alienated themselves from their public rather than the more common interpretation of "alienation" being citizens feeling alienated from government. It is a subtle difference, but it reveals a great deal about the problems with political communication.

A group in Kansas City, Kansas, expounded on another aspect of alienation and that was the failure of politicians to keep promises and their focus on those with money:

Male: [In response to the prompt "politicians"] A bunch of lies. They promise all kinds of things, and then when it comes time to do it, it never happens. And when it's brought up to them, they either try to get around to it or say, "We'll face that problem soon," so to me it's just a bunch of lies.

Male: It's more along the lines of who can help me now and who can help me later type of thing. It's more of an ally system. They basically overwhelm people that can help them get accomplished what they want accomplished.

Male: Like he said, the only people they care about are the ones with the money. They don't touch them on taxes, but when it comes to their middle and lower class, we have to take out of our pockets. It's a dull-faced roaring monster. They're nice to your face, but they reach around your back and pull out your wallet and your money and take off.

The responses provide insight into voters' and nonvoters' attitudes about voting and toward the individuals whose names are on the ballot. In order to get more specific information as to why individuals stay home from the polls, especially since many of the responses to specific statements on the attitude questionnaire did not produce significant differences between voters and nonvoters, a set of questions was asked regarding nonparticipation.

REASONS FOR NONPARTICIPATION

Three open-ended questions were designed to determine if voters and nonvoters attribute different reasons for nonparticipation. Nonvoters were asked to explain why they did not vote in 1996. Nonvoters in 1996 who had voted in previous elections were asked what was different in 1996 that kept them home. A final question asked all respondents to speculate as to why they thought other people did not vote. Open-ended responses were placed into one of eight categories: apathy, disempowerment, ineligibility, voting and registration process, personal inconvenience, disillusioned with the system, candidate choices, and lack of information to make an informed decision. Contrary to conventional wisdom that would suggest alienation-related issues would be the most frequent responses, only 6 (2.2%) of the respondents cited disillusionment as the reason and only 23 (8.3%) didn't like the candidate choices. While separated into discrete categories, the most common reasons overlap. The most common responses for nonparticipation were as follows: ineligibility (28.3%), which included being underage at the time of the election or registration; problematic voting process (24%), which included not knowing how to get registered, not getting an absentee ballot in time, not being in the state where registered on election day, and changing addresses and not reregistering (which is also an eligibility issue but was not coded as such); and personal inconvenience (16.4%), which covered being too busy, not having a car, or being too lazy to make the effort. Only 10.9 percent of the respondents cited a lack of information or knowledge as their reason for not voting. For those who had voted in the past, none of the reasons dominated, with apathy receiving the smallest number of mentions (5.7%) and personal inconvenience (20%) the most.

The focus group comments were more in keeping with the popular view that people do not vote because they are disillusioned with the system. However, some individuals cited a move to a new city that made them ineligible, not having time to get off work, a lack of convenience for registering and voting, and a lack of information. Several participants who registered reasons more in keeping with expectations did not vote because they wanted to register a protest or not contribute to what they found disagreeable about politics and politicians. They expressed the opinion that by voting they suggested the system was all right and that was not a message they wanted to send. Many of the nonvoters in the focus groups who were once voters but had not voted for many years saw voting for the "lesser of two evils" as a way of perpetuating the problem. One individual in Wilmington, Delaware, was part of an organized movement to protest. He explained, "I chose to concede my vote and not vote, you know, out of protest. In '96 because of the church I'm affiliated with, they chose not to vote, and I feel comfortable with that." A woman in Detroit explained the protest nonvote this way:

The reason that I actively chose not to vote is because you're giving your consent. Like by your effort to go out there, you are consenting to give over your power to these people. And I don't wanna do that. I mean, I do a lot of things in my everyday life to try and let it be known and to put my voice out there and help other people put their voice out there, and that's what I'm doing, and that's where my consent is. I don't even want my consent associated with any of those people running for office.

Other individuals discussed the causes of their disillusionment with the people who run for office being a major one. A male in Bellingham, Washington, explained:

I think I've gotten really cynical about the choices that are offered. If somebody said, "You're given the choice of 'Tweedle Dum' and 'Tweedle Dee,'" well, why vote? To me it's like a food analogy—like being in a restaurant where everything on the menu is garbage. Why would you order anything at all? There's nothing there that looks even edible.

A woman in Detroit echoed the theme:

Yeah, I hear people use the phrase, "lesser of two evils," in elections all the time. Like everyone I know who DOES vote is like, "Well, I hate this guy. I don't trust him. I don't think he's going to do anything I want. I DON'T think he should be in power, but I like the other guy LESS." So why would you spend time out of your day to go and do that and say, "Okay, I really hate you, but there you go, run my life, please, because I hate the other guy even more." I mean, yeah, why give your consent to that? And that leaves a bad taste in my mouth.

Halfway across the country, a male in Las Vegas admitted,

I voted in '92, and it was kind of like I was listening to stuff and trying to figure out who would be the best, but I didn't really like anyone who was running so I just picked what I thought would be the lesser of two evils without really thinking of what kind of consequence that would have. And I think, come '96 I'd learned my lesson, and that's why I didn't vote in '96.

Another reason for not voting had nothing to do with elections at all: not wanting to be in a jury pool. One woman who reported this reason indicated that at least 15 people she knew didn't vote for the same reason; others in the group agreed that it was a reason.

The third question in this set asked respondents to speculate as to why others don't vote. It yielded interesting results as well. There were no significant differences between the reasons given by student voters and nonvoters; however, the reasons given by both survey respondents and focus group participants that were attributed to others did not correlate with the reasons given by nonvoters for why they did not vote. Both student groups listed apathy and disempowerment as the two major reasons, with 34.2 percent of the voters and 36.8 percent of the nonvoters citing the former, and 53.7 percent of the voters and 41 percent of the nonvoters citing the latter. Only 0.9 percent of voters and 0.8 percent of nonvoters attributed ineligibility as the reason. Of the nonvoters, 3.2 percent cited the process as did 2.8 percent of the voters. Personal inconvenience was the only top reason cited by both voters (23.8%) and nonvoters (25.2%) at levels that were consistent with the self-reports from the nonvoting students (see Table 2 in Appendix B).

The focus group members' analysis was similar to that of the students'. They cited apathy and frustration with the system as the major reasons for nonparticipation, with jobs, registration, and other process issues contributing to a lesser extent. This excerpt from the Las Vegas group is representative of the gap between self-reports and subjects' perceptions of others:

Female 1: Frankly, I think the people I know just don't care. They're just like, "Whatever!" It's just like walking down the street and kicking a can, you know? You don't pick it up, you just keep going. "Whatever…" And that's how they see it. They don't even look at it. They don't think about politics. They just don't.

Male 1: As far as presidential elections go, I think a lot of people think that not much is going to change no matter who's in office. There's going to be criticisms, and some people are not going to like what they do, and I think people just don't care.

Female 2: I think going back to the survey questions, it's kind of a feeling of apathy that whatever happens as far as politics go and who is the president is not going to have a direct effect on their life. So, they don't.

Female 1: Whatever happens is just going to happen. Regardless of what you do or what you say, it's going to happen.

Male 2: Also, it's kind of in the abstract…people don't know these people. Like, somewhere 3000 miles to the east of us, so what? How is that going to be impacting me? even on a local level I mean people don't go to city council meetings or things like that. They don't see any type of trickle down to the masses. So, why should they really care who it is? That's how I think a lot of people view it.

Female 3: Well, I know a lot of my friends who are minorities that didn't vote because of the history of the country. They don't care anymore because of the history of the country. They don't care anymore. They are really upset and frustrated.

While more focus group nonvoters than student nonvoters admitted to disillusionment and apathy, they were more likely to attribute apathy to others ("Just don't care," "Whatever…") than to themselves. Their explanations for their alienation or apathy versus that of others' were also more sophisticated. For instance, others were seen as being alienated because they were tired of the whole system and had given up, but many of the group members, as the quotations indicate, were making a conscious effort to communicate a message to those in power by refusing to participate. They considered this anything but apathy or disengagement and as noted previously, the alienation was not theirs but belonged to the politicians.

POLITICAL INFORMATION

Since few nonvoters cited a lack of information or knowledge as the reason for not voting, it was assumed that there would be few differences in the types and levels of information available to both groups, and that proved to be the case.

There were no significant differences in the types of media from which student voters, student nonvoters, and focus group members drew their information. However, there was a significant difference in their level of media consumption as indicated by the top three news sources reported previously in the section on news sources. While the majority from both groups indicated they regularly followed the news, either daily or several times per week, 14 percent more student voters than student nonvoters followed on a regular basis (51% versus 36.9%). When comparing the students' and focus group members' level of attention to the news, the percentage who follow daily or several times per week was 32 percent, while those in the three to four times per month category was nearly identical to the other two groups with 23 percent listing this level of attention. The 19-point difference between student voters and focus group members was significant. Given that most participants read local newspapers and watched nightly network news, the type of information available to both groups is similar.

LANGUAGE ABOUT POLITICS

The language people use to discuss politics and politicians typically reflects their attitudes. The study was designed to identify language differences, if any, between voters and nonvoters when describing the attributes of politics and politicians. Word association questions in the open-ended section of the survey and the focus group responses provided examples of language choices. Subjects were asked to state what came to mind when seeing or hearing the following words or phrases: politics, politician, news media elections/campaigns, and political advertising. There were no significant differences in the ratios of positive, negative, and neutral statements listed by the two student groups, with over 50 percent of the terms listed by each group falling into the negative category (voters = 53.7%; nonvoters = 58.7%), and only 4 percent of the voters' and 3 percent of nonvoters' comments fell into the positive category. The terms listed by both groups in all three categories were essentially the same (see Appendix B for a summary). For example, positive statements usually dealt with the ideal. "A way of bettering society" was used to explain politics, and a politician was described as "a person who listens to the public and tries to make positive changes in the laws." Neutral language commonly included definitions. "Politics" was used interchangeably with "government" and "laws." For the term, "politicians," definitions included "an elected official" or "the people behind the politics." Both groups tended to see politics as "complex" or "complicated," and not necessarily because of its inherent nature but due to the way that politics and campaigns are conducted.

The word association section of the focus group discussion produced nearly identical ratios of positive, negative, and neutral terms to those on the student surveys. In fact, most of the language was very similar for the word association discussion. In the more extensive discussions within the focus groups, the terms that were given at the outset of the discussions were used frequently throughout. Two of the more common referents for politicians by both students and focus group members were "rich white guys" and "men in suits;" often they were combined. Even when these terms weren't used per se, the discussion quoted in previous sections suggests that many nonvoters think of elected officials and those involved in politics as being wealthy or different from them. A common theme on both the surveys and in the discussions was the corruption that results from the large amounts of money in politics—either from personal wealth, interest groups, or political parties. This exchange in Detroit is illustrative:

Female: If you talk about presidential politics—even local politics—you don't get on the ballot unless you've got a lot of money…and once you get there, even if you DIDN'T come from a lot of money, all of a sudden, you're surrounded by a lot of money. So the decisions—with the way this system works—the decision will always be made by big money. Whether I vote for this guy or whether I vote for that guy, I can think he's representing me, but he's not gonna. After I get him the job, he's gonna be representing whoever can pay him the most, like, to take big vacations. No matter who I vote for, money is still gonna control it!

Male: It's like the lobbyists. I mean I think I'm as personable as any of them, but how can you get a job making like $200,000 and all you have to do is walk up and talk to somebody and be real personable and ask them to vote our way and they can go over here to Palm Beach and play 18 holes.

A male in Kansas City, Kansas, echoed this theme when he said, "If you've got the most money, then you've got my UNDIVIDED attention. I'll clear everybody else that's standing out in the hallway." A male in Wilmington, Delaware, was equally cynical with his comment that "billionaires that control money in a corporation are not going to let just anybody become President." And a male in Martin, Tennessee, related money to the importance of a single vote when he commented, "And only money people seem to have their views heard the best, too. I'm not saying one vote doesn't make a difference. I'm just saying my vote with $200,000,000 behind it makes a whole lot of difference."

Both survey responses and focus group discussions were filled with emotional and colorful responses, especially to the word association questions. Voters and nonvoters alike expressed frustration and an overall sense of negativity based on themes that are common in the media—scandals, corruption, broken promises, influence of big money, lack of issues that affect the average citizen, and political gamesmanship.

SOLUTIONS TO POLITICAL PROBLEMS

The study also sought to determine if voters and nonvoters offer similar solutions to the problems they identified. Four open-ended questions on the survey addressed this topic: "What are the major problems, if any, with American politics today?"; "What can be done to resolve the problems?"; "What would it take to get you more interested in politics?"; and "Do you have any other comments to make about politics, political campaigns or media coverage of campaigns?" Examples of statements illustrating responses to each of the four questions on the student survey are provided in Appendix B. As stated in the methods section, statements fell into one of six categories (numbers indicate how many respondents identified this as a problem): flawed candidates (262), negative and costly campaign process (185), failure to address citizens' and the country's needs (78), media (75), public apathy (46), and specific issues that need to be resolved (32). There were no significant differences in the terms listed among the three groups or in their frequency.

There were also no significant differences in the solutions offered. The recommendations fell into the following categories: campaign and political process reform (158), more accountability by politicians and media (97), broaden the candidate base (93), reform the media (76), nothing can be done (59), and unsure of the solution (45). Problems and solutions offered by the focus group members were phrased nearly identically and fell into the same categories. One solution discussed as a candidate reform measure that was offered by the focus groups but not by the students was the need for a new party or stronger third parties because of the breakdown of the two-party system.

Both student voters and student nonvoters gave similar responses to the third question asking what needed to be done to increase their interest in politics. The top responses included better candidates (132), relevant issues to life (120), access to useful information (111), already interested (87), nothing (64), having more power and voice in the system (58), and reformed media (22). The last item included many specific suggestions such as more useful information, less analysis and more facts about candidates' histories and positions, more focus on the issues and on positive accomplishments and attributes, and more accountability for information reported by media and given by candidates. These suggestions reinforce the DebateWatch comments discussed in chapters five and eight that people want substantive information from candidates that reflects past records and clear policy positions. The final open-ended question asking for additional comments yielded too few comments to provide for meaningful analysis. Most of the statements were repetitive of answers to other questions.

The focus group discussions yielded similar responses on all questions to those given by the student participants with an emphasis on money as the major problem. They recommended equalizing the playing field as a solution through spending limits or public financing. Money was also seen as giving the two parties power to restrict voters' choices of candidates. While participants knew they were discussing the ideal when it came to solutions, they were also able to inject reality. This excerpt from the Las Vegas group was representative of discussions that took place in most of the groups:

Male: I think the parties have too much power.... Simply because of the overwhelming Republican/Democrat dichotomy all over the news and everywhere, you didn't hear about the Green party or the economic reformists or any of the other people that like, you know, had like one single issue they were fighting for. And in our "all or nothing" political arena, the small fries and the underdogs are just washed over by the gigantic tidal waves of political propaganda and advertising and campaigning that the gigantic Democrats have or that the Republicans have with all the money and contributions they have. I mean when supporters that can pay $50,000 for a dinner to come and hear Gore talk about something, how are the people that are out handing out hand-made pamphlets on street corners going to compete with that?

Male: They can't.

Male: Exactly. That's a problem, I think.

Female: That just hits the nail right on the head. It's all my way or no way and that's for both sides. It's really really screwed up.

Female: But if we could somehow get money completely out of it....

Female: One hundred percent out of it and just have it be that the best person will get that job. The most effective, best leader who stands for what everyone else in the country wants should have the job, not the guy with the most money to have the best platform. But I don't think, in a capitalist society, that it's possible.

In addition to discussion of money, for which there was no admitted easy solution, group members had more pragmatic solutions as well. Several groups discussed the need to make registration easier or information about voting laws more accessible. The problem of not having time to vote was discussed by several participants and comparisons to other countries that have holidays were made. A Detroit participant noted, "Although it might not change whether or not I vote, I think a National Voting Day—everybody has the day off from work—I think that would be an incentive for more people than currently vote to vote."

Echoing comments heard in the 1992 presidential debates focus groups and the 1996 DebateWatch groups, several groups commented on the need to know what and how someone would solve a problem as well as the desire for less partisanship. This comment from a Martin, Tennessee, nonvoter is representative:

Male: Can we put the word "solutions" in there? It seems like we concentrate constantly where there's a line here, and you're either on one side or the other, and there has to be this conflict. And you can't be a Democrat and agree with a Republican on this issue or that issue because fundamentally you just can't because of the danger of not getting elected. You have to oppose. And I would really like to see more solutions discussed instead of "Why I'm against it and why it's horrible."

Overall, the solutions were practical, thoughtful, and reasonable responses to the problems they outlined. The fact that both the students and focus group participants readily listed multiple solutions suggests that the public does think about these problems and does more than just complain even if some of them choose not to vote. Participants in our study obviously wanted to be heard in way that spoke differently than a vote or else they would not have given up their time.

CAMPAIGN MESSAGES AND MEDIA COVERAGE

In the discussion of problems and solutions, the media and political advertising were mentioned frequently. The final topic addressed in the study was whether or not voters and nonvoters differed in their assessments of the value of campaign messages and news about politics. Three statements addressed this topic: "political issues are too complicated for the average person to understand," "there is too much negative advertising in campaigns," and "news media coverage of politics is too negative." There were no significant differences on student responses to any of the three statements. On the statement regarding issue complexity, 66.2 percent of the voters disagreed or strongly disagreed that the issues are too complicated, and 68.4 percent of the nonvoters responded in a similar fashion. On the two statements dealing with negativity, both voters and nonvoters agreed that there is too much negative campaigning and that news media coverage is too negative. Responses related to the media were nearly identical. While fewer nonvoters than voters thought that the advertising was negative (63.7% versus 73.6%), more nonvoters had no opinion (23.2% versus 14.9%). The differences were not statistically significant at the .05 level, however. The suggestions regarding a reformed media that were reported in previous section also revealed respondents' attitudes toward the media and show a consistency of opinion.

When responses from focus group participants were compared to those of the student sample, there were significant differences regarding the complexity of the issues and negative advertising. Thirty-four percent of the focus group members agreed or strongly agreed that the issues are too complex as compared to 18.7 percent of the student voters and 17.7 percent of the student nonvoters. The difference in opinion about negative advertising is explained by the fact that a higher percentage had no opinion on the subject because they don't pay attention to the advertising. As noted in the discussion in the previous section, the negativity of campaigns and media coverage of campaigns and politics was cited by all three groups as a major problem that needs correcting.

The open-ended questions asked if the media and candidates provide enough and the right kind of information to make an informed choice as a voter and what was needed that isn't currently provided. Over half of both student voters and nonvoters said that the media provides enough and the right kind of information (53.3% for voters and 59.3% for nonvoters). The top six suggested improvements and the percentage of respondents identifying them were: accountability for information (29.3%), more on candidate positions and record (20.7%), more focus on issues (13%), less analysis and more facts (10.7%), better access to information (10%), and more focus on candidate positives (9%). Focus group participants believed the information was available, but that it took work to find it all. Focus group perceptions of media messages are borne out by research cited previously in the book that while candidate messages are primarily issue-oriented, media coverage emphasizes nonissues such as horse race and campaign strategy.

WHAT DOES IT ALL MEAN?

In the final sentence of his book, *Why Americans Hate Politics*, E. J. Dionne claims, "A nation that hates politics will not long survive as a democracy."[9] However, the focus group participant in Wilmington, Delaware, who wanted to stage a coup and clean up government saw his outrage over the state of American politics as a means to return the country to democracy. Nonvoters in this study did not believe that it was their hatred of politics and their nonparticipation that threatens democracy. They see those who are at the center of American political life—politicians, those with money, and the media—as the real threats.

Three possible explanations were given for low voter turnout in 1996 when this study was inspired: people are satisfied with current economic conditions, they are disenchanted with politics and politicians, or the race was a foregone conclusion so why bother. Many of the participants in this study were not entirely satisfied with the current political and economic environment. In fact, many expressed concern that they are not benefiting from the robust economy and that the political system overlooked middle-class wage earners. It did appear from the data reported in this study that nonvoters and voters, alike, were disenchanted, frustrated, and critical of the political system and for a variety of reasons sat out the election. There was no discussion of the inevitability of Bill Clinton's reelection, but the fact that they did not feel they had real choices suggested a sense of inevitability on a different level.

In examining the surveys and focus group transcripts, it is also clear that some of the conventional wisdom concerning both voters and nonvoters requires re-examination. This study suggests that voters and nonvoters are more similar than dissimilar in their political attitudes, and that nonvoters define political participation or fulfillment of civic responsibility as more than the act of voting. The phenomenon described as "voter rage,"[10] which sends some individuals to the polls, is exactly the thing that keeps others away. The results, however, do support other studies and theories posited in popular and academic analyses of contemporary American politics. For example, the increased emphasis on negative campaigning and negative political reporting contributed to a growing cynicism among the population as a whole.[11] Partisanship and the swing between liberal and conservative philosophies leave many feeling excluded.[12] The findings that were consistent with previous research and theories, and those that suggest we should view voting differently are examined as a means of suggesting new approaches to voter education, political dialogue, and definitions of civic responsibility.

Common and Uncommon Ground among Voters and Nonvoters

Relatively few significant differences were found between voters and nonvoters in their attitudes about politics and the language they used to discuss it. Where significant differences did exist, the reasons for the differences were not necessarily what were expected. Significant percentages of both voters and nonvoters in our study believe that government does affect their everyday lives, and most of their examples were economic ones. Many feel powerless to influence who is elected and also don't believe they can influence those who are in power or that there is much difference among the candidate choices. The powerlessness is not something that they believe voting relieves even if the candidate they support wins. Statements by both voters and nonvoters regarding control of the process by those with money and failure of candidates and the media to raise salient issues explain why there is a commonality of perceptions, but not why there is a difference in actions.

One explanation may be found by looking at profiles of voters, both in our sample and in the population overall. Our sample of voters was taken largely from 18- to 25-year-olds who tended to be white, middle and upper middle class. They may be critical of the system, using the same language to disparage it that nonvoters use, but the system essentially works for them and those outside believe it does benefit this group. The voters also represent the socioeconomic groups whose parents tend to vote, and they are more likely to vote as a result. In fact, some of their answers on the surveys and in the student focus group referred to the sense of "duty" their parents had instilled in them about voting. While many in our nonvoter focus groups had voted at one point in time, they were not individuals who considered themselves as part or beneficiaries of the system. Interestingly, a majority of nonvoters disagreed with the statement that politicians don't care. However, their discussion revealed that they believe politicians care about individuals unlike themselves. Based on criticisms of the media for providing little positive information, this suggests to us that they do not believe they have the "facts" to make a valid judgment about elected officials' intent.

Media and Technology Effects

One possible explanation for the similarities in perceptions about the system and the overwhelmingly negative language used by all three groups is the media itself, which has convinced most Americans that the system is corrupt, controlled by money, and inhabited by individuals who are nothing like the public. As was discussed in chapter five, the media serve an agenda setting function, and their emphasis on the negative definitely is mirrored in comments from voters and nonvoters alike. The word association exercise with only three or four positive responses reflects the negativity in the media. Students were less likely to have experienced the personal disappointments that focus group members reported and were more likely to be repeating the conventional wisdom based on media reports.

Agenda setting also explains why both voters and nonvoters attributed reasons why others do not vote that were dissimilar to their own explanations for not voting. They have heard and read that people don't vote because they are apathetic; thus, that is the expected explanation for others. The self-report could also explain why they chose more socially acceptable explanations, but the focus group members listed apathy more than did those on the survey. Students, especially, have more logistical problems related to voting than do individuals who are not living away from home. This explains why the process and eligibility issues dominated. However, it also provides insights into what needs to be done and what actually has been done to increase voter turnout for 18- to 25-year-olds. Since 1996, the growth of the Internet has impacted youth participation. They used technology to mobilize for John McCain in 2000, for Howard Dean and John Kerry in 2004, and for Barack Obama in unprecedented numbers for primaries and caucuses. It also provided a way for individuals supporting all candidates in 2004 and even more so in 2008 to make small donations online or to become part of a campaign organization. Individuals who had never given to a campaign before combined to break numerous fundraising records in 2008 through small contributions.

Some might argue that while nonvoters say they want more information and want candidates to address their agendas, there is no assurance they will actually vote. However, the increased turnout in the 1992 and 2004 general elections and the 2008 primaries suggests what can happen when citizens believe that their agenda is at the center of a campaign, when their voices are heard in the process, and when they have choices that they consider different or better than in the past. The 1992 surge in voters occurred largely because Ross Perot, whose presence in the campaign forced an economic agenda and more discussion of issues, was able to command media attention and had the money to get his message across. Many focus group participants discussed Perot, especially those who had voted in 1992 but sat out 1996, as an example of the rare situation in which citizens are in the driver's seat. In 2004 the war in Iraq and the faltering economy mobilized voters of all ages. In 2008, the presence of a woman and an African American male as serious candidates created levels of interest and registration of new voters in record-breaking numbers. When one reflects on the word association reactions to "politicians" as "rich white men," it is easier to understand the attraction to individuals who don't fit the stereotypical mold. The general election in 2008 provides additional insights into the impact of technology, new players, and old players with a maverick streak on voter participation. The 2008 campaign is different from previous ones because of the candidates and because there is more contact with voters and more opportunity for their input.

TURNING NONVOTERS INTO VOTERS: CAN IT BE DONE?

All research takes place within a context and the post-1996 focus groups certainly had theirs. However, not much changed in 2000 in terms of voter turnout, especially among younger voters. It took the prolonged election of 2000 and the 9/11 attacks and their aftermath to produce increased turnout for all age cohorts in 2004. Increased participation did not translate into satisfaction with politics or politicians. Expressions of dissatisfaction with the candidates, their campaigns, and the media were still voiced in focus groups as reported in previous chapters. The 2008 election garnered earlier and increased interest because of new technologies and new approaches to politics. The media, however, continued to devote most of its attention to the horse race, campaign strategies, and character issues. On the positive side, there were record numbers of debates and candidates such as John McCain used town hall meetings in New Hampshire to his advantage to jump-start what was seen as a moribund campaign.

If there is an implication for the future of political participation that goes beyond a snapshot analysis of the post-1996 political climate, it is one that has been reported by others: we need to find new means of creating a public sphere that either encourages politicians to discuss the public agenda, as the presidential debate town hall meetings, alternative media, and the Internet have progressively done since 1992, or we need to find alternative ways to discuss civic issues that return politics to the grassroots levels and separate it from elections. Perhaps there is a need to do both.

How the latter is done is not simple because our research also indicates that people are busy and have to deal with the mundane elements of their lives. The fact that nonvoters participated in the focus groups indicates that they do want to talk and are willing to take the time if they think it might change the process. For some, participating in the focus group and survey was a way of contributing that went beyond simply voting. Many participants said it gave them a chance to air their opinions and justify their actions in a way they hadn't be able to before. Similar to the original DebateWatch research participants, who punctuated their comments with "thank yous" for listening, many participants in this study were grateful for the opportunity to discuss politics with others in a civil manner. Blogs and interactive Web sites enable citizens to take part in the political conversation and the Internet's power is just beginning to be realized to create a virtual public sphere.

While this study examined voting, future research should do more to discover how to expand participation and dialogue by average citizens outside of elections. In research and news reporting, people tend to focus on voting as the most ideal, and sometimes the only way of participating. However, as many of the participants were quick to point out, it is not the only way, or even necessarily the most effective way of participating in a representative democracy. Nonvoters indicated that being active in a variety of ways, including community service and correspondence with representatives, as well as discussions with others, contributes to the well-being of democratic institutions. Participation takes different forms for each person, and limiting the judgment of citizenship to voting patterns discounts the civic contributions of average citizens in the larger democratic arena.

Along with altering the way civic participation is perceived and information is made available, a final area needing to be covered deals with voter research and how we approach it in the future. First and foremost, we need to be paying much more attention to the nonvoters. Rather than having pollsters disregard people who do not intend to vote, we need to be asking why they are not. We need to be getting feedback from nonvoters immediately after the elections are over to verify why they sat the election out. This will help publicize the "protest" nonvotes and further an understanding of the messages they are trying to send.

With technology that can create a virtual gathering of people from across the country, the media should capitalize on the public's desire to shape candidates' agendas. Citizens will be engaged if they are invited to participate on many levels, especially in ways that enable them to make their voices heard. The 2008 election, again, stands as proof of that. If there is a lesson from the nonvoter study and from DebateWatch, in general, it is that people welcome a chance to be heard and to contribute. There are unlimited ways to make that happen in the political process and the political climate since 1996 suggests that it is happening.

Sustaining interest and participation is difficult as the ebb and flow of turnout over the past 16 years indicates. One reason that was given for not participating was a lack of choices or new voices. Chapter 10 examines an element of voter frustration that relates to the desire for alternative voices through third parties.

Chapter Ten

The Majors and the Minors: Who Should Participate in Debates?

Third parties are a regular part of U.S. elections despite their relative lack of success at the polls. Since the founding of the Republican Party in 1854, no third party has achieved major party status. When Abraham Lincoln was elected the first Republican president in 1860, the party had virtually subsumed the Whigs to become the new member of the two-party system that has dominated U.S. politics for over two hundred years. While the founders had no intention of creating political parties, they were complicit in their development and in fostering the two-party system. Political scientists Paul Herrnson and John Green explained, "The seeds for the two-party system came from the British Parliament. They were sown during the Colonial era and firmly rooted by the time the Federalists and Anti-Federalists battled over ratification of the U.S. Constitution."[1]

The existence of the two-party system does not deter other parties from forming. Typically when they do appear, it is as "an expression of discontent with the major parties and their candidates."[2] The ebb and flow of third parties and independent candidates is well documented. Between 1992 and 2000 there was a flow; by 2004, and clearly in 2008, the ebb set in. After Ross Perot's historic 19 percent finish in 1992, the total number of votes cast for all non-major candidates in 1996 was 10.1 percent, with Perot receiving 8.3 percent. In 2000, 3.75 percent of the ballots went to non-majors, with Ralph Nader receiving 2.74 percent. The total dropped again in 2004 when only 1 percent of the popular vote went to all non-major party candidates. Nader garnered only 0.3 percent that year.[3]

When presidential debates occur during the flow period, the issue of whether or not candidates other than the major party candidates should be included has led to considerable controversy, which is reflected in viewers' discussions of the debates. The minor party controversy serves as a larger barometer of public thinking about the parties and the role of debates in elections. Two of the debate cycles discussed in this book included media and public reaction to the issue of third party inclusion; thus, the issue needs to be addressed.

In order to fully appreciate the decisions related to third party inclusion and to put the citizen comments into perspective, this chapter deviates from the others in that it includes considerable historical and contextual information before presenting citizens' viewpoints. Debate sponsors of both primary and general election debates have come under attack regarding their policies for determining inclusion; thus, it is important to uncover the issues surrounding past decisions and legal opinions regarding those decisions. Some of the context is provided from the perspective of one of the book's authors, Diana Carlin, who played a role in the decisions regarding third party inclusion from 1988 until 1996.

Since third party inclusion is a contentious and litigious issue, it is important to frame the issue historically and legally before examining citizen talk about it. The historical information that follows includes a summary of the issues faced by sponsors prior to 1996 and then examines the arguments candidates and citizens made in 1996 and 2000. Since arguments included criticism of the sponsor, the Commission on Presidential Debates, a brief history of the Commission and its process for candidate selection is outlined. The citizen voices shared in this chapter include both e-mail and DebateWatch comments. In fact, this was an issue that was given more life via e-mails than in the DebateWatch groups.

THIRD PARTIES AND PRESIDENTIAL DEBATES

Beginning with the first televised general election presidential debates in 1960, the issue of third party and independent candidate inclusion has been a recurring one. The Kennedy-Nixon debates proceeded as major party debates through an act of Congress that suspended the equal time provision—Section 315—of the Federal Communications Act of 1934. The act required broadcasters to give free airtime equally to all candidates for political office. With well over 100 presidential candidates, each of whom was on at least one state's ballot, any debate would be impossible if all participated. The suspension made a two-party debate possible. Justice Anthony M. Kennedy wrote a majority opinion in a Supreme Court decision several years after the 1960 debates that upheld the right of public television stations to place restrictions on who is invited to debate: "Were it faced with the prospect of cacophony, on the one hand, and First Amendment liability on the other, a public television broadcaster might choose not to air candidates' views at all," but Kennedy further noted that such a decision would "not promote speech but repress it."[4] There were no debates between 1960 and 1976, due in part to Section 315 and the need for Congressional action to pave the way for major candidate debates. Front-runners played politics with attempts to suspend Section 315 in order to avoid debates.[5] Between 1960 and 2004 several changes affected how the decision regarding independent and minor party inclusion was made.

A HISTORY OF CANDIDATE SELECTION

In 1975, the Federal Communications Commission ruled in its *Aspen* decision that debates were not subject to the equal time provision if they were "bona fide news events" not sponsored by the media, were not held in broadcast studios as were the Kennedy-Nixon matches, were covered live, were covered in their entirety, and met a journalistic standard of being newsworthy.[6]

In 1976, the League of Women Voters stepped forward as the sponsor and announced in May of that year that the debates would be limited to candidates from the two major parties. According to an account of the League's decision making, "The solution to the third party dilemma was, and is, beyond the League's problem solving ability—it lies with Congress, the courts, and the Federal Election Commission."[7] Independent candidate Eugene McCarthy, American party candidate Thomas Anderson, American Independent party candidate Lester Maddox, and Socialist Workers candidate Peter Camejo challenged the League's decision to include only the major party candidates. McCarthy and Anderson filed suits in federal court, and Maddox and Camejo took their cases to the FCC. The League's decision was upheld by both bodies.[8]

In reaching their decision to limit participation, the League acknowledged a political reality about debates that continues to affect the decisions regarding inclusion: "To invite every legally qualified candidate was a patent impossibility [there were 160 in 1976]; to select one or two of the major 'minor' party contenders would have been arbitrary and less defensible than the course it chose."[9]

The situation in 1980 was more difficult for the League. In August, the League announced three criteria for inclusion that were used in 1980 and 1984: (1) constitutional eligibility, (2) demonstrated ballot eligibility in enough states to have a mathematical possibility of winning a majority of electoral votes, and (3) demonstrated voter interest in the candidacy by meeting a 15 percent threshold in public opinion polls.[10] Independent candidate John Anderson, who had run in the Republican primaries against Ronald Reagan, continued to hold public interest. Anderson met the League's three criteria and was invited. The criteria did not stop complaints from other candidates, however. Libertarian Ed Clark called the 15 percent decision "unreasonable and narrowly partisan."[11]

The controversy was not limited to complaints by candidates deemed ineligible to debate in 1980. President Carter did not want a three-way debate. He and his advisors feared that Anderson would gain at Carter's expense. Reagan insisted on having Anderson in the first debate but was willing to do a second without him.[12] The League held its first scheduled debate without Carter. What resulted was historic: a debate without one major party candidate and with an independent challenging a nonincumbent major party candidate. When Anderson's ratings fell below 15 percent after the debate, Carter agreed to a single debate with Reagan.

In 1981, the FCC altered its original view of the *Aspen* decision to allow debates to be held in studios for "technical convenience" so long as a qualified sponsor made the arrangements. Two years later, the FCC further altered its original decision when it ruled that radio and television stations had the right to sponsor debates with selected candidates for an office without violating the equal time provision. These changes in the FCC ruling failed to eliminate legal challenges to the League's selection of only the two major party candidates in 1984—Ronald

Reagan and Walter Mondale. While no one of the national stature of McCarthy, Maddox, or John Anderson was running in 1984, Citizens Party candidate Sonia Johnson petitioned the FCC to be included. The request was denied.

THE COMMISSION ON PRESIDENTIAL DEBATES

Between 1984 and 1988 the issue of inclusion in debates took another twist with the establishment of the Commission on Presidential Debates (CPD) in 1987. To fully understand the changes made in selection of participants from 1996–2004, a brief history of the CPD is necessary. The CPD was formed as a result of two studies. The Commission on National Elections, a group formed by Georgetown's Center for Strategic and International Studies, conducted the first study in 1985. Melvin Laird, former chair of the Republican National Committee and former Secretary of Defense, and Robert Strauss, former chair of the Democratic National Committee, co-chaired the Commission.

In 1986, the Twentieth Century Fund (now the Century Fund) and Harvard's Institute of Politics sponsored the second study. Newton Minow, a former FCC commissioner who was instrumental in securing the 1960 suspension of Section 315, and 30 participants in and observers of presidential debates convened to study the future of presidential debates. The League of Women Voters participated in both studies. The Commission on National Elections' final report in April 1986 included a recommendation for party sponsorship of future debates to achieve institutionalization.[13] As suggested by the report, then Republican Chair Frank Fahrenkopf and Democrat Chair Paul Kirk, signed a Memorandum of Agreement on Presidential Candidate Joint Appearances indicating that they would pursue the recommended course.

The Twentieth Century Fund's recommendations for future sponsorship were included in its report, *For Great Debates: A New Plan for Future Presidential TV Debates* by Newton N. Minow and Clifford M. Sloan. The authors concluded that:

> political parties are the most likely vehicle for institutionalizing debates. Because of their close relationship to the candidates, political parties can accomplish much of the debate planning well in advance of the actual campaign, and to a great extent, commit the candidates to the planning of the details.[14]

To accomplish this goal, the report recommended establishment of a "not-for-profit, tax-exempt, bipartisan Presidential Debates Organization to plan and administer a series of presidential debates."[15] The structure was envisioned as having "a broadly based committee, composed of various citizens and groups to help advise on the sponsorship of debates."[16]

The Twentieth Century Fund's study provided much of the framework for the Commission on Presidential Debates once it was organized. The one major exception is that there is no direct connection to the major parties other than the CPD originally being organized by past party chairs. The Commission is a nonpartisan—not bipartisan—not-for-profit, tax-exempt organization with a two-fold mission: to sponsor presidential and vice presidential general election debates and to serve as a source of voter education through the debates.[17] Based on its mission, the CPD has sponsored the debates since 1988 and has supported voter education through preparation of debate history materials distributed to schools in 1988; development of a video and brochure on how to sponsor a debate; sponsorship of postelection seminars on debate formats and issues surrounding sponsorship in 1990, 1993, and 1997; sponsorship of research in 1992 on debate formats and voter education; and sponsorship of Debate Watch '96, 2000, and 2004. The CPD has also advised debate sponsors in numerous countries throughout the world.

Tax ordinance 501 (c) (3) states that as a tax exempt organization the Commission "may not attempt to influence legislation as a substantial part of its activities and it may not participate in any campaign activity for or against political candidates."[18] As such, it is funded through private donations. No party or government funds were used in carrying out the debates between 1988 and 2004. The CPD makes public the list of direct contributors to its work and the contributors who were solicited by the host sites to defray their expenses. The media and critics of the CPD refer to it as bipartisan and it is easy to understand why given its genesis and the role of former party chairs as CPD chairs. However, the tax status requires nonpartisanship, which essentially means that the CPD cannot and does not take political stances on issues or directly engage in any aspect of partisan politics.

The Commission on Presidential Debates was originally composed of 12 directors, an executive director, and a 40-member advisory board consisting of representatives from business, the arts, academe, public policy, and the media. Over the years, the formal advisory board ceased to exist; however, outside advisors representing a broad spectrum of backgrounds and over one hundred voter education partners assist the CPD in the arrangements for and production of the debates, use of technology, and other voter education activities. The membership of the board at the time this was written consisted of Howard Buffett, John C. Danforth, Antonia Hernandez, Caroline Kennedy, Michael D. McCurry, Newton N. Minow, Dorothy Ridings, Alan K. Simpson, and H. Patrick Swygert. While some of these individuals are clearly partisans, others such as Minow, who is known for his work with the Federal Communications Commission, Ridings who is a past-president of the League of Women Voters, and Swygert, the President of Howard University, are not readily associated with partisan issues.[19]

During the summer of 1987, the advisory board was appointed by the co-chairmen. The advisory board met on October 1, 1987, to discuss procedures for selection of a panel of questioners and guidelines for inclusion of third party candidates. As a result of the meeting, a subcommittee composed of Richard Neustadt, Anne Wexler, and then-Senator Pete Wilson developed a set of criteria for determining participation by third party candidates based on research presented by Neustadt at the October meeting. This was an important step to meet the Federal Election Commission (FEC) and Federal Communications Commission (FCC) requirements and also to demonstrate that the CPD would not limit debate to the two major parties when inclusion criteria were met. It also provided a consistent philosophy for inclusion that transcended any single campaign cycle.

THE COMMISSION'S THIRD PARTY CRITERIA

The subcommittee, headed by Neustadt and based on the guiding principle that the criteria should allow an individual who has "more than a theoretical chance" of being elected an opportunity to debate, developed the following set of criteria: (1) evidence of a national organization as determined by declaration of candidacy, ballot access to make it mathematically possible to win sufficient electoral votes, and eligibility for matching funds; (2) signs of national newsworthiness and competitiveness based on media coverage and opinions of electoral experts; and (3) signs of national enthusiasm or concern, editorials by leading commentators, and inclusion in polling data.[20]

Using the criteria, the Neustadt Committee[21] reviewed information on all candidates who had filed with the Federal Election Commission for the offices of president and vice president. The committee concluded that no independent or minor party candidates met the criteria for inclusion. Dr. Lenora B. Fulani, a third party candidate representing a coalition of groups, filed a suit in federal court in North Carolina (site of the first debate) two days before the first debate asking to be included. The CPD's decision was upheld, as was an appeal the following day.

In 1992, the first serious test of the Commission's criteria took place. Prior to Ross Perot's reentry into the race on October 1, 1992, the Neustadt Committee[22] determined that no viable independent or minor party candidates qualified for debate participation. With Perot's decision to return, the committee again met via phone on October 5, 1992, and recommended to the Board of Directors that an invitation be issued to Ross Perot and James Stockdale. The recommendation was made with the proviso that the invitation be reviewed between debates. The recommendation was accepted; however, the schedule of four debates in nine days did not allow for collection of sufficient feedback or time to reassess the Perot candidacy and the board accepted the recommendation for inclusion but issued the invitation for all four debates. As in 1988, Fulani challenged her exclusion through the courts but was again denied a slot in the debates.

Critics of the CPD alleged that Perot's inclusion resulted from pressure by the two parties and even fear that another sponsor would take over.[23] Diana Carlin was part of the advisory group that met on October 5 and recalls that early on in the discussion, the question was posed to CPD representatives: "If we decide against inclusion, will the board stand behind the decision even if it means losing debate sponsorship?" The committee was told that loss of sponsorship was not a consideration. With the assurance that the deliberations and resulting recommendation would be taken seriously by the board regardless of its impact on the CPD's sponsorship, the committee spent approximately two hours applying the Neustadt criteria to the Perot-Stockdale ticket. The discussion included a summary of interviews conducted by Neustadt and Carlin with media and academic experts. Each element of the criteria was reviewed and the conclusion that Perot should be included was based on his past standing in the polls (he was the front-runner at 39% in May 1996), the immediate positive reaction to his reentry, his ability to finance a national campaign, his name recognition and media accessibility, his grassroots support, and his potential (based on interviews with experts) to possibly win a state or two and throw the election into the Electoral College. At no time in the discussions were the wishes of either major party candidate to have Perot included considered. The committee took its task seriously and based its recommendation on application of the criteria it was asked to consider.

Given that the level of public interest in the 1996 election was low and that the polls had remained relatively constant since February,[24] the only real excitement centered on whether anyone other than the major party candidates, and specifically Ross Perot, would participate. In the wake of his 19 percent showing in 1992, Perot established a new party, the Reform Party, and was its standard-bearer in '96. In addition to Perot, Green party candidate Ralph Nader, Libertarian Harry Browne, and Natural Law Party candidate John Hagelin were also garnering national attention and claiming a place at the debates. As in past years, dozens of other lesser known candidates appeared as well and the types of issues they were supporting varied.[25]

Using the same criteria as in 1988 and 1992, the Neustadt Committee, which was composed of the same five individuals from 1992, met via conference call in September and reviewed the list of over one hundred individuals who had filed candidacy papers with the Federal Election Commission. Prior to the call, committee members received notebooks with information relevant to the criteria for each of the candidates. Many were not affiliated with a party but with a cause or idea, and only four—Perot, Browne, Hagelin, and Howard Phillips of the Taxpayers Party—met the first test of being on a sufficient number of ballots to achieve a majority in the Electoral College. The committee reviewed the two major party candidates and decided that they both had more than a theoretical chance of winning. In applying each of the 11 indicators to the four minor party candidates, the advisory committee concluded that none of the candidates met a sufficient number of criteria to meet the "more than theoretical" standard. In issuing the advisory committee's recommendation to the board, Neustadt summarized that group's deliberations:

> We begin with Mr. Ross Perot, now of the Reform Party. We have reviewed the data your staff has assembled for us, supplemented by telephonic inquiries of our own [of] political scientist and political journalists across the country. We have concluded that, at this stage of the campaign, Mr. Perot has no realistic chance either of popular election in November or of subsequent election by the House of Representatives, in the event no candidate obtains an Electoral College majority. None of the expert observers we have consulted thinks otherwise. Some point to possibilities of extraordinary events later in the campaign, but grant that those possibilities do not change the likelihood as of today.
>
> Four years ago, we confronted an unprecedented condition when Mr. Perot rejoined the campaign in October. We were mindful that the preceding Spring,

before his withdrawal, he had registered approximately 40 percent in the polls,[26] and that upon rejoining the campaign, he could spend unlimited funds on television campaigning. Unable to predict the consequences of this combination, we agreed that he must be presumed to have a remote chance of election, should he do well enough so that no one else won a majority of electoral votes. His chance in the House of Representatives we found incalculable. So, we concluded that his prospect of election was unlikely but not unrealistic.

With the 1992 results and the circumstances of the current campaign before us, including Mr. Perot's funding limited by his acceptance of a federal subsidy, we see no similar circumstances at the present time. Nor do any of the academic or journalistic individuals we have consulted. Moving on to other minor party candidates, we find no one with a realistic chance of being elected President this year. Applying the same standard and criteria to them individually as to Mr. Perot, our response is again "no."[27]

The decision touched off a major storm of controversy and severe criticism of the CPD including legal action by Perot and others. The Perot campaign criticized the Neustadt Committee for what they described as inconsistent application of polling data. Perot argued that his numbers were identical in the two election cycles. Examination of the polls supplied to the committee disproves the claim. During the October 5, 1992, conference call, the polls showed Perot with a low of 9 percent (*Newsweek*) and a high of 20 percent (Gannett/Harris). A *Washington Post* poll from October 2 had him at 14 percent. Given that Perot reentered the race on October 1, those numbers were significant. In contrast, the data received in 1996 showed Perot in single digits in all but one poll taken in September. The exception was the *Los Angeles Times*, which had him at 10 percent. Most polls showed him in the 4–6 percent range despite his 1992 finish and continued media attention for the Reform Party.

Perot was not the only one complaining, as citizen voices reveal later in this chapter. The expansion of the Internet fueled the controversy in 1996 and gave many citizens an opportunity to voice their opinions to the CPD, to members of the Neustadt Committee, and to DebateWatch headquarters about minor party inclusion. The Natural Law Party filed a complaint against the CPD in September 1996 as a result of its decision to limit the debates to the major party candidates. The CPD's decision was upheld by the U.S. District Court for the District of Columbia.

Between 1996 and 2000 the CPD changed its standards for inclusion by adopting the League of Women Voter's 15 percent rule as part of its three criteria: (1) evidence of constitutional eligibility; (2) evidence of ballot access, which includes being on enough ballots to make it mathematically possible to win in the Electoral College; and (3) indicators of electoral support, which is translated as having at least 15 percent as determined by five selected national public opinion polling organizations, using the average of those organizations' most recent publicly reported results at the time of the determination.[28]

In both 2000 and 2004, no third party candidate met the 15 percent threshold. Controversy once again surfaced, especially in 2000 with Ralph Nader's candidacy. Between the 2000 and 2004 debates, John Hagelin, the Natural Law Party candidate, led a group of third party candidates in filing an FEC complaint on June 17, 2003, to stop the CPD from sponsoring. The FEC dismissed the complaint.

In 2004, there was far less attention given to excluded third party candidates by the media or citizens. Cornell University sponsored a third party debate. Media coverage was primarily local, through print outlets and a National Public Radio affiliate. C-SPAN provided a delayed broadcast several days after the event. The best-known third party candidate, Ralph Nader, chose not to participate in the debate.[29]

The war in Iraq and the uncertain domestic economy were at the forefront of voters' minds, and the two major party candidates were addressing the issues that mattered. The need for alternative voices appeared to be of less concern based on media attention and the eventual 1 percent of votes cast for independent and minor party candidates. The fact that George W. Bush became the first president in 16 years to win over 50 percent of the vote in 2004 and Ralph Nader went from 2.7 percent of the vote in 2000 to 0.3 percent in 2004 also indicates that focus was on the two major parties.

In spite of the focus on the two major parties during the campaign and far less public attention, the third party debate controversy did not go away. Prior to the election in 2004, a new group called Open Debates was formed to challenge the CPD's sponsorship role. The formation was announced in a news release on January 12, 2003.[30] The group included 2000 third party candidate Pat Buchanan's sister, Bay, and former candidates John Anderson and Allen Keyes.[31] It was headed by a Harvard law student, George Farah. Farah published a book shortly before the general election campaign that suggested the two parties controlled the debates rather than the nonpartisan commission.[32] The group presented its own debate schedule and sites at a news conference on May 24, 2004.[33]

Farah received media attention for the book and for filing two complaints against the CPD. The first complaint with the FEC charged that the major parties "collude with the CPD to dictate the terms of the presidential debates and exclude third party and independent challengers" in violation of FEC regulations.[34] The second complaint was filed with the IRS and claimed that the Commission's tax-exempt status should be removed because "it executes the joint demands of the Republican and Democratic nominees concerning the presidential debates, and shields the Republican and Democratic nominees from public accountability."[35] Both complaints were decided in the CPD's favor.

On August 12, 2004, the U.S. District Court for the District of Columbia reviewed the 2003 Hagelin decision and found that the FEC acted "contrary to law."[36] The case was in the courts until June 10, 2005, when the original FEC decision was upheld. Open Debates used the August 2004 filing as the springboard for inviting candidates to participate in their debates rather than the CPD's.

Ultimately, Open Debates's creation, the proposed alternative debate schedule, and the legal actions had no impact on the continued sponsorship by the CPD. While it is not possible here to examine all of the claims Farah's book made, it is important to note that many of the criticisms of the CPD's debates were also made about the networks' and League of Women Voters' debates, as indicated in chapters two and four. One of the suits against the League even suggested collusion between the League and the parties. Farah ignored the history of the debates and previous findings about their legality. He also overlooked the evolution of the CPD into an organization that did more to publicly discuss the structure of debates and to gather systematic research about the debates to improve them than did its predecessor. The participation of Ridings, a past League president, on the Neustadt committee was also overlooked.

It is important to note that even when attempts are made to produce a third party debate, as was done in 1996 by the International Center for Economic Justice and George Mason University,[37] cries of unfairness go up against the sponsors. An individual who did not meet the criteria of being on enough ballots to have a mathematical possibility to win disrupted the moderator's opening comments. Monica Moorehead, the Workers World Party candidate, and her supporters stormed the stage and engaged in a heated protest. Moorehead argued that the rules favored white male candidates and that she was the only black woman in the race and the only representative of poor working people. Moorehead claimed that she had a right to be heard and the rules were undemocratic. After making her point, she and her supporters left the stage and the debate proceeded.

There is no doubt that the CPD has had and most likely will continue to have its critics and conspiracy theorists, but there is also significant positive public reaction to the debates as sources of important information for voters that denies Farah's overall claim that the public is not served by the debates. The Pew research cited in chapters two and four also supports the importance of debates for the public and their overall satisfaction with them.

The remainder of this chapter presents citizen voices heard during the 1996 and 2000 election cycles regarding third party inclusion. Because there was little interest in third party candidates in 2004, there were virtually no DebateWatch discussions about their lack of inclusion. Comments are taken from e-mail messages submitted to the DebateWatch address, letters sent to Diana Carlin, and comments made in postdebate discussion groups.

CONTEXT FOR MINOR PARTY ARGUMENTS FOR INCLUSION

The CPD's 1996 criteria for third and Independent Party inclusion in the debates, cited previously in this chapter, were released on October 31, 1995, and later posted on the CPD's Web site. The widespread availability of the criteria to minor party supporters guided the nature of their arguments prior to the September 1996 recommendations by the Neustadt Committee. The Libertarian party was the most active via e-mail. The Libertarian Web site included the criteria for inclusion in the debates along with addresses and phone numbers for sending comments. Most of the messages received at the DebateWatch '96 Research Center from Perot and Nader supporters were in the form of phone calls as opposed to letters or e-mails. The calls were not recorded; thus, a less than complete record of arguments exists. However, the extant record of letters and e-mails includes sufficient numbers to identify major themes for Perot and Browne. For Nader, however, there were insufficient comments to generalize. It is important to note that there were hundreds of messages to the Center on behalf of minor party candidates. Many, especially in the case of the Libertarian candidates' supporters, were verbatim copies of a sample letter sent via e-mail to Browne supporters.

In 2000, the 15 percent average over five major polls was the criteria for inclusion along with constitutional requirements and sufficient ballot access to provide a mathematical possibility for victory. The third party controversy in 2000 centered primarily on Ralph Nader, who was seen as an alternative to the business as usual of the two major parties. A split in the leadership of the post-Perot Reform Party had Pat Buchanan, a former Republican contender, and John Hagelin, the perennial Natural Law Party standard-bearer, both seeking funding, ballot access, and support as the Reform Party candidate.[38]

Of the over 400 e-mails received at the DebateWatch 2000 Research Center at the University of Kansas that addressed the third party issue, the most dominant theme centered on the preservation of democratic principles, free speech, and choice (87 e-mails)—a theme that also dominated discussion in 1996. The need to change the 15 percent threshold was a theme of 75 e-mails; this was a new focus due to the change in requirements to qualify for the debates. The need for new ideas and a differentiation from the major parties was expressed in 36. The majority of the other e-mails were very general or very brief—usually "put Nader and Buchanan (or Browne) in the debates" or were a combination of all three of the major themes.

The 9/11 attacks in 2001 changed the political climate in the United States on many fronts. As noted in chapter five, foreign policy was on the list of top issues, unlike in the previous three elections. Voter turnout had an upsurge. In 2004, 122,295,345 votes were cast compared to 96,277,634 eight years earlier and turnout increased for every age cohort. As noted in the introduction to this chapter, third party candidates garnered few votes (1%) and little attention from citizens. Since the research center in 2004 was organizing research groups composed of National Communication Association members and feeding that data into the online results compiled by the CPD, there was no direct e-mail communication with citizens prior to the debates as there had been in 1996 and 2000 and no discussion. As a result, the examples of the citizen voices that follow cover only 1996 and 2000, when third party issues were discussed. The analysis that follows includes the best examples of thematic arguments across the two cycles: meeting CPD criteria, democracy and free speech issues, and the need for new ideas or more interesting debate.

MEETING THE CPD CRITERIA

The arguments made for Libertarian nominees Harry Browne and Jo Jorgensen in 1996 were similar throughout the letters and e-mails received. The letters were organized to clearly show the candidates met the criteria or were more deserving than other third party candidates. The following letter from a Browne supporter in Michigan illustrates the major arguments for the Libertarian ticket's inclusion (comments in brackets refer to CPD criteria):

> I am writing this letter to request that the commission include Libertarian candidate Harry Browne in the Presidential debates. Mr. Browne is a well known writer and an interesting and intelligent speaker. The Libertarian Party will be on the ballot in all 50 states and will run many other candidates for other offices [evidence of national organization and mathematical chance of winning]. The popularity of libertarian philosophy can be seen on the Internet where Harry Browne usually wins the presidential polls [indicator of national public enthusiasm].
>
> The Libertarian party is much larger than Ross Perot's reform party [national organization and indicator of national public enthusiasm]. Harry Browne and vice-presidential candidate Jo Jorgenson are not millionaires yet they turned down the offer of federal matching funds that Mr. Perot accepted [qualification for matching funds]. They are the ones that do not believe political campaigns should be funded by the taxpayers.
>
> Some prominent members of the media such as David Broder, Hugh Downs, Gil Cross, Coleman McCarthy, Bill Press, Mary Matalin, Rush Limbaugh, and even Ross Perot, have supported including Harry Browne in the debates [signs of national newsworthiness and competitiveness].

Perot's supporters were also vocal, but the quantity of written messages received from them at DebateWatch headquarters at the University of Kansas paled in comparison—approximately one to five—to those for Browne largely because of the Libertarians' widespread use of the Internet to organize, inform, and recruit followers. Representative arguments for Perot, however, were similar to those for Browne in that they touted his presence on ballots in all states, his qualification for matching funds, and his performance in 1992. The fact that he had taken taxpayers' money caused some individuals to express the belief that he should be heard for that reason alone. This e-mail from Hawaii opined: "while I am not a supporter of ross [*sic*], I do think if the u.s. [*sic*] felt that he qualified for 30 million dollars…and since that is taxpayers money (read mine, my wifes [*sic*], mother, two sons, etc.), I really don't see how 'the system' can keep him out."

One 1996 Browne supporter from Florida was more direct in applying the criteria than the Michigan writer cited previously. The Florida writer took issue with the criterion that had been considered controversial since 1980 when the League first introduced it—polling data:

> According to my understanding of your eleven qualifying criteria, Mr. Browne has met all. The issue of the polls is one on which his exclusion may be based and, on this, I take issue. As you know, the polls ask "for which presidential candidate are you most likely to vote; Robert Dole or Bill Clinton?" The respondent would have to comment outside of the query "Harry Browne." In 1992, Ross Perot made a showing of only 7% and was included in the debates. The survey questions at that time, as well as many today, include his name. I ask you to consider only those political surveys which do NOT slant the respondent's reply, but ask only "for whom will

you vote?" or list the names of all four qualified candidates. You will find, I am quite certain, that Mr. Browne will appear in those results.

While many Browne supporters expressed similar dissatisfaction with the use of polling data, references to the Internet poll showing Browne in the lead were common while ignoring the polls' lack of a representative sample of the voting population.

Polling data was a major argument in 2000 for Nader supporters. Criticism of the 15 percent policy constituted a high percentage of the e-mails sent from Nader supporters. An e-mail from a Nader supporter in Ohio argued that the bar should be set at 5 percent since it is "equal to the amount needed to receive federal funding." That argument was a common one. Another person supporting the 5 percent threshold drew a comparison to democracies with multiparty parliamentary systems and noted "in most democracies, 5 percent is all it takes to get representation in the governing body." A California writer wanted the 5 percent guideline but also indicated that if that wasn't changed, "allow at least the two 'larger' minor parties—the Green Party and Reform Party—to be equal participants in at least one of the three scheduled debates." A Massachusetts supporter of change simply wrote in the subject line: "What would it take for you to change the 15% rule?" Finally, a Michigan writer tied the difficulty of achieving 15 percent to a lack of coverage by the media: "Perhaps he doesn't have the necessary 15% because he doesn't get enough press—these debates would allow his ideas to proliferate at a greater rate." The argument that the debates were needed for any minor party candidate to secure 15 percent was presented by others as well.

Browne supporters in 1996 also based arguments on the relationship between levels of support and media attention. Some writers such as one in Florida argued that "His support grows as his media exposure grows" and proceeded to list the media figures supporting Browne's inclusion. Some writers included lists of radio talk show hosts, newspapers, Internet sites, and political figures who supported Browne in the debates. Implicit within the argument was that additional media attention in the form of inclusion in the debates would increase Browne's popularity with the electorate and increase his viability. This is a common argument despite the fact that John Anderson's numbers dropped after participating in 1980 and focus groups after the 1992 debates became less interested in Ross Perot as the debates proceeded.[39] Clearly the writers were well informed of the "rules" and had their data in hand to support how candidates were either meeting the rules or how the polling threshold simply could not be met given the circumstances third party candidates face. Other writers took a more philosophical approach.

ARGUMENTS BASED ON DEMOCRATIC PRINCIPLES

Common in both 1996 and even more so in 2000 were arguments stressing the need for application of democratic principles and free speech. A writer from Texas expressed support for widespread use of debates as an informational tool of democracy: "In fact, let's have more of them, and include even more candidates, which represents an even wider spectrum of voters and electors: This is the true heart of our particular form of democracy, the Republic!"

A writer from Arkansas spoke passionately of the symbolic nature of the decision regarding inclusion:

> America was founded upon free and fair elections. To exclude a candidate solely because they are not one of the two "major" parties is arbitrary at best, censorship at worst. And to censor the presidential debates, the bastion of freedom and democracy, is patently unfair to the American people and dangerously akin to subversion of the whole democratic process.

Several writers cited polling data that showed Americans wanted a third party candidate in the debates as a way of claiming that the decision of inclusion should be a democratic one rather than one based on a set of criteria. A writer from California summarized the argument:

> Several polls have shown that the majority of Americans are receptive to the idea of a third party. A new poll released last week shows that 68% of those most likely to vote want to see a four-way debate with Bill Clinton, Bob Dole, Ross Perot, and Harry Browne. Only 19% believed that the debates should be restricted to only Clinton and Dole. This poll was conducted by Grassroots Research, an independent public polling firm from Charlotte, NC and was a scientific survey of 1000 registered voters who vote in "all or almost all" presidential elections.

In 2000, the democracy argument was equally strong and came mainly from Nader supporters. A Florida writer wrote one of the longest e-mails we received— two full pages—and democracy was the theme. Here are excerpts:

> Every time I turn around this Democracy is eroding. 15% Poll-rating requirement to be admitted into the Presidential Debates? Oh, I get it! Why don't we just eliminate the popular vote entirely, and let the pollsters elect our government officials?... Debates are about the open discussions of legitimate public issues. Once you stifle that debate process you have eviscerated this Democracy. There is nothing more fundamental to a Democracy, which is why "Free Speech" has always been deemed the cornerstone of a Democracy. Let Ralph Nader into these debates.

Other letters were shorter but made the same point as this comment from a North Carolina Nader supporter illustrates: "Our democracy is based on more voices and more ideas, not fewer." While some argued for multiple voices from a philosophical perspective, others argued from more pragmatic positions as discussed in the next section.

NEW IDEAS AND BETTER DEBATES

In addition to arguments for the inclusion of a particular candidate, there were also comments related to the general need to improve the debates and political dialogue by allowing diverse voices. Many writers were concerned that the marketplace of ideas had shrunk at a time when many individuals were dissatisfied with the ideas generated by the major party candidates. A letter from an individual in South Carolina during the 1996 campaign is representative:

> There is little substance in the national political dialogue these days, partially due to a number of factors, but primarily due to the fact that the media only focuses on personalities (e.g. Ross Perot) and the two biggest parties. Debating is one of the greatest contributions of the Greeks to the art of political discourse, and I would like to see our presidential debates reflect a true clash in the marketplace of ideas, as opposed to the sterile positioning of two candidates who actually differ very little in what they are saying to the public.

Because the 1996 campaign was not generating much interest due to the fact the candidates were well known and Clinton's lead was consistent, some individuals wanted other voices included to add interest. A writer from California was representative of that perspective:

> Anecdotally, in talking to friends and family, I have yet to hear anyone say they need to know more about Clinton, Dole or Perot to judge them as candidates. If the debates involve only them, the debates will not be newsworthy. I watched in 1992, but if it's the same old faces this year, I, for one, would feel it a waste of time to watch.

Others noted that Browne's media exposure came because of his ideas, in contrast to Perot's, and they argued for his inclusion over Perot's. An Ohio supporter was quite blunt: "Unlike Perot, Mr. Browne cannot afford to buy his way into the spotlight. It isn't money or ego, but ideas and principles." One writer echoed this sentiment with comparisons such as the following: "Harry Browne is polling at 3% while Ross Perot with 30 million dollars and free media coverage only has from 2% to 7%. This CLEARLY shows Harry Browne is more viable." Thus, even proponents of third party inclusion did not necessarily support inclusion of all candidates.

Finally, Browne supporters emphasized his clear stand on the issues and the desire of many Americans to have less government in their lives. This was noted by a writer in Florida: "How refreshing it would be to see Libertarian Harry Browne in the debates; a defender of individual liberty, personal responsibility, and freedom from government on all issues, at all times." Another in Seattle wrote, "I saw Harry Brown on TV and I am excited about someone that really knows what the working people want. I don't want government to take care of me; I want government to leave me alone!"

Perot's supporters also stressed issues in 1996:

> Please include Ross Perot! He's the only one talking about the economic disaster we're facing, has written books about The Dollar Crisis, Medicare/Medicaid, is the only one outside the two party duopoly who has the courage to say the politically unpopular but necessary things about the bankruptcy we face.

A writer in Florida echoed the sentiment: "I urge you to seize this opportunity to bring a different point of view to the American public, and make the 1996 presidential debates something worth watching." Many supporters of both Browne and Perot argued that another set of voices would make "an ideal catalyst for interesting debate," "would give the other candidates an excellent opportunity to stand their ground and clearly state their beliefs before the American public," and would provide a better opportunity for "ALL MAJOR CANDIDATES [to] discuss, debate, and CHALLENGE each other on their positions and past actions." Still others noted that the entrance of a third candidate, as was the case with Perot in 1992, changed the agenda of the debates.

Nader and Buchanan supporters in 2000 also relied heavily on arguments related to improving the debates and public discourse. Many of the writers expressed a need to provide "opinions that differ from those of the two dominant political parties, and this is the perfect opportunity to make that happen. Include Nader in the debates, and you might just find that more people are interested in politics." Another writer from Florida also suggested that minor voices would enliven the debates: "Jazz it up. Open it up. What are you afraid of? Give yourself some real credibility. Let Nader and Buchanan speak."

A third writer opined, "The point is, one-half of the country is tuning out the election because the two institutional candidates are boring and have no opinions of their own. Put Ralph and Pat in."

While nearly all of the writers in 1996 and 2000 were supporting the inclusion of minor party candidates, some writers did argue for exclusion in 1996. This message from Mississippi, asking that Perot not be included, argued that having Perot in the debate would actually reduce the opportunity to explore the important issues:

I supported Ross Perot in 1992 (until he dropped out of the race), graduated from Vanderbilt with his son, and think highly of the man's intellect, drive and history of patriotic commitment to this country. Nonetheless, I am taking time out of my day to express hope that the CPD will not employ its selection criteria to deem Mr. Perot "a principle rival" (using your language) of the incumbent and, thus, will exercise its discretion to exclude Mr. Perot from the debates. He cannot win, regardless of how many times the TODAY show chooses to air something about his candidacy. In my opinion, placing Mr. Perot on the same stage or platform with Messrs. Clinton and Dole will detract from the goal of reasonably informing voter choice through clear communication of the positions of those with "more than a theoretical" chance of becoming the next president. Please consider these sentiments in determining whether to include Mr. Perot. In 1996, Ross Perot is becoming an irrelevancy: a sad outcome for one with such a distinguished history of family, business and patriotic service. Thank you.

Messages such as this, while few in number, do suggest the complexity of the selection process in balancing the need to inform and educate voters with the practicality of having them hear from those who are likely to be president.

DEBATEWATCH GROUPS WEIGH IN

Moderators for DebateWatch groups did not have a specific question about third party inclusion in the debates on the common interview schedule; however, group discussions go the direction that the participants want them to take. When a specific question was asked about inclusion, it was a result of a comment. The question of expectations was the most likely one to elicit a remark about third party candidates. An examination of the transcripts indicated that most groups touched on the topic at least briefly. Opinions were offered as to whom should have been included and why, why third parties would help revitalize politics, the role of the media in perpetuating the two-party system, and the difficulties of deciding who gets in. Many of those supporting inclusion made similar arguments to those who e-mailed or wrote. Many, however, concluded that while alternate voices were needed, making them workable in a debate was not easy. A discussion in Murray, Kentucky, after the Hartford debate in 1996 demonstrates how many of the focus group members grappled with the third party issue and came to the same conclusion as U.S. Supreme Court Justice Anthony Kennedy, Richard Neustadt, and many others quoted in this chapter:

Male 1:	I wish Perot could be there but it is not realistic for him to win so I do agree that he's out for now. Maybe next election we could have three.
Female Moderator:	Does anyone feel that he just had a basic right to be there regardless of the fact whether or not he is going to win? Does anybody feel that he should have been there because he's running for president?
Male 2:	You've got to earn it.
Male 3:	If I had his money, I guess I could claim that I wanted to be on there, too.
Male Moderator:	Now I know it's hard to imagine what did not happen but do you think the debates would have been more interesting if he had been there or it wouldn't have made a difference?
Female 1:	I think he would have just argued and thrown analogies that would have just watered down all the issues.
Female 2:	In my opinion, it would have been more a circus and more comical in ways.
Male Moderator:	Let me take a show of hands here. How many people feel that it was fine not to have him?
Female Moderator:	Interesting.
Male Moderator:	So overwhelmingly people feel that it was just fine without him.
Female 3:	They could have another debate with two lesser parties where you could see their views on the issues. But I think to have a four-way split.... they were already juggling things so.

The *St. Petersburg Times* hosted their own version of DebateWatch in 1996 with multiple experts and audience members exchanging questions and comments about the debate and the campaign. After the first debate in Hartford, this dialogue occurred that illustrates a lack of closure on the third party issue even after the debates had begun:

Male: How would you comment on Ross Perot's exclusion from these events, especially since Mr. Perot can be counted on to bring up subjects that mainstream candidates choose to avoid, seemingly?

Moderator: Ross Perot. The Commission, as you know, said he was not a viable candidate and therefore was not included in the debates. What does that say, Peter [Ruby Wallace, the Speaker of the Florida House of Representatives]?

PRW: He ought to be here tonight. It was his performance in the debate four years ago that lifted his recognition and resulted in his receiving almost twenty percent of the national vote, which was extraordinary. Even though he's fallen behind in the polls this year, he is a credible candidate; he is clearly a national candidate. He is on the ballot in fifty states. The Dole campaign should not have said, "no," to including Perot in the debates.

Moderator: The Clinton campaign was for including Perot; the Dole campaign was not. Charlie [Crist, who was a Republican state legislator from St. Petersburg in 1996 and was elected governor in 2006] why not?

CC: Maybe that's accurate. I wasn't privy to those negotiations.

Moderator: Well, that's what we've been told.

CC: News reports indicate that. I would say that I think he should be present. I think it's very important that people have a right to speak. Obviously he is a candidate who has tremendous support; he got close to 20 percent in 1992. Just because his polling numbers aren't as strong as somebody else thinks they ought to be, I don't think that's a reason for excluding him....

Moderator: I want to go down this row. Ross Perot—should he be included in the debate?

Female: I think he should....

Moderator: How about you?

Female: Sure. I think he should have a chance to speak.

Moderator: Does anybody not think so on this row? No? So everybody thinks he should be included. Well, he's not going to be included.

Comments such as these reflected arguments made by third party candidates and those reported in the media.

A member of the Hartford discussion group turned to the issue but discussed it from a broader perspective than the debate itself. This individual is representative of the disgruntled electorate that catapults third parties onto the stage during the "flow" periods in the nation's history:

I'm eager for a time to have more than what I refer to as a one party system—the Republicrats. I'm actively promoting a third party campaign....There's so much apathy in the public....Until we get some third parties that are actually to the left of these Republicrats, you're going to continue to have more apathy which is in the Republicrats best interest because the only people who still vote are the ones who want to keep them in charge anyhow.

Although a male in Denver, Colorado, did not use the term "Republicrats," he also addressed the issue of a lack of real difference between the two major parties when he said: "I'm kind of disappointed the Commission chose to exclude any independent party candidates from the debates. I think that's a problem that has to be addressed because I think the independent parties have a lot to offer—a lot of innovative ideas. And I'm not really hearing any from the Republicans or the Democrats."

After the San Diego debate, a group in San Francisco also discussed the role of third parties on political discourse. A female reacted to discussion about a lack of new information in the debates with this observation: "I think what the problem is in this country is that you have only two parties...maybe if you had more parties you would be forced to take a stand on some of the important issues. There would be one party that would do that if there were more parties, or the likelihood is at least bigger."

Later in the discussion, when asked if the debates affected how they would vote, another woman noted that "I think that I would probably still vote for the same party as earlier. But, as people have been saying earlier, if I had more information about other parties, I would probably change. The problem is the media is focused on those two parties."

A different group in San Francisco after the first 1996 debate discussed solutions to the third party problem. However, they also recognized the difficulties:

Female: I think that Ross Perot should have been allowed. I think Ralph Nader should have been allowed. In the first debate they should have because they all have something to say, and it would have given us a better idea of what each candidate really stood for.

Moderator: Anybody else agree or disagree with that?

Female 2:   I don't know if I would let Perot in, because of all the hoopla he made and all the "look at me," but I would have let some of the other quieter candidates in on it if they wanted.

Male: So in other words, it would be kind of nice to have like a pre-debate. Not exactly a presidential debate, but a preliminary, to have a group of people get down to the brass tacks.

Moderator: How large would this group be ideally?

Female: How many candidates are there?

Moderator: It depends. Each state has a different number, depending on who filed to get on their ballots in time. In the state of California, I think it's seven.

Female: That would be tough then, because you could end up with like 200.

Female 2:   You could. Maybe we should do it on a state-by-state basis first, and then have eliminations until we get to the nationals.

Comments such as these by DebateWatch groups around the country indicated that average citizens recognized that there are no easy answers about how to choose candidates, how many third-party candidates should share the stage with the major party candidates, or how to organize a third party debate.

In examining the public talk about Nader's participation in 2000, it was interesting to note that the third agenda very closely paralleled what the media was writing about Nader and what Nader was saying, just as comments in 1996 were very similar to news media and candidate language. The general themes, however, were very consistent with the conditions that political scientists identify as needing to exist for third party interest to grow: public interest in issues being ignored, an attempt to influence the major parties' agendas, and major party candidates who are not especially attractive.[40]

CONCLUSION

The complexities of third party politics in the United States are amplified when considering their inclusion in the national televised presidential debates. Statements by citizen participants in DebateWatch reveal the strong emotional commitment to issues, candidates, and the larger democratic process—which, in the watershed years of interest in third party inclusion, meant for many citizens the addition of candidates to the national televised debates. For others, it was about having a more responsive and robust political process, whether or not any additional candidates appeared on the stage. It is doubtful the issue will go away in future election years when the major party candidates fail to captivate the electorate. While the solutions are not easy to come by and are likely to leave someone complaining, chapter eleven examines some alternatives that should be considered, including some suggested by DebateWatch groups. The reality, however, is that the issue of third party inclusion in the debates, will be, as the League suggested in 1976, something that will be left to the courts and regulators to decide.

Chapter Eleven

Presidential Debates and Public Talk: The Next Chapter

After the first presidential debate in 2004, which focused on the war in Iraq and national security, the group gathered in College Station, Texas, was asked to identify the most useful questions or topics in the debate. As they identified the issues that resonated, they did more than provide a laundry list; they explained why. The following excerpt provides a succinct summary of the value of debates:

Male 1:   Maybe the way they phrased their most important point, proliferation, weapons of mass destruction, and I think a more fundamental understanding of really where the disparity lies concerning ideology.

Male 2:   That was the most interesting part of it for me, on the issue of Iran and North Korea. Those were two issues that hadn't been talked about and hadn't been in the media as much at least from what I've seen, and to see the two of them at opposite sides and talking about why they are.

Debate, according to nearly every definition, should be an exposition of two sides of an issue. At the end of the debate, a person listening to or participating in the war of words should have sufficient information to make a decision about the issue, whether it be guilt or innocence, aye or nay on a piece of legislation, who gets the trophy, or who holds the office of President of the United States. The two men in College Station made it clear that the ideological differences between President Bush and Senator Kerry were highlighted and clarified. The debate provided information that can't be found simply by following the news. Everyone's agenda—media, candidate, and public—can be broadened and deepened through a debate.

If DebateWatch proved nothing else, it proved that even for those who wanted a "real" debate like Lincoln and Douglas had or thought that cross-examination would add interest and distinguish positions more clearly, televised political debates are indeed debates and they provide tremendous educational value.

DebateWatch intensifies the value because it helps people sort out what they heard and saw. DebateWatch also does something that a survey, poll, or even a facilitator's response form cannot do—it gets into the heads of viewers to understand the why of what they think and how they use information.

There is no doubt that the debates are not perfect, but even with their imperfections they provide insight and content that can be discussed afterwards whether it is in a formal setting such as DebateWatch or in casual conversation while turning out the lights or having a morning cup of coffee. It is also clear from the DebateWatch feedback that a candidate's debate skills, mastery of the media, or command of language matter less than what they say and what they project via the genre and the medium about who they are, what they believe, why they believe it, and how that will affect the nation, the world, and a person's everyday life.

The DebateWatch project addressed a set of questions, and the previous ten chapters provided lengthy and detailed answers. A brief summary of those answers sets the stage for looking toward the future and how to continue to improve political debates—because the lessons learned about presidential debates have implications for those at other levels—and how to improve DebateWatch. Although this book was completed 12 years after the project was initiated, feedback to the Commission on Presidential Debates, the media, and the public took place after every cycle. News releases with results were issued after each debate. Dozens of DebateWatches were covered by local and national media outlets. Facilitators from universities around the country gave interviews about their local events and wrote about their research in the form of conference papers, journal articles, and book chapters. This book provides a means to draw the collective information and wisdom together with more depth than a news release or even a scholarly article can provide. It privileges the words of citizens in ways that numbers or lists of topics cannot. It benefits from being an analysis of more than one debate cycle and having distance from "the moment." Thus, this final chapter reviews the questions presented in chapter one and makes suggestions for how to continue to improve debates and DebateWatch.

QUESTIONS AND ANSWERS

There was no shortage of answers to the question about viewers' expectations of political debates as information sources about candidates and issues. Several chapters included references to expectations and gratification or the lack thereof. There were also expectations about the debate itself, which were discussed in chapter four. Many participants had a preconceived idea of where the candidates stood on the issues or how well they would debate, and those comments were scattered throughout chapters four through eight. The bottom line response to the research question was that nearly everyone learned something new. Even individuals who came in highly informed about the issues indicated that there was a topic covered in more depth than the news media had covered it or that there was something about a candidate's personal background they didn't know before the debate. All of the pieces of the debate revealed something about the candidates as people and potential presidents, which could only be gleaned from the face-to-face encounters. Countless quotations throughout the book highlight that finding, and the dialogue at the beginning of this chapter makes the point.

It was clear that the formats vary in their ability to inform. Too short answers, insufficient follow-up, moderators who don't keep the candidates on the subject and questions aimed at revealing a deeper side of the candidate, but which the public view as a waste of time, all reduce the overall usefulness of the debates. Chapter four made it clear that debates have been around long enough that viewers compare and contrast the various formats and they know what they want. But even with their flaws, people learn from the debates. Since the DebateWatch groups had a disproportionate number of first-time and less experienced voters in comparison to voter turnout, it was clear that the learning dimension of the debates was especially powerful for them. Countless times, younger participants indicated that watching the debates and talking about them "got me excited" or "will cause me to look for more information" or "will motivate me to vote." For more seasoned voters and the majority of viewers who had their minds made up, the reinforcement value was undeniable. Reinforcement can provide the comfort level needed to turn a viewer into a voter, and as individuals in the postelection groups told us, it even made them evangelists of sorts, sharing what they had learned and motivating others, thus expanding the learning value of debates.

Getting into viewers' heads to find out what information resonates and helps them determine presidential fitness was one of the more interesting aspects of the project. Chapter five examined what people look for in a leader in terms of leadership qualities and issue positions. It provided insights as to why viewers consistently list "character" or personal questions such as what one learns from women in their families as irrelevant or not useful. Because debates are high risk, have moments of spontaneity, and force candidates to look voters in the eye, they do reveal a vast array of personal characteristics without ever asking a question or raising doubts about an opponent's trustworthiness. There was considerable consistency as to what issues are important to viewers. People do vote their pocketbooks, even when a war on terror is being waged, and the economy and health care are perennial favorites. The issue/image dichotomy discussed in chapter five supported previous research that the two are not separate dimensions. Numerous comments in that chapter and in chapter seven on vice presidential candidates indicated that judgments about fitness for office are rooted in policy positions because of what they reflect about shared values.

The participant surveys asked viewers if they had a predebate choice but not to identify it. Postdebate and postdiscussion surveys also asked about choice. Chapter three presented those results and confirmed what other research has shown: debates move few preferences from one candidate to another; they are more likely to move undecided voters to a candidate; very few viewers move to undecided from a candidate; and the major impact is reinforcement.

Chapter six provided explanation behind the survey data reported in chapter two that debates usually top the list of information sources when compared to news, advertising, or other candidate messages. The direct encounter that is live, unedited with the exception of shot choices, spontaneous, high risk, and comparative has no equal for weighing issue and image factors. As was learned in 1992 when the pilot that created DebateWatch was run, the debates can motivate viewers to seek out other information from news sources or candidates' Web sites. News reports of the debates also have an impact on learning. For example, news reports on Al Gore's behavior in the first debate in 2000 or the "box" on George Bush's back in the first debate in 2004 affected how the candidates were viewed in subsequent debates. It was clear that viewers thought that much of the news reporting on debate strategy, gaffes, or winners and losers did not do justice to the issue content in the debates and would not be as useful as watching the debates themselves. The DebateWatch discussions were considered helpful in clarifying information and learning why others support a candidate. They provided a measure of comfort with the candidate not supported, which group members indicated was valuable if their candidate didn't win.

Part of the DebateWatch project in the initial year—1996—addressed what was a real problem that year—low voter turnout, high apathy and cynicism about the political process. Chapters eight and nine on youth and nonvoters included results from surveys and focus groups composed of representatives of the two groups. Findings revealed that many nonvoters and young people are not disinterested in politics or public policy issues, but they are disenchanted with the political process, see no difference among candidates, don't expect anything to change in their lives regardless of who is elected, don't have time for the process, and don't believe representative democracy represents them. In spite of these feelings, they participated in the study. They wanted to be heard. What was learned from the youth and nonvoter segments of the 1996 study and from participation in 2000 and 2004 by younger viewers was that the simple act of inviting a person to be part of the research stimulated interest and created efficacy for them. We learned that nonvoting is a form of protest against a system. We found that special appeals to the groups work, as evident from increased numbers in 2008 when previously disenfranchised groups were targeted by several campaigns through a combination of personal politics and technology. DebateWatch is highly personal and technology can expand its reach.

Each debate cycle had a vice presidential debate and DebateWatch activities. Chapter seven summarized the reactions to the running mates and deemed the encounters valuable. The chapter explored theories about vice presidential debates and tested them against the debates themselves and viewers' reactions. The expectation that the debates would be more aggressive than presidential debates was theorized and was borne out with participants' comments. There was a fine line between a desire for a more spirited debate and civility. The debates each cycle met at that line, and in the case of 1996, may have disappointed. There was clear consensus that it is important to see the running mates to learn more about them and how their choice reflects on the person at the top. The heartbeat away aspect of the vice presidency was clearly on viewers' minds. The discussions demonstrated, once again, the thoughtfulness and perceptivity of DebateWatch participants as they were quite aware that running mates must compromise and they saw signs of it in answers and in a person's ability to support and defend the presidential candidate.

Finally, in chapter ten we waded into the very controversial subject of who should be included in debates. DebateWatch did not ask the question specifically, but the beauty of focus groups is that they provide detailed information on selected research questions—they do focus—but they also focus on what a researcher has overlooked. A focus group is a perfect way to reveal the third agenda, and one aspect of that agenda, especially in 1996 with Ross Perot in the wings, was minor party participation. The chapter is lengthy and reveals why the issue is so emotional. Recommendations later in this chapter provide more detail on the subject.

Answers to research questions should provide direction for improvement of whatever status quo is investigated, and the remainder of this chapter does that. Both the debates and DebateWatch can be improved, and the groups had no shortage of suggestions throughout the book for how to do that. The future-oriented aspect of this chapter summarizes the ideas from groups and addresses the debate formats, third party issues, DebateWatch, and motivating previously disenfranchised groups.

HOW CAN PRESIDENTIAL DEBATES
CONTINUE TO IMPROVE?

It was clear from the discussions that changes over the past 16 years have improved the debates. The town hall, single moderator, and use of extension time were all seen as positive. After the 1996 DebateWatch project was completed, a report was submitted to the Ford Foundation, and to the Commission on Presidential Debates. That report included the following comments about format:

Debate Formats. The groups preferred the single moderator to the panelist format. They did not like the restrictions in the town hall that prevented the moderator from asking follow-up questions. They believe that the citizen questions are good, but there needs to be an expert to clarify and focus. While the town hall is still a popular format, there were criticisms of the lack of representativeness among the Gallup group. Minorities and individuals at both ends of the age spectrum were underrepresented. There were also complaints that by having individuals only from the area where the debate is held that localized issues come into play at times. There was criticism of the time limits 60–90–30 seconds. Almost to a person, participants believed that the time limits allowed the candidates to do no more than repeat their sound bytes. They felt that these debates were far less useful that the '92 debates. As was the case in '92, they want fewer topics and more time spent on each topic. They want different issues covered in each debate. They want a variety of formats, and they want the questions asked to reflect the public agenda more than the media's or the candidates'.

Recommendations. Limit the general topic areas for each debate by first identifying the 8–10 top issues among the public and the candidates. Polling data can assist with the public agenda, and a survey of the candidates' speeches, ads, etc., will indicate their major issues. Include a place on the CPD and DW Web sites for individuals to list questions they would ask if they were in the Gallup group. These can be content analyzed and the summary given to moderators. In a post-election interview I had with Jim Lehrer, he said that his staff was doing some research on lead stories in the news and front-page news stories to help him determine topics. They also did look at polling data. While this is a good gauge, also giving him or whoever the moderator is a summary of the questions on the CPD survey would be useful. Announce prior to the debate what the topic areas will be. This was done with the Arizona Republican primary debate, and it has been done in the past with primary debates. The categories can be broad enough to incorporate several specific questions. This might encourage candidates to actually give more information and rely less on sound bytes if they know the general areas ahead of time. It will also eliminate the "gotcha" type questions and the questions of little interest to the public such as the horse race questions. Include a variety of formats with a single moderator. Include follow-up questions. Provide an opportunity for the candidates to question one another. There are many different ways that this can be done. It doesn't have to be done for the entire debate but could be part of it. This would add interest. Consider as part of the town hall having individuals from various parts of the country who are hooked up via two-way interactive video to participate. Candidates do this now. The technology is there, and it would eliminate the parochial nature of the questions and would add a new twist to the town hall. You don't want to get in the same rut that the League did with only using a panel. At some point, the town hall is going to become passé as well unless it continues to develop as technology develops. We are in a high tech world, and the debates need to use some of that or the Internet with candidate chat rooms, etc. will be touted by some as a better way to communicate. What debates offer cannot be found with the Internet, but there are those who will try to make debates appear irrelevant.

Twelve years after the memorandum was written, many of the suggestions were implemented and others are proposed for 2008. A news release from the Commission on Presidential Debates on November 19, 2007, revealed several proposed changes to the format and continuation of popular changes such as a single moderator, a separate debate on foreign policy, and the town hall. The recommendations include having the candidates seated for all but the town hall. The major recommended change is one that was emphasized starting with the pilot group in 1992 to divide the debate into segments. Other suggestions from past DebateWatch groups are also reflected in the proposal, which includes "8 ten-minute issue segments; the moderator will introduce each segment with an issue on which each candidate will comment, after which the moderator will facilitate further discussion of the issue, including direct exchange between the candidates, for the balance of that segment."[1] The town hall debate is also getting a face lift that will address concerns about the parochial nature of the Gallup Group. The CPD postdebate facilitators' report after the town hall indicated that only 32 percent of the DebateWatch participants considered the format more valuable than the traditional formats—a clear indicator that the town hall needs to continue to evolve. The town hall will include "the introduction of Internet access to the presidential town meeting debate. Questions solicited by Internet will be included with those from citizens on the stage with the candidates."[2]

The proposed changes, if accepted by the candidates, are the most significant since the introduction of the single moderator and the town hall in 1992. The gradual changes each cycle and these more dramatic proposals indicate that the CPD is determined to improve the debates and that the DebateWatch feedback has been heard.

Candidates would be wise to accept the proposals. The research on format indicates that the seated staging contributes to civility; thus, any potential problems from direct cross-examination are significantly reduced because of the setting and the presence of a moderator. The clear segments and the looser time structure will provide an opportunity for more closure on a topic and will prevent the need to go back to a past question when taking on a new one in order to make a point. Twenty-minute segments would be preferable to 10, but this is a start in the right direction. The research on issues provides some justification for an expansion. There are a limited number of big issues that people want to hear about, and, after three debates, they still want to hear about some of them. One recommendation was that the town hall should be the first debate, not the middle one. Since the third debate is suggested to be foreign policy in 2008, there is a possibility for repetition from the eight topics discussed in the first debate unless the moderator does some screening to either find questions that attack the issue differently or avoids the topic altogether if there is limited potential for new information. The foreign policy questions for the third debate could be guided by what was asked in the town hall. However, if the town hall were first, the public agenda would be front and center and expansion or new topics would be easier to achieve on domestic issues—which are likely to be at the top of the public agenda.

The addition of moderator questions for clarification in 2000 also reflected that the CPD heard the suggestions for change; however, the town hall format would also benefit from more direct follow-up questions rather than just those for clarification. The DebateWatch groups were clear on that issue. Overall, the incremental changes and the more dramatic proposals for 2008 indicate that debates do not have to be static in their formats. The main considerations for format improvements are first to find ways to obtain feedback, second to take advantage of technology, third to have a variety of formats as a means of providing fairness for candidates and variety for viewers, fourth to provide depth of analysis on an issue, and finally to help the candidates' representatives understand why format proposals are made and why they are to their advantage.

With the rise of the Internet, as ABC news found out during the primaries, it is easy to get feedback. There is no shortage of critics and clear opinions about what works and what doesn't. Sponsors are wise to listen to the viewers. If a format works one election cycle, that doesn't mean it will work again; sponsors have to be willing to tweak what has worked. Getting candidates to buy-in to the new format ideas, especially cross-examination, is the key to evolving formats into something that works for everyone equally well. Whatever can be done to reduce risk for candidates is usually accepted. This is why having separate debates for foreign and domestic policy makes sense. For candidates, they only have to prepare on one area for those two debates. For the public, they can hear more detail and can tune in or not depending on their primary interests. There is no reason why some or all of the topic areas for the traditional debates cannot be announced for the same reason. Sound bytes are always going to be an issue because the one element of a debate that cannot be controlled is what the candidates are willing to say or what they are coached to say. However, when some of the guesswork about questions is removed, then there is a greater likelihood for more depth.

Moderators should have latitude in what questions they ask or how they ask a question, but the debates are not about what the moderator wants to know, and the public made that very clear both in the DebateWatch groups and in the response to the ABC 2008 Democrat primary debate. While moderators may think that questions about baseball players or women in the candidates' lives will reveal deep-seated character traits, the jury—the public—says they don't and that there are better ways to reveal those traits. With so many major, complex issues, moderators would be better served and would serve the public better to concentrate on the key issues. This doesn't mean that they shouldn't delve into issues that aren't on the top three list or that aren't headlining the news because they do have a responsibility to raise issues that potentially could be problems, as we learned from 9/11. They need to be studied and judicious in making those choices, however.

Candidates and their handlers should consider listening to the people who run the debates and know something about doing them rather than closing themselves up in rooms playing out power games among the staff. Staff don't always know what is best for their candidates. For example, George H.W. Bush would have been far better served by his staff in 1992 if the negotiators had accepted the original proposal of a single moderator for all of the debates. That was by far President Bush's strongest suit. More importantly, if the candidates want to curry favor with the public, then they need to appear to have some recognition of the public's agenda. The candidate's goal is to win, but a candidate is more likely to win if he or she is answering questions or at least explaining why a certain level of detail cannot be provided rather than repeating a message *ad nauseam*. If they don't do this, nauseated viewers are more likely to turn off the debate in favor of something that does provide gratification. Candidates who say less also accomplish less based on the feedback from the groups.

Debates as they were presented in 1996, 2000, and 2004 were certainly not broken. The DebateWatch project put the microscope on what flaws did exist and even in doing so found much that was right about them when it came to the ultimate goal of voter education. Continued experimentation and attention to the public's needs by all parties will make the debates more useful to everyone because the public is the hub in this wheel.

IMPROVING DEBATEWATCH

Just as the debates need to continually adjust and change, so does Debate-Watch. As chapter three indicated, adjustments were made each cycle, and after three runs and considerable feedback from the groups and from the 1996 postelection groups on how to improve DebateWatch, there are definitely some changes needed to sustain the program. There is no doubt that the program is successful. The 40,000 participants in 2004 are proof of that, and the usefulness of their feedback to the CPD that has resulted in changes in debates is further validation of the program's success and utility. What is most obvious is that comments made in groups and on surveys indicated that participants appreciated the opportunity to have a voice in the process, especially the facilitator's report, which allowed for news media reports on the groups and put the public's agenda front and center. Citizens are looking for ways to discuss political issues in a constructive manner and to learn about the issues, and DebateWatch does that. A survey of Debate-Watch partners indicated that they had a high level of satisfaction with the program and most of the original partners continued in 2000 and 2004. The overseas DebateWatch groups were reported to make those who are outside the country feel more a part of the process.

While the 18- to 25-year-old cohort was consistently larger than their share of the voting market, it is important to reach out to this group to begin developing a voter base for the future. Overall, the demographic data showed that there was much broader participation in 2004 on most measures. The breadth of partner institutions can expand those numbers even more.

The program should continue by building on past relationships and looking for organizations that represent nonstudents. Unions are one avenue for reaching more working-class voters. Projects such as those undertaken in some cities in 1996 where the mayors led efforts and opened community centers will take DebateWatch to the neighborhoods. Successful community efforts can also be led by the media with newspapers or broadcast outlets sponsoring a DebateWatch in a community center and then having trained volunteers lead smaller group discussions. This creates local interest in the debates and DebateWatch. The debate sites have all done an excellent job of organizing DebateWatch groups, and there is every indication that they are planning to do so again in 2008. Most DebateWatch activities took place in schools, and there are definite advantages to these locations in terms of accessibility, parking, and safety. Communities need leaders to get everything started, and government teachers and political science or communication professors in communities with higher education institutions can be catalysts. The League of Women Voters and the American Association of University Women have sponsored meetings in many locations, and they are a natural, as are civic groups. Individuals who have run the groups in the past from universities should consider going to civic organizations such as Rotary, Kiwanis, and Optimists to talk about the program and encourage their members to become involved. People can host small groups in their homes to the same effect as the large public groups—they will get people talking and thinking. The beauty of DebateWatch is that it doesn't require much planning or work. Most of the planning is already done and organizational materials are online. The main need is to get the word out and make it clear that people are invited, that they will have an educational experience, and that they will have a good time.

The Internet has been extremely useful in spreading the word and in collecting data, and its use should definitely be expanded. The CPD announced the launch of a new Internet project in conjunction with MySpace for 2008 to complement the DebateWatch project. The Web site, MyDebates.org, is designed to "enhance the educational value of the televised debates, engage new audiences, and facilitate ongoing online conversation throughout the general election period."[3] In announcing the new project, CPD co-chairs Frank Fahrenkopf and Paul Kirk listed among its features "innovative tools and materials for users to make scorecards of issues important to them and to track these issues throughout the debates, using video-tapes and transcripts in both real time and archival fashion. Citizens can submit questions to MyDebates.org for possible inclusion in the town meeting debate and offer feedback on the new debate formats that will explore a smaller number of topics for longer periods of time."[4] This initiative adds a new dimension to the third agenda that goes beyond the night of the debates or even online solicitation of potential topic areas.

The new online activities should enhance the opportunities for public participation and input and are likely to attract younger voters. There are limitations, however, to online discussions compared to face-to-face interactions. In comparing the transcripts from two online discussion groups in 1996 with the traditional groups, it was obvious that the depth of discussion was much greater in the face-to-face groups. Shorthand is the norm with online discussions, as is a much less guarded approach to language. Most posts by-passed one another. If there was engagement, it was often ruder than anything that was said in a group. One of the benefits of DebateWatch is that it creates community and increases tolerance for opposing views. A good monitor can do that with a virtual group, and a study of online projects should be undertaken after the 2008 debates to further develop good models for online DebateWatch-type activities.

Now that the research to learn more about the debates themselves has been done over four cycles, there were suggestions from the groups to ask some different types of questions. It was suggested to have fewer questions on format and more on issues. In addition to asking what issues were important or not important, news releases should include some of the comments that give meaning to the lists. As one person said, "give them [the media] newsworthy information, then it [DebateWatch] will become news" (Detroit group member in 1996). Since the DebateWatch groups indicated they don't want to hear about winners or losers, sports metaphors, or debate strategies—the common subjects covered in postdebate news stories, DebateWatch provides far more substance even than the postdebate focus groups many news outlets assemble in their studios. Those groups often respond to media agenda questions such as about who won.

The Detroit group also suggested that there needs to be "a separate Debate-Watch organization with a staff that devotes full time to it." The CPD does have staff members brought on right before the debates to coordinate the project, but identifying a few specific partner organizations to form an advisory group that develops models for spreading the word would take some of the burden off of an organization whose primary responsibility is to broadcast the debates. Most organizations have public service projects and so partner organizations could work with other local organizations to expand the DebateWatch base. There is no limit to the ways that DebateWatches can be organized, and the significant growth in 2004 demonstrates the power of the Internet to spread the word. However, it takes people on the ground to make the groups actually happen.

THIRD PARTY ISSUES

The chapter on this topic made it clear that third party issues are historically important when certain larger political conditions exist. The CPD is perceived as not inclusive and controlled by the two parties. One of the authors, Diana Carlin, has extensive personal experience with the CPD and knows that to not be true. But in politics, perceptions are reality and critics and conspiracy theorists make good press. This is a highly complex issue and the media doesn't usually treat it that way. It would be helpful if a journalist took on the issue and read through the court cases going back to 1976 and did a thorough investigative piece. That would only solve part of the problem, however. The other problem is that people do want to hear alternative voices—more some cycles than others—and there will always be a minority of the population that prefers minor party candidates.

C-SPAN and other organizations have hosted third party debates in the past, but they get little attention. One of the major arguments for inclusion is that third party positions won't be known unless the candidates are in the debates. Ross Perot showed that if an independent or third party candidate has a message that resonates and gets media attention early, he or she is heard long before the debates and then has the popular support to be included. That is how it should be. Largely unknown and unvetted candidates most likely don't belong on center stage to be introduced to the American public in late September. It is the media's responsibility to educate the public on third party candidates, and they should do it well before the debates begin. There is a chicken and egg element to all of this, and the omelet can best be made with the media mixing it.

The major media outlets should consider hosting a prime-time third party debate about the time of the national conventions. Most third parties select their candidates prior to the major party conventions, and if there were such a debate, they are likely to move up their selection dates. It could be done in a studio just as the primary debates are held. The debate should be covered as closely as other debates. If there is a candidate with a message who is missing in the regular campaign, the message can still be spread. Polls need to include the minor party candidates to reflect changes before and after the debates. There should be periodic reporting on the status of the third party campaigns after the debate.

The media should vet the minor party candidates just as they vet the major party candidates—reveal as much as possible about their past public records if they have one, their business or professional dealings, their families, their tax records, their health status, and so on. With a more level playing field in the treatment of the candidates overall, the minor party candidates can be judged alongside the major party candidates, and if the public judges their ideas as superior, they, like John Anderson and Ross Perot, will show up in the fall debates.

CONCLUSION

There were thousands of pages of DebateWatch transcripts, hundreds of e-mails and letters, and thousands of comments on facilitator and participant reports from which to choose in writing this book. Some of the transcripts were so rich in insightful dialogue that it was tempting to include the entire discussion. There was no way that this book did justice to all of the careful responses that were made to facilitators' questions, but the comments that are included are a fair representation of what the public was thinking at three unique periods in the nation's political history. Someone asked one of the authors if she thought debates would ever go out of style and if 50 or 100 years from now there would be some other way to judge the candidates. Perhaps the best answer is in the dedication to this book—"To the memory of Abraham Lincoln and Stephen A. Douglas in recognition of the 150th anniversary of their historic debates." Debate has been with us since the Greeks, and, as a vital component of a democracy and democratic society, debate in all of its forms is not going to go away. The forms may change, and they have changed. The Lincoln-Douglas debates were nothing like today's debates, and today's debates are different from the first televised debates that John Kennedy and Richard Nixon experienced. The formats may change, but the fundamental goals of debates won't. The DebateWatch project demonstrated that the public expects to have debates, they learn from the debates, and they appreciate the opportunity to talk about what they have learned, but they also want their voices to be heard so that debates and democracy flourish. We believe they have been.

Appendix A

DebateWatch '96
Research Materials

PREDEBATE TELEPHONE SURVEY SCRIPT

FIPS CODE _____

Good evening, my name is _____(insert name) _____, I am calling from the University of Kansas as part of a national research project called DebateWatch '96 aimed at finding out what topics you and other citizens would like to hear about in the upcoming presidential debates. Your phone number was selected at random and can in no way be connected to your name and address. Would you like to take 3–5 minutes to help us?

1. Are you 18 years of age or older?

   (1) Yes
   (2) No (Ask if someone of the same gender 18 or older is available—If no one is available, thank and terminate.)

2. What three topics or issues do you want the candidates to discuss in the presidential and vice presidential debates? (Record responses verbatim. Do not change or correct grammar or word usage. If the respondent volunteers fewer than three, ask if there are any other topics or issues.)

   a. _____
   _____
   b. _____
   _____
   c. _____
   _____

3. Are there any topics or issues you would prefer not be discussed in these debates? (Record responses verbatim. Do not change or correct grammar or word usage.)

   _____
   _____

4. One presidential debate will be conducted like a town hall meeting where citizens selected by a national polling agency will question the candidates. If you were one of those citizens, what question would you ask? (Record responses verbatim. Do not change or correct grammar or word usage.)

    _____
    _____
    _____

Next, I need some information about your background.

5. Sex of respondent (if possible, infer from voice—don't ask)
    1   Male
    2   Female

6. What is your approximate age? Are you between
    1   18–24
    2   25–34
    3   35–44
    4   45–54
    5   55–64
    6   65–74
    7   75 or older

7. Are you currently registered to vote?
    1   Yes (Skip to 8)
    2   No (Continue with 7A)

7A. Do you plan to register to vote before this fall's election?
    1   Yes (Continue with 8)
    2   No (Skip to 10)

8. (Did/Will) you give a political party preference when you register(ed) to vote?
    1   Yes (Continue with 9)
    2   No (Skip to 10)

9. What (was/will be) that party preference?

    _____

10. What is the highest grade or year of regular school or college you have completed?
    1   Grade School (0–8 years)
    2   Some High School (9–11 years)
    3   High School Graduate (12 years)

    4   Some College or Technical School (13–15 years)

    5   Associate Degree

    6   Bachelor's Degree (16 years)

    7   Post Graduate Study (17+ years)

11. How would you describe your current employment status? Are you

    1   Employed full-time

    2   Employed part-time

    3   Self-employed

    4   Unemployed, seeking work

    5   Homemaker

    6   Full-time student

    7   Retired

12. So that we may represent everyone fairly, which of the following ethnic groups do you fall into?

    1   White

    2   African American/Black

    3   Native American

    4   Asian or Pacific Islander—Specify Origin _____

    5   Mixed Race

    6   Other—Specify _____

13. Do you consider yourself to come from a Hispanic or Latin American background?

    1   Yes

    2   No

14. In 1995, what was your approximate total annual *household* income?

    ___Less than $10,000

    ___$10,000 to $24,999

    ___$25,000 to $39,999

    ___$40,000 to $54,999

    ___$55,000 to $69,999

    ___$70,000 or More

15. Do you plan to watch the debates?

    1   Yes

    2   No

Thank you for your time.

INSTRUCTIONS TO SURVEY STAFF

Consistency is what we are striving for; thus, the following prompts and suggestions should assist you in achieving that goal.

1. Read all statements as written.

2. If someone has a question, answer it as completely as possible without giving him or her a suggestion of an answer. On the questions where they are to list a topic, any examples you supply should be neutral and should not prompt them to give your example as a response. For example, if someone wants you to give them an example of an issue or topic use "U.S./Soviet relations" or "immunization against childhood diseases." (If someone suggests that there is no Soviet Union, simply say, "I realize that, I am simply giving you an example of the type of response we are after but not one that you might give.")

3. On the lists of demographics read until they tell you that you have reached the correct range. You do not need to read the entire list if they give you a positive response.

4. If someone refuses to respond to any of the demographic questions, simply go on to the next one. This is a voluntary survey, and they have the right to refuse.

5. On the question related to the Town Hall meeting, if the respondent does not understand, ask if they watched the 1992 debates. If they did, remind them of the Richmond debate where undecided voters were selected by Gallup to ask the candidates questions. Explain that this is a town hall meeting.

6. If anyone asks what DebateWatch is, explain that it is

    A national voter education project, which is non-partisan and not affiliated with any political party or special interest group, designed to learn what citizens want discussed in the presidential debates and that it is being run out of the University of Kansas and is funded with grant money from a private foundation. For more information, call 1-800-340-8109.

7. If they want to know how the research is being used, tell them that it will be part of a report combined with group discussion data collected during the debates and will be released in a book within the next 18 months.

8. If they want to know how you got their number, explain that

    The number was randomly generated by a computer and we were presented with a list of numbers which does not discriminate between businesses, residences, active and inactive numbers. Your number was randomly generated for research purposes and will not be passed along to anyone or sold to anyone.

9. If they want to engage you in a discussion of the issues, candidates, schedule of the debates, etc. simply explain that you do not know anything about them and that you are just responsible for making phone calls for the survey which is under the direction of several faculty members at the University of Kansas. Don't mention any names.

SCA PARTICIPANT PACKET INFORMATION

Dear SCA participant:

Thank you for agreeing to be one of the official SCA coordinators for Debate-Watch '96. This is an exciting project that could change the tenor of the 1996 elections at not only the presidential level but also at state and local levels. The opportunity for citizens to have a voice in setting the political agenda is one that is needed in the current political environment.

As an SCA coordinator, there are several things we would like for you to do. There are also several optional projects. If you choose to participate in the optional projects, please indicate which projects on the attached information form. We are asking coordinators to do the following:

1. Organize at least one DebateWatch group per debate that is for research purposes. This group should represent a cross-section of the community rather than be composed of students and faculty. You can either invite the same individuals for each debate, have a new group for each, or have the same individuals for the first and last debate and different members for the VP and the second presidential. We will send you a report before the debates begin for you to describe your structure.

    Group members should complete the survey forms (of course, with the disclaimer that they can withdraw from doing so at any point), and you should complete the facilitator's report and fax it to us at 913-864-5046 within 24 hours of completing the discussions. DO NOT USE THE FAX NUMBER PRINTED ON THE DEBATEWATCH PACKETS as we are having all SCA reports go to a dedicated number. A reminder notice is included with the number. These reports will be used in a news release issued within 48 hours of the debate. Mail the hard copy to us along with the individual surveys. Audio or video tape the group and send us the tape.

2. Help organize DebateWatch groups on campus and throughout the community. This can best be done by delegating through a steering committee. The University of Maryland is serving as the model for organizing campuses. They will have a web site that can be reached through www.debates96.org. Enclosed are several lists of suggestions for how to organize groups on campus and within the community. This is an excellent project for a political communication class.

3. Give speeches, write an op-ed piece for the campus and local paper, and make media contacts to publicize DebateWatch within the community. National NPR wants to coordinate coverage through local affiliates by making SCA contacts their new sources. Your name will be given to NPR as the contact person in your state.

We are on a limited budget, but we can provide you with $75 to defray fax, phone, and refreshment costs for the groups. You will need to keep all of your receipts in order to be reimbursed. Please send a statement of expenses and invoices after the last debate.

In return for your hard work, you will receive a special place in heaven AND an opportunity to use data for your research if you desire. The Ford Foundation grant requires me to address a set of research questions; however, there are thousands of others that need to be asked and answered. If you want to design research on your own, please indicate what it is on the attached form. I will provide whatever data you need from what we collect nationally. Let me know what you need and when you need it. If you have questions about the research, please let me know.

You will continue to receive information from us as the project progresses. Please call us on the 800 number or e-mail to save expenses at your end. If you can't reach me, Kelly McDonald, Susan Buehler, and Tammy Vigil are graduate assistants on the project.

Your packet should include the following materials:

1.   Three DebateWatch packets (you can make as many copies as you wish). If you need originals for groups you enlist, call or e-mail.

2.   The press kit that was distributed at the news conference in Washington announcing DebateWatch. This will help you answer media questions.

3.   Suggestion sheets for how to involve groups.

4.   An information sheet.

5.   Recruitment suggestions for organizing DebateWatch groups.

6.   Fax number reminder notice.

Once again, thank you for your assisting with the project.

Sincerely,
Diana Carlin
National Project Director, DebateWatch '96

FACILITATOR'S QUESTIONS (RESEARCH AND PUBLIC GROUPS)

The following questions are designed to stimulate discussion. Feel free to add your own. *It is not necessary to ask all of the questions.*

1.   Why did you decide to participate in DebateWatch?

2.   What role does politics play in your everyday life?

3.   What were your expectations of the debate? Were they met?

4.   What did you learn about the candidates or issues that you did not know prior to viewing the debate?

5.   Did the debate influence your attitudes about the issues or the candidates?

6.   Were there any issues of interest that were not discussed during the debate?

7. Were there any issues raised that you considered irrelevant or unimportant?

8. How do debates compare with other campaign information sources (e.g. news, ads, speeches, conventions, call-in shows, online resources, etc.) in helping you learn about the candidates and the issues?

9. What are your reactions to the debate format (i.e. time limits, moderator, citizen participants, questions)?

10. If you could change one feature of the debate format, what would it be? Why?

11. Will this debate and discussion influence the way you vote?

12. How will participating in DebateWatch affect the way you read, watch, or listen to news of the campaign?

13. How will it affect the way you discuss the campaign at work, home, etc.?

Use these additional questions for the second and third presidential debates:

14. What did you learn from this debate that you hadn't learned from previous debates?

15. How, if at all, did the press coverage of the previous debate(s) influence your attitudes about the candidates or the issues in this debate?

16. How would you compare this format to previous formats (if the format differs?)

Use this question for the vice presidential debate:

17. Do you think vice presidential debates are useful? What can be done to make them more useful?

FACILITATOR'S REPORT

Thank you for participating in DebateWatch '96. You and the members of your groups joined thousands of other Americans across the country in being active participants in the democratic process. To enable the organizers of DebateWatch '96 to prepare a summary of the project's impact, we would appreciate your completing the following set of questions. Participation is voluntary, however. To return by mail, send to DebateWatch '96, P.O. Box 3467, Lawrence, KS 66046-0467. But to ensure that your report will be included in postdebate press releases, email your responses to presdeb@falcon.cc.ukans.edu or fax to 800-403-2358. If you want a copy of the final DebateWatch summary, please print your name and address below:

Name: _____

Address: _____

City and state where DebateWatch was held:

_____

Place of discussion (school, library, home, etc.):

_____

Debate discussed:

❑ 1st Pres   ❑ 2nd Pres   ❑ 3rd Pres   ❑ Vice Pres

Total number of participants _____

Indicate the number of participants representing the following demographic groups:

Female____   Male____

Age (estimate):   Under 18____   18–25____

26–40____   41–55____   Over 55____

Race:

Black-African Native Descent____

Asian or Pacific Islander____

Hispanic____   White (not Hispanic)____

American Indian or Alaska Native_____

Other (Please specify)_____

How or where did you or the group organizer learn about DW '96?

_____

Is your group connected with any organizations participating in DW '96 (National League of Cities, AAUW, Kids Voting, etc.)?

❑ Yes   ❑ No

If yes, which one? _____

Please rate the materials in the packet on a 1–5 scale

	(1-poor;	2-fair;	3-good;	4-very good;	5-excellent)
Q&A on DebateWatch '96	1	2	3	4	5
Viewer's Guide	1	2	3	4	5
Debate Notes	1	2	3	4	5
Facilitator's Guide	1	2	3	4	5
Resource list	1	2	3	4	5

Based on the group discussion, please briefly describe people's reactions to the topics or issues raised during the debates.

    (a) Which questions or topics did participants find most useful?
    (b) Were any questions considered irrelevant or unimportant to participants?
    (c) Were any topics overlooked by debate questioners or candidates which DW participants wanted to hear discussed?

PARTICIPANT SURVEY

Thank you for participating in DebateWatch. *Completion of this survey is optional and responses anonymous.*

PART 1—PREDEBATE

Complete this section before the debate begins.

Which debate are you watching and discussing?

❏ 1st Pres   ❏ 2nd Pres   ❏ 3rd Pres   ❏ Vice Pres

1. How did you first learn about DebateWatch?

    ❏ Television   ❏ Friend, co-worker, family   ❏ Newspaper
    ❏ Radio Announcement   ❏ Information in Library   ❏ School
    ❏ Other _____

2. Who invited you to participate?

    ❏ Friend   ❏ Club/organization   ❏ Family member
    ❏ Neighbor   ❏ Co-worker   ❏ Public Announcement
    ❏ Other _____

3. How many DebateWatch groups have you attended including this one?

    ❏ 1   ❏ 2   ❏ 3   ❏ 4

4. Rank your top three sources of campaign information, with 1 being your most useful source.

    ___ Nightly network news (ABC, CBS, CNN, NBC, PBS)

    ___ C-SPAN

    ___ Weekday or evening talk shows (*Nightline, Larry King Live, Rush Limbaugh,* etc.)

    ___ Sunday talk shows/special news shows (e.g. *This Week, Face the Nation, Meet the Press, Washington Week in Review, Crossfire, Equal Time,* etc.)

    ___ Local newspaper

    ___ National newspaper such as the *New York Times, Christian Science Monitor, Washington Post*

    ___ News magazines

    ___ Commercial radio news

    ___ National Public Radio

    ___ Internet

    ___ Direct mail from candidates, parties, organizations, or interest groups

    ___ Other _____

5. What was your level of exposure to campaign coverage during the past 6–8 months?

    ___ regular—daily/weekly

    ___ 3–4 times per month

___ one per month or less

___ began following regularly the past two months

___ began following regularly the past month

___ have followed irregularly up until the debates

6. Before watching the debate, do you have a candidate preference?

❏ YES   ❏ NO

7. Age (check one):

❏ under 18   ❏ 18–25   ❏ 26–40   ❏ 41–55   ❏ over 55

8. ❏ Male   ❏ Female

9. Occupation: _____

10. Ethnic Background (check most appropriate box):

❏ Black-African Native Descent   ❏ Asian or Pacific Islander
❏ Hispanic   ❏ White (not Hispanic)
❏ American Indian or Alaska Native

11. Party affiliation (if unaffiliated, please indicate):_____
_____

Stop here until after the debate.   STOP

PART 2—POSTDEBATE

Complete this section before group discussion.

If before the debate you indicated YES to having a candidate preference, go to question 12-A below.

If before the debate you indicated NO to having a candidate preference, go to question 12-B below.

12-A. After watching the debate, are you:

❏ still leaning toward your predebate preference

❏ now undecided

❏ now leaning toward another candidate

12-B. After watching the debate, are you:

❏ still undecided

❏ now leaning toward a candidate

13. Please evaluate *the debate itself* by responding to the statements below on the following scale:
1-strongly disagree; 2-disagree; 3-no opinion; 4-agree; 5-strongly disagree

A. The debates taught me something new about one or more candidates

❑ 1   ❑ 2   ❑ 3   ❑ 4   ❑ 5

B. The debates taught me something new about one or more issue

❑ 1   ❑ 2   ❑ 3   ❑ 4   ❑ 5

C. The debates clarified my understanding of one of more candidates' position on an issue or issues.

❑ 1   ❑ 2   ❑ 3   ❑ 4   ❑ 5

D. The debates reinforced my attitudes about one or more candidates

❑ 1   ❑ 2   ❑ 3   ❑ 4   ❑ 5

E. The debates helped me to evaluate one or more candidates differently than prior to the debate.

❑ 1   ❑ 2   ❑ 3   ❑ 4   ❑ 5

F. The debates helped me decide for whom to vote or helped firm up my decision

❑ 1   ❑ 2   ❑ 3   ❑ 4   ❑ 5

G. The debates gave me ideas to discuss in the group

❑ 1   ❑ 2   ❑ 3   ❑ 4   ❑ 5

H. The debates made me more likely to vote

❑ 1   ❑ 2   ❑ 3   ❑ 4   ❑ 5

I. The debates increased my interest in following the remainder of the campaign more closely.

❑ 1   ❑ 2   ❑ 3   ❑ 4   ❑ 5

Stop here until after the discussion   STOP

PART 3—POSTDISCUSSION

Complete this section after group discussion.

14. After participating in the discussion, has your position on the candidates changed from what was indicated as your position after the debate?

❑ Yes   ❑ No

If YES, have you:

❑ gone from undecided to a candidate

❑ gone from a candidate to undecided

❑ changed from one candidate to another

15. Please evaluate *the postdebate discussion* by responding to the statements below on the following scale:
1-strongly disagree; 2-disagree; 3-no opinion; 4-agree; 5-strongly disagree

A. The discussion taught me something new about one or more candidates

❑ 1 ❑ 2 ❑ 3 ❑ 4 ❑ 5

B. The debates taught me something new about one or more issue

❑ 1 ❑ 2 ❑ 3 ❑ 4 ❑ 5

C. The discussion clarified my understanding of one of more candidates' position on an issue or issues.

❑ 1 ❑ 2 ❑ 3 ❑ 4 ❑ 5

D. The discussion reinforced my attitudes about one or more candidates

❑ 1 ❑ 2 ❑ 3 ❑ 4 ❑ 5

E. The discussion caused me to evaluate one or more candidates differently than prior to the debate.

❑ 1 ❑ 2 ❑ 3 ❑ 4 ❑ 5

F. The discussion helped me decide for whom to vote or helped firm up my decision

❑ 1 ❑ 2 ❑ 3 ❑ 4 ❑ 5

G. The discussion gave me ideas to discuss in the group

❑ 1 ❑ 2 ❑ 3 ❑ 4 ❑ 5

H. The discussion made me more likely to vote

❑ 1 ❑ 2 ❑ 3 ❑ 4 ❑ 5

I. The discussion increased my interest in following the remainder of the campaign more closely.

❑ 1 ❑ 2 ❑ 3 ❑ 4 ❑ 5

COMMENTS

A Viewer's Guide to Political Debates

Voters typically identify candidate debates as the most influential source of information received during a campaign. Because of their importance, this guide gives suggestion for getting the most out of a debate. Focus your attention on a few key points. Know what it is you want in an office holder, than watch and listen to see which candidate best fits your ideal. The following suggestions will help you focus:

- *Prepare ahead.* Try to follow the campaign at least a few weeks before the first debate.

- *Watch more than one debate.* No debate can cover every issue; try to watch multiple debates to learn the most.

- *Watch with others.* Once the debate is over discuss what you heard and saw. Research shows that discussion helps clarify points made in the debate.

- *Set aside your partisan views.* Use the debates to learn as much as possible about all candidates and their positions.

- *Don't worry about who won or lost.* Both sides will claim victory. Since there are no criteria for determining a political debate winner, concentrate more on issues and ideas rather than on strategies. Focus on the question, "Who would make a better president, senator, governor, legislator, county clerk?"

- *Pay close attention to the candidates when they talk about how to solve problems.* Listen carefully for comparisons candidates make between or among their programs and their opponents'.

- *Identify the candidate's debate goals.* Does the candidate speak directly to the issues, provide specifics, and present new policies or information? Or does the candidate evasively interpret questions to suit his/her agenda?

- *Identify the images that candidates try to create for themselves.* Most candidates try to portray themselves as leaders and identify themselves with cherished American values while suggesting that their opponents lack these qualities. What in the responses supports their claims?

- *Be aware of the limitations of televised debates.* Television works by showing action. To create action and minimize monotony, directors sometimes include "reaction shots" to show one candidate's response to an opponent's statement. This can distract your attention from what is being said. It is wise to remember the role of action shots when watching the debates.

- *Try to learn more after the debate.* Because most formats provide for brief responses, it is difficult to get a complete understanding of a candidate's position or the issues discussed. Follow up on the issues by watching and reading the news or visiting candidate's Internet Web sites.

About the Guide

This guide was adapted from material by the following National Communication Association members: Diana Carlin, University of Kansas; Robert Friedenberg, Miami University, Hamilton, OH; James Guadino, Speech Communication Association; Susan Hellweg, San Diego State University; John Morello, Mary Washington College; Michael Pfau, University of Wisconsin.

DebateWatch '96 Partners

American Association of Community Colleges

American Association of homes and Services for the Aging

American Library Association

American Association of University Professors

American Association of University Women

American Medical Student Association

American Pharmaceutical Association Academy of Students of Pharmacy

Arizona State University, Communication Department

Beloit College

Black Entertainment Network (BET)

Boys & Girls Clubs of America—TEENSupreme Keystone Clubs

Bush Presidential materials Project/Texas A&M Speech Communication Dept./ Presidential Rhetoric Program

Campus Green Vote

Jimmy Carter Library

Catholic Community at the University of California at San Diego

Center for Policy Alternatives—National Student Voter Education Day

Child Welfare League of America

Children's Defense Fund

Close Up Foundation

College Democrats

College Republicans

Congressional Asian Pacific American Caucus Institute

Congressional Hispanic Caucus Institute

Connecticut Council of Municipalities/Secretary of State/League of Women Voters/ Hartford Debate '96

Council for the Advancement of Citizenship

Council of American Private Education

Dwight D. Eisenhower Presidential Library

Episcopal Church House

Faith and Politics Institute

Federal Voting Assistance Program

Gerald R. Ford Library

Florissant Valley Community College, Phi Theta Kappa

Franklin & Marshall College, Department of Government

Front lash

Fraternal Order of Police

General Federation of Women's Clubs

George Mason University, Communication Department

George Washington University

Georgetown University Student Government

Hebb & Gitlin, Attorneys at law

Hispanic Association on Corporate Responsibility

Howard University, Political Science Department

Illinois State University, Communication Department

Institute of Governmental Studies, University of California at Berkley

John Fitzgerald Kennedy Library

Johns Hopkins University

Kansas State University, Speech Department

Kids Voting USA

Lutheran Volunteer Corps

George C. Marshall Foundation

Mayor's Office, Charlotte, NC

Mayor's Office, Dallas, TX

Mayor's Office, Detroit, MI

Mayor's Office, Jackson, MS

Mayor's Office, Oklahoma City, OK

Mayor's Office, Orem, UT

Mayor's Office, Primera, TX

Mayor's Office, Robbinsdale, MN

Mayor's Office, Rutland, VT

Mayor's Office, Wichita, KS

Mexican-American Legal Defense and Education Fund (MALDEF)

The Miller Center at the University of Virginia

Minnesota E-Democracy

National Archives and Records Administration

National Association of Black School Educators

National Association of Broadcasters

National Association of Colored Women's Clubs, Inc.

National Association of Graduate and Professional Students

National Association of Hispanic Publications

National Association of Retired Federal Employees

National Association of Secretaries of State

National Association of Towns and Townships

National Association of Truck Stop Owners

National Cable Television Association

National Catholic Schools Education Association

National Conference of Black Political Scientists

National Council for the Social Studies

National Democratic Institute

National Forensic League

National League of Cities

National Network for Youth

National Newspaper Association

National Pan-Hellenic Council

National Puerto Rican Forum

National Student/Parent Mock Election

Northwestern University, School of Speech

Organization of Chinese Americans

Phi Theta Kappa

Project Vote Smart

Rock the Vote

Ronald Reagan Library

Southeast Missouri State University, Department of Speech Communication

Speech Communication Association

Stand for Children

St. Petersburg Times/City of St. Petersburg/University of South Florida/St. Petersburg-Clearwater Area Convention and Visitors Bureau/WTVT Ch 13, Tampa

Stennis Center for Public Service

Study Circles Resource Center

Tarleton State University, Fine Arts & Speech Department

Harry S. Truman Scholarship Foundation

Unitarian Universalist Association

United Artists Theatre Circuit

United States Chamber of Commerce

United States Hispanic Chamber of Commerce

United States Pan Asian American Chamber of Commerce

University of California at Los Angeles

University of Cincinnati, Communication Department

University of Kansas, Department of Communication Studies

University of Maryland, Center for Political Leadership and Participation/Speech Communication Department

University of New Hampshire

University of Oklahoma/Oklahoma League of Women Voters

University of Richmond

University of San Diego

University of Tennessee at Martin, School of Arts and Sciences/Honors Program

Unruh Institute of Politics, University of Southern California

Urban Family Institute

Villanova University, Communication Arts Department

Voice of America

Wake Forest University

Washington University in St. Louis

Wayne State University, Department of Communication

West Chester University, Communication Studies Department
Wichita State University, Elliott School of Communication
Women's Vote Project
Young Democrats
Young Republicans
Youth Vote '96

1996 and 1997 Postelection Study Surveys and Tables

LETTER TO RESEARCHERS

October 29, 1996

Dear Researcher:

Thank you for all of your help and support of DebateWatch over these last several weeks. We are getting more and more data in all the time from facilitators and participants across the country. This process has been very exciting as we begin to analyze the data and see what participants across the nation had to say about the debates.

We would very much appreciate your assistance in completing one remaining part of the project. This involves convening a postelection DebateWatch group to help provide feedback about the discussion process.

If you could reconvene a stable group which you had during a particular debate or a composite group of individuals from different debates, we have just a few questions we would like to investigate. The discussion itself will probably not be too long, likely no more than 45 minutes. If the group could come together one week to ten days following the election, the debates and DebateWatch discussion will still be salient in their minds.

Please record the discussion on audio and/or video tape and mail it to the PO Box address with any comments or feedback you have about the process. The grant will provide $100.00 for your participation in this stage of the project.

As we are coordinating participation in this phase of the project, could you please fax us a note indicating you will be able to conduct a postelection group or give us a call and leave a message on the 800 number in the next couple of days? We would really appreciate knowing what is happening where.

Again, thank you so much for your time and effort in this project. The KU reception at SCA will be Sunday from 5–7 in the convention hotel and we are having a coffee in the morning for everyone involved. We look forward to seeing everyone in a month.

Sincerely,
Diana Carlin   Kelly McDonald
National Project Director   Assistant Project Director

POSTELECTION DEBATEWATCH QUESTIONS

1. Now that you have had time to reflect on the debates, how valuable were they for
   a. guiding how you followed the campaign? (i.e. did they make you read or look for additional information)
   b. helping you reach a decision as to whom you supported?
   c. helping you decide whether to vote?
2. Did your participation in DebateWatch help you feel more comfortable talking to coworkers, friends, or others about the debates?
3. Did you follow the campaign differently as a result of participating in Debate-Watch? How?
4. Did you seek out different news sources?
5. What was the benefit of participating in DebateWatch'96?
6. Do you think the public benefits from political discussion projects like DebateWatch?
7. Did you feel you had more of a voice in the campaign as a result of participating in DebateWatch?
8. Should we have DebateWatch for the election in 2000? How would you improve DebateWatch for 2000? Do you have any suggestions about how Debate-Watch could reach out to more people?
9. Any suggestions about how DebateWatch could reach out to more people?

LETTER TO FOCUS GROUP PARTICIPANTS

Dear Focus Group Participant:

Thank you for agreeing to participate in this voter education study. The principal researcher for this study is a faculty member at the University of Kansas who is conducting this research under a grant from the Ford Foundation. The Department of Communication Studies at the University of Kansas supports the practice of protection for human subjects participating in research. The following information is provided for you to decide whether you wish to participate in the study. You should be aware that even if you agree to participate, you are free to withdraw at any time.

I am interested in learning about public attitudes about politics. You will participate in a 60–75 minute focus group discussion and will complete a brief survey. The discussion will be taped for purposes of data analysis.

Your participation is solicited although it is strictly voluntary. We assure you that your name will not be associated in any way with the research findings. I will receive only the taped interview and your survey and will not have your complete name on my list.

If you would like additional information about the study feel free to contact me.

Thank you for participating.

Sincerely,
Diana B. Carlin, Ph.D.
Principal Investigator
3090 Wescoe Hall
University of Kansas
Lawrence, KS 66045

_____

Signature of subject
By signing, the subject certifies that he or she is a least 18 years of age.

FOCUS GROUP PROCEDURES

1. Please arrive at the designated location by _____ p.m.
2. Upon arriving you will be asked to complete a brief questionnaire to obtain demographic information to be used in data analysis. You will also be given an informed consent agreement form from Dr. Carlin which indicates that you are aware of the purpose and procedures for the research.
3. The group discussion should last approximately 60–75 minutes.

FOCUS GROUP QUESTIONS

1. What is the first thing that comes to mind when you hear the following:

   Politics

   Politicians

   Elections or campaigns

   Media

   (Ask everyone to respond to this question as an ice breaker)

2. Why do you feel that way?
3. Why did you not vote in the last election?
3a. If they indicate that their vote doesn't matter, ask: Why do you think your vote doesn't matter?
4. If you have voted in the past, what was different in 1996 that caused you not to vote?
5. What do you think is the major reason why other people don't vote?
6. Do you follow politics in the news? What news sources do you follow?

7. For anyone who doesn't follow, ask, "Is there a reason?"

8. (If no one listed political ads as a problem, ask:) What do you think of political ads?

9. What, if anything, would you like to see changed about news coverage of politics?

10. What are the major problems with the U.S. political system? with the parties? with campaigns specifically?

11. Do you think most of the problems are national or are they at all levels?

12. What should be done to correct the problems?

13. What would it take to get you more interested in politics?

14. Do you think you can find out enough about the candidates and issues to make an informed decision if you choose to vote?

15. What else do you need to know to be better informed?

16. Do you think that what politicians decide in city, state, or national governments affect you? Why or why not.

17. What other comments do you have about politics and elections that you want to share?

GUIDELINES FOR CONDUCTING THE FOCUS GROUP

For consistency among the groups being conducted nationally, it is essential that you ask all of the questions. There will be probes and follow-ups that emerge, but you need to be sure that you cover the basic questions. This research is designed to elicit responses on public attitudes about politics and elections from those who feel alienated from the process. You will receive a check to cover your honorarium and a check to cover expenses and participant honoraria. It will be available before you conduct your group. I will notify you by e-mail or phone when the check will arrive. You should cash the honoraria expense check and place $25 in cash in each envelope along with the thank you letter. Each participant needs to sign a form for the University of Kansas business office. The following suggestions should assist you in conducting the focus groups. If you have a better system that works for you, that is fine so long as you follow the first three basic guidelines to ensure consistency in data collection.

1. Since this is a relatively short time period, it is not necessary to have more than coffee, soft drinks, and cookies.

2. Have group members complete the questionnaire and consent forms before beginning the discussion. They are to keep one copy of the consent letter. Collect the other copy and the questionnaire, and send them to me with the tape. Answer any questions they have.

3. Begin the focus group by informing them of the following:

    The purpose of the focus group is to study public attitudes about politics and elections. This research is part of a nonpartisan voter education project supported by a grant from the Ford Foundation. I am interested in your candid responses to the questions I will ask. Your opinion is important. We are not seeking to reach agreement; thus, feel free to disagree with comments made by others. We will discuss a topic until everyone has said everything desired and then we will proceed to the next topic. We are tape recording this session, so please speak up. The tape will be sent to Dr. Carlin at the University of Kansas. She will not be able to associate names with comments. No names will be used in reporting about the project.

4. It is possible that in the course of answering one question, another question on the list will be answered by a group member. Solicit reactions from other group members on that topic at that point.

5. Have two *audio* recorders. Have an assistant run the recorders. Begin the second recorder before the first side of the tape has been completed so that you do not have to switch sides. Have all audio equipment set up in advance. Try to place the recorder in the center of the group so that everyone can be heard. You might want to test this ahead of time as we have tapes from some groups that are inaudible. You do not have to video tape.

6. At the conclusion of the focus group, thank everyone. Give them the envelope with the honorarium and thank you letter as they leave.

7. There is one question that focus group participants might ask. Although the informed consent letter states that the participant's name will not be associated in any way with the research findings, someone may question this assurance of anonymity since they are asked to sign their consent letter and the business department's form. You should explain that all consent forms and budget forms from the ten cities will be merged and not matched up with tapes or identified by site.

8. Put the tapes, surveys, and the consent forms in the FedEx envelope and return to us within 24 hours of completing the group.

RECRUITMENT OF FOCUS GROUP PARTICIPANTS

Size and Composition of Groups

1. Recruit only individuals who were eligible but did not vote in 1996.

2. Each group should have 8–10 members. You should recruit 11–12 people to account for attrition.

3. There should be equal numbers of men and women if possible.

4. Do not recruit students (at least not the typical 18–25 year olds as we will do a student group here).

5. Try to have a diverse set of individuals, if possible.

Suggestions for Recruiting

There are several methods you can use. Be creative. The following have been used by others for past groups:

1. Random digit dialing. If this is done, alternate among exchanges in your area if you have more than one.

2. Use the "Rolodex Model." Think about individuals you know through work, church, community activities, etc. that fit a wide demographic range and include them if they meet the nonvoting criteria.

3. Systematic sampling from the phone book.

4. Random sampling of individuals from voter registration lists who did not vote.

5. Selecting people from the phone book based on where they live in the city (assuming that there are socioeconomic differences by section of the city).

6. Some combination of the above.

PARTICIPANT SCREENING

Telephone Script

(for participants in "Public Attitudes About Politics" focus groups)

Hello... My name is _____ and I'm a professor from *(Insert College/University)*. I am involved with a research project on public attitudes about politics and elections. May I please speak with a male/female {alternate between m/f to keep groups even} of voting age who did not vote in the 1996 election.

{If no one fits description} Thank you for your time. Good-bye.

{If the person answering fits the description, then continue below. If a different person is called to the phone, then add the following before proceeding: Hello... My name is _____ and I'm a professor from *(Insert College/University)*.}

I am involved in a voter education project to study public attitudes about politics and elections. I am interested in assembling a small group of citizens from the *(insert city name)* area on *date* to discuss their views about politics and elections. The discussion will last 60–75 minutes and you will receive $25 for participating. Would you be interested in participating?

{if no} Thank you for your time. Good-bye.

{if yes, continue}

Let me first describe my research and then I would like to get your name and address so that I can send you additional information concerning the group discussion.

The discussion will take place on *(insert date)* and is scheduled to begin at *(insert local time)*. On the evening of the discussion, I would like for you to join 10–12 other residents of *(city)* at *(local viewing site)* so that we can discuss your opinions about politics. You will need to arrive by *(time)* and our discussion should last approximately 60–75 minutes.

The focus group discussion will be audio taped; however, the principal researcher at the University of Kansas will have no way of knowing whose voice is on a particular tape.

I am working with researchers throughout the nation to examine the public's attitudes about politics. Your participation will help us determine how to describe the reasons behind current public attitudes about politics and elections and to formulate suggestions for improvements.

Do you have any questions about the project?

Let me get your full name, address, and phone number so that I can send you some follow-up material on the discussion, along with a map of how to get to *(insert local site),* where we will be having the discussion.

{Record name, address, and phone number.}

Mr./Ms. *(insert last name),* I appreciate your willingness to participate in this important project, and you should receive the follow-up material in the mail within the next few days. I look forward to seeing you on *(date of discussion).* Thank you. Good-bye.

PARTICIPANT REMINDER

Telephone Script

May I please speak with Mr./Ms. _____. Mr./Ms._____, this is _____ from _____. I am just calling to remind you about the voter education focus group discussion that will take place on _____ _____. Did you receive the follow-up information that I sent to you? Are you familiar with _____, the location where we will conduct the focus group? Do you have any questions concerning the project?

I appreciate your participation and I look forward to seeing you at *(insert time)* on *(insert date).*

Thank you. Good-bye.

Participant Confirmation Letter

(type on your university's letterhead)

Dear _____:

Thank you for agreeing to participate in the voter education focus group research. You will be joining individuals in ten other communities throughout the country in this research project which is being coordinated by Dr. Diana Carlin at the University of Kansas and is funded through a grant from the Ford Foundation.

As stated in our telephone conversation, the purpose of the focus group is to determine public attitudes about politics and elections.

You will need to arrive at *(Building and room number)* by _____ p.m. on the evening of _____. A map is included to assist you in locating the site.

Upon arriving, you and other focus group members will have a discussion lasting approximately 60–75 minutes. The session will be tape recorded so that Dr. Carlin can transcribe your comments and suggestions. You will not be identified by name on the tape. At the conclusion of the discussion you will receive $25 to show our appreciation for taking time to help us.

Those of us involved in the research appreciate your willingness to participate in this very important study.

If you have any questions between now and _____, or if you learn that you cannot participate, please call me at _____.

Sincerely,
Enclosures

ATTITUDES ABOUT POLITICS SURVEY

(Note: Student groups completed the entire survey; focus groups completed a version without questions 14–23; these were asked in the groups.)

1. Age (check one):
    ____ 18–25   ____26–40   ____ 41–55   ____ over 55

2. ____ Male   ____ Female

3. Occupation: _____

4. Ethnic Background (check most appropriate box)
    ____ African-American
    ____ Asian or Pacific Islander
    ____ White (not Hispanic)
    ____ Hispanic
    ____ American Indian or Alaskan native
    ____ Other

5. Are you a registered voter?   Yes_____ No_____

6. Did you vote in the 1996 elections?   Yes_____ No_____

7. Political party affiliation (if unaffiliated, please indicate):
    _____

8. Have you voted in any of the following elections?
    initiative/referendum   ____ yes ____ no
    city or county   ____ yes ____ no
    school board   ____ yes ____ no
    statewide offices   ____ yes ____ no
    U.S. Senate or House   ____ yes ____ no
    presidential election   ____ yes ____ no

9. When was the last election year in which you voted? _____

10. Rank your *top three* sources of news information, with *1* being your most useful source.
    ____ nightly network news (ABC, CBS, CNN, NBC, PBS)
    ____ C-SPAN

_____ Weekday or evening talk shows (*Nightline, Larry King Live,* etc.)

_____ Sunday talk shows/special news shows (e.g. *Face the Nation, Crossfire*)

_____ Local newspaper

_____ National newspaper such as the *New York Times, Christian Science Monitor, Washington Post*

_____ News magazines (*Time, Newsweek, U.S. News,* etc.)

_____ Commercial radio news

_____ National Public Radio

_____ Internet

_____ Direct mail from groups, organizations, or individuals

_____ Other _____

11. In 1996, which if any, presidential debate(s) did you view?

_____ Clinton/Dole debate from Hartford, CT

_____ Gore/Kemp debate from St. Petersburg, FL

_____ Clinton/Dole town hall meeting from San Diego, CA

_____ None—did not view debates

12. What was your level of exposure to campaign coverage during the 1996 campaign?

_____ regular—daily/weekly

_____ 3–4 times per month

_____ once per month or less

_____ began following regularly during last two months of campaign

_____ began following regularly during last month of campaign

13. Please respond to the following statements about politics and elections using the following scale:

1-strongly disagree   2-disagree   3-no opinion   4-agree   5-strongly agree

a.	A single vote doesn't matter.	1	2	3	4	5
b.	Politicians do not listen to the public.	1	2	3	4	5
c.	Politicians do not care about the public.	1	2	3	4	5
d.	Politicians only care about people with money.	1	2	3	4	5
e.	Politicians forget campaign promises.	1	2	3	4	5
f.	Politicians should not be trusted.	1	2	3	4	5
g.	Political issues are too complicated for the average person to understand.	1	2	3	4	5
h.	I do not have time for politics.	1	2	3	4	5
i.	What goes on in Washington does not affect my life.	1	2	3	4	5
j.	What goes on in the state capital does not affect my life.	1	2	3	4	5
k.	What goes on in the city/county government does not affect my life.	1	2	3	4	5
l.	Elected officials try to do the right thing.	1	2	3	4	5

m.	Politicians will say anything to get elected.	1	2	3	4	5
n.	There is too much negative advertising in campaigns.	1	2	3	4	5
o.	News media coverage of politics is too negative.	1	2	3	4	5

14. Write the first thing that comes to mind when you see or hear the following words (your answer can be a word or phrase) and follow the word or phrase with a brief explanation as to why you answered as you did.

    politics

    politician

    elections/campaigns

    news media

    political advertising

15. If you did not vote in 1996, explain why not.

16. If you have voted in past elections, but didn't vote in 1996 what was different about the 1996 election that caused you not to vote?

17. What do you think is the major reason other people don't vote.

18. What are the major problems, if any, with American politics today?

19. What can be done to resolve the problems?

20. What would it take to get you more interested in politics?

21. Do you think the news media and candidates provide you with enough and the right kind of information to make an informed choice as a voter? If not, what information do you need that you don't get?

22. Do the decisions politicians make at local, state, and national levels affect you personally? If yes, on what particular issues and how?

23. Do you have any other comments to make about politics, political campaigns or media coverage of campaigns?

Table 1. Attitudes about Politics Survey

Question	Student Voters						Student Nonvoters	
	1	2	3	4	5	X	1	2
13a. Single vote doesn't matter	128 39.6%	131 40.5%	18 5%	33 10.2%	13 4%	1.98	67 26.5%	99 39.2%
13b. Pols don't listen	28 8.6%	155 47.8%	52 16%	80 24.6%	9 2.7%	2.65	8 3.1%	104 40.7%
13c. Pols don't care	31 9.5%	166 51.2%	70 21.6%	47 14.5%	10 3%	2.50	18 7%	122 47.8%
13d. Pols care $s	17 5.2%	104 32.1%	76 23.5%	96 29.7%	30 9.2%	3.05	6 2.3%	66 25.8%
13e. Pols forget promises	8 2.4%	77 23.7%	58 17.9%	143 44.1%	38 11.7%	3.39	2 0.7%	56 21.9%
13f. Can't trust pols	12 3.7%	101 31.1%	117 36.1%	79 24.3%	15 4.6%	2.95	7 2.7%	71 28%
13g. Issues too complex	73 22.8%	138 43.2%	48 15%	49 15.3%	11 3.4%	2.33	53 20.9%	120 47.4%
13h. No time for politics	69 21.2%	142 43.8%	57 17.5%	47 14.5%	9 2.7%	2.34	24 9.4%	86 33.7%
13i. Washington doesn't affect life	182 56.1%	120 37%	16 4.9%	6 1.8%	0	1.52	102 40.1%	117 46%
13j. State gov doesn't affect life	173 53.3%	128 39.5%	16 4.9%	6 1.8%	1 0.3%	1.56	110 43.1%	113 44.3%
13k. Local gov doesn't affect life	190 59%	114 35%	15 4.6%	4 1.2%	1 0.03%	1.49	120 47.2%	111 43.7%
13l. Elected officials do right thing	7 2.2%	38 11.8%	122 37.8%	147 45.5%	9 2.7%	3.35	9 3.5%	40 15.7%
13m. Pols say anything	3 0.9%	38 11.9%	74 23.2%	151 47.3%	53 16.7%	3.67	4 1.6%	15 5.9%
13n. Too many neg ads	8 2.5%	29 9%	48 14.9%	133 41.3%	104 32.3%	3.92	10 3.9%	23 9%
13o. News media too negative	10 3.1%	63 19.5%	116 35.9%	102 31.6%	32 9.9%	3.26	8 3.1%	53 20.8%

$*p = .05, **p = .025, ***p = .01, ****p = .001, *****p = .0001$

	Student Nonvoters				Focus Group Nonvoters				
3	4	5	X	1	2	3	4	5	X
24 9.5%	40 15.8%	22 8.7%	2.40****	21 30.9%	19 28%	6 8.8%	11 16.2%	11 16.2%	2.59***
60 23.5%	68 26.6%	15 5.8%	2.91***	6 8.8%	22 32.3%	14 20.6%	22 32.3%	4 5.9%	2.94***
62 24.3%	43 16.8%	10 3.9%	2.63	5 7.4%	34 50%	9 13.2%	18 26.5%	2 2.9%	2.68
74 29%	74 29%	35 13.7%	3.25	6 9%	15 22.8%	10 15.1%	22 33.3%	13 19.7%	3.32
40 15.6%	111 43.5%	46 18%	3.56	3 4.5%	11 16.4%	6 9%	31 46.3%	16 23.9%	3.69**
97 38.3%	53 20.9%	25 9.8%	3.07	3 4.5%	14 20.9%	20 29.9%	23 34.3%	7 10.4%	3.25*
35 13.8%	40 15.8%	5 1.9%	2.30	10 14.7%	22 23.3%	12 17.6%	16 23.5%	8 11.8%	285**
70 27.4%	60 23.5%	15 5.8%	2.83*****	12 17.6%	23 33.8%	12 17.6%	17 25%	4 5.9%	2.68***
18 7%	10 3.9%	7 2.7%	1.83	30 45.5%	27 41%	8 12.1%	1 1.5%	0	1.7
22 8.6%	6 2.3%	4 1.5%	1.75	25 36.8%	32 47.1%	8 11.8%	2 2.9%	1 1.5%	1.85
13 5%	7 3%	3 1%	1.70	36 53%	29 42.6%	3 4.4%	0	0	1.51
96 37.7%	104 40.9%	5 1.9%	3.22	6 8.8%	15 22%	27 39.7%	18 26.5%	2 2.9%	2.93**
49 19.2%	110 43.3%	76 29.9%	3.94****	4 6%	14 20.9%	10 14.9%	22 32.8%	17 25.4%	3.51***
59 32.2%	89 35%	73 28.7%	3.76	5 7.5%	7 10.4%	21 31.3%	12 17.9%	22 32.8%	3.58***
92 36.1%	69 27%	32 12.9%	3.26	6 8.8%	10 14.7%	25 36.8%	14 20.6%	13 19.1%	3.26

RESPONSES TO WORD ASSOCIATIONS

In both the student survey on attitudes about politics and the focus groups, participants were asked to write or say the first thing that came to mind when they heard or saw five words or phrases. The answers fell into the three categories of positive, negative, or neutral. A fourth category, "cost" was added for the fifth term, "political ads." The following is a list of the terms, followed by the content categories and sample responses.

Politics

A. *Positive*—1 (A way of bettering society)

B. *Neutral*—71 (Foundation of our government; the process of elections and serving in an office. It is how the government operates. Republicans and Democrats)

C. *Negative*—89 (The slow destruction of our country, boring, complicated, I don't understand half the things that go on)

Politicians

A. *Positive*—3 (People who try to make people's lives better, a person who listens to the public and tries to make positive changes in the laws)

B. *Neutral*—77 (The people behind the politics, an elected official, the names and faces that actually run the government)

C. *Negative*—82 (Rich—it seems that all politicians are rich, rich white men, men in suits, a guy who will say anything to get elected, slick)

Elections/Campaigns

A. *Positive*—26 (Ways of becoming informed about candidates)

B. *Neutral*—92 (Process of getting into office; talking and giving information about issues)

C. *Negative*—55 (Mud slinging, a way to bash your opponent, nothing more than useless polls)

News Media

A. *Positive*—37 (Good coverage, a good job of showing both sides, the best source of information on politics)

B. *Neutral*—28 (A tool for information, 5 o'clock news, national news)

C. *Negative*—97 (Circus, always looks for something bad to bring out, nit-pick, pulling bones out of someone's closet, biased)

Political Ads

A. *Positive*—2 (Information source on a specific candidate)

B. *Neutral*—34 (During election campaigns you will see ads for candidates everywhere you turn; signs in front yards)

C. *Negative*—115 (Lies, they are just out to get other people, bashing other candidates

Table 2. Reasons Others Do Not Vote with Comparison to Self-Reports

Reasons	Voter Responses	Nonvoter Responses	Self-Reports of Nonvoters
1. Disempowerment	171 (53.7%)	101 (41%)	11 (4%) [7]
2. Apathy	109 (34.2%)	91 (36.9%)	18 (6.6%) [6]
3. Personal inconvenience	76 (23.8%)	62 (25.2%)	40 (14.7%) [3]
4. Lack of knowledge/information	55 (17.2%)	41 (16.6%)	30 (11%) [5]
5. Disillusionment	37 (11.6%)	25 (10.1%)	6 (2.2%) [8]
6. Disliked choices	29 (9.1%)	28 (11.3%)	23 (8.4%) [4]
7. Process	9 (2.8%)	8 (3.2%)	64 (23.4%) [2]
8. Ineligibility	3 (0.9%)	2 (0.8%)	81 (29.7%) [1]

D. *Cost*—10 (Expensive, too much money runs through the advertising, a big waste of everyone's money because they cost millions for only a few seconds)

Responses to Open-Ended Questions

Question 15: If you did not vote in 1996, explain why not.

Question 16: If you have voted in past elections, but didn't vote in 1996 what was different about the 1996 election that caused you not to vote?

Question 17: What do you think is the major reason other people don't vote?

A. *Apathy* (I was too lazy to go wait in a line and vote for someone when I didn't really care who won, apathetic, no concern for the country, people don't care)

B. *Empowerment* (I knew Clinton would win so it didn't really matter, my one vote would have been meaningless, they think their one vote won't change the election in any way, shape, or form, I never vote, I don't think one vote matters)

C. *Ineligibility* (My birthday was about a week too late, I am not eligible, I was not a citizen yet)

D. *Process* (Somehow the paperwork got crossed and I received the absentee ballot after it was too late, not in state where I am registered, I changed addresses and didn't change quick enough to be able to vote, I only turned 18 on October 10th that year and the deadline to register came up before I had time to go register, I never knew how or where to sign up)

E. *Personal Inconvenience* (Had too much to do—never got around to registering, I wanted to, but I just did not get around to actually voting, too busy with college classes, I don't have a car, a lot of people are really lazy.)

F. *Disillusioned with System* (The Electoral College takes the power of vote away from citizen, they don't like politics or politicians or just the whole idea in general, people are frustrated by a system that provides benefits only to the very poor and rich.)

G. *Candidate Choices* (I did not like either of the presidential choices, I am not into choosing the better of two evils)

H. *Lack of Information* (I feel left in the dark as to who these people really are, I felt I did not pay attention enough to just go out and vote when I could be voting for or against something I'm not aware of, I was not educated enough to make the proper vote, people are uninformed and uneducated and have no idea about political system)

Question 18: "What are the major problems, if any, with American politics today?"

A. *Public apathy* (People don't care, people don't participate, don't have enough time)

B. *Failure to address citizen and country's needs* (It's not citizen oriented, only good for the rich, politicians don't care about government)

C. *Campaign process: negative and costly* (Too many lies against opponents, too much focus on money, too complicated and drawn out)

D. *Media* (The media encourages the capable not to run, heavy focus on controversy, media focuses on the negative aspects of politics)

E. *Candidates are flawed* (Electing bad politicians, candidates lack personal values, lack of integrity)

F. *Issues* (Education, court system)

Question 19: "What can be done to resolve the problems?"

A. *Accountability* (Make candidates sign contracts stating their campaign promises, hold politicians to their word, make government accountable to the people)

B. *Broaden Candidate Base* (Encourage more minorities and women to run, elect a female president, let anybody run, not just those with money)

C. *Campaign/process reform* (Limit campaign spending, throw out the entire system and start again, eliminate PACs and special interest groups, reform the government)

D. *Education* (Increase education on issues, give more information to the public, learn from mistakes and history, make it seem interesting to people)

E. *Reform media* (Put the news media back in their place—to inform the public on two sides to every issue, media needs to be more ethical and back off, more positive reflections to the audience, focus on issues; not on people)

F. *Nothing can be done*

G. Unsure of solution

Question 20: "What would it take to get you more interested in politics?"

A. *Already interested* (I couldn't be more interested, I follow politics now, I'm a political science major—how much more interested could I be?)

B. *Nothing* (I will never be interested in that stuff, only money could get me interested in politics)

C. *Access/Ease of information* (More user-friendly voting system, presenting issues in ways that are easier to understand, more readily available information, campaigns that are easy to understand, more time to pay attention)

D. *Candidates* (Somebody who actually has something to say, candidates should answer the questions clearly, a candidate I could believe in and who could actually make a difference, they need to have an agenda and see it through, bring Reagan back.)

E. *Increase empowerment* (If I believed that I wouldn't be pressured by the general consensus and could voice my opinion freely, if I thought my vote really mattered, knowing my opinions, as a minority, are appreciated)

F. *Relevance of Issues* (Less political jargon, more issues discussed that affect my age group, more action toward the public good, exposure to topics that affect me more closely)

G. *Reformed media* (More intelligent debates; let it be politics, not a game, honest representations of candidates)

Question 21: "Do you think the news media and candidates provide you with enough and the right kind of information to make an informed choice as a voter? If not, what information do you need that you don't get?"

A. *More focus on issues* (Issue relevant topics, delving into issues and exploring them for what they are worth)

B. *More positive* (Stop focusing on all the negatives, more positive information, more on the good things candidates do)

C. *Less analysis, more fact* (More info and less opinion, let the audience draw their own conclusions, real informative numbers and actual working of the bills to be presented, too much information and too analyzed—let the audience analyze)

D. *Candidate: stance & history* (We need to know more about their views and opinions, bipartisanship of candidates, the individual's exact stance on many of the key issues, rap sheets on issues, standings, and past votes)

E. *Access to information* (Needs to be more convenient, you can probably go to public files and find info yourself, more debates, more local information)

F. *Accountable information* (I still don't believe half of what I am told, explain *how* changes *will* be made, ask better questions)

DebateWatch 2000 Research Materials

MATERIALS FOR CONDUCTING FOCUS GROUPS

DebateWatch 2000

Conducting Focus Groups

A *common sequence* of events for many focus groups goes something like this: (The leader usually takes responsibility for carrying them out.)

- Thank people for coming.
- Review the purpose of the group, and the goals of the meeting. Set the stage.
- Go over the flow of the meeting—how it will proceed, and how the members can contribute. Lay out the ground rules. Encourage open participation.
- Set the tone.

This is important, because probably few of your participants will have been in a focus group before.

- Ask an opening question. This could be a very general question ("What are your general thoughts about X?"), or something more specific. Both choices are justifiable; and both types of questions might be asked before the group ends.
- Make sure that all opinions on that question get a chance to be heard. How do you do this?

Some common techniques:

- Summarize what you think you have heard, and ask if the group agrees;
- Phrase the same question in a different way;

- Ask if anyone else has any comments on that question;
- Ask a follow-up question;
- Look around the room, and make brief eye contact, especially with those who may not have spoken.

Reminder #1: Be sure to record. If the group is not being tape-recorded, someone should be writing the key points down.

Reminder #2: Of course, the leader's job is to *elicit* opinion, and not judge it. All opinions should be supported. Judgments come later.

- Ask your next question—and proceed with other questions in the same general manner.

The phrasing of the questions, the follow-ups, the ordering of the questions, and how much time to spend on each one are points that the leader will have to decide—sometimes on the spot. An experienced leader will be able to do this. This is why you have spent time preparing for this!

- When all your questions have been asked, and before the group ends, ask if anyone has any other comments to make. This can be an effective way of gathering other opinions that have not yet been voiced.
- Tell the member about any next steps that will occur, and what they can expect to happen now.
- Don't forget to thank the group for coming!

The above was adapted from Chapter 3, Section 6: Conducting Focus Groups of the Community Tool Box, a project of the KU Work Group on Health Promotion and Community Development. The entirety of the Tool Box can be viewed at http://ctb.lsi.ukans.edu.

PROJECT DESCRIPTION: DEBATEWATCH 2000

DebateWatch 2000

WHAT—A project to get Americans *talking* about the election, not just *listening*. DebateWatch asks people to come together to watch the presidential debates and discuss them. It is a way to strengthen communities, build civic participation, and *make your voice heard.*

HOW—is your voice heard?—Each DebateWatch turns in a summary of the participants' discussion. The results will be immediately tabulated and released the next day to the public, the media, and DebateWatch sponsors.

WHO—Anyone! You, your friends, neighbors, business colleagues, teens.

WHERE—Anywhere with a television. Living rooms, public libraries, community centers, schools, etc.

WHEN—October 2000.

Presidential debates:
October 3, 11, and 17
Vice-presidential debate:
October 5.

Organizing a DebateWatch

- Anyone can host a DebateWatch.
- It can be a small event in your home or a larger community meeting.
- Organize it by yourself or in conjunction with a civic group or business.
- Invite people of all ages—even teens not yet of voting age.
- Choose a facilitator to keep the discussion going.
- Ideally, DebateWatch groups will have between 6–12 people. If there are more in your group, watch the debate together and break into smaller groups afterward for discussions.
- If you are unable to hold a DebateWatch at the time the debates are aired, simply record the debates to watch and discuss them the next day.

Sign Up Today!
To register your event, get a "How to do" a DebateWatch packet, or if you have questions, contact the DebateWatch Research Center at:
Toll-free Phone: 1-888-864-9875
E-Mail: presdeb@ukans.edu, or download the packet via the
Internet: http://www.debates.org/pages/debwatch.html
If you are interested in attending a DebateWatch already organized in your area, please contact us and we will try to find one near you.

FACILITATOR'S REPORT: DEBATEWATCH 2000

Group responses must be received by midnight Eastern Time the night of the debate to be included in the next day's press release. Responses received after 12:00 a.m. will be tallied and posted on the CPD web site.

Submit your group's responses in one of the following ways:
PREFERRED OPTIONS
Internet: The fastest and easiest way—log onto www.debates.org and click the link for DebateWatch.
Email: Send to debatewatch@debates.org
ALSO AVAILABLE
Phone: Please submit your answers online or by email. If you cannot, please call toll free at 1-888-864-9875.
Fax: Please submit your answers online or by email. If you cannot, please fax to 1-877-780-7987.

Mail: Please submit your answers online or by email. If you cannot, please mail to:

DebateWatch 2000, Communication Studies Dept., University of Kansas, Lawrence, KS 66045

1. City and state where DebateWatch was held:

    _____

2. Place of discussion (school, library, home, etc.):

    _____

3. Debate discussed:
    ❏ 1st Pres   ❏ 2nd Pres   ❏ 3rd Pres   ❏ Vice Pres
    Tues, Oct. 3   Thu, Oct. 5   Wed, Oct. 11   Tue, Oct. 17

4. Total number of participants _____

    For questions 5–7, indicate the number of participants representing the following demographic groups:

5. Female_____   Male_____

6. Age (estimate): Under 18_____   18–25_____
    16–40_____   41–55_____   Over 55_____

7. Race:
    ___Black/African American
    ___Hispanic
    ___Native American
    ___Asian or Pacific Islander
    ___White
    ___Other (please specify)

8. How or where did you or the group organizer learn about Debate Watch 2000?

    _____

9. Is your group connected with any organizations participating in DebateWatch 2000?
    ❏ Yes   ❏ No
    If yes, which one? _____

    Based on the group discussion, please answer the following questions. Make sure the group agrees with the answers.

10. Which topics or issues in the debate did participants find most useful or informative?

11. Were any issues or topics considered irrelevant or unimportant to participants?

12. Did participants want to hear about any topics or issues that were not included in the debate? Please list.

13. How many members of your group said participating in DebateWatch would influence the way they read about, watch, or discuss the election?

To receive a copy of the final DebateWatch summary, please print your name and address below:

_____

_____

_____

PARTICIPANT SURVEY

Thank you for participating in DebateWatch 2000. *Completion of this survey is optional and responses anonymous.*

PART 1: PREDEBATE

Complete this section before the debate begins

Which debate are you watching and discussing?

❑ 1st Pres   ❑ 2nd Pres   ❑ 3rd Pres   ❑ Vice Pres

1. How did you first learn about DebateWatch?

   ❑ Television   ❑ Friend, coworker, family

   ❑ Newspaper   ❑ Radio Announcement

   ❑ Information in Library   ❑ School

   ❑ Other _____

2. Who invited you to participate?

   ❑ Friend   ❑ Club/organization   ❑ Family member

   ❑ Neighbor   ❑ Coworker   ❑ Public Announcement

   ❑ Other _____

3. How many DebateWatch groups have you attended including this one?

   ❑ 1   ❑ 2   ❑ 3   ❑ 4

4. Rank your top three sources of campaign information, with 1 being your most useful source.

   ____ Nightly network news (ABC, CBS, CNN, NBC, PBS)

   ____ C-SPAN

   ____ Weekday or evening talk shows (*Nightline, Larry King Live, Rush Limbaugh,* etc.)

   ____ Sunday talk shows/special news shows (e.g. *This Week, Face the Nation, Meet the Press, Washington Week in Review, Crossfire, Equal Time,* etc.)

___ Local newspaper

___ National newspaper such as the *New York Times, Christian Science Monitor, Washington Post*

___ News magazines

___ Commercial radio news

___ National Public Radio

___ Internet

___ Direct mail from candidates, parties, organizations, or interest groups

___ Other _____

5. What was your level of exposure to campaign coverage during the past 6–8 months?

___ regular—daily/weekly

___ 3–4 times per month

___ one per month or less

___ began following regularly the past two months

___ began following regularly the past month

___ have followed irregularly up until the debates

6. Before watching the debate, do you have a candidate preference?

   ❏ Yes   ❏ No

7. Age (check one):

   ❏ under 18   ❏ 18–25   ❏ 26–40   ❏ 41–55   ❏ over 55

8. ❏ Male   ❏ Female

9. Occupation: _____

10. Ethnic Background (check most appropriate box):

    ❏ Black-African Native Descent   ❏ Asian or Pacific Islander
    ❏ Hispanic   ❏ White (not Hispanic)
    ❏ American Indian or Alaska Native

11. Party affiliation (if unaffiliated, please indicate):

    _____

Stop here until after the debate.   STOP

PART 2: POSTDEBATE

Complete this section before group discussion

If before the debate you indicated YES to having a candidate preference, go to question 12-A below.

If before the debate you indicated NO to having a candidate preference, go to question 12-B below.

12-A. After watching the debate, are you:
- ❏ still leaning toward your predebate preference
- ❏ now undecided
- ❏ now leaning toward another candidate

12-B. After watching the debate, are you:
- ❏ still undecided
- ❏ now leaning toward a candidate

13. Please evaluate *the debate itself* by responding to the statements below on the following scale:

1-strongly disagree; **2**-disagree; **3**-no opinion; **4**-agree; **5**-strongly disagree

A. The debates taught me something new about one or more candidates

❏ 1   ❏ 2   ❏ 3   ❏ 4   ❏ 5

B. The debates taught me something new about one or more issue

❏ 1   ❏ 2   ❏ 3   ❏ 4   ❏ 5

C. The debates clarified my understanding of one of more candidates' position on an issue or issues.

❏ 1   ❏ 2   ❏ 3   ❏ 4   ❏ 5

D. The debates reinforced my attitudes about one or more candidates

❏ 1   ❏ 2   ❏ 3   ❏ 4   ❏ 5

E. The debates helped me to evaluate one or more candidates differently than prior to the debate.

❏ 1   ❏ 2   ❏ 3   ❏ 4   ❏ 5

F. The debates helped me decide for whom to vote or helped firm up my decision

❏ 1   ❏ 2   ❏ 3   ❏ 4   ❏ 5

G. The debates gave me ideas to discuss in the group

❏ 1   ❏ 2   ❏ 3   ❏ 4   ❏ 5

H. The debates made me more likely to vote

❏ 1   ❏ 2   ❏ 3   ❏ 4   ❏ 5

I. The debates increased my interest in following the remainder of the campaign more closely.

❏ 1   ❏ 2   ❏ 3   ❏ 4   ❏ 5

Stop here until after the discussion.   STOP

PART 3: POSTDISCUSSION

Complete this section after group discussion

14. After participating in the discussion, has your position on the candidates changed from what was indicated as your position after the debate?
- ❏ Yes   ❏ No

If YES, have you:

❑ gone from undecided to a candidate

❑ gone from a candidate to undecided

❑ changed from one candidate to another

15. Please evaluate *the postdebate discussion* by responding to the statements below on the following scale:

1-strongly disagree; 2-disagree; 3-no opinion; 4-agree; 5-strongly disagree

A. The discussion taught me something new about one or more candidates

❑ 1   ❑ 2   ❑ 3   ❑ 4   ❑ 5

B. The debates taught me something new about one or more issue

❑ 1   ❑ 2   ❑ 3   ❑ 4   ❑ 5

C. The discussion clarified my understanding of one of more candidates' position on an issue or issues.

❑ 1   ❑ 2   ❑ 3   ❑ 4   ❑ 5

D. The discussion reinforced my attitudes about one or more candidates

❑ 1   ❑ 2   ❑ 3   ❑ 4   ❑ 5

E. The discussion caused me to evaluate one or more candidates differently than prior to the debate.

❑ 1   ❑ 2   ❑ 3   ❑ 4   ❑ 5

F. The discussion helped me decide for whom to vote or helped firm up my decision

❑ 1   ❑ 2   ❑ 3   ❑ 4   ❑ 5

G. The discussion gave me ideas to discuss in the group

❑ 1   ❑ 2   ❑ 3   ❑ 4   ❑ 5

H. The discussion made me more likely to vote

❑ 1   ❑ 2   ❑ 3   ❑ 4   ❑ 5

I. The discussion increased my interest in following the remainder of the campaign more closely.

❑ 1   ❑ 2   ❑ 3   ❑ 4   ❑ 5

Comments:

INFORMED CONSENT STATEMENT

The Department of Communication Studies at the University of Kansas supports the practice of protection for human subjects participating in research. The following information is provided for you to decide whether you wish to participate in the present study. You should be aware that even if you agree to participate, you are free to withdraw at any time without affecting opportunities for participation in other projects offered by this department.

As a subject in this study you will watch a presidential debate for two political candidates and will participate in a discussion group and complete a survey related to what you saw. The study will take approximately one hour to complete. This research involves no risk to subjects. Benefits of the study may involve new information regarding the improvement of information provided by political candidates to potential voters.

This investigation is being conducted by Dr. Diana Carlin and her graduate research assistants as part of a larger research project organized by the Commission on Presidential Debates and the University of Kansas. We do solicit your participation, but it is strictly voluntary. Do not hesitate to ask any questions about the study before, during, or after the research is complete. Be assured that your name will not be associated with the research findings in any way. For any additional information on this research, please contact Dr. Carlin at 785-864-6161 or the DebateWatch Research Center at 785-864-9875.

You must be 18 years of age or older to participate in this project. Your signature indicates that you agree to participate in this research project as described above.

Diana B. Carlin, Ph.D.
Department of Communication Studies/
Graduate School and International Programs
300 Strong Hall

_____

Subject's Signature

ACADEMIC PARTNERS: DEBATEWATCH 2000

Alabama A & M University
Allegheny College
Appalachian State University
Arizona State University
Augsburg College
Beloit College
Boston University
Bridgewater College
Centre College
Chicago State University
Clarion University
College of DuPage
College of William and Mary
College of Wooster
Cottey College
Duquesne University

Eastern University

Eastern Washington University

Elon University

Emerson College

Emporia State University

Florida State University

Franklin and Marshall College

George Mason University

George Washington University

Georgetown University Student Government

Henderson State University

Howard University

Illinois State University

Indiana University

Iowa State University—Carrie Chapman Catt Center

Ithaca College

James Madison University

Kansas State University

Lewis and Clark College

Manchester College

Marshall University

Mary Washington College

Mercyhurst College

Monmouth University

New Mexico State University

Normandale Community College

North Carolina Agricultural and Technical State University

Northern Kentucky University

Northwestern University

Ohio University

Portland State University

Providence College

Purdue University

Randolph Macon College

Rockhurst University

Russell Sage College

Southeast Missouri State University

State University of New York-Albany

State University of New York-Fredonia

State University of New York-New Paltz

Stephen F. Austin University

Syracuse University

Tarleton State University

Texas A & M University

Truman State University

University of Akron

University of Arizona

University of Arkansas

University of California-Berkeley Unruh Institute of Politics

University of Cincinnati

University of Florida

University of Georgia

University of Kansas

University of Maryland Center of Political Leadership & Participation

University of Massachusetts-Boston

University of Minnesota-Humphrey Center

University of Nebraska-Lincoln

University of New Hampshire

University of New Haven

University of Northern Iowa

University of Oklahoma

University of Portland

University of Puget Sound

University of Richmond

University of Southern California- Unruh Institute of Politics

University of Southern Mississippi

University of Tennessee-Martin

University of Texas-Permian Basin

University of Tulsa

University of Virginia-center Miller Center

University of Wisconsin

Vanderbilt University

Villanova University

Wabash College

Wake Forest University

Washington University

Wayne State University

West Chester University

West Virginia University

Wichita State University-Elliott School of Communication

DebateWatch 2004
Research Materials

GUIDE TO HOSTING A DEBATEWATCH

Welcome to the 2004 DebateWatch research project. This is the third election cycle for DebateWatch and the third time that members of the National Communication Association have coordinated efforts to gather data from DebateWatch discussion groups specifically for research purposes. If you would like to become involved in this NCA research project, there are only a few steps and many options. They are as follows:

Before Debate

- Organize discussion group. Review and print out the guidelines for running your group from Commission on Presidential Debates website at www.debates.org.

Night of Debate

- Download all these Participant Questionnaires and Facilitator Reports:
- Note: Bullets represent links for Reports and Questionnaires.

  - Participants Questionnaire
  - International Participants Questionnaire
  - Post Debate Voter's Choice Questionnaire
  - Facilitator's Final Report (2 pages)

- Disseminate the questionnaires to the participants in your group. Note, there are sections of the questionnaire that must be completed prior to the debate and then after the debate and after the discussion.

After Debate

- Immediately following the debate, turn your televisions off. Ask the participants in your group to complete the Postdebate sections of their questionnaires, as well as the *Postdebate Voter's Choice Questionnaire.*

- Facilitate a Discussion! Follow the suggested questions. Note: Link for Suggested questions will be here or create your own. However, encourage group participants to also ask questions.

- Ask the participants in your group to complete the Postdiscussion section of their questionnaire.

- Send the *Participant Questionnaire* and the *Post Debate Voter's Choice Questionnaire* to Diana Carlin, Graduate School and International Programs, Strong Hall 1450 Jayhawk Blvd., Room 300, Lawrence, KS 66045. Postage will be reimbursed.

- Complete the Facilitator's report on the CPD Web site (www.debates.org).

- Complete both NCA Facilitators' Reports—the *Facilitator's Final Report* and the *Voting Choice Changes Facilitator's Report*—and submit them to the national data collection center no later than the next morning. If you cannot get them in by the next morning, please send them anyway since we will do a final summary after all of the debates. You can cut and paste your results into an email message and send them to the National DebateWatch Center at DW2004@ku.edu. Or you may also fax your results to 1-785-864-4555. *Be sure to submit your responses by 10:00 AM Central Time the day following the debate if you want them in the NCA news release. If you cannot make the deadline, send them when you can for the final report on October 15.*

DEBATEWATCH 2004: DISCUSSION QUESTIONS FOR POSTDEBATE GROUPS

Below are questions for facilitators to use in their small group discussions. Each discussion group should have one facilitator. We encourage you to tape one or more of your groups (if you have multiples in your project) and send the tape to Diana Carlin, Graduate School and International Programs, Strong Hall 1450 Jayhawk Blvd., Room 300, Lawrence, KS 66045. If you need to be reimbursed, we will do so. We would prefer audio tapes and ask that you have people pass the microphone or small recorder around or that someone hold it near the speaker so that the quality is good for transcription.

1. What were your expectations for the debate? Were they met?
2. What did you learn about the candidates or issues that you did not know prior to viewing the debate?
3. Which topics or issues in the debate did you find most useful or informative?
4. Did the debate influence your attitudes about the issues or the candidates?
5. Were there any issues of interest that were not discussed during the debate?
6. Were there any issues raised that you considered irrelevant or unimportant?
7. How do debates compare with other campaign information sources (e.g., news, ads, speeches, conventions, call-in shows, online resources, etc.) in helping you learn about the candidates and the issues?
8. If you could change one feature of the debate format, what would it be? Why?
9. Will the debate and discussion influence the way you vote?

10. How will it affect the way you discuss the campaign at work, home, etc.?

11. How will it influence how you follow the campaign (e.g., will you read/watch more news, search websites, etc.)?

12. As a member of a particular demographic group (e.g., students, young parent, senior, etc.), how effective were the questions and answers in addressing your interests and needs?

13. Will watching the debates make you more or less likely to vote?

Possible additional questions for the second, third or vice presidential debates:

1. What did you learn from this debate that you did not learn from the previous debate(s)?

2. How, if at all, did the press coverage of the previous debate(s) influence your attitudes about the candidates or the issues in this debate?

3. What did you learn from the vice presidential debate that was different from the presidential debate?

DEBATEWATCH 2004: FACILITATOR'S FINAL REPORT

Make your voice heard by participating in the National Communication Association's DebateWatch 2004 research project. Complete the following questions and submit your group's responses by e-mail to DW2004@ku.edu or by fax to 1-785-864-4555. Be sure to submit your responses by 10:00 A.M. Central Time the day following the debate.

1. City and state where DebateWatch was held:

   _____

2. Place of discussion (school, library, home, etc.):

   _____

3. Debate discussed:

   ___ First Presidential   ___ Vice Presidential   ___ Second Presidential
   ___ Third Presidential

4. Number of participants: _____

   For questions 5–8 indicate the number of participants representing the following demographic groups:

5. Female _____   Male _____

6. Age (estimate):

   _____ Under 18   _____ 18–25   _____ 26–40
   _____ 41–55   _____ Over 55

7. Race:

  _____ White   _____ American Indian or Alaska Native

  _____ Asian   _____ Native Hawaiian or other Pacific Islander

  _____ Other   _____ Black or African-American

  _____ International/Non-U.S. Citizens

8. How would members describe their preference before and after the debate?

  Before: _____ Decided   _____ Undecided

  After: _____ Decided   _____ Undecided

9. How did the group organizer learn about DebateWatch 2004?

  _____

10. Is your group connected with any organization participating in DebateWatch 2004?

  _____ Yes _____ No If yes, which one?

  _____ National Communication Association

  _____ Campus Compact

  _____ National Campaign

  _____ Other. If other, please list: _____

  Based on the group discussion, please answer the following questions. Make sure the group agrees on the answers.

11. Which topics or issues in the debate did participant find most useful or informative?

  _____
  _____
  _____

12. Were any issues or topics considered irrelevant or unimportant to participants?

  _____
  _____
  _____

13. Did participants want to hear about any topics or issues that were not included in the debate? Please list.

  _____
  _____
  _____

14. How many members of your group said participating in DebateWatch would influence the way they read about, watch, or discuss the election?

  _____
  _____
  _____

For members of your research group, indicate the total number who fit the following categories:

Pre-Debate Voting Choice

_____ Have a candidate preference
_____ Undecided

Postdebate Voting Choice

For those who had a candidate preference, how many were
_____ Supporting the same candidate
_____ Supporting a different candidate
_____ Undecided

For those who did not have a candidate preference prior to the debate, how many were
_____ Still undecided
_____ Supporting a candidate

Postdiscussion Voting Choice

After the DebateWatch discussion, how many of those who had a candidate preference after the debate were
_____ Supporting the same candidate
_____ Supporting a different candidate
_____ Undecided

After the DebateWatch discussion, how many of those who did not have a candidate preference were
_____ Still undecided
_____ Supporting a candidate.

INFORMED CONSENT STATEMENT

The Department of Communication Studies at the University of Kansas supports the practice of protection for human subjects participating in research. The following information is provided for you to decide whether you wish to participate in the present study on political debates. Your completion of the surveys indicates your willingness to participate. You should be aware that even if you agree to participate, you are free to withdraw at any time.

Purpose of the Study

The purpose of this study is to find out what you have learned about the candidates from the presidential debate, how you learn about political issues, and if the debates influenced your voting choice. You are to complete the predebate part of the survey before the debate begins and other sections after the debate and after the discussion. You will participate in a discussion, led by a trained facilitator, after the debate. There are no risks connected with this research. All surveys are completely anonymous. If you are in a group that is being taped, your name will not be associated with the tape. All data collected will be compiled along with data from throughout the country so there is no way of tracking your responses to you.

Through your participation in this study you will assist a national research project that is designed to make the debates better voter education tools for citizens in the future.

Thank you for participating.
Diana B. Carlin, Ph.D.
University of Kansas
Department of Communication Studies
National Communication Association

DEBATEWATCH 2004: PARTICIPANT QUESTIONNAIRE

PART I: PREDEBATE WATCH

Please complete this section *before* the debate begins.
Which debate are you watching and discussing?

_____ 1st Pres _____ 2nd Pres _____ 3rd Pres _____ Vice Pres

1. How did you first learn about DebateWatch

   ___ TV   ___ Friend/Colleague

   ___ Newspaper   ___ Radio

   ___ Info in library   ___ School/Teacher

   ___ CPD website

   ___ Other internet source _____

   ___ Other _____

2. How many DebateWatch groups have you attended, including this one?

   ___ 1 ___ 2 ___ 3 ___ 4

3. Please rank your *top three* sources of campaign information, with #1 being your most useful.

   ___ Nightly network news (ABC, CBS, CNN, Fox, NBC, MSNBC, PBS etc.)

   ___ Weekday or evening talk shows (*Nightline, Larry King Live, Hannity & Colmes,* etc.)

   ___ Sunday talk shows / special news shows (*This Week, Face the Nation, Meet the Press,* etc.)

   ___ Local newspaper

   ___ National newspaper (*New York Times, Washington Post, USA Today, Wall Street Journal,* etc.)

   ___ Commercial news radio

   ___ National Public Radio

___ Internet

___ Debates

___ Direct mail from candidates, parties, organizations or interest groups

___ Other _____

4. What has been the frequency of your exposure to campaign coverage over the past six to eight months?

___ Regular (Daily/Weekly)

___ Three to four times per month

___ Once per month or less

___ Began following regularly within the past two months

___ Began following regularly within the past month

___ Have followed irregularly/sporadically prior to the debates

5. Age (Please check one)

___ Under 18   ___ 18–25   ___ 26–40   ___41–55   ___Over 55

6. Sex

___ Male ___ Female

7. Occupation _____

8. Ethnicity (Please check the most appropriate box)

___ White (non-Hispanic)   ___ International Student/Non U.S. Resident

___ Black or African American

___ Hispanic or Latino

___ American Indian or Alaskan Native

___ Asian

___ Hawaiian or other Pacific Islander

___ Multiracial

9. Political Party Affiliation (If unaffiliated, please indicate)

_____

10. State: _____

Stop here until after the debate.

PART II: POSTDEBATE

Complete this section after the debate.

11. Please evaluate the debate itself by responding to the statements below on the following scale.

1-Strongly disagree 2-Disagree 3-No opinion 4-Agree 5-Strongly agree

A. The debates taught me something new about one or more of the candidates.

___1   ___2   ___3   ___4   ___5

B. The debates taught me something new about one or more issues.

___1   ___2   ___3   ___4   ___5

C. The debates clarified my understanding of one or more candidate's position on an issue or issues.

___1   ___2   ___3   ___4   ___5

D. The debates reinforced my attitudes about one or more candidates.

___1   ___2   ___3   ___4   ___5

E. The debates caused me to evaluate one or more candidates differently than prior to the debate.

___1   ___2   ___3   ___4   ___5

F. The debates helped me to decide for whom to vote, or helped firm up my decision.

___1   ___2   ___3   ___4   ___5

G. The debates gave me ideas to discuss in the group.

___1   ___2   ___3   ___4   ___5

H. The debates made me more likely to vote.

___1   ___2   ___3   ___4   ___5

I.   The debates are a valuable voter education tool.

___1   ___2   ___3   ___4   ___5

J.   I will watch future debates.

___1   ___2   ___3   ___4   ___5

K. The debates increased my interest in following the remainder of the campaign more closely.

___1   ___2   ___3   ___4   ___5

Stop here until after the discussion.

PART III: POSTDISCUSSION

Complete this section after the group discussion

12. Please evaluate the postdebate discussion by responding to the statements below on the following scale:

1-Strongly disagree 2-Disagree 3-No opinion 4-Agree 5-Strongly agree

A. The discussion taught me something new about one or more of the candidates.

___1   ___2   ___3   ___4   ___5

B. The discussion taught me something new about one or more issues.

___1   ___2   ___3   ___4   ___5

C. The discussion clarified my understanding of one or more candidate's position on an issue or issues.

___1   ___2   ___3   ___4   ___5

D. The discussion reinforced my attitudes about one or more candidates.

___1   ___2   ___3   ___4   ___5

E. The discussion caused me to evaluate one or more candidates differently than prior to the debate.

___1   ___2   ___3   ___4   ___5

F. The discussion helped me to decide for whom to vote or helped firm up my decision.

___1   ___2   ___3   ___4   ___5

G. The discussion helped me understand why others view the candidates or issues differently than I do.

___1   ___2   ___3   ___4   ___5

H. The discussion made me more likely to vote.

___1   ___2   ___3   ___4   ___5

I. DebateWatch is a valuable voter education tool.

___1   ___2   ___3   ___4   ___5

J. I will participate in future DebateWatches.

___1   ___2   ___3   ___4   ___5

K. The discussion increased my interest in following the remainder of the campaign more closely.

___1   ___2   ___3   ___4   ___5

L. The information discussed in the debates differed from that presented by news media.

___1   ___2   ___3   ___4   ___5

Thank you for completing this questionnaire. Please return your questionnaire to the group facilitator.

DEBATEWATCH 2004: INTERNATIONAL PARTICIPANT QUESTIONNAIRE

PART I: PREDEBATE WATCH

Please complete this section before the debate begins.

1. Which debate are you watching and discussing?

____1st Pres   ____2nd Pres   ____3rd Pres   ____Vice-Pres

2. Nationality: _____

3. Age (check one):

____under 18   ____18–25   ____26–40   ____41–55   ____over 55

____Male   ____Female

4. Length of Stay in the U.S.: ____years ____months

5. Rank your *top three sources* of the U.S presidential campaign information.

___Your home country's media (broadcasting, radio, newspaper, Internet, etc)

___Weekly or evening talk shows (*Nightline, Larry King Live, Rush Limbaugh,* etc)

___Sunday talk shows/special news show (e.g., *This Week, Face the Nation, Meet the Press, Washington Week in Review, Crossfire, Equal Time,* etc.).

___Local newspaper

___National newspaper such as *New York Times, Christian Science Monitor, Washington Post*

___Commercial Radio News

___National Public Radio

___Internet as a U.S. media

___Presidential debates

___other_____

6. What has been the frequency of your exposure to campaign coverage over the past six to eight months?

___ Regular (Daily/Weekly)

___ Three to four times per month

___ Once per month or less

___ Began following regularly within the past two months

___ Began following regularly within the past month

___ Have followed irregularly/sporadically prior to the debates

7. Before watching the debate, do you have a candidate preference?

_____Yes   _____No

8. Have you watched the U.S presidential debate before?

_____Yes   _____No

9. Please respond to the following statements by checking on a 5 point scale:

1-strongly disagree 2-disagree 3-no opinion 4-agree 5-strongly agree

I am interested in U.S. politics.

___1   ___2   ___3   ___4   ___5

In general, I know each candidate's position on major issues.

___1   ___2   ___3   ___4   ___5

In general, I understand well the U.S. political processes.

___1   ___2   ___3   ___4   ___5

The result of the 2004 U.S presidential election will strongly impact my country.

___1   ___2   ___3   ___4   ___5

Stop here until after the debate.

PART II: POSTDEBATE

Complete this section *after* the debate.

10-A. If before the debate you indicated *YES* to having a candidate preference, after watching the debate do you:

___still lean toward your predebate preference

___have no candidate preference

___lean toward another candidate

10-B. If before the debate you indicated *NO* to having a candidate preference, after watching the debate do you:

___still have no candidate preference

___now lean toward a candidate

11.   Please evaluate the debate itself by responding to the statements below on the following scale:

1-strongly disagree 2-disagree 3-no opinion 4-agree 5-strongly agree

A. The debates taught me something new about one or more candidates.

___1   ___2   ___3   ___4   ___5

B. The debates taught me something new about one or more issues.

___1   ___2   ___3   ___4   ___5

C. The debates enhanced my understanding of U.S. politics.

___1   ___2   ___3   ___4   ___5

D. The debates changed positively my image of U.S. politics or politicians.

___1   ___2   ___3   ___4   ___5

E. The debate adopted a proper format for candidates to discuss main issues.

___1   ___2   ___3   ___4   ___5

F. The debates reinforced my attitudes about one or more candidates.

___1   ___2   ___3   ___4   ___5

G. The debates caused me to evaluate one or more candidates differently than prior to the debate.

___1   ___2   ___3   ___4   ___5

H. The debates are a valuable voter education tool.

___1   ___2   ___3   ___4   ___5

I. I will watch future debates.

___1   ___2   ___3   ___4   ___5

J. The debates increased my interest in following the remainder of the campaign more closely.

___1   ___2   ___3   ___4   ___5

K. The U.S. presidential debate style can be applied to my country.

___1   ___2   ___3   ___4   ___5

Stop here until after the discussion.

PART III: POSTDISCUSSION

Complete this section *after* the group discussion.

12. After participating in the group discussion, has your position on the candidates changed from what was indicated as your position after the debate?

___Yes   ___No

If Yes, have you:

___gone from no preference to a candidate

___gone from a candidate to no preference

___changed form one candidate to another

13. Pleased evaluate the postdebate discussion by responding to the statements below on the following scale:

1-strongly disagree 2-disagree 3-no opinion 4-agree 5-strongly agree

A. The discussion taught me something new about one or more candidates.

___1   ___2   ___3   ___4   ___5

B. The discussion taught me something new about one or more issues.

___1   ___2   ___3   ___4   ___5

C. The discussion enhanced my understanding of U.S. politics.

___1   ___2   ___3   ___4   ___5

D. The discussion changed positively my image of U.S. politics or politicians.

___1   ___2   ___3   ___4   ___5

E. The discussion reinforced my attitudes about one or more candidates.

___1   ___2   ___3   ___4   ___5

F. The discussion caused me to evaluate one or more candidates differently than prior to the debate.

___1   ___2   ___3   ___4   ___5

G. The discussion is a valuable voter education tool.

___1   ___2   ___3   ___4   ___5

H. I will attend another Debate Watch discussion group if I have an opportunity.

___1   ___2   ___3   ___4   ___5

I. The discussion increased my interest in following the remainder of the campaign more closely.

___1   ___2   ___3   ___4   ___5

J. The information discussed after the debates differed from that presented by the news media.

___1   ___2   ___3   ___4   ___5

Thank you for completing this questionnaire. Please return your questionnaire to the group facilitator.

DEBATEWATCH 2004: POSTDEBATE VOTER'S CHOICE QUESTIONNAIRE

1. Age (Please check one)
    ___ Under 18   ___ 18–25   ___ 26–40   ___ 41–55   ___ Over 55

2. Sex
    ___ Male ___ Female

3. Political Party Affiliation (If unaffiliated, please indicate)

    _____

4. State: _____

5. *Prior* to watching the debate, did you have a candidate preference?
    ___ Yes   ___ No

6A. If you indicated *YES* to having a candidate preference, *after watching the debate,* are you
    ___ still leaning toward your predebate preference
    ___ now undecided
    ___ now leaning toward a different candidate

OR

6B. If you indicated *NO* to having a candidate preference, *after watching the debate,* are you
    ___ still undecided
    ___ now leaning toward a candidate

7. *After participating in the group discussion,* did your position on the candidates change from what was indicated as your position immediately after the debate?
    ___ Yes ___ No

8.   If yes, have you

    ___ gone from undecided to a candidate

    ___ gone from a candidate to undecided

    ___ changed from one candidate to another

Notes

CHAPTER ONE

1. Marilyn Jackson-Beeck and Robert G. Meadow, "The Triple Agenda of Presidential Debates," *Public Opinion Quarterly* 5 (1979): 173–80.

2. David J. Lanoue and Peter R. Schrott, *The Joint Press Conference: The History, Impact, and Prospects of American Presidential Debates* (Westport, CT: Greenwood Press, 1991), 152.

3. William L. Benoit and Glenn J. Hansen, "Presidential Debate Questions and the Public Agenda," *Communication Quarterly* 49 (2001): 135.

4. E. J. Dionne, *Why Americans Hate Politics* (New York: Simon & Schuster, 1991).

5. Robert D. Putnam, "Bowling Alone: America's Declining Social Capital," *Journal of Democracy* 6, no. 1 (1995): 65–78 and Robert D. Putnam, *Bowling Alone: The Collapse and Revival of American Community* (New York: Simon & Schuster, 2000).

6. Stephanie Greco Larson, "Public Opinion in Television Election News: Beyond Polls," *Political Communication* 16 (1999): 133.

7. David Zarefsky, "The Postmodern Public: Revitalizing Commitment to the Public Forum," *Vital Speeches of the Day* 60 (1993): 309.

8. For a complete discussion of the ideal public sphere and its development, see Jürgen Habermas, *The Structured Transformation of the Public Sphere* (Cambridge, MA: MIT Press, 1989).

9. See Diana B. Carlin and Mitchell S. McKinney, *The 1992 Presidential Debates in Focus* (Westport, CT: Praeger Publishers, 1994).

10. Richard R. Lau and David P. Redlawsk, *How Voters Decide: Information Processing during Election Campaigns* (New York: Cambridge University Press, 2006), 3.

11. Carlin and McKinney, 212–13.

12. James W. Carey, "Abolishing the Old Spirit World," *Critical Studies in Mass Communication* 12 (1995): 89.

13. Curtis Gans, "1994 Congressional Elections: An Analysis," http://www.fairvote.org/reports/1995/chp3/gans.html.

14. Gallup, "Honesty Ratings of Pharmacists, State Officeholders Reach New Highs," http://www.gallup.com/poll/14290/Honesty-Ratings-Pharmacists-State-Officeholders-Reach-New-Highs.aspx.

15. Thomas E. Patterson, *Out of Order* (New York: Alfred A. Knopf, 1993), 135.

16. See Marion R. Just et al., *Crosstalk: Citizens, Candidates, and the Media in a Presidential Campaign* (Chicago: University of Chicago Press, 1996) and James S. Fishkin, *Voice of the People: Public Opinion and Democracy* (New Haven, CT: Yale University Press, 1995). Just et al. examined candidate, media and citizen talk in the 1992 election to determine how each group reacts to and anticipates the others' messages. Fishkin experimented with several groups to determine if discussion would impact views on issues. As a result of his research, he created a public sphere through The National Issues Convention in 1996 in which 459 citizens converged on Austin, Texas, for a televised discussion of three key issues: the economy, the state of the American family, and the United States in a post–Cold War world. Using a deliberative polling technique, Fishkin gauged opinions prior to and after participants listened to and interacted with experts and one another.

CHAPTER TWO

1. See Kate Kenski and Natalie Jomini Stroud, "Who Watches Debates? A Comparative Analysis of Presidential Debate Viewing in 2000 and 2004," *American Behavioral Scientist* 49 (2005): 213–28. Their analysis of viewers and nonviewers indicates that those who view the debates "were more likely to express interest in politics, to discuss politics with friends and family, and to consume news at high levels compared to people who did not watch debates" (p. 225).

2. For a discussion of debates as focal points in campaigns, see Diana B. Carlin, "Presidential Debates as Focal Points for Campaign Arguments," *Political Communication* 9 (1992): 251–65 and John M. Murphy, "Presidential Debates and Campaign Rhetoric: Text within Context," *Southern Communication Journal* 57 (1992): 219–28.

3. Thomas M. Holbrook, "Presidential Campaigns and the Knowledge Gap," *Political Communication* 19 (2002): 449.

4. Richard R. Lau and David P. Redlawsk, *How Voters Decide: Information Processing during Election Campaigns* (New York: Cambridge University Press, 2006), 182.

5. Diana B. Carlin and Mitchell S. McKinney, *The 1992 Presidential Debates in Focus* (Westport, CT: Praeger Publishers, 1994), 30.

6. See Diana B. Carlin, "A Rationale for a Focus Group Study," in *The 1992 Presidential Debates in Focus,* ed. Diana B. Carlin and Mitchell S. McKinney (Westport, CT: Praeger Publishing, 1994), 3–19; Mitchell S. McKinney and Diana B. Carlin, "Political Campaign Debates," in *Handbook of Political Communication Research,* ed. Lynda Lee Kaid (Mahwah, NJ: Lawrence Erlbaum Associates, Publishers, 2004), 203–34; The Racine Group, "White Paper on Televised Political Campaign Debates," *Argumentation and Advocacy* 38 (Spring 2002): 199–218; and Peter L. Francia, "Debate Literature: Previous Findings," in *The Debate Book,* ed. Ronald A. Faucheux (Washington, DC: Campaigns & Elections Publishing Company, 2003), 179–97.

7. Lynda L. Kaid, Mitchell S. McKinney, and John C. Tedesco, *Civic Dialogue in the 1996 Presidential Campaign: Candidate, Media, and Public Voices* (Cresskill, NJ: Hampton Press, 2000), 135.

8. Diana Owen, *Media Messages in American Presidential Elections* (New York: Greenwood, 1991).

9. Racine Group, 211, 212.

10. Media Tenor, "Monitoring the Presidential Debates: How the Debates Affected the Candidate's Image on TV News," October 13, 2004, np.

11. Ibid., 212.

12. Hillary Clinton, "The Democratic Debate in Cleveland," *The New York Times,* February 26, 2008, http://www.nytimes.com/2008/02/26/us/politics/26text-debate.html? pagewanted=5&r=1.

13. Dave Itzkoff, "Laughs Have Impact on Campaign Trail," *The Kansas City Star,* March 8, 2008, E3.

14. Nielsen ratings for all presidential debates since 1960 can be found at http://www. debates.org.

15. Don Aucoin, "Low Ratings Mark Slim Convention Coverage," *The Boston Globe,* August 5, 2000, F1.

16. Journalism.org, "The State of the News Media," http://www.stateofthenewsmedia. com/2005/chartland.asp?id=471&ct=col&dir=&sort=&col1_box=1&col2_box=1.

17. Saeed Ahmed, "Obama the Choice of Democrats in Indonesia," *CNN.com,* February 5, 2008, http://www.cnn.com/2008/POLITICS/02/5/indonesia.usvote (accessed February 24, 2008).

18. U.S. Department of Defense Federal Voting Assistance Program, "Voting Information News," Vol. 14, 10, October 2004, http://www.fvap.gov/pubs/vin/html04vins/oct-04vin.html (accessed September 30, 2006).

19. *USA Today,* "Best Voter Information on TV," July 30, 1997, A1.

20. Times Mirror Center for the People and the Press, "The People, the Press and Politics: Campaign '92," November 15, 1992, News Release.

21. Ronald A. Faucheux, "Nationwide Poll: What Voters Think about Candidate Debates," in Faucheux, *The Debate Book,* 81.

22. Ibid., 83.

23. The Pew Center for the People and the Press, "When Presidential Debates Matter," September 24, 2004, http://people-press.org/commentary/display.php3?AnalysisID=98.

24. McKinney and Carlin, 210.

25. For a discussion of research and findings from 2004 that confirm the reinforcement effect, see Jeffrey W. Jarmen, "Political Affiliation and Presidential Debates: A Real-Time Analysis of the Effect of the Arguments Used in the Presidential Debates," *American Behavioral Scientist* 49 (2005): 229–42.

26. Ibid., 210–11.

27. Robert Friedenberg, "The 2004 Presidential Debates," in *The 2004 Presidential Campaign: A Communication Perspective*, ed. Robert E. Denton Jr. (Lanham, MD: Rowman & Littlefield Publishers, 2005), 127.

28. James B. Lemert et al., *News Verdicts, the Debates, and Presidential Campaigns* (New York: Praeger, 1991), 216.

29. J. Jeffrey Auer, "The Counterfeit Debates," in *The Great Debates: Background, Perspective, and Effects*, ed. Sidney Kraus (Bloomington: Indiana University Press, 1962), 142–50.

30. Lloyd F. Bitzer and Theodore Reuter, *Carter vs. Ford: The Counterfeit Debates of 1976* (Madison: University of Wisconsin Press, 1980).

31. Diana P. Carlin, "A Defense of the 'Debate' in Presidential Debates," *Argumentation and Advocacy* 25 (1989): 208–13.

32. *CNN.com,* "Transcript of GOP Debate at Reagan Library," January 30, 2008, http://www.cnn.com/2008/POLITICS/01/30/GOPdebate.transcript/.

33. William L. Benoit's functional theory of presidential debates is explained and tested in numerous publications: William L. Benoit and William T. Wells, *Candidates in Conflict: Persuasive Attack and Defense in the 1992 Presidential Debates* (Tuscaloosa: University of Alabama Press), 1996; William L. Benoit et al., *Campaign 2000:*

A Functional Analysis of Presidential Campaign Discourse (Lanham, MD: Rowman & Littlefield, 2004); William L. Benoit, "Retrospective Versus Prospective Statements and Outcome of Presidential Elections," *Journal of Communication* 56 (2006): 331–45; William L. Benoit, Kevin A. Stein, and Glenn J. Hansen, "*New York Times* Coverage of Presidential Campaigns, 1952–2000," *Journalism & Mass Communication Quarterly* 82 (2005): 356–76; William L. Benoit and Glenn J. Hansen, "Presidential Debate Watching, Issue Knowledge, Character Evaluation, and Vote Choice," *Human Communication Research* 30 (2004): 121–40.

34. David O. Sears and Steven H. Chaffee, "Uses and Effects of the 1976 Debates: An Overview of Empirical Studies," in *The Great Debates: Carter vs. Ford, 1976*, ed. Sidney Kraus (Bloomington: Indiana University Press, 1978), 223–61.

35. Senja Post, "Monitoring the Presidential Debates: Post-debate Panels Did Not Focus on Hard Issues," October 14, 2004, 5, http://www.mediatenor.com/newsletters.php?id_news=153.

36. Commission on Presidential Debates, *Proceedings of "Debate '88": A Symposium*, (Washington, DC: Commission on Presidential Debates, 1990).

37. Racine Group, 204.

38. Diana B. Prentice, Janet K. Larsen, and Matthew J. Sobnosky, "A Comparison of Clash in the Dual Format," paper presented at the Speech Communication Association Convention, Anaheim, CA, November 1981; Diana B. Carlin, Eric Morris, and Shawna Smith, "The Influence of Format and Questions on Candidates' Strategic Argument Choices in the 2000 Presidential Debates," *American Behavioral Scientist* 44 (2001): 2196–2218; Diana B. Carlin et al., "The Effects of Debate Formats on Clash: A Comparative Analysis," *Argumentation and Advocacy* 27 (1989): 126–36. Michael Pfau, "A Comparative Assessment of Intra-Party Political Debate Formats," *Political Communication Review* 9 (1984): 1–23.

39. Carlin and McKinney, 73.

40. Racine Group, 205.

41. Edward Hinck, *Enacting the Presidency: Political Argument, Presidential Debates and Presidential Character* (Westport, CT: Greenwood Publishing, 1993).

42. Racine Group, 204–5. See also William Eveland Jr., Douglas McCleod, and Amy Nathanson, "Reporters v. Undecided Voters: An Analysis of the Questions Asked during the 1992 Presidential Debates," *Communication Quarterly* 42 (1994): 390–406, and Rodrick Hart and Sharon Jarvis, "Political Debates: Forms, Styles & Media," *American Behavioral Scientist* 40 (1997): 1095–1122.

43. All quotations from the 1996, 2000, and 2004 debates are taken from the transcripts provided by the Commission on Presidential Debates at their Web site http://www.debates.org.

44. Eveland, McCleod, and Nathanson, 390–406.

45. John Meyer and Diana B. Carlin, "The Impact of Formats on Voter Reaction," in Carlin and McKinney, 82.

46. Benjamin R. Barber, *Strong Democracy: Participatory Politics for a New Age* (Berkeley: University of California Press, 1984), 173.

47. James Benjamin, "The Greek Concept of Dialectic," *The Southern Speech Communication Journal* 48 (1983): 364.

48. Fay Lomax Cook, Michael X. Delli Carpini, and Lawrence R. Jacobs, "Who Deliberates? Discursive Participation in America," *Working Paper Series* (Evanston, IL: Institute for Policy Research Northwestern University, 2005). Used with permission from the first author.

49. Ibid., 4.

50. Ibid., 12.

51. Ibid., 11–12.

52. Vault.com, "Politics in the Workplace Survey 2007," 2008. http://www.vault.com/surveys/politics/politicsindex.jsp.

53. Diana B. Carlin et al., "The Post-9/11 Public Sphere: Citizen Talk about the 2004 Presidential Debates," *Rhetoric & Public Affairs* 8 (2005): 619.

54. David G. Levasseur and Diana B. Carlin, "Egocentric Argument and the Public Sphere: Citizen Deliberations on Public Policy and Policymakers," *Rhetoric & Public Affairs* 4 (2001): 407–31.

55. Drew Westen, *The Political Brain: The Role of Emotion in Deciding the Fate of the Nation* (New York: Public Affairs, 2007), 14.

56. William P. Eveland Jr., "The Effect of Political Discussion in Producing Informed Citizens: The Roles of Information, Motivation, and Elaboration," *Political Communication* 21 (2004): 177.

57. Ibid., 180.

58. David Zarefsky, "The Postmodern Public: Revitalizing Commitment to the Public Forum," *Vital Speeches of the Day* 60 (1993): 309.

59. Gerald A. Hauser, *Vernacular Voices: The Rhetoric of Publics and Public Spheres* (Columbia: University of South Carolina Press, 1999), 280.

CHAPTER THREE

1. Kids Voting, a national voter education project for children and young adults was a DebateWatch partner or ganization. Many of those under 18 were involved though Kids Voting recruitment or through local schools or other civic organizations. Parents typically participated with those under 18.

2. The percentage of Libertarian versus Reform party participation for the three debates was as follows: Hartford, 0.6% versus 0.1%; San Diego, 0.4% versus 0.3%; and St. Petersburg, 0.4% versus 0.4%.

3. The six states not represented in this portion of the study were Alaska, Delaware, Hawaii, Maine, West Virginia, and Wyoming. With the sole exception of West Virginia, requests for packets were filled from every state.

4. Participants were asked only whether or not they had a preference. They were never asked to identify which candidate they supported, though most did indicate which candidate they specifically supported through the discussions.

5. CPD data was posted at http://www.debates.org.

6. The CPD's final DebateWatch results for 2004 are available at http://www.debates.org/pages/news.

CHAPTER FOUR

1. David J. Lanoue and Peter R. Schrott, *The Joint Press Conference: The History, Impact, and Prospects of American Presidential Debates* (New York: Greenwood Press, 1991), 150, 152.

2. "Kennedy-Nixon Debate Organizers Take a Critical View," *Broadcasting*, October 15, 1984, 36.

3. David Zarefsky, "The Lincoln-Douglas Debates Revisited: The Evolution of Public Argument," *Quarterly Journal of Speech* 72 (1986): 162.

4. John Splaine, *A Companion to the Lincoln-Douglas Debates* (Washington, DC: C-SPAN, 1994), 9.

5. Zarefsky, 181.

6. All transcripts are taken from the Commission on Presidential Debates Web site at http://www.debates.org.

7. Diana B. Prentice, Janet K. Larsen, and Matthew J. Sobnosky, "A Comparison of Clash in the Dual Format," paper presented at the Speech Communication Association Convention, Anaheim, CA, November 1981; Diana B. Carlin, Eric Morris, and Shawna Smith, "The Influence of Format and Questions on Candidates' Strategic Argument Choices in the 2000 Presidential Debates," *American Behavioral Scientist* 44 (2001): 2196–2218; Eric Morris, *A Clash Strategy Analysis of Contemporary General Election Presidential Debates* (PhD diss., University of Kansas, 2004); and Patty Riley and Thomas Hollihan, "The 1980 Presidential Debate: A Content Analysis of the Issues and Arguments," *Speaker and Gavel* 18 (1981): 47–59.

8. Jack Kay and Timothy A. Borchers, "Children in a Sandbox: Reaction to the Vice Presidential Debate," in *The 1992 Presidential Debates in Focus*, ed. Diana B. Carlin and Mitchell S. McKinney (Westport, CT: Praeger Publishers, 1994), 99.

9. For a report on this debate, which occurred prior to the 1948 Oregon Republican primary and was based on the topic, "Shall the Communist Party in the United States be Outlawed?," see Tom Swafford, "The Last Real Presidential Debate," *American Heritage* 37, no. 2 (1986): 66–71.

10. Robert V. Friedenberg, "The 2004 Presidential Debates," in *The 2004 Presidential Campaign: A Communication Perspective*, ed. Robert E. Denton Jr. (Lanham, MD: Rowman & Littlefield Publishers, 2005), 113.

11. Diana B. Carlin, "DebateWatch: Creating a Public Sphere for the Unheard Voices," in *Communicating Politics: Engaging the Public in Democratic Life*, ed. Mitchell S. McKinney et al. (New York: Peter Lang, 2005), 227–28.

12. Michael D. Schaffer, "ABC Gets an Earful after the Debate," *The Philadelphia Inquirer*, April 18, 2008, http://www.philly.com/inquirer/front_page/20080418_ABC_gets_an_earful_after_debate.html.

13. Jim Lehrer, interview with Diana Carlin and Kelly McDonald, June 18, 1997.

14. John T. Morello, "Questioning the Questions: An Examination of the 'Unpredictable' 2004 Bush-Kerry Town Hall Debate," *Argumentation & Advocacy* 41 (Spring 2005): 214.

15. Carlin, Morris, and Smith, 2211.

16. Mitchell S. McKinney, "Let the People Speak: The Public's Agenda and Presidential Town Hall Debates," *American Behavioral Scientist* 49, no. 2 (2005): 199.

17. Commission on Presidential Debates, http://www.debates.org/pages/news_041025.html.

18. Morello, 214.

19. Ibid., 222.

20. Ronald A. Faucheux, "Nationwide Poll: What Voters Think about Candidate Debates," *Campaigns & Elections* 23 (2002): 99.

21. Ibid.

22. See John Meyer and Diana B. Carlin, "The Impact of Formats on Voter Reaction," in Carlin and McKinney, 70–83.

CHAPTER FIVE

1. Francis X. Clines, "Character Issue Is Dead as an Issue, Voters Say," *New York Times*, October 28, 1996, http://query.nytimes.com/gst/fullpage.html?res=9F01E3DF1439F93BA15753C1A5753CIA960958260&sec=&spon=&pagewanted=2.

2. Ibid.

3. Judith S. Trent and Robert V. Friedenberg, *Political Campaign Communication: Principles & Practices*, 5th ed. (Lanham, MD: Rowman & Littlefield Publishers, 2004), 131–32.

4. Bernard C. Cohen, *The Press and Foreign Policy* (Princeton, NJ: Princeton University Press, 1963), 13.

5. Trent and Friedenberg, 134.

6. Susan A. Hellweg, "Introduction," *Argumentation and Advocacy* 30 (1992), 59–61, in Mitchell S. McKinney and Diana B. Carlin, "Political Campaign Debates," in *Handbook of Political Communication Research*, ed. Lynda Lee Kaid, 203–34 (Mahwah, NJ: Lawrence Erlbaum Associates, Publishers, 2004), 212.

7. See McKinney and Carlin, 212–13.

8. McKinney and Carlin, 212.

9. Diana B. Carlin, "Watching the Debates: A Guide for Viewers," in *Televised Election Debates: An International Perspective*, ed. Stephen Coleman (New York: St. Martin's Press, 2000), 170.

10. The most commonly cited work on the impact of nonverbal communication is Albert Mehrabian. The percentages cited are found in his writings, including Albert Mehrabian and Susan R. Ferris, "Inference of Attitudes from Two Channels," *Journal of Consulting Psychology* 31 (1967): 248–52.

11. Alan Schroeder, *Presidential Debates: Forty Years of High Risk TV* (New York: Columbia University Press, 2000).

12. Evan Cornog, "High Noon in Prime Time," *Columbia Journalism Review* 39, no. 4 (2000): 80–81.

13. Chris Wallace, *Character: Profiles in Presidential Courage* (New York: Rugged-Land, 2004), viii.

14. The Racine Group, "White Paper on Televised Political Campaign Debates," *Argumentation and Advocacy* 38 (Spring 2002): 210.

15. Adam Nagourney, "The Strategy: Dole Tries to Make an Issue of Clinton's Trustworthiness," *New York Times*, June 2, 1996, http://query.nytimes.com/gst/fullpage.html?res=9F04E3DE1F39F931A35755C0A960958260.

16. Kathleen Hayden, "Second Debate. Last Chance?," CNN AllPolitics, October 16, 1996, http://www-cgi.cnn.com/ALLPOLITICS/1996/news/9610/16/debate.prenews/.

17. The Racine Group, 210.

18. Online NewsHour, "Presidential Debate Preview," September 30, 2004, http://www.pbs.org/newshour/bb/political_wrap/july-dec04/debatepreview_9–30.html.

19. Swift Vets and POWS for Truth, http//:www.swiftvets.com/index.php.

CHAPTER SIX

1. See Elihu Katz and Jacob Feldman, "The Debates in the Light of Research: A Survey of the Surveys," in *The Great Debates: Kennedy vs. Nixon, 1960*, ed. Sidney Kraus (Bloomington: Indiana University Press, 1962), 173–223.

2. David L. Vancil and Sue D. Pendell, "The Myth of the Viewer-Listener Disagreement in the first Kennedy-Nixon Debate," *Central States Speech Journal* 38 (1987): 16–27.

3. Sidney Kraus, "Winners of the First 1960 Televised Debate between Kennedy and Nixon," *Journal of Communication* 46 (1996): 78–96.

4. Susan A. Hellweg, Michael Pfau, and Steven R. Brydon, *Televised Presidential Debates: Advocacy in Contemporary America* (Westport, CT: Greenwood, 1992), 73.

5. Robert K. Tiemens, "Television's Portrayal of the 1976 Presidential Debates: An Analysis of Visual Content," *Communication Monographs* 45 (1978): 362–70.

6. See John T. Morello, "Visual Structuring of the 1976 and 1984 Nationally Televised Presidential Debates: Implications," *Central States Speech Journal* 39 (1988): 233–43; John T. Morello, "Argument and Visual Structuring in the 1984 Mondale-Reagan Debates: The Medium's Influence on the Perception of Clash," *Western Journal of Speech Communication* 52 (1988): 277–90; and John T. Morello, "The 'Look' and Language of Clash: Visual Structuring of Argument in the 1988 Bush-Dukakis Debates," *Southern Communication Journal* 57 (1992): 205–18.

7. For example, Tiemens, et al. concluded the opposite of Morello regarding the 1980 Carter-Reagan debate. See Robert K. Tiemens, Susan A. Hellweg, Philip Kipper, and Steven. L. Phillips, "An Integrative Verbal and Visual Analysis of the Carter-Ford Debate," *Communication Quarterly* 33 (1985): 34–42. Davis did not detect any differences between Carter and Ford in terms of eye contact in 1976. See Leslie K. Davis, "Camera-Eye Contact by the Candidates in the Presidential Debates of 1976," *Journalism Quarterly* 55 (1978): 431–37, 455.

8. Memorandum of Understanding, September 27, 2004, 16–17, http://www.gwu.edu/~action/2004/deb04main/debateagreement.pdf.

9. "Networks Balk at Bush-Kerry Debate Agreement," http://www.cnn.com/2004/ALLPOLITICS/09/28/debates.television/index.html.

10. Yariv Tsfati, "Debating the Debate: The Impact of Exposure to Debate News Coverage and Its Interaction with Exposure to the Actual Debate," *The International Journal of Press/Politics* 8 (2003): 70.

11. Frederick T. Steeper, "Public Response to Gerald Ford's Statements on Eastern Europe in the Second Debate," in *The Presidential Debates: Media, Electoral, and Policy Perspectives,* ed. George F. Bishop, Robert G. Meadow, and Marilyn Jackson-Beeck (New York: Praeger, 1978), 84.

12. William P. Eveland, "The Effect of Political Discussion in Producing Informed Citizens: The Roles of Information, Motivation, and Elaboration," *Political Communication* 21 (2004): 179.

CHAPTER SEVEN

1. Robert V. Friedenberg, "Patterns and Trends in National Political Debates: 1960–1996," in *Rhetorical Studies of National Political Debates—1996,* ed. Robert V. Friedenberg (Westport, CT: Praeger, 1997), 61–90.

2. David W. Romero, "Requiem for the Lightweight: Vice Presidential Candidate Evaluations and the Presidential Vote," *Presidential Studies Quarterly* 31, no. 3 (2001): 454–64.

3. Thomas M. Holbrook, "The Behavioral Consequences of Vice-Presidential Debates: Does the Undercard Have Any Punch?" *American Politics Quarterly* 22, no. 4 (1994): 481.

4. Mari Boor Tonn, "Flirting with Perot: Voter Ambivalence about the Third Candidate," in *The 1992 Presidential Debates in Focus*, ed. Carlin and McKinney (Westport, CT: Praeger Publishers, 1994), 122–23.

5. Katharine Q. Seelye, "Searing Images from Debates Past Are Continuing to Haunt Dole," *New York Times*, October 17, 1996, http://query.nytimes.com/gst/fullpage.html?res=9A02E5DB1231F934A25753C1A960958260&sec=&spon=&pagewanted=all.

6. For a discussion of strategy, see Diana B. Carlin, "Presidential Debates as Focal Points for Campaign Arguments," *Political Communication* 9 (1992): 251–65 and

"Debating our Destiny," a PBS special on presidential debate history, http://www.pbs.org/newshour/debatingourdestiny/interviews/quayle.html#1988.

7. Bernard Shaw asked Governor Dukakis the following question at the second presidential debate on October 13, 1988: "Governor, if Kitty Dukakis were raped and murdered, would you favor an irrevocable death penalty for the killer?" Dukakis began his response as follows and throughout the entire answer did not address the personal and visceral nature of Shaw's question: "No, I don't, Bernard. And I think you know that I've opposed the death penalty during all of my life. I don't see any evidence that it's a deterrent, and I think there are better and more effective ways to deal with violent crime. We've done so in my own state. And it's one of the reasons why we have had the biggest drop in crime of any industrial state in America; why we have the lowest murder rate of any industrial state in America. But we have work to do in this nation. We have work to do to fight a real war, not a phony war, against drugs."

8. William L. Benoit and David Airne, "A Functional Analysis of American Vice Presidential Debates," *Argumentation and Advocacy* 41 (2005): 225–36.

9. Diana B. Carlin and Peter J. Bicak, "Toward a Theory of Vice Presidential Debate Purposes: An Analysis of the 1992 Vice Presidential Debate," *Argumentation and Advocacy* 27 (1993): 122.

10. Ibid., 122–23.

11. Mark Sherman and Ken Herman, "Debate a Gentlemen's Disagreement: Cheney, Lieberman Spar Gently, Keep Vow to Stay Positive While Differing on Policy," *The Atlanta Journal and Constitution*, October 6, 2000, 1A.

12. Helen Kennedy and Thomas M. DeFrank, "Veep Hopefuls' Fight Is Polite: Cheney, Lieberman Keep Debate Civil," *New York Daily News*, October 6, 2000, 5.

13. James O'Toole, "High Stakes Debate: Cheney-Edwards Clash Could Well Affect Newly Closer Race," *Pittsburgh Post-Gazette*, October 5, 2004, A1.

14. Walter Shapiro, "The Ruckus at the Roundtable: There Was No Mincing Words Here," *USA Today*, October 6, 2004. Retrieved from Lexis Nexis.

15. See Online NewsHour, "The Cheney Factor," March 12, 2001, http://www.pbs.org/newshour/bb/white_house/jan-june01/cheney_3–12.html and John Bolton, "Book World" (online chat), *The Washington Post,* January 30, 2008, http://www.washingtonpost.com/wp-dyn/content/discussion/2008/01/27/DI2008012700816.html.

16. Romero, 454–64.

CHAPTER EIGHT

1. Citizens aged 21 to 24 were previously allowed to vote. Since 1972, the U.S. Census Bureau has classified the youngest voting block as "18–24 year olds." All voting data was retrieved from U.S. Census Bureau reports unless otherwise noted. Kelly Holder, *Voting and Registration in the Election of 2004*, U.S. Census Bureau, Population Division, Education & Social Stratification Branch (Washington, DC: GPO, 2006), http://www.census.gov/population/www/socdemo/voting.html.

2. In 1980, 39.9 percent of eligible 18- to 24-year-olds voted. In 1984, the number rose to 40.8 percent. See Holder.

3. Of 18- to 20-year-olds, only 33.2 percent voted in 1988. See Holder.

4. Julie Apker and Cary Voss, "The Student Voter," in *The 1992 Presidential Debates in Focus*, ed. Diana Carlin and Mitchell McKinney (Westport, CT: Praeger Publishers, 1994), 187–204.

5. The "card playing" metaphor changed in the 2008 campaign when the "cards" were associated with characteristics of the candidates rather than the issues being discussed.

6. Jim Hoagland, "The Youth Card," *Washington Post*, September 1, 1996, C7.

7. Frank Sesno, "Young Democrats Size Political Opportunity," *Inside Politics, CNN*, (Transcript #309–4, Lexis/Nexis), April 12, 1993.

8. The 1988 elections in Great Britain saw an increase in participation among 16- to 25-year-olds when a Green Party candidate gained high popularity.

9. Primary turnout increased from 9 percent in 2004 to 17 percent. Counting the 2006 midterm, turnouts for those 18–30 increased three election cycles in a row—2004, 2006, and 2008. For a full discussion of the trends, see Jose Antonio Vargas, "Millennials at the Polls," *The Washington Post*, June 17, 2008, A7.

10. David Von Drehle, "It's Their Turn Now," *Time*, February 11, 2008, 37.

11. League of Women Voters, *Get Out and Vote: Encouraging Participation in Your Community* (Washington, DC: League of Women Voters, 1996), 70.

12. Apker and Voss, 187–204.

13. Federal Election Commission, *1996 Electoral Vote and Popular Vote Summary* (Washington, DC: FEC, 1997), http://www.fec.gov/pubrec/fe1996/summ.htm.

14. George Will, "Who Votes? Who Cares?," *Washington Post*, October 31, 1996, A21.

15. Will Durst, "Happy National Apathy Day," *New York Times*, November 2, 1998, A27; Eric Alterman, "Clinton Rocked the Vote, Now It's Rocking Him," *Rolling Stone*, February 23, 1995, 41–42; Owen Ullman, "Why Voter Apathy Will Make a Strong Showing," *Business Week*, November 4, 1996, 57.

16. Michael DeCourcy Hinds, "Youth Vote 2000: They'd Rather Volunteer," *Carnegie Reporter*, 2001, http://www.carnegie.org/reporter/02/vote2000/index.html.

17. Sydney Hyman, *Youth in Politics: Expectation and Realities* (New York: Basic Books, 1972), 369–70.

18. See Hinds.

19. For a complete presentation of the results of the intergenerational comparative study, see Diana B. Carlin and Karen Anderson, "Across the Ages: Views of the 2000 Debates from College Freshmen to Senior Citizens," in *The Millennium Election: Communication in the 2000 Campaign*, ed. Lynda Lee Kaid et al. (Lanham, MD: Rowman & Littlefield Publishers, 2003), 229–41.

20. Julia Spiker, Yang Lin, and Scott D. Wells, "The Voice of Young Citizens: A Study of Political Malaise in Campaign 2000," in Kaid et al., 243–56.

21. Ibid., 249.

22. In 1972, Richard M. Nixon, the former reserve officer and incumbent president, faced George McGovern, the World War II veteran and Vietnam opponent. In 2004, George W. Bush, the former national guardsman, opposed John Kerry, the Vietnam veteran who proposed diplomatic interaction in Iraq.

23. In 1996, 32.4 percent of nonvoters participated in the focus groups, and 24.5 percent of them expressed belief in the disempowering idea.

24. Annenberg Public Policy Center, "Majority of 18 to 29 Year Olds Think Bush Favors Reinstating the Draft, Annenberg Data Show," News Release, October 8, 2004, 1.

25. Mitchell McKinney and Sumana Chattopadhyay, "Political Engagement through Debates: Young Citizens' Reactions to the 2004 Presidential Debates," *American Behavioral Scientist* 50 (2007): 1169–82.

26. Ibid.

CHAPTER NINE

1. An earlier version of this chapter was presented under the title, "The Disaffected Electorate: What Separates Voters from Nonvoters?" at the 1998 Annual Meeting of the American Political Science Association by Diana B. Carlin, Tammy R. Vigil, and Susan E. Buehler. A notation on the paper indicated that "Research reported in this paper is part of a larger study to be published in *The Third Agenda*."

2. Several books referenced in chapter one described the political climate in the 1990s. In addition to those books, see also Gordon S. Black and Benjamin D. Black, *The Politics of American Discontent: How a New Party Can Make Democracy Work Again* (New York: John Wiley & Sons, 1994); Joseph N. Cappella and Kathleen H. Jamieson, *Spiral of Cynicism: The Press and the Public Good* (New York: Oxford University Press, 1997); Jean B. Elshtain, *Democracy on Trial* (New York: Basic Books, 1995); Suzanne Garment, *Scandal: The Culture of Mistrust in American Politics* (New York: Doubleday, 1992); William Greider, *Who Will Tell the People: The Betrayal of American Democracy* (New York: Touchstone, 1992); and Susan J. Tolchin, *The Angry American: How Voter Rage Is Changing the Nation* (Boulder, CO: Westview Press, 1996).

3. The universities participating in this survey were the University of Kansas, George Washington University, New Mexico State University, State University of New York at New Paltz, University of Nevada–Las Vegas, Western Washington University, Southern University (Louisiana), and Normandale Community College (Minnesota).

4. Communication studies scholars in Martin, Tennessee; Bellingham, Washington; Detroit, Michigan; Kansas City, Kansas; Lawrence, Kansas; Las Vegas, Nevada; Wilmington, Delaware; and Minneapolis, Minnesota, conducted focus groups. Two focus groups were held in both Kansas City and Wilmington.

5. One of the focus groups was comprised of all student nonvoters as a means of getting richer data to supplement the survey data from that specific cohort group.

6. These results were all comparable with the responses from the student group.

7. Steven J. Rosenstone, Donald R. Kinder, and Warren E. Miller, *National Election Studies, 1996: Pre- and Post-Election Study* [dataset], 3rd ed. (Ann Arbor: University of Michigan Center for Political Studies, 1998).

8. Frequencies were calculated for each of the five categories of agreement for each question (1-strongly disagree to 5-strongly agree). Determination of significant differences between voters and nonvoters or across the three groups of student voters, student nonvoters, and focus group members was determined by use of the chi square statistic, which compares observed frequencies for each response with theoretical frequencies (those that would indicate no difference). Chi square statistics were computed two ways: (1) using the five categories from the Likert scale and (2) collapsing the two agreement and two disagreement categories on items for which there was a significant difference. If there was still a significant difference based on three rather than five categories, then significance was reported. Frequencies were also calculated for the 15 questions on the focus group survey.

9. E. J. Dionne, Jr., *Why Americans Hate Politics* (New York: Simon and Schuster, 1991), 355.

10. See Tolchin.

11. See Capella and Jamieson.

12. See Dionne, Greider, and Tolchin.

CHAPTER TEN

1. Paul S. Herrnson and John C. Green, *Multi-Party Politics in America: People, Passions, and Power*, 2nd ed. (Lanham, MD: Rowman & Littlefield Publishers, 2002), 10.

2. Steven J. Rosenstone, Roy L. Behr, and Edward H. Lazarus, *Third Parties in America*, 2nd ed. (Princeton, NJ: Princeton University Press, 1996), 5–6.

3. Results were taken from the Federal Election Commission.

4. Joan Biskupic, "Public Broadcasters Given Choice in Candidate Debates," *Washington Post*, May 10, 1998, A2.

5. Newton N. Minow and Clifford M. Sloan, *For Great Debates: A New Plan for Future Presidential TV Debates* (New York: Priority Press Publications, 1987), 23.

6. Myles Martel, *Political Campaign Debates: Images, Strategies, and Tactics* (New York: Longman, 1983), 174.

7. Peggy Lampl, "The Sponsor: The League of Women Voters Education Fund," in *The Great Debates: Kennedy vs. Nixon, 1960*, ed. Sidney Kraus (Bloomington: Indiana University Press), 88.

8. See Minow and Sloan, 23; Lampl, 87.

9. Lampl, 88.

10. See Minow and Sloan, 28.

11. Ibid.

12. "The Great Debates Debate: Jockeying for Advantage Is the Name of the Game for all the Contenders," *Time,* September 8, 1980, 16.

13. Minow and Sloan, 38.

14. Ibid.

15. Ibid.

16. Ibid.

17. Commission on Presidential Debates, "Mission," http://www.debates.org.

18. Internal Revenue Service, "Exemption Requirements," http://www.irs.gov/charities/charitable/article/0,,id = 96099,00.html.

19. Commission on Presidential Debates, http://www.debates.org.

20. Diana Prentice Carlin, "The Past and Future of Presidential Debate Sponsorship," paper presented at the annual meeting of the Speech Communication Association, New Orleans, LA, November 3, 1988. The complete set of guidelines are as follows:

> The goal of the Commission's debates is to afford the members of the voting public an opportunity to sharpen their views of those candidates from among whom the next President or Vice President will be selected.
>
> In light of the large number of declared candidates in any given presidential election, the Commission has determined that its voter education goal is best achieved by limiting debate participation to the next President and his or her principal rival(s)....
>
> In order to further the educational purpose of its debates, the Commission has developed nonpartisan criteria upon which it will base its decisions regarding selection of non major party candidates, if any, who have a realistic (i.e., more than theoretical) chance of being elected the next President of the United States and who properly are considered to be among the principal rivals for the Presidency. The realistic chance of being elected need not be overwhelming, but it must be more than theoretical....
>
> The criteria contemplate no quantitative threshold that triggers automatic inclusion in a Commission-sponsored debate. Rather, the Commission will employ a

multifaceted analysis of potential electoral success, including a review of (1) evidence of national organization, (2) signs of national newsworthiness and competitiveness, and (3) indicators of national enthusiasm or concern, to determine whether a candidate has a sufficient chance of election to warrant inclusion in one or more of its debates (CPD, Candidate selection, 1996, p. 1).

Each of the three areas included specific indicators against which candidates were judged. They are as follows:

1. Evidence of National Organization

The Commission's first criterion considers evidence of national organization. This criterion encompasses objective considerations pertaining to the eligibility requirements of Article II, Section I of the Constitution and the operation of the Electoral College. This criterion also encompasses more subjective indicators of a national campaign with a more than theoretical prospect of electoral success. The factors to be considered include:

a. Satisfaction of the eligibility requirements of Article II, Section 1 of the Constitution of the United States.

b. Placement on the ballot in enough states to have a mathematical chance of obtaining an Electoral College majority.

c. Organization in a majority of congressional districts in those states.

d. Eligibility for matching funds from the Federal Election Commission or other demonstration of the ability to fund a national campaign, and endorsements by federal and state officeholders.

2. Signs of National Newsworthiness and Competitiveness

The Commission's second criterion endeavors to assess the national newsworthiness and competitiveness of a candidate's campaign. The factors to be considered focus both on the news coverage afforded the candidacy over time and the opinions of electoral experts, media and non-media, regarding the newsworthiness and competitiveness of the candidacy at the time the Commission makes its invitation decisions. The factors to be considered include:

a. The professional opinions of the Washington bureau chiefs of major newspapers, news magazines, and broadcast networks.

b. The opinions of a comparable group of professional campaign managers and pollsters not then employed by the candidates under consideration.

c. The opinions of representative political scientists specializing in electoral politics at major universities and research centers.

d. Column inches on newspaper front pages and exposure on network telecasts in comparison with the major party candidates.

e. Published views of prominent political commentators.

3. Indicators of National Public Enthusiasm or Concern

The Commission's third criterion considers objective evidence of national public enthusiasm or concern. The factors considered in connection with this criterion are intended to assess public support for a candidate, which bears directly on the candidates prospects for electoral success. The factors to be considered include:

a. The findings of significant public opinion polls conducted by national polling and news organizations.

b. Reported attendance at meetings and rallies across the country (locations as well as numbers) in comparison with the two major party candidates.

The criteria were released at the October 31, 1995 news conference and were posted on the CPD's web site.

http://www.debates.org/pages/candsel2004.html.

21. The committee was chaired by Neustadt and included Vernon Jordan, a Washington attorney and member of the CPD board of directors, and Diana Carlin, a communication studies professor at the University of Kansas and a member of the CPD advisory board.

22. The 1992 committee was chaired by Neustadt and included Carlin; Dorothy Ridings, former President of the League of Women Voters and Publisher and President of the *Bradenton Herald* (Florida); Eddie Williams, President of the Joint Center for Political and Economic Studies; and Kenneth Thompson, Director of the Miller Center at the University of Virginia. The same committee was used in 1996.

23. George Farah, *No Debate: How the Republican and Democratic Parties Secretly Control the Presidential Elections* (New York: Seven Stories Press, 2004), 52–53.

24. Polls in March 1996 showed Clinton winning a three-way race with Dole and Perot by 11 points. A story on the eve of the election showed Clinton ahead anywhere from 4 to 16 points. For coverage of the polls throughout the campaign see Richard Benedetto, "Perot Run Not Necessarily a Boon to Clinton," *USA Today*, March 22, 1996, 4A, and Richard Benedetto, "One Constant in Race Has Been Clinton's Lead," *USA Today*, November 4, 1996, 8A.

25. See Sam Walker, "When Anyone Can Run, Everyone Does," *The Christian Science Monitor*, September 26, 1995, http://www.csmonitor.com/1995/1995/0926/26014.html.

26. According to a Gallup poll conducted in June 1992, "Mr. Perot was supported by 39 percent, Mr. Bush by 31 percent, and Mr. Clinton by 25 percent." "The 1992 Campaign: On the Trail; Poll Gives Perot a Clear Lead," *New York Times*, June 11, 1992, http://query.nytimes.com/gst/fullpage.html?res = 9E0CE7DB133EF932A25755C0A964958260.

27. Richard Neustadt, Text of a letter from the Neustadt Committee to the Commission on Presidential Debates Board of Directors, September 16, 1996.

28. Commission on Presidential Debates, Candidate Selection Criteria, 2004, http://www.debates.org/pages/candsel2004.html.

29. Roger Segelken, "Diversity Abounds at Debate of 'Alternative' Party Candidates," *Cornell Chronicle*, October 14, 2004, http://www.news.cornell.edu/chronicle/04/10.14.04/prez_debate_cover.html.

30. Open Debates, http://www.opendebates.org/news/pressreleases/06253003.html.

31. Pat Choate, Jon Hanson, Larry Noble, Jamin B. Raskin, Randall Robinson, and Paul M. Weyrich are the other directors. For complete information on Open Debates, see http://www.opendebates.org.

32. See Farah.

33. http://www.opendebates.org/news/pressreleases/05242004.html.

34. Open Debates, "Open Debates Files FEC Complaint against the Commission on Presidential Debates," Press Release, February 19, 2004. http://www.opendebates.org/news/pressreleases.02192004.html.

35. Open Debates, "Open Debates Files IRS Complaint against the Commission on Presidential Debates," Press Release, April 14, 2004, http://www.opendebates.org/news/pressreleases.04122004.html.

36. Open Debates, "Following Court Ruling, Civic Leaders and Elected Officials Call on Candidates to Participate in Debates Proposed by the Citizens' Debate Commission," Press Release, August 16, 2004, http://www.opendebates.org/news/pressreleases/08162004.html.

37. C-SPAN broadcast the third party debate on October 17, 1996.

38. See Herrnson and Green, 22.

39. See Mari Boor Tonn, "Flirting with Perot: Voter Ambivalence about the Third Candidate," in *The 1992 Presidential Debates in Focus*, ed. Carlin and McKinney (Westport, CT: Praeger, 1994), 109–23. The chapter chronicled the growing disenchantment with

Perot after Admiral James Stockdale's performance in the vice presidential debate and concluded that after the last debate, "missing in general was substantial discussion of him as a genuine, prospective president. Reasons offered for dismissing him as viable repeated concerns voiced earlier: his evasive clichés and generalizations, his lack of political experience and understanding, his withdrawal from the campaign, his failure at General Motors, and his running mate" (121). Focus group members did acknowledge the contribution he made to forcing a discussion of economic issues.

40. Herrnson and Green, 25–26.

CHAPTER ELEVEN

1. Commission on Presidential Debates, "Commission on Presidential Debates Announces Sites, Dates, Formats and Candidate Selection Criteria for 2008 General Election," News Release, November 19, 2007, http://debates.org/pages/news_111907.html.

2. Ibid.

3. Commission on Presidential Debates, "Commission on Presidential Debates Announces Internet Educational Partnership with MySpace," news release, August 6, 2008, http://debates.org/pages/news_111909.html.

4. Ibid.

Selected Bibliography

Angle, Paul M. *Created Equal? The Complete Lincoln-Douglas Debates of 1858*. Chicago: University of Chicago Press, 1958.

Auer, J. Jeffrey. "The Counterfeit Debates." In *The Great Debates: Background, Perspective, and Effects*, ed. Sidney Kraus, 142–50. Bloomington: Indiana University Press, 1962.

———. "Great Myths about Great Debates." *Speaker and Gavel* 18 (1981): 14–21.

———. "Presidential Debates: Public Understanding and Political Institutionalization." *Speaker and Gavel* 24 (1986): 1–7.

Barber, Benjamin R. *Strong Democracy: Participatory Politics for a New Age*. Berkeley: University of California Press, 1984.

Benjamin, James. "The Greek Concept of Dialectic." *The Southern Speech Communication Journal* 48 (1983): 364.

Benoit, William L. "Retrospective versus Prospective Statements and Outcome of Presidential Elections." *Journal of Communication* 56 (2006): 331–45.

Benoit, William L., and David Airne. "A Functional Analysis of American Vice Presidential Debates." *Argumentation and Advocacy* 41 (Spring 2005): 225–36.

Benoit, William L., and Glenn J. Hansen. "Presidential Debate Watching, Issue Knowledge, Character Evaluation, and Vote Choice." *Human Communication Research* 30 (2004): 121–40.

Benoit, William L., John P. McHale, Glenn J. Hansen, P. M. Pier, and John P. McGuire. *Campaign 2000: A Functional Analysis of Presidential Campaign Discourse*. Lanham, MD: Rowman & Littlefield, 2004.

Benoit, William L., Kevin A. Stein, and Glenn J. Hansen. "New York Times Coverage of Presidential Campaigns, 1952–2000." *Journalism & Mass Communication Quarterly* 82 (2005): 356–76.

Benoit, William L., and William T. Wells. *Candidates in Conflict: Persuasive Attack and Defense in the 1992 Presidential Debates*. Tuscaloosa: University of Alabama Press, 1996.

Berquist, Goodwin F., and James L. Golden. "Media Rhetoric, Criticism and the Public Perception of the 1980 Presidential Debates." *Quarterly Journal of Speech* 67 (1981): 125–37.

Bishop, George F., Robert Oldendick, and Alfred J. Tuchfarber. "Debate Watching and the Acquisition of Political Knowledge." *Journal of Communication* 28 (1978): 99–113.

Biskupic, Joan. "Public Broadcasters Given Choice in Candidate Debates," *Washington Post*, May 10, 1998, A2.

Bitzer, Lloyd F., and Theodore Reuter. *Carter vs. Ford: The Counterfeit Debates of 1976*. Madison: The University of Wisconsin Press, 1980.

Bryon, Steven R. "The 'Town Hall' Presidential Debate of 1992: The Candidates Meet the People." Paper presented to the annual meeting of the Speech Communication Association. San Diego, California, November 23, 1996.

Cappella, Joseph N., and Kathleen Hall Jamieson. *Spiral of Cynicism: The Press and the Public Good*. New York: Oxford University Press, 1997.

Carlin, Diana B. "A Defense of the 'Debate' in Presidential Debates." *Argumentation and Advocacy* 25 (1989): 208–13.

———. "Presidential Debates as Focal Points for Campaign Arguments." *Political Communication* 9 (1992): 251–65.

———. "A Rationale for a Focus Group Study." In *The 1992 Presidential Debates in Focus*, ed. Diana B. Carlin and Mitchell S. McKinney, 3–19. Westport, CT: Praeger Publishing, 1994.

———. "DebateWatch: Creating a Public Sphere for the Unheard Voices." In *Communicating Politics: Engaging the Public in Democratic Life*, ed. Mitchell McKinney, 227–28. New York: Peter Lang, 2005.

Carlin, Diana B., and Karen Anderson. "Across the Ages: Views of the 2000 Debates from College Freshmen to Senior Citizens." In *The Millennium Election: Communication in the 2000 Campaign*, ed. Lynda Lee Kaid, John C. Tedesco, Dianne G. Bystrom, and Mitchell S. McKinney, 229–41. Lanham, MD: Rowman & Littlefield Publishers, 2003.

Carlin, Diana B., and Peter J. Bicak. "Toward a Theory of Vice-Presidential Debate Purpose: An Analysis of the 1992 Vice Presidential Debate." *Argumentation and Advocacy* 30 (1993): 119–30.

Carlin, Diana B., Charles Howard, Susan Stanfield, and Larry Reynolds. "The Effects of Debate Formats on Clash: A Comparative Analysis." *Argumentation and Advocacy* 27 (1990): 126–36.

Carlin, Diana B., and Mitchell S. McKinney. *The 1992 Presidential Debates in Focus*. Westport, CT: Praeger Publishers, 1994.

Carlin, Diana B., Eric Morris, and Shawna Smith. "The Influence of Format and Questions on Candidates' Strategic Argument Choices in the 2000 Presidential Debates." *American Behavioral Scientist* 44 (2001): 2196–218.

Carlin, Diana B., Dan Schill, David G. Levasseur, and Anthony S. King. "The Post-9/11 Public Sphere: Citizen Talk about the 2004 Presidential Debates." *Rhetoric & Public Affairs* 8 (2005): 619.

Chaffee, Steven A. "Presidential Debates: Are They Helpful to Voters?" *Communication Monographs* 45 (November 1978): 330–45.

Conrad, Charles. "Political Debates as Television Form." *Argumentation and Advocacy* 30 (Fall 1993): 62–76.

Cook, Fay Lomax, Michael X. Delli Carpini, and Lawrence R. Jacobs. "Who Deliberates? Discursive Participation in America." *Working Paper Series*. Evanston, IL: Institute for Policy Research Northwestern University, 2005.

Crocker, Lionel. *An Analysis of Lincoln and Douglas as Public Speakers and Debaters*. Springfield, IL: Charles C. Thomas, 1968.

Davis, Leslie K. "Camera-Eye Contact by the Candidates in the Presidential Debates of 1976." *Journalism Quarterly* 55 (1978): 431–37, 55.

Denton, Robert E., Jr., and Rachel Halloway. "Clinton and the Town Hall Meetings: Mediated Conversation and the Risk of Being 'In Touch.'" In *The Clinton Presidency: Images, Issues and Communication* Strategies, ed. Robert E. Denton, Jr. and Rachel Halloway, 17–42. Westport, CT: Praeger, 1996.

Dionne, E.J., Jr. *Why Americans Hate Politics*. New York: Simon and Schuster, 1991.

Durst, Will. "Happy National Apathy Day." *New York Times*, November 2, 1998, A27.

Elshtain, Jean B. *Democracy on Trial*. New York: Basic Books, 1995.

Eveland, William P., Jr. "The Effect of Political Discussion in Producing Informed Citizens: The Roles of Information, Motivation, and Elaboration." *Political Communication* 21 (2004): 177–93.

Eveland, William P., Jr., Douglas McCleod, and Amy Nathanson. "Reporters v. Undecided Voters: An Analysis of the Questions Asked during the 1992 Presidential Debates." *Communication Quarterly* 42 (1994): 390–406.

Fallows, James. *Breaking the News: How the Media Undermine American Democracy*. New York: Vintage Books, 1997.

Faucheux, Ronald A. *The Debate Book*. Washington, DC: Campaigns & Elections Publishing Company, LLC, 2003.

———. "Nationwide Poll: What Voters Think about Candidate Debates." *Campaigns & Elections* 23 (2002): 99.

Fishkin, James S. *Democracy and Deliberation: New Directions for Democratic Reform*. New Haven, CT: Yale University Press, 1991.

———. *The Voice of the People: Public Opinion and Democracy*. New Haven, CT: Yale University Press, 1995.

Friedenberg, Robert V. "The 2004 Presidential Debates." In *The 2004 Presidential Campaign: A Communication Perspective*, ed. Robert E. Denton, Jr., 113. Lanham, MD: Rowman & Littlefield Publishers, 2005.

———. "Patterns and Trends in National Political Debates: 1960–1996." In *Rhetorical Studies of National Political Debates: 1996*, ed. Robert V. Friedenberg, 61–90. Westport, CT: Praeger, 1997.

Gallup, George. "The Impact of Presidential Debates on the Vote and Turnout." In *Presidential Debate and Beyond*, ed. J. L. Swerdlow, 34–42. Washington, DC: Congressional Quarterly, 1986.

Garment, Suzanne. *Scandal: The Culture of Mistrust in American Politics*. New York: Doubleday, 1992.

Germond, Jack W., and Jules Witcover. *Mad As Hell: Revolt at the Ballot Box, 1992*. New York: Time Warner Books, 1993.

Gersh, Debra. "Improving Presidential Debates." *Editor and Publisher* 40 (April 1993): 66–77.

Gill, Mary M. "Presidential Debates: Political Tool or Voter Information?" *Speaker and Gavel* 24 (1986): 36–40.

Grossman, Lawrence K. *The Electronic Republic: Reshaping Democracy in the Information Age*. New York: Viking, 1995.

Hahn, Dan F. "The 1992 Clinton-Bush-Perot Presidential Debates." In *Rhetorical Studies of National Political Debates: 1960–1992*, ed. Robert V. Friedenberg, 187–210. Westport, CT: Praeger, 1998.

Harrison, Teresa, Timothy D. Stephen, William Husson, and B. J. Fehr. "Images Versus Issues in the 1984 Presidential Election: Differences between Men and Women." *Human Communication Research* 18 (December 1991): 200–27.

Hart, Rodrick, and Sharon Jarvis. "Political Debates: Forms, Styles & Media." *American Behavioral Scientist* 40 (1997): 1095–122.

Hauser, Gerald A. *Vernacular Voices: The Rhetoric of Publics and Public Spheres*. Columbia: University of South Carolina Press, 1999.

Heckman, Richard Allen. *Lincoln vs. Douglas, the Great Debates Campaign*. Washington, DC: Public Affairs Press, 1967.

Hellweg, Susan A., Michael Pfau, and Steven R. Byron. *Televised Presidential Debates: Advocacy in Contemporary America*. New York: Praeger, 1992.

Herrnson, Paul S., and John C. Green. *Multi-Party Politics in America: People, Passions, and Power*. 2nd ed. Lanham, MD: Rowman & Littlefield Publishers, 2002.

Hinck, Edward. *Enacting the Presidency: Political Argument, Presidential Debates and Presidential Character*. Westport, CT: Greenwood Publishing, 1993.

Hinds, Michael DeCourcy. "Youth Vote 2000: They'd Rather Volunteer." *Carnegie Reporter* 1, no. 2 (January 21, 2008), http://www.carnegie.org/reporter/02/vote2000/index.html.

Holbrook, Thomas M. "The Behavioral Consequences of Vice-Presidential Debates: Does the Undercard Have Any Punch?" *American Politics Quarterly* 22 (October 1995): 469–82.

Hyman, Sydney. *Youth in Politics: Expectation and Realities*. New York: Basic Books, Inc., 1972.

Ifzkoff, Dave. "Laughs Have Impact on Campaign Trail." *The Kansas City Star*, March 8, 2008, E3.

Jackson-Beeck, Marilyn, and Robert G. Meadow. "The Triple Agenda of Presidential Debates." *Public Opinion Quarterly* 5 (1979): 173–80.

Jamieson, Kathleen Hall, and David S. Birdsell. *Presidential Debates: The Challenge of Creating an Informed Electorate*. New York: Oxford University Press, 1998.

Johannasen, Robert W. *The Lincoln-Douglas Debates of 1858*. New York: Oxford University Press, 1965.

Just, Marion R., Ann N. Crigler, Dean E. Alger, Timothy E. Cook, Montague Kern, and Darrell M. West. *Crosstalk: Citizens, Candidates, and the Media in a Presidential Campaign*. Chicago: University of Chicago Press, 1996.

Kaid, Lynda L., Mitchell S. McKinney, and John C. Tedesco. *Civic Dialogue in the 1996 Presidential Campaign: Candidate, Media, and Public Voices*. Cresskill, NJ: Hampton Press, 2000.

Katz, Elihu, and Jacob J. Feldman, "The Debates in the Light of Research: A Survey of the Surveys." In *The Great Debates: Kennedy vs. Nixon, 1960*, ed. Sidney Kraus, 173–223. Bloomington: Indiana University Press, 1962.

Kay, Jack, and Timothy A. Borchers. "Children in a Sandbox: Reaction to the Vice Presidential Debate." In *The 1992 Presidential Debates in Focus,* ed. Diana B. Carlin and Mitchell S. McKinney, 99. Westport, CT: Praeger, 1994.

Kennedy, Helen, and Thomas M. DeFrank. "Veep Hopefuls' Fight is Polite: Cheney, Lieberman Keep Debate Civil." *New York Daily News*, October 6, 2000, 5.

Kenski, Kate, and Natalie Jomini Stroud. "Who Watches Debates? A Comparative Analysis of Presidential Debate Viewing in 2000 and 2004." *American Behavioral Scientist* 49 (2005): 213–28.

Kraus, Sidney, ed. *The Great Debates: Carter vs. Ford*. Bloomington: Indiana University Press, 1979.

———. *The Great Debates: Kennedy vs. Nixon, 1960*. Bloomington: Indiana University Press, 1962.

Kraus, Sidney. "Winners of the First 1960 Televised Debate between Kennedy and Nixon." *Journal of Communication* 46 (1996): 78–96.

Lang, Gladys E., and Kurt Lang. "The First Debate and Coverage Gap." *Journal of Communication* 28 (Fall 1978): 93–98.

Lanoue, David J., and Peter R. Schrott. *The Joint Press Conference: The History, Impact, and Prospects of American Presidential Debates*. Westport, CT: Greenwood Press, 1991.

Lemert, James B. *News Verdicts, the Debates, and Presidential Campaigns*. New York: Praeger, 1991.

Leon, Mary-Ann. "Revealing Character and Addressing Voters' Needs in the 1992 Presidential Debates: A Content Analysis." *Argumentation and Advocacy* 30 (Fall 1993): 88–105.

Levasseur, David G., and Diana B. Carlin. "Egocentric Argument and the Public Sphere: Citizen Deliberations on Public Policy and Policymakers." *Rhetoric & Public Affairs* 4 (2001): 407–31.

Martel, Myles. *Political Campaign Debates: Images, Strategies, and Tactics*. New York: Longman, 1983.

McKinney, Mitchell S. "Building Community through Communication: Expressions of Voter Anger and Alienation in the Political Process." Ph.D. dissertation, University of Kansas, 1996.

McKinney, Mitchell S., and Diana B. Carlin. "Political Campaign Debates." In *Handbook of Political Communication Research*, ed. Lynda Lee Kaid, 203–34. Mahwah, NJ: Lawrence Erlbaum Associates, Publishers, 2004.

McKinney, Mitchell, and Sumana Chattopadhyay. "Political Engagement through Debates: Young Citizens' Reactions to the 2004 Presidential Debates." *American Behavioral Scientist* 50 (2007): 1169–82.

Middleton, Russell. "National TV Debates and Presidential Voting Decisions." *Public Opinion Quarterly* 26 (1962): 426–34.

Miller, Arthur H., and Michael MacKuen. "Learning about the Candidates: The 1976 Presidential Debates." *Public Opinion Quarterly* 43 (Fall 1973): 326–46.

Minow, Newton N., and Clifford M. Sloan. *For Great Debates: A New Plan for Future Presidential TV Debates*. New York: Priority Press Publications, 1987.

Morello, John T. "Argument and Visual Structuring in the 1984 Mondale-Reagan Debates: The Medium's Influence on the Perception of Clash." *Western Journal of Speech Communication* 52 (1988): 277–90.

———. "The 'Look' and Language of Clash: Visual Structuring of Argument in the 1988 Bush-Dukakis Debates." *Southern Communication Journal* 57 (1992): 205–18.

———. "Questioning the Questions: An Examination of the 'Unpredictable' 2004 Bush-Kerry Town Hall Debate." *Argumentation and Advocacy* 41 (Spring 2005): 214.

———. "Visual Structuring of the 1976 and 1984 Nationally Televised Presidential Debates: Implications." *Central States Speech Journal* 39 (1988): 233–43.

Morrow, Gary R. "Changes in Perceptions of Ford and Carter Following the First Presidential Debate." *Perceptual and Motor Skills* 45 (1977): 423–29.

Muir, Janette Kenner. "Clinton Goes to Town Hall." In *Bill Clinton on Stump, State, and Stage: The Rhetorical Road to the White House*, ed. Stephen A. Smith, 341–64. Fayetteville: University of Arkansas Press, 1994.

Murphy, John M. "Presidential Debates and Campaign Rhetoric: Text within Context." *Southern Communication Journal* 57 (1992): 219–28.

Nimmo, Dan. "The Electronic Town in Campaign '92: Interactive Forum or Carnival of Buncombe?" In *The 1992 Presidential Campaign: A Communication Perspective*, ed. Robert E. Denton, Jr., 207–26. Westport, CT: Praeger, 1994.

Owen, Diana. "The Debate Challenge; Candidate Strategies in the New Media Age." In *Presidential Campaign Discourse*, ed. Kathleen E. Kendall, 135–56. Albany: State University of New York Press, 1995.

———. *Media Messages in American Presidential Elections*. New York; Greenwood Press, 1991.

Page, Benjamin J. *Who Deliberates? Mass Media in Modern Democracy*. Chicago: University of Chicago Press, 1996.

Patterson, Thomas E. *Out of Order*. New York: Alfred A. Knopf, 1993.

Payne, J.G., James Golden, John Marlier, and Scott C. Ratzan. "Perceptions of the 1988 Presidential and Vice-Presidential Debates." *The American Behavioral Scientist* 32 (1989): 425–35.

Pfau, Michael. "A Comparative Assessment of Intra-Party Political Debate Formats." *Political Communication Review* 9 (1984): 1–23.

Popkin, Samuel L. *The Reasoning Voter: Communication and Persuasion in Presidential Campaigns*. Chicago: University of Chicago Press, 1991.

Prentice, Diana B., Janet K. Larsen, and Matthew J. Sobnosky. "A Comparison of Clash in the Dual Format." Paper presented at the Speech Communication Association Convention, Anaheim, CA, November 1981.

Protess, David L., and Maxwell McCombs. *Agenda Setting: Readings on Media, Public Opinion and Policymaking*. Hillsdale, NJ: Lawrence Erlbaum Association, 1991.

Racine Group, The. "White Paper on Televised Political Campaign Debates." *Argumentation and Advocacy* 38 (Spring 2002): 199–218.

Ragsdale, Gaut. "The 1996 Gore-Kemp Vice-Presidential Debates." In *Rhetorical Studies of National Political Debates: 1996*, ed. Robert V. Friedenberg, 31–60. Westport, CT: Praeger, 1997.

Ritter, Kurt, and Susan Hellweg. "Televised Presidential Primary Debates: A New Functional Forum for Political Debating." *Journal of the American Forensic Association* 23 (Summer 1986): 1–14.

Romero, David W. "Requiem for the Lightweight: Vice Presidential Candidate Evaluations and the Presidential Vote." *Presidential Studies Quarterly* 31 (September 2001): 454–64.

Rosenstone, Steven J., Roy L. Behr, and Edward H. Lazarus. *Third Parties in America*. 2nd ed. Princeton, NJ: Princeton University Press, 1996.

Ruggiero, Thomas E. "Uses and Gratifications Theory in the 21st Century." *Mass Communication & Society* 3 (2000): 3–37.

Sabato, Lawrence J. *Feeding Frenzy: How Attack Journalism Has Transformed American Politics*. New York: Free Press, 1991.

Schroeder, Alan. *Presidential Debates: Forty Years of High Risk TV*. New York: Columbia University Press, 2000.

Schudson, Michael. *The Good Citizen: A History of American Civil Life*. New York: The Free Press, 1998.

Schwartz, John, and Howard Kurtz. "Internet, Talk Radio Let Citizens Sound Off." *The Washington Post*, April 23, 1995, A22.

Sears, David O., and Steven H. Chaffee. "Uses and Effects of the 1976 Debates: An Overview of Empirical Studies." In *The Great Debates: Carter vs. Ford, 1976*, ed. Sidney Kraus, 223–61. Bloomington: Indiana University Press, 1978.

Sigelman, Lee, and Carol K. Sigelman. "Judgments of the Carter-Reagan Debate: The Eyes of the Beholders." *Public Opinion Quarterly* 48 (1984): 624–28.

Spiker, Julia, Yang Lin, and Scott D. Wells. "The Voice of Young Citizens: A Study of Political Malaise in Campaign 2000." In *The Millennium Election: Communication in the 2000 Campaign*, ed. Lynda Lee Kaid, John C. Tedesco, Dianne G. Bystrom, and Mitchell S. McKinney, 243–256. Lanham, MD: Rowman & Littlefield Publishers, 2003.

Splaine, John. "A Companion to the Lincoln-Douglas Debates." Washington, DC: C-SPAN, 1994.

Steeper, Frederick T. "Public Response to Gerald Ford's Statements on Eastern Europe in the Second Debate." In *The Presidential Debates: Media, Electoral, and Policy Perspectives*, ed. George F. Bishop, Robert G. Meadow, and Marilyn Jackson-Beeck, 84. New York: Praeger, 1978.

Tiemens, Robert K. "Television's Portrayal of the 1976 Presidential Debates: An Analysis of Visual Content." *Communication Monographs* 45 (1978): 362–70.

Tiemens, Robert K., Susan A. Hellweg, Philip Kipper, and Steven. L. Phillips. "An Integrative Verbal and Visual Analysis of the Carter-Ford Debate." *Communication Quarterly* 33 (1985): 34–42.

Tolchin, Susan J. *The Angry American: How Voter Rage Is Changing the Nation*. Boulder, CO: Westview Press, 1996.

Trent, Judith, and Robert V. Friedenberg. *Political Campaign Communication: Principles & Practices*. 5th ed. Lanham, MD: Rowman & Littlefield Publishers, 2004.

Tsfati, Yariv. "Debating the Debate: The Impact of Exposure to Debate New Coverage and Its Interaction with Exposure to the Actual Debate." *The Harvard International Journal of Press/Politics* 8 (2003): 70–86.

Vancil, David L., and Sue D. Pendell. "The Myth of the Viewer-Listener Disagreement in the First Kennedy-Nixon Debate." *Central States Speech Journal* 38 (1987): 16–27.

Williams, Wenmouth, and William D. Semlak. "Structural Effects of TV Coverage in Political Agendas." *Journal of Communication* 28 (1978): 114–19.

Winkler, Carol L., and Catherine F. Black. "Assessing the 1992 Presidential and Vice-Presidential Debates: The Public Rationale." *Argumentation and Advocacy* 30 (Fall 1993): 77–87.

Zarefsky, David. *Lincoln-Douglas and Slavery; In the Crucible of Public Debate*. Chicago: University of Chicago Press, 1990.

———. "The Lincoln-Douglas Debates Revisited: The Evolution of Public Argument." *Quarterly Journal of Speech* 72 (1986): 162.

———. "The Postmodern Public: Revitalizing Commitment to the Public Forum." *Vital Speeches of the Day* 60 (1993): 309.

Zhu, Jian-Hua, J. Ronald Milvasky, and Rahul Biswas. "Do Televised Debates Affect Image Perception More Than Issue Knowledge?: A Study of the First 1992 Presidential Debate." *Human Communication Research* 20 (1994): 302–33.

Index

About the Authors

Diana B. Carlin is a professor of Communication Studies at the University of Kansas. She has conducted research on presidential debates since 1980 and created the DebateWatch project. Carlin served on the advisory board for the Commission on Presidential Debates from 1987 until 2000. Carlin is the co-editor of and contributor to *The 1992 Presidential Debates in Focus*. She has authored or co-authored articles on presidential debates that appeared in *Argumentation & Advocacy, Political Communication, American Behavioral Scientist*, and *Rhetoric & Public Affairs*, and had book chapters in *The Handbook of Political Communication Research, The Millennium Election, Communicating Politics: Engaging the Public in Democratic Life, The Debate Book, Televised Election Debates: An International Comparison*, and *The Electronic Election: Perspectives on the 1996 Campaign Communication*. Carlin has served as an advisor on debate projects in Africa and Eastern Europe.

Tammy Vigil received her Ph.D. from the University of Kansas where she served as a research assistant on the DebateWatch '96 project and led an on-site group in Boston in 2000. She is currently an Assistant Professor at Boston University's College of Communication. Her research interests include political communication, rhetoric, and popular culture.

Susan Buehler earned her Ph.D. in Communication Studies from the University of Kansas in 2004. Her dissertation focused on how college students interpret political messages. She served as a graduate research assistant on the 1996 Ford Foundation grant project that started DebateWatch. A part-time administrator for the University of Kansas, Buehler lives in Lawrence, Kansas, with her husband and 10-year-old daughter.

Kelly McDonald earned his Ph.D. from the University of Kansas in 1998. He was the senior graduate research assistant on the 1996 DebateWatch project and led groups in subsequent years in Bellingham, Washington and Tempe, Arizona. He is an assistant professor at The Hugh Downs School of Human Communication where he served as Director of Forensics for five years. He is active in the Consortium for Strategic Communication, an initiative focused on national security and terrorism-related questions from a message-based perspective. He has published in *Argumentation & Advocacy* and in proceedings from the Conference on Argumentation.